Comics Art
in China

University Press of Mississippi / Jackson

Comics Art in China

John A. Lent
and Xu Ying

The color reproductions in this book are funded by a generous
donation from the Huang Yao Foundation and Carolyn Wong.

www.upress.state.ms.us

The University Press of Mississippi is a member
of the Association of American University Presses.

First printing 2017
∞

Library of Congress Cataloging-in-Publication Data

Names: Lent, John A., author. | Xu, Ying, 1959– author.
Title: Comics art in China / John A. Lent and Xu Ying.
Description: Jackson : University Press of Mississippi, 2017. |
Includes bibliographical references and index.
Identifiers: LCCN 2017003509 (print) | LCCN 2017007881
(ebook) | ISBN 9781496811745 (hardback) | ISBN 9781496811752
(epub single) | ISBN 9781496811769 (epub institutional) | ISBN
9781496811776 (pdf single) | ISBN 9781496811783 (pdf institutional)
Subjects: LCSH: Caricatures and cartoons—China—History.
| Animated films—China—History and criticism. | Arts and soci-
ety—China—History. | BISAC: LITERARY CRITICISM / Comics &
Graphic Novels. | SOCIAL SCIENCE / Popular Culture. | HISTORY
/ Asia / China.
Classification: LCC NC1690 .L46 2017 (print) | LCC NC1690
(ebook) | DDC 741.5/6951—dc23
LC record available at https://lccn.loc.gov/2017003509

British Library Cataloging-in-Publication Data available

To my many cartoonist friends
worldwide and the research community
that studies them: you have made
it a magnificent adventure

Fang Cheng at work

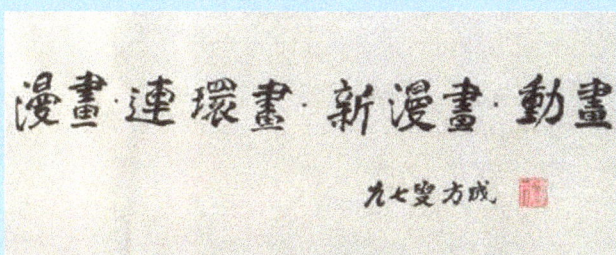

漫畫·連環畫·新漫畫·動畫

九七叟方成

Manhua, lianhuanhua, xinmanhua, and donghua

Cartoons, picture books, comics, and animation

Calligraphy by Fang Cheng, 2016, age ninety-seven

Contents

Every book has a history of its own.

This one originated in the late 1980s when I met archaeologist and professor Alfonz Lengyel and his wife, HongYing Liu-Lengyel. Soon after, HongYing enrolled as a PhD student under my supervision at Temple University. For her dissertation, HongYing and I fashioned a survey of China's cartoonists, certainly a new topic in academia at that time. Before embarking on her fieldwork, I instructed her to interview as many cartoonists as possible, starting with the oldest. She took my advice seriously, even interviewing Zhang Leping in his hospital bed shortly before he died. HongYing and Alfonz talked to about 100 cartoonists, quite a feat at a time when networking was not as facile as later in the internet era.

HongYing was the first of a number of doctoral candidates, who under my direction, researched cartoons, comics, and animation in South Korea (two), Taiwan (two), Japan, India, Turkey, Cuba, and Kenya. Others who studied comic art with me for purposes other than the completion of PhD dissertations wrote about Nepal, Bangladesh, Thailand, Peru, South Korea, Taiwan, and China.

In 1993, during the second of at least thirty trips to China, I began interviewing cartoonists and animators in Shanghai. With much help from HongYing, Alfonz, and cartoonist/animator Zhan Tong, I got a "feel" for the Shanghai cartooning scene, which was intensified and expanded to all of China after I met Xu Ying in 1996. During the past fifteen years, Ying and I, either together or solely, interviewed at least 121 comic art-related personnel in many cities of China. Some were interviewed multiple times (see Appendix).

Thus, interviewing was a major research technique used for this book. In most cases, loosely structured interview schedules were used, allowing the artists and managers leeway in how they responded to questions and at what length. Interviews were done wherever the interviewees chose: their homes, restaurants, my hotel room, their offices or studios. Some were conducted at festivals, conferences, universities, and museums where either one of us or both were invited to speak.

Preface

Because almost all interviews were with mainland cartoonists and animators, the overall tenor of the discourse leans to that of the People's Republic of China and the Communist Party. The senior author interviewed cartoonists and animators in Taiwan and Hong Kong on several occasions, but dwelt primarily on contemporary, not historical, issues during those discussions. Whenever possible, the Guomindang perspective is given, accessed from the many interviews conducted with senior Taiwanese political cartoonists by Hsiao Hsiang-wen, whose doctoral dissertation I supervised, and from secondary sources. Although we do not apologize for our heavy reliance on the interviews (to the contrary, we consider the interviews with the giants of mainland cartooning to be a major strength of this book), we do recognize that interviews have pitfalls and do not tell the whole story. We attempt to account for that issue by critically appraising what we were told by interviewees, and, in some instances, offering alternative perspectives.

Observation was also a useful research technique, allowing us to see where artists worked (studios, offices, and homes) and to view their works (in private collections, exhibitions, and museums). We were invited guests to museums dedicated to individual cartoonists Bi Keguan, Ding Cong, Feng Zikai, and Liao Bingxiong, as well as to the Frog Cartoon Group's galleries housing works by Hua Junwu and Ying Tao. We gathered information at Shanghai University, Communication University of China, Nanjing University of Finance and Economics, and Jilin College of the Arts Animation School, where I hold visiting professorships.

As already stated, both of us were involved in most interviews, which Xu Ying interpreted; she was also responsible for finding and translating Chinese-language resources, and for verifying facts and names in the final manuscript. I was responsible for researching/reading English-language books, articles, and internet postings, for locating non-English-language sources, for analysis of the gathered information, and for all of the writing, editing, and preparation of the manuscript.

In these pages, "comic art" is an all-encompassing term. More specifically, "cartoons" normally refer to political and social commentary drawings; "comic strips" are sole or multiple panels used in newspapers to tell a humorous episode or continue a serialized story; "comic books" and "*xinmanhua*" are periodicals with a number of stories that can be serialized or completed in one issue; "*lianhuanhua*" are palm-size books that usually tell one story with one image per page; "animation" consists of filmed cartoons using movement and sound; and "caricature" means a likeness of an individual that is highly exaggerated.

As already implied, the study is primarily confined to mainland China and does not, in any measurable sense, include Hong Kong, Taiwan, or diasporic Chinese communities scattered around the world. Occasional references to Hong Kong and Taiwan are unavoidably included, because both have served as havens during times of crises, such as in World War II, the China Civil War, and the 1949 overthrow of the Guomindang Party; some of the early Chinese cartoons started in Hong Kong and moved to the mainland, and vice versa, and Hong Kong often served as mainland China's bridge to the West.

Names are given in Pinyin (Mao Zedong, Guomindang, etc.). Birth and death dates are provided for most individuals discussed, but there were instances where we could not determine these dates.

The objectives of this project were to present the most comprehensive overview possible of China's comic art; to highlight key historical and contemporary events, personnel, issues, and trends; to set the story of China's comic art in the contexts of Chinese politics, culture, society, and economics; to critically deal with both the business/industrial and artistic/literary dimensions of cartoons, comics, and animation; and to include as many aspects of comic art as possible, including lianhuanhua, xinmanhua, comic books, newspaper strips, political and social commentary cartoons, humor/cartoon magazines, pictorial periodicals, and animation.

The arguments that we intend to support are based on answers to: 1. Are there common threads throughout the history of Chinese comic art, and if there are, what are they? 2. What outside factors played roles in the development and nourishment of Chinese comic art? 3. How is Chinese comic art linked historically to the structure and function of the country's art and literary professions generally? 4. What is the relationship of art (specifically, comic art) to Chinese society?

Comics Art in China is dedicated to the memory of He Wei and Wang Fuyang, prominent cartoonists who encouraged us in this endeavor and granted us many favors along the way; it is a pity neither lived long enough to see the book in print. We are thankful to all of the comics/cartoons personnel who gave freely of their time and, in some cases, materials. They are listed in the Appendix. Singled out for special thanks are the individuals who helped arrange interviews and meeting places, transported us through China's horrendous traffic jams, provided books, articles, images, and papers, and offered us unforgettable hospitality. Among these are Fang Cheng, who at ninety-seven years old, painted the calligraphy title that adorns a front matter page; Zheng Huagai, who provided research materials and many images; Xu Pengfei, Ding Cong and Shen Jun, Liao Bingxiong and daughter Ling-er, Feng Yiyin, Chen Jianyu, Chang Guangxi, Bi Weimin, Sun Jihong, Li Qingai, Chen Yuli, Li Binsheng, and Ma Kexuan.

Others who helped in various capacities were Hong-Ying Liu-Lengyel, Alfonz Lengyel, Shi Chuan, Jin Tianyi, David Ehrlich, my co-director of Asian Youth Animation and Comics Competition, Wang Liuyi, Huang Yuanlin, Miao Yintang, HaeLim Suh, and my colleagues and doctoral students at Communication University of China—President Liu Jinan, Lu Shengzhang, Zhang Jun, Zhang Huilin, Jia Fou, Wang Jizhong, Wang Lei, Liu Mingjun, Chen Jingwei, Yan Han, and Sun Hongyang—as well as the excellent staff at University Press of Mississippi. We also express our deepest appreciation to the Huang Yao Foundaton and its dedicated founder and head, Carolyn Wong of Singapore, for providing a grant (no strings attached) to enable the use of color illustrations in the book. We thank all of you for making the history of this book pleasurable and memorable.

—John A. Lent

Comics Art
in China

Dynastic Visual Humor and Narrative

Taking into consideration some of its characteristics, such as caricature, satire and parody, humor, wit and playfulness, and narration/storytelling, cartoon art existed in China thousands of years ago. It was not yet called *manhua* (cartoon); that term, meaning "painting with free strokes" or "drawing as dictated by a free will," likely was first used in the eighteenth century to describe the exaggeration and satire found in painter Jin Nong's "Mr. Dong Xin's Inscriptions for Miscellaneous Paintings" (Liu-Lengyel 2001: 43; Barmé 2002: 91). Nor was it as conspicuously "cartoonish" in format and style as contemporary cartoons and comics, but the rudiments of the art form were definitely present.

Caricature

Exaggeration of facial and other bodily characteristics and grotesqueries have been found in Chinese art existent many dynasties ago. As early as the Yangshao Dynasty (5000–3000 BC), grotesque figures adorned burial materials; one burial jar of that period found in Shaanxi Province displayed a cartoon-like image of a human face (Li 1985: 20; quoted in Liu-Lengyel 1993). Also uncovered have been a number of stone statues and reliefs from about 1100 BC that featured humans in humorous ways (Lent 1999: 6, 8). For centuries, popular New Year's pictures (*nianhua*), according to Bo (1995: n.p.), were "expert at using exaggeration and distortion to highlight forms."

There have been those who disagree with the idea that China had caricature before the twentieth century, chief among them being A. L. Bader (1941: 229), who wrote, "The Chinese racial genius has always been for the indirect, for suggestion, for compromising rather than for outspoken from which caricature stems. Second, caricature demands freedom of expression. . . . Finally, caricature presupposes social and political consciousness in its audience." However, evidence contradicts Bader's assertion. Writing in 1877, James Parton told of a printer attached to an American mission

Chapter 1

Cradle of Chinese Cartooning

in China who brought back a "caricature" showing an English foraging party that dated to the 1840s. Believing that the Chinese had been caricaturing for decades, Parton (1877: 196) wrote:

> Caricature, as we might suppose, is a universal practice among them; but, owing to their crude and primitive taste in such things, their efforts are seldom interesting to any but themselves. In Chinese collections, we see numberless grotesque exaggerations of the human form and face, some of which are not devoid of humor and artistic merit.

Satire and Parody

For centuries, Chinese painters poked fun at the social and political systems under which they worked. As with artists of dissent in similar authoritarian circumstances, they veiled their meanings. Murck (2000: 2) reported that, in the eleventh century, "painted allusions to poetry became a vehicle for lodging silent complaint." Drawn on scrolls, they were meant for private viewing to "empathize with those who had been punished, to ridicule imperial judgments, and to satirize contemporaries for the amusement and edification of a trusted circle of friends" (Murck 2000: 3). The ways that dissent was imparted varied; some scrolls illustrated the poem's main point, while others either lyrically summarized a "revelation central to the referenced poem" or "treated visual imagery in ways analogous to poetry" (Murck 2000: 4). As an example of a "sarcastic quatrain" applied to a painting, Murck (2000: 127) showed a scroll of snails crawling up a wall, accompanied by these poetic lines:

> Rancid saliva inadequate to fill a shell,
> Barely enough to quench its own thirst,
> Climbing high, he knows not how to turn back,
> And ends up stuck on the wall—shriveled.

As Murck (2000: 127–28) explained, the poet, Su Shi, used the snail as a metaphor for Wang Anshi, a close advisor to Emperor Shenzong (1048–1085), "whose

greed had over reached his inner resources. If the humor delighted like-minded men who were disgusted with ambitious officials, those who were the target of the jokes must have been infuriated. Both witty and accessible, the quatrains circulated widely."

In the mid-thirteenth century, books of paintings with verse also had political allusions, some satirical in intent. Clunas (1997: 135–37) singled out Song Boren's *Meihua xishenpu* (*Register of Plum-Blossom Portraits*) as a book with political allusions encoded in poetry. *Meihua xishenpu* supposedly was the earliest Chinese printed book in which illustrations did more than merely support the text.

Satire was plentiful in Ming Dynasty (1368–1644) paintings, Clunas (1997: 135) even claiming that the color that marked these works was for satirical effect. As an example, he said that the novel *Jinpingmei* (*The Plum in the Golden Vase*) was replete with color that described furnishings, architecture, clothing, etc., satirically implying that the owners of these things had no taste. Also in the Ming Dynasty (in 1465), according to Bi (1988: 1), an emperor "executed a royal masterpiece entitled Great Harmony, satirizing the bogus harmonious relationship among court officials."

Zhu Da (1626–1705; pen name, Bada Shanren) and Luo Liangfeng (1733–99) are often cited as early Qing Dynasty painters who used political satire and caricature to make a point. A leading painter of his time, Zhu Da, because of his royal heritage, lived a precarious existence, hiding out in a monastery for decades until the uncertainty between the Ming and Qing (1644–1911) dynasties was settled. His "Peacocks," drawn in 1690, displayed local government officials as ugly peacocks standing on an unstable egg-shaped rock as they waited for the emperor to pass by. Symbolically, the officials' positions were portrayed as very shaky, despite their flattery of the emperor. Luo Liangfeng's "Ghosts' Farce Pictures" (about 1771) made fun of unacceptable human behavior of the Qing Dynasty.

Throughout the Ming and Qing dynasties, political satire in art was abundant, found in nianhua (New Year's pictures), colored woodblock prints based on historical stories, folklore, and current events (Flath 2004). Wong (2002: 11) agreed that nianhua were often humorous or satirical, but, as she said, seldom were they political. However, New Year's pictures of the late Qing Dynasty, according to Bo (1995: n.p.), often exposed the "grimness of society and even directly skewered the authorities." Examples he provided were the Wuqiang New Year's picture, "Pointy Heads (wicked and powerful people) Bring a Lawsuit," which used "biting humor to render venal officials in sinister and diabolic form"; "The Ten Desires," which ridiculed "avarice behavior"; and "Witticisms," which satirized "degenerate worldly behavior."

Humor, Wit, Playfulness

Humor and sarcasm figured in early Chinese stone etchings (*shike*), an example being an inscription found in Shandong Province, dating to the Eastern Han Dynasty (25–220), that pictured the tyrannical and licentious last king of the Xia Dynasty (c. 2070–c. 1600 BC) holding a spear while sitting on the shoulders of two women (Bi and Huang 1986). In at least one case, an emperor, Xianzong, made a humorous drawing for political purposes. The brush drawing, "Keeping Good Terms with Everyone," appeared when Xianzong succeeded his tyrannical father in 1465; it was meant to lighten the public mood and announce that a different style of rule was on the way. The print showed three men's faces on a common body; together, they formed a single smiling face that gave the impression that the men were holding one another.

In Chinese art, humor regularly has revolved around puns, wordplay, and connotative meanings attached to verses and other text accompanying drawings, and around folktales and artists' philosophies. Even today, this is the case; to avoid trouble with authorities, artists employ traditional approaches of indirection and symbolism to "express satirical intent, inject humor in their art, or elicit a laugh or smile from the viewer" (Fu 1994: 61).

A figure very often used in traditional (and modern) Chinese drawings for humorous appeal is Zhong Kui,

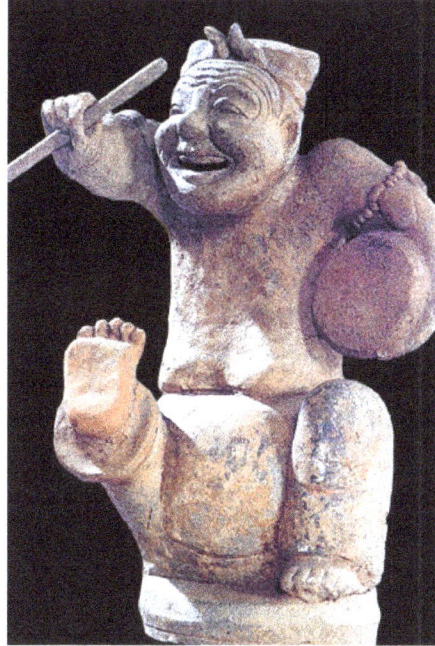

Fig. 1.1. *Jigu shuochangyong* (*Drum Playing and Singing Figure*), Eastern Han Dynasty burial tomb figure, happy to serve his master in the afterlife. Courtesy of Zheng Huagai. *Zhongguo manhua* (*Chinese Cartoon*), May 2005. http://www.ndcnc.gov.cn/jingpinzy/manhua.

Fig. 1.2. *Jihuangpiao eyindan jingzhong* (*Hungry Men Eating Everything*), North Wei mural in Ming temple built in 1503. Exaggerated depiction of one man holding a boar and biting its stomach; another with a whole bird in his mouth; others eating a man's leg or chewing roots. Courtesy of Zheng Huagai. *Zhongguo manhua* (*Chinese Cartoon*), May 2005. http://www.ndcnc.gov.cn/jingpinzy/manhua.

known as the "demon queller." Supposedly, the character first appeared in a dream Tang (618–907) Emperor Ming Huang had while he had a fever. After Zhong Kui dispelled the fever, the emperor asked painter Wu Daozi to do a portrait of his healer (Forrer 1966: 66). Zhong Kui's

Fig. 1.3. Humor played a pivotal role in early erotic art. This Qing print shows a young woman who has been stung by a scorpion while using the night chamber pot. Bertholet Collection in *Dreams of Spring*, 1997, 144.

ugly face, heavy beard, and intoxicated demeanor have been the gist for many artists' works since then.

Also exhibiting a great deal of humor and playfulness were the Chinese Spring Palace Paintings from the late Ming (from 1560 to about 1640) and succeeding Qing Dynasty, all erotic and irreverent. Many dealt with husbands getting caught while trying to seduce, or when copulating with, the servant girl or concubine; others portrayed a jealous child disrupting his parents' lovemaking by pulling the father's queue while the couple was entwined, a naked spouse trying to entice her studious husband to bed, a bashful bride wanting to escape the bridal chamber, or a fat lady bitten on her sex organ by a scorpion while using the chamber pot (Yimen 1997; see also de Smedt [1981]). The anonymous author of *Dreams of Spring* (1997: 43–45) pointed out that humor is an "important ingredient" of erotic art and that some popular booklets of late Ming "even become comics, where legends are added to the scenes."

Narration/Storytelling

The tradition of telling a story with cartoon-like illustrations goes back to at least the Western Han Dynasty (206 BC–25 AD). A 1972 excavation found two picture stories on a coffin from that time (Zhu 1990). During the Eastern Han Dynasty, door gods (*menshen*) designed to ward off evil featured pictures of legendary heroes. Serial stories were prominently displayed on stone slabs and colorful frescoes during the Wei (386–534) and Sui (581–618) dynasties of the sixth and seventh centuries; they were usually interpretations of Buddhist scriptures or biographical sketches of Sakyamun (Peng 1980: 2). In 527, three episodes of Jataka stories were carved in a single sculpture of Jianbozhi; in 543, twelve episodes of Sakyamun were sculpted (Chen 1996: 66). Those that appeared during the Wei Dynasty were not fully developed as stories; that came about in the Sui Dynasty (Ah Ying 1982). Buddhist narrative paintings of the fifth through tenth centuries are plentiful in 492 decorated caves in Dunhuang, Gansu Province. The early caves depict narrative tales based on the lives of Buddha, illustrated for didactic purposes. Pekarik (1983: 24) said that some caves are both visionary and narrative, featuring "graceful elongated people, exaggerated swaying scarves and vividly colored bursting flames [that] give these paintings a remarkable sense of animation."

Other forerunners of the modern serial story pictures can be found during the Song (960–1279) and Yuan (1279–1368) dynasties, when fictional works flourished. Artists were asked to decorate storybooks with illustrations at the top of pages; some from the Song Dynasty had cartoon characteristics (Shi 1989: 12). Also coming out of the Song Dynasty was *Gengzhitu* (Pictures on Farming and Weaving), first given to Emperor Ningzong and then successively carved on stone and woodblock prints. *Gengzhitu* and similar works aimed to increase productivity among farmers and weavers (Chen 1996: 72). Another Chinese painting of the tenth century, "Han Xizai yeyantu" (Han Xizai's Night Banquet)—depicting five sequential pictures of the rich nightlife of government officials—has been labeled comic strip-like ("China's Cartoon" 2008). In the Yuan, Ming, and Qing dynasties, popular romantic novels carried portraits of the main characters on the front and sometimes at the beginning of each chapter (Hwang 1978: 52). Some novels were richly illustrated with the upper half of each

Fig. 1.4. *Laoshu jianü* (*Rat's Quest for His Daughter's Marriage*), late Qing Dynasty New Year's picture; a story of false hopes, deception, and an arranged marriage gone awry. Courtesy of Zheng Huagai. *Zhongguo manhua* (*Chinese Cartoon*), May 2005. http://www.ndcnc.gov.cn/jingpinzy/manhua.

page featuring a picture or an illustrated page following every page of text (see also Chiang 1959).

Independent picture stories representing biographies, novels, operas, and even the news appeared as New Year's pictures during the Qing Dynasty. Flath (2004: 82) wrote that nianhua had a "profound effect on how people saw history." Before 1736, they were made up of a single panel or a story spread over several pages; after that, they were usually one page with sixteen, twenty-four, or thirty-two panels, relating stories of legendary heroes and episodes of operas. These were credited with subsequently influencing picture storybooks. The serial wall paintings had similar themes; among the most prominent were the 112 paintings portraying the life of Confucius in the temple at Qufu in Shandong Province (Hwang 1978: 52, see also Lent 1994: 280).

Picture stories that were antecedents to lianhuanhua (illustrated storybooks) date to "classical times," according to Nebiolo (1973: Introduction), carrying themes dealing with historical events and everyday life. He elaborated:

The story of Viceroy Lin Ze-xu, who destroyed the opium convoys and made war on the English, dates from 1839. The revolutionary moves which the Taipings directed against the imperial troops, as seen from the rebels' point of view, date from 1854. From the same year but from the government viewpoint is an account of the struggle of General Zeng Guo-fan against the Taipings, where the captions are long excerpts from Zeng's harangues to his men, coming out of his mouth in a form that is a forerunner of

contemporary comics' balloon. In 1901 there were many series on the Boxer Rebellion, showing the "righteous harmony band" attacking Tientsin, setting fire to missionary trains and houses and putting Europeans to flight. Early in the century there was a series on the destructive effects of opium upon the families of the smokers; another on the anachronism of Confucian principles in a developing society (the girl compelled to marry a dead fiancé, the son deficient in respect for his father who is drowned in a well by the other members of the family).

Nebiolo (1973: Introduction) thought one lianhuanhua had to have had an underground circulation because

it sympathized with young men who had been thrown into prison for having cut off the pigtails imposed upon them by their Manchu rulers; one that related the exploits of students who broke the law by going to brothels during the period of mourning for the death of the Emperor Hu [Guangxu]; and others about the phenomena of progress—the woman barber of Peking who cleaned her clients' ears, the ladies of Shanghai who used sewing machines, and the young sportsman falling off a bicycle. All these were printed on large sheets, one sheet for each story, or as strips in newspapers.

Although the aforementioned examples of humor, satire, and narrative do not exactly conform to what we now think of as cartoons and comics, they were precursors whose characteristics were similar to what existed in the Western world.

Forging a New Nation, Incorporating Modern Cartooning

Chinese humorous and narrative drawing began to take on the characteristics of Western-defined cartooning at the juncture of the nineteenth and twentieth centuries. Major catalysts for this transformation were the growing dissatisfaction with Qing dynastic rule leading up to the 1911 revolution (with attendant issues of imperialism and such social evils as opium, gambling, etc.) and the increased contact with the outside world that brought in different ideas and modern printing technology, including lithography. During this period, satirical and political cartoons about these and other topics proliferated, found in cartoon/humor magazines, pictorial magazines, partisan newspapers, and lianhuanhua that sprouted in profusion in cities such as Shanghai, Hong Kong, Beijing, Tianjin, and Guangzhou. Many of these publications carried what they called "funnies" ("huaji"), "burlesques," "current pictures" ("shihua"), or "emblems."

The thousands of political caricatures in these media during the end of the nineteenth century (many dealing with foreign imperialism) were labeled "overelaborate and ill-drawn" by art historian Michael Sullivan (1996: 119), who granted that they improved as the anti-Manchu revolutionary movement spread after 1900.

In what he called "the age of irreverence," historian Christopher Rea (2015) maintained that, from the 1890s to the 1930s, what Chinese people considered funny changed. Early in the twentieth century, literary people and illustrators used veiled, allegorical statements to criticize the new Republican government; however, the critiques became so offensive, loaded with cursing, scatology, pornography, and in-your-face punches, that some literati sought a new dimension to funniness. The result was popular writer Lin Yutang's invention of *youmo* (humor), which stood for a "new comedic sensibility that sought to displace the irreverence of the early 1900s" (Rea 2015: 12). The most important trends of the first four decades of the twentieth century were outlined by Rea as *xiaohua* (jokes), *youxi* (play), *maren*

(mockery), *huaji* (farce), and youmo (humor), with the latter two becoming popular in the 1930s (9).

Cartoon/Humor Magazines

China had at least four cartoon/humor periodicals during its formative period of comic art: *The China Punch* (1867–68, 1872–76), *Puck, or the Shanghai Charivari* (April 1871–November 1872), *Raoshe zazhi* (*The Rattle*, 1896–1903), and *Shanghai Puck* (aka *Bochen huaji huabao*, or *Bochen's Comic Pictorial*) (1918–19). As their names testify, all emulated either Britain's *Punch* (1842–2002) or the United States' *Puck* (1871–1918). There may have been other cartoon magazines in the Qing and Republican eras, but because they usually appeared in English, they and other foreign-language or -owned periodicals are practically absent from the histories (Rea 2013: 392). For example, Rea (2013: 418–19) wrote that, in the 1880s, the *Japan Gazette* in Yokohama wrote a scathing review of a magazine called *Quis, the Shanghai Charivari*, but apparently, Rea was not able to determine whether it had connections to *Puck, or the Shanghai Charivari*. Rea (2013: 418–19) was able to elaborate more on *The Rattle*, an illustrated humor magazine, which was published by Kelly and Walsh in Shanghai's International Settlements and closely followed the style and format of the earlier *Puck, or the Shanghai Charivari*. According to Rea (2015: 43), the magazine ceased to exist for a couple of years—having, in its words, "absolutely drained Shanghai of humour"—and was revived in November 1900 in time to mock the Boxer Rebellion. Rea (2015: 43–44) contended that *The Rattle*'s humor, "often at the expense of the Chinese for the benefit of expatriate Westerners, was aimed at the easily amused—those 'pleased with a rattle, tickled with a straw,' a line from Alexander Pope's 'Essay on Man' (1734)." H. W. G. Hayter supervised *The Rattle*'s cartoons (Zhang 2001: 130).

The China Punch and *Puck, or the Shanghai Charivari* had other similarities besides imitating London's *Punch*; they used "whole-page caricatures, comedic verses, wry commentaries on local society and politics, filler jokes, and editorials written in the voice of their

Fig. 1.5. *The China Punch*, Vol. 1, No. 1, China's first cartoon/humor magazine, May 28, 1867.

Fig. 1.6. *Puck, or the Shanghai Charivari*, April 1, 1871, featuring foreigners being served drinks by Chinese, while drunkards fall down the sides, and other foreigners bow to one another at the top.

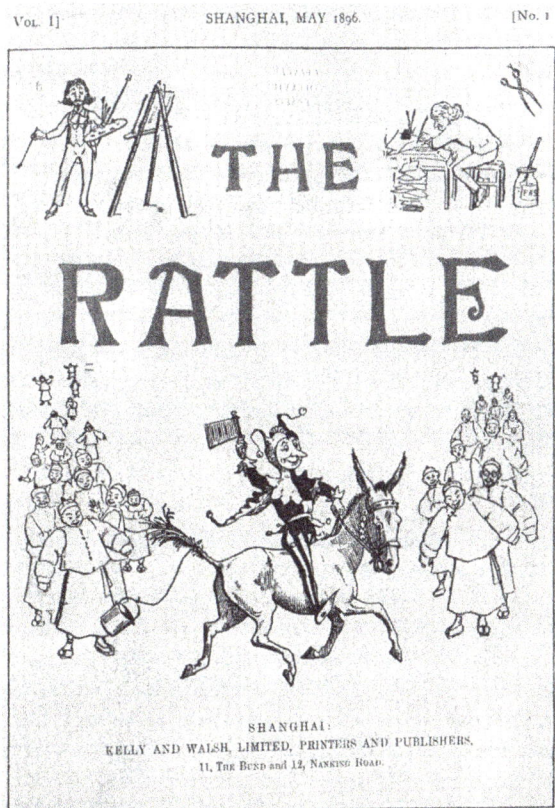

Fig. 1.7. Inaugural issue of *The Rattle*, May 1896. Published in Shanghai. Widener Library, Harvard University.

namesake trickster [Mr. Punch]" (Rea 2013: 289). Both had short lives, stopping publication upon the "abrupt departure of a proprietor" (389); they were amateurishly done, depended on the literary and artistic contributions from the tiny Anglophone community, employed a type of whimsy closely related to farce, and promoted readers' prejudices and cultural stereotypes. Although they used a condescending attitude towards the Chinese, they also poked fun at the Irish, Germans, Portuguese, and other British rivals in the region (Rea 2013: 407). One writer, reporting in 1877, said that for the most part, the British ridiculed themselves in *Puck*, although occasionally they made fun of Chinese ceremonies. He claimed that some Chinese patriots translated the British self-humor and printed it in anti-British flyers, making it appear that the "English barbarians" were criticizing themselves (Parton 1877: 196). Both *The China Punch* and *Puck* made extensive use of "satirical caricature in a mimetic idiom, in which distorted representatives of officials and society types presume correspondence to a 'real' referent" (Rea 2013: 390). In Rea's analysis, neither magazine had influences on China's cartoons or humor periodicals (2013: 419).

Published in Hong Kong, *The China Punch* was a subsidiary of *The China Mail*, founded in 1845 as the "Official Organ of All Government Notifications in Hong Kong." *The China Punch* labeled its parent newspaper "The China Snail." One of the delusions *Punch* continually sought to puncture was that Hong Kong was a city of dreams. As Rea (2013: 398) wrote: "He [Mr. Punch] takes an interest not only in the surreal official proceedings of the colonial government . . . , but also in the fantasies that the Oriental dream world engenders among Europeans." Westerners coming to Hong Kong to seek fortunes were called naïve by Mr. Punch.

Rea (2013: 398) described Mr. Punch's "topsy-turvy world" as a place where "government officials can do no right, gender norms are suspended (if not inverted), and Europeans are at the mercy of their supposed inferiors, the Chinese." The regular contents of *The China Punch*, according to Rea (2013: 399), were, "caricatures of colonial government officials and their Chinese

Fig. 1.8. Shen Bochen, who, in a lifespan of just over thirty years, started *Bochen huaji huabao* and published more than 1,000 (mostly) political cartoons. Courtesy of Zheng Huagai. *Zhongguo manhua* (*Chinese Cartoon*). May 2005. http://www.ndcnc.gov.cn/jingpinzy/manhua.

counterparts, roundups of fictitious social events, parodic telegrams and letters to the editor, witty rhymes on financial, political, commercial and social topics, and copious one-off puns."

Puck, or the Shanghai Charivari was issued by F&C Walsh, a British printing and stationery firm, on April 1 (Fools' Day), 1871. Like *The China Punch*, *Puck* delighted in quoting or referring to Shakespeare; the first issue carried the words "A Midsummer Night's Dream" on the cover. Interestingly, the title of the magazine, *Puck, or the Shanghai Charivari*, incorporated parts of two Western humor journals, although it is unlikely, because of time and transportation constraints, that the magazine was spun off from the American *Puck*, whose inaugural issue came out less than a month earlier. Published every three months, there were seven known numbers of *Puck, or the Shanghai Charivari* (Wu 2013: 368).

The circulations of *Punch* and *Puck, or the Shanghai Charivari* were limited because of their use of English; although *Puck* was read by inhabitants of other treaty ports in Asia, it is likely the circulation was only in the hundreds since there were only 1,149 English-speaking foreigners in Shanghai in 1870.

Ever--lasting memory to our late contemporaries.

讜 驚 界 文 射 泉
論 三 光 九

Fig. 1.9. Shen Bochen cartoon paying tribute to newspapers closed due to censorship. *Shanghai Puck*. September 1, 1918. Courtesy of Zheng Huagai. *Zhongguo manhua* (*Chinese Cartoon*), May 2005. http://www.ndcnc.gov.cn/ jingpinzy/manhua.

Early in the Republican period (1918), *Shanghai Puck*, also called *Bochen huaji huabao* (*Bochen's Comic Pictorial*), appeared as a bilingual (English and Chinese) monthly, this time, the product of a Shanghai cartoonist, Shen Bochen (1889–1919). Only four numbers, each circulating about 10,000 copies, were published before Shen's premature death in 1919. *Shanghai Puck* "positioned itself neither as a direct descendant of *Punch* [England] nor of *Puck* [United States and Japan], although both were acknowledged as important models" (Wu 2013: 367). Throughout its brief existence, *Shanghai Puck* incorporated ideas from, and exchanged caricatures and cartoon styles with, other *Punch* and *Puck* magazines globally (see Scully 2013, for an overview of *Punch* magazines worldwide); in some instances,

cartoons from the American *Puck* were unashamedly copied in almost all details except for added Chinese elements (Wu 2013: 372–73).

Shen (1918: 2, quoted in Shen 2001: 109) gave his magazine's responsibilities as, "first, to give advice and warning to both governments of the south and the north, and spur them to work in concerted efforts to create a unified government; second, to let Westerners understand Chinese culture and customs, and thus, raise the positions of China in the world; and third, to promote the new morality and practices and discard the old." In line with these objectives, most of the cartoons related to current political issues—colonialism, imperialism, militarism, and China's weaknesses and victimization; the use of English helped Westerners to know

China better and served as a safety device for Shen, allowing him to voice more critical statements in a language probably unfamiliar to most government officials (Wu 2013: 378). From its inaugural number, *Shanghai Puck*, in an editorial and a cartoon entitled "Ever-lasting Memory to Our Late Contemporaries"—showing the character Puck bowing to tombstones of newspapers killed by censorship—vowed to make the wishes of its banned contemporaries "come true" (Wu 2013: 371). Overall, *Shanghai Puck* cartoons differed, because they were "more helpful . . . with regard to raising China onto the global stage" (Wu 2013: 381).

One of the most prolific and influential cartoonists of his time, Shen drew nearly all of the cartoons in *Shanghai Puck*; during the 1910s, he is credited with more than 1,000 cartoons, many in other periodicals, such as *Shenbao*, *Shenzhou huabao* (*Shenzhou Pictorial*), *Minquan huabao* (*Human Rights Daily*), *Dagonghe ribao* (*Great Republic Daily*), and *Shishi xinbao* (*Current News*) (Wu 2013: 365). Other painters—among them, Chen Baoyi and Wang Dun'gen—contributed cartoons to *Shanghai Puck*.

Pictorial Magazines and Newspapers

The advances in printing brought to China in the last quarter of the nineteenth century ushered in pictorial magazines that provided space for cartoons and illustrations. Although the pictorials were purveyors of cartoons, they were "entirely dissimilar" from cartoon/humor magazines such as *Punch* and *Puck* in "layout, content, and visual composition" (Rea 2013: 419). They were thought to have a special impact, as the editor of *Wushen quannian huabao* (*The 1908 Pictorial*) later said: "[They] can greatly enhance the people's wisdom and broaden their horizons."

Ernest Major (1841–1908), a British businessman resident in Shanghai, pioneered in producing illustrated magazines, first with *Yinghuan huabao* (*Yinghuan Pictorial*, 1877–80), which mainly reprinted foreign pictorials' images, and then with *Dianshizhai huabao* (*Lithographic Studio Pictorial*,[1] 1884–98), called "one

of the most significant pictorials in late Qing China" (Mittler 2007). *Dianshizhai huabao* was a Chinese-language supplement of the very important daily *Shenbao* (1872–1949), also founded by Major. The pictorial was issued every ten days and was available as a stand-alone periodical or as bound twelve-issue volumes;[2] there were 528 issues containing more than 4,600 illustrations, drawn in a "mixed style that combined traditional techniques of the brush with perspectives seen in contemporary photographies" (Theobald 2012).

Dianshizhai huabao's main artist was Wu Youru (1850–93). Some contend that Wu's illustrations were not comic art, because they were too realistic and did not contain elements of exaggeration or satire. Bi Keguan was of that belief, relegating Wu to a footnote in his history of Chinese cartooning (Bi 1982). However, using a broad definition (as done in the previous section, "Dynastic Visual Humor and Narration"), a case can be made that certain drawings in *Dianshizhai huabao* constituted comic art. First, some were news-oriented pictures (occasionally sensational in nature), with tinges of anecdotal humor that "recreated vividly and imaginatively the everyday life of the denizens of varied social strata and nationalities" of Shanghai (Zhang 2001: 122). Although Mittler (2007) did not think illustrations in *Dianshizhai huabao* depicted "everyday life and everyone's lives" in Shanghai, but rather "peak periods, peak figures, and peak events," she did write that many contained "elements of caricature and exaggeration." Second, *Dianshizhai huabao* was probably the first of many pictorial magazines to use lianhuanhua, normally associated with comic art. In 1884, *Dianshizhai huabao* printed ten illustrations in narrative form to describe a Korean rebellion (Shen 2001: 100; for more about *Dianshizhai huabao*, see Zürcher 1994; Theobald 2012).

Dianshizhai huabao and other Chinese illustrated periodicals were aware of similar publications outside of China and followed their pictorial modules. Chinese and foreign pictorials reprinted one another's illustrations and quoted one another's articles as a way "to improve and authenticate their global coverage," according to Mittler (2013).

Any doubt about pictorial magazines' connections to comic art were irrelevant by the early 1900s as there were increasing numbers of such periodicals which published drawings political in content (attacking the Qing Dynasty) and cartoon-like in style. In fact, they nourished what is considered the first generation of Chinese cartoonists. Among these pioneers were Pan Dawei, Gao Jianfu (1879–1951), Xie Yingbo, He Jianshi (1877–1915), and Zheng Nuquan, all members of Tongmenghui (Chinese Alliance)[3] who drew for *Journal of Current Pictorial*, followed by others such as Zhang Yuguang (1885–1968), Ma Xingchi (1873–1934), Qian Binghe (1874–1944), Zhang Guangyu (1900–1964), Dan Duyu (1896–1972), and Ding Song (1891–1972).

Beginning in 1905, *Journal of Current Pictorial* published thrice monthly and was staffed by artist members of Tongmenghui. Because of its very critical stand against the Qing government, the magazine was banned in 1907, at which time it moved from Guangzhou to Hong Kong. After only a few issues there, the British colonial authorities in Hong Kong caved in to Qing pressure and *Journal of Current Pictorial* was banned once again. Back in Guangzhou, the artists used pseudonyms to continue their criticism in *Shixie huabao* (*Current Jokes Pictorial*) and *Pingwen huabao* (*People Pictorial*) (Wong 2002: 33). In 1912, former staff members of the banned *Journal of Current Pictorial*, including He Jianshi and Zheng Nuquan, inaugurated *The True Record*, published in Guangzhou and distributed in Shanghai. The magazine harshly criticized the new government, especially struggles within the Guomindang Party, for which opinions, its publication was stopped in 1913, resulting in its artists fleeing to the mainland (Wong 2002: 14, 33).

Among the many issues that the *Journal of Current Pictorial* brought attention to was the maltreatment of Chinese workers in the United States. When a delegation of Americans, including President Theodore Roosevelt's daughter, visited Guangzhou in 1905, *Journal of Current Pictorial* cartoonists called upon palanquin (a conveyance to transport people, carried on men's shoulders) carriers not to serve them. One of the cartoonists,

He Jianshi, painted a dozen large, anti-American cartoons and posted them in the streets. When one of the cartoons particularly offensive to the Americans was republished in a Hong Kong newspaper, its editor was expelled by British and Hong Kong officials (Jiang 1989).

As the revolutionary fervor grew more heated, additional pictorials with vitriolic cartoons appeared, usually staffed by the already-mentioned, pioneering cartoonists, as well as some newcomers. The painter Zhang Yuguang, though a cartoonist only from 1909 to 1911, nevertheless contributed immeasurably to the nationalist cause. In a 1911 cartoon, Zhang showed the power-hungry Yuan Shikai on a rocking horse, implying that, despite his claims to advancing with reforms, Yuan was actually standing in place. Zhang also pioneered in social cartooning, often drawing about people's miserable living conditions. As chief editor of Shanghai's *Fairy Land Pictorial*, founded in 1907, Ma Xingchi used the weekly newspaper supplement to point out the people's deplorable living conditions resulting from officials' corruption. He became the main artist of *National Herald*'s (founded 1907) twice-weekly pictorial supplement where "many talented Chinese cartoonists cut their teeth," including Shen Bochen, most doing cartoons heavily dependent upon "allegory, visual punning, and word-play" (Rea 2015: 54). A Revolutionary Party member who was forced into a decade-long exile by Qing government suppression, Ma became editor of the paper's supplement in 1910, and shortly after, was drawing for *Truly Pictorial* and Shanghai's largest daily, *Sin Wan Pao* (Xinwanbao), becoming editor of its graphics section in 1918 (Rea 2015: 56). Before and after the 1911 revolution, Qian Binghe published cartoons in the revolutionist-sponsored *Minquan huabao (Civil Rights Pictorial)* in Shanghai, including the popular series, "A Hundred Appearances of the Old Gibbon," also carried by *Minguo xinwen* and later collected in a book of more than 100 works. Based on the cartoon's title, the homonym of the Chinese words for "ape" and "yuan," the latter the family name of the president and self-appointed emperor, it was apparent that Qian did not pull his punches (Shen 2001: 109). A cartoonist who later changed the face of

13

Fig. 1.10. Zhang Yuguang's cartoon showing Yuan Shikai as a non-advancing rocking horse rider.

Fig. 1.11. *Guanlifei baixingshou* (*Fat Officials, Skinny Common People*), ca. 1911, drawn by Shu Mingang. Cartoons depicting the corruption of officials at the expense of the poor were common at the time.

Fig. 1.12. Freedom of the press was the theme of this 1909 cartoon in *Minhu huabao* showing four editors attempting to hold up the press building with their brushes.

the profession, Zhang Guangyu was only eighteen years old in 1918, when he began submitting cartoons to *Shijie huabao* (*World Pictorial*). A year later, he edited *Huaji huabao* (*Comic Pictorial*). As with many pictorials from 1918 through the early 1920s, both succumbed rather quickly—*Shijie huabao* after ten issues, *Huaji huabao*, two issues (Laing 2004: 141). Zhang later founded cartoon magazines, established cartoon associations, and continued to draw a wide range of cartoons.

An issue befitting the revolutionary cause that was taken up by some pictorial magazine cartoonists was freedom of the press. Probably the first such cartoon was a reaction against a 1908 imperial authority-enacted press law meant to suppress revolutionists' publications. Published in 1909 in *Minhu huabao* (*Minhu Daily Pictorial*), the cartoon shows

> a military officer, portrayed as a huge wine jar standing on the right side, [who] puts a piece of paper with the caption "Press Law" on a building. On his body is the word *Gaolianghong*, which is a kind of Chinese liquor, and on his cap is the Chinese word *Dao*, which means morality. This metaphorical image signified that the authorities had unreasonably enacted the Press Law in the name of morality as if drunk. On the plaque of the building is the word *Baoguan* (i.e. newsroom), and under the heavy load of Press Law, the newsroom is about to collapse. Only four editors near the newsroom struggle to sustain the building with their brushes. (Yi Guo 2015: 219)

Yi Guo (2015) mentioned about a half-dozen similar cartoons defending press freedom in *Civil Rights Pictorial* during 1912 alone.

Chinese cartoonists did not limit their work to magazines; they also took advantage of the increasing numbers of newspapers in the late Qing Dynasty. Because of the aforementioned advances in printing technology—as well as the politics and wars of the Manchu court, which provided subject matter—the number of dailies in China mushroomed from nineteen in 1895 to 500 by 1912 to 628 by 1926 (Lin 1936: 146, quoted in Hung 1994: 40). The tabloid (*xiaobao*)

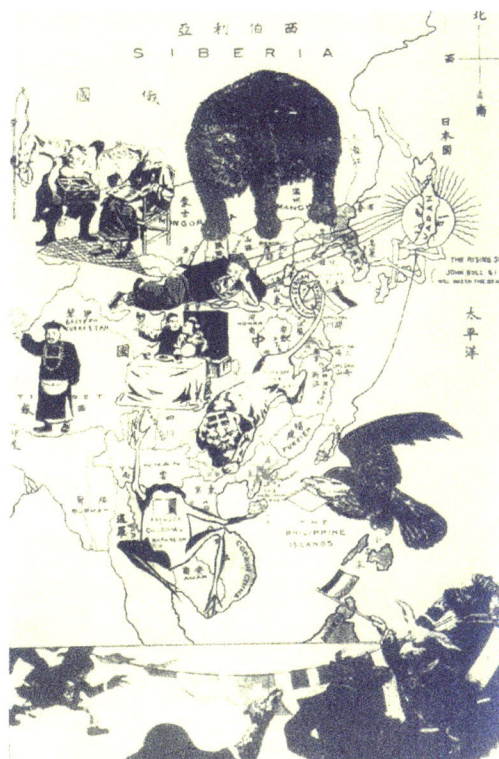

Fig. 1.13. Probably the first political cartoon by a Chinese artist, Xie Zantai, was "The Situation in the Far East" (July 19, 1899), which showed outside powers as animals piecing up China while the Chinese government and public nonchalantly looked on.

made up a large proportion of the dailies. From the time of the first tabloid in Shanghai on June 24, 1897, until 1952, the total number of tabloids in Shanghai was 1,266, or 70.88 percent of the total number of newspapers of 1,786 (Hong 2007: 1, 27).

With this proliferation of Chinese-language newspapers, especially city tabloids, and the "incessant demand for copy with immediate appeal," titles started to appear such as *Laughter Stage* (1918), *Absurd World* (1926–27), *Absurd Laughter* (1927), *Xiasan huasi* (*Shooting the Breeze*, 1927), *Addled-Brained* (1927–28), *Xinxiaolin* (*New Forest of Laughs*, 1928), *New Laughter* (1928), *Nonsense* (1929), two different versions of *Chaplin* (1926; 1930) and *Really Happy* (1927; 1928), and three papers called *Happy World* (1914; 1926–27; 1927). These and other major dailies carried humorous content, including comic strips (Rea 2015: 10). In the 1930s, humor/cartoon magazines, such as Lin Yutang's (1895–1976) *The Analects Fortnightly* (1932–37), began to appear, as will be discussed later.

By now, it is obvious that because of nomenclature and cultural factors, it is difficult to pinpoint the earliest political cartoon in China. Often given as the first drawn by a Chinese artist is "The Situation in the Far East," created on July 19, 1899, by the revolutionary organizer Xie Zantai (1872–1937). Xie resided in Hong Kong, but his cartoon had to be printed in Japan because of Chinese and British censorship. Wong (2002: 31) wrote that the cartoon was reprinted several times, most notably on December 15, 1903, in *Eshi jingwen (Russian Issues Alarming News)*, a Shanghai-based, anti-Russian periodical. The cartoon, using Chinese and English, was described by Wong (2002: 31) as depicting

> the political dangers then facing China. Various animals represent the countries that had a presence in China: a bear for Russia, a dog for Britain, a frog for France, an eagle for the United States, a round sausage for Germany, and a sun for Japan. A Qing government official waves invitingly at the Chinese border. Near Beijing, another official lounges calmly. Below him, a wealthy citizen enjoys a lavish meal. Together, these three figures illustrate the nonchalant attitude of the people and the government toward the situation.

The animals' powers were reflected in their sizes.

In the upper left corner of one of the versions of the cartoon is a passage in Chinese chastising the people for being asleep and imploring them to awaken:

> Deep in sleep is our China,
> how should they know that loving one's country is as natural as loving one's family!
> [You] citizens / The Nation should know that as to waking up you have to wake up now
> and not wait until the land is carved up like a melon!
> (Wagner 2011; translation is Wagner's)

As the number of progressive newspapers grew, so did political cartooning. The influential *People's Journal*, published in Japan by the Chinese Alliance and smuggled into China, used many hard-hitting cartoons, especially in a 1907 issue entitled "Heaven Condemns." High-ranking Qing officials were depicted

in some cartoons as snakes and fish, and, according to Liu-Lengyel (2001: 43), "their double-faced personalities were symbolized by splitting their heads into two halves"[4] (see also Lent 1994: 282).

Like the cartoon and pictorial magazines, these newspapers were havens for young artists who went on to become important cartoonists. Zhang Yuguang, called one of the "most prolific, influential, and multitalented" artists of early twentieth-century China (Laing 2004: 140–41), heightened anti-Qing feelings between 1909 and 1911, when he drew political cartoons for three partisan newspapers, *Minxubao (The People's Sigh)*, *Minhubao (The People's Cry)*, and *Minli bao (The People's Stand)* (Sullivan 2006: 141). Cartoons calling for reform also dotted issues of *Dongfang shibao (The Eastern Times)* (1904–39), a popular newspaper started by literati with Japanese experience (see Judge 1996).

In pictorial magazines and newspapers of the period immediately preceding the 1911 revolution through the 1930s, cartoons were often difficult to understand despite comic art analysts' propensity to claim without reservation that visual symbols are more decipherable than textual matter, especially for illiterates. It is extremely unlikely that illiterates could comprehend the *Minhu Daily Pictorial* described above. Furthermore, illiterate Chinese were usually not motivated to "read" these periodicals' visual matter because they lacked the interest and the ability to afford them. As Guo (2015) pointed out, "the main aim of these political cartoons was to make Chinese literates who were politically apathetic resonate around the theme and awaken them to the importance of civil rights, specifically freedom of speech and of the press, and further to motivate them to struggle for civil rights."

In addition to magazines and newspapers, cartoons occasionally came out in flyer form. During the patriotic movement of Yihetuan (the Boxers) in 1899, poster-sized cartoons drawn by self-taught cartoonists were strategically placed on streets, denouncing imperialism and foreign missionary activity. The cartoons contained familiar allusions to folklore and symbolic messages. Later, about the time of the revolts in China during the 1910s, cartoon leaflets drawn by amateurs were dispersed. One such leaflet, entitled "Do Not Let Us Be Laughed at by the Japanese," implored the Chinese to boycott Japanese imports because of the country's occupation of parts of China. As will be seen later, cartoon leaflets figured in World War II propaganda.

Lianhuanhua

Lianhuanhua have been compared to United States-style comic books such as the Big Little Books (see Inge 2004: 10–15) and *Classics Illustrated* from the mid-twentieth century. However, the lianhuanhua differ in size, format, message, and purpose. They are palm size (five inches long, three-and-a-half inches wide, and one-fourth inch thick), contain one image per page and carry a paragraph description usually at a given page's bottom, and more often than not dispense messages to promote social and political campaigns and educate and mobilize people.

How then can they be classified as comic art? They combine the verbal with the visual and converge *gushihua* (storytelling picture) with *lianxuhua* (sequential picture) to tell stories. Chen (1996: 31) explained that separately, gushihua capture one moment at a time, while lianxuhua allow separate but related scenes and activities to appear all at once. Lianhuanhua also have close semblances to pre-twentieth century, Western drawings labeled as comics, such as those of the Swiss artist of the 1840s, Rodolphe Töpffer.

Historically, the mini-books have taken on different names by region: *tuhuashu* (picture book) or *xiaoshu* (little book) in Shanghai, *yayashu* (children's book) in Wuhan, and *gongzaishu* (kid's book) in Guangdong (Zhong 2004: 107).

As discussed previously, picture stories existed in China for a long time, but they evolved into lianhuanhua when published as separate books. When this first happened is up for debate. Shen (2001: 100) thought it could have been when Zhu Zhixuan's *Sanguozhi* (*The Legend of Three Kingdoms*) was published by Wenyi Book Company[5] in 1908; Huang and Wang (1993: 17–18)

said it was when the newspaper *Chaobao* (*Wave*) bound its single-page pictorials into an album in 1916; and Cao (2002, cited in Pan Lingling 2008: 694) credited *Xiyouji* (*Journey to the West*) in 1925 as the first (see also Huang Yuanlin 1981: 17–18). Other sources have taken their origins back to the late nineteenth century.

Peking opera played a pivotal role in changing the content of lianhuanhua, which previously was mainly news and current events. When a famous Peking opera serial, *Limao huan taizi* (*Exchange the Prince with a Leopard Cat*), played in Shanghai for a few months in 1918, some publishers capitalized on its success by seeking painters to draw illustrated books based on the opera's script. Roughly and quickly drawn to be ready for scheduled performances, this type of book proliferated because of the familiarity and continuity of the narrated stories and their readability (Shen 2001: 101). Chen (1996: 64) wrote that the beginning stages of lianhuanhua grew

> spontaneously, absorbing whatever was available in the cultural soil without much recognition or encouragement from the political or intellectual elite. To meet the people's taste, lianhuanhua changed styles constantly, struggling to shape itself into a stable format that was acceptable to the public. In the process of formalization, lianhuanhua assimilated characteristics from other forms of popular art, such as novels, stage performances, movies, especially New Year's pictures.

Liu Boliang and Zhu Runzhai (1890–1936) pioneered the adaptation of novels to lianhuanhua. In 1920, Liu painted *Xue Rengui zhengdong* (*Xue Rengui Going on an Eastern Expedition*), published by Youwen Book Company as likely the first novel turned into a lianhuanhua. The format he used became the template adopted by other lianhuanhua artists of the 1920s (Shen 2001: 101). Liu and fellow cartoonist Li Shuchen encouraged Zhu to make lianhuanhua, most of which were based on novels and historical romances. By the 1930s, Zhu was one of Shanghai's main cartoonists, turning out more than thirty comic serials, including *Sanguo yanyi* (*Historical*

娛樂大觀　男老女幼

連環圖畫三國志

全部三集　每集八冊　第一集　第五冊

上海世界書局出版

Fig. 1.14. *Lianhuan Tuhua Sanguozhi* (*Comic Strip Romance of the Three Kingdoms*) by Chen Danxu, 1927. Published by Shanghai Shijie Shuju (Shanghai World Publishing House).

Romance of Three Kingdoms), *Tianbaotu* (*Heavenly Treasures*), and *Dibaotu* (*Earthly Treasures*), all very popular with the public (Shen 2001: 101–3).

As sales of lianhuanhua climbed, large publishers took an interest in publishing them; for example, in 1927, Shijie shuju (World Book Company) brought out *Lianhuan tuhua sanguozhi* (*Illustrated History of Three Kingdoms*). Shen (2001: 103) claimed that this was the first use of the term lianhuanhua for these books.

Besides being published by larger firms, lianhuanhua in the 1920s and '30s also benefited from the increased availability of Western publications in China and an elaborate distribution system. Andrews (1997: 18) claimed "the appearance of lianhuanhua was part

of the Chinese response to and adoption of new forms of publishing from the West." Hwang (1978: 53) had thought the same, stating that many foreign comics [strips] were translated into Chinese at the time, and that, "before long, original Chinese comics [lianhuanhua] modeled after the foreign ones were rolling off the press of specialized publishing houses." Stories continued to feature plots from Chinese dramas and, by the 1920s, movies. Those based on current running dramas and films were often drawn and printed the night of the opening performance and distributed the next morning (Andrews 1997: 18–19). Chen (1996: 66) said that balloons were added to lianhuanhua with the appearance of sound movies.

18

志道沒錢不與你這
道我將錢來還你
楊志道你偏要買我這刀
你不買休要買他
買牛二道你殺得人
殺人殺你這口刀與你
楊志道禁城中難殺人我如何敢殺你看
三件我不信你再說殺人
二道我不信再試第
劈如灰不曾壞了吹毛利刃再看
吹氣如灰求人吹
銅錢又剁鐵如泥斷他
血泊牛二不信叫他剁
過第三段人叫他剁
口不捲第二吹毛利得
道第一砍銅錢楊志上漬
二道第一刀砍銅錢上渴
是白鐵刀楊志道不
如得肉是買刀楊志道這不
我三十文買一把也
牛二喝道甚麼高刀

Fig. 1.15. *Lianhuan Tuhua Shuihu* (*Comic Strip of Water Margin*) by Li Pengzheng, 1928. Published by Shanghai Shijie Shuju (Shanghai World Publishing House).

No less important for spurring lianhuanhua's success was the newly instituted distribution system. Because the small books were considered vulgar by intellectuals, most bookstores did not stock them. Instead, publishers sold lianhuanhua to street booth vendors in Shanghai, who, in turn, rented them to low-income readers. Nightly, the vendors went to the small publishers to buy the two new volumes of each comic serial issued every day in 2,000-copy press runs. Once twenty-four volumes of a serial appeared, publishers bound them and put them in a box to be sold as "old-style books" (Shen 1997: 5; Huang and Wang 1993: 18–19). In 1935, the publishers and street book stalls formed a comic book exchange in the Taoyuanli district of Shanghai, where new lianhuanhua were brought by publishers at two o'clock in the afternoon daily, from whence they would appear in street book booths by six o'clock (Huang and Wang 1993: 115–19).

The demands brought about by this more efficient distribution system required a different way of producing the books. Production in the 1920s and '30s was handled by several large and approximately twenty small publishers, all dependent upon a master-apprentice workforce. Because speed was essential, the commissioned masters were expected to finish works daily. In an assembly-line type of operation, the master composed and drew the main images, after which the apprentices completed the details, each person in charge of a specific

Fig. 1.16. Customers reading lianhuanhua at a street vendor stand.

aspect—clothes patterns, flora, fauna, architecture, etc. (Shen 1997: 5).

Quite famous among the masters were Zhu Runzhai, Zhou Yunfang, Shen Manyun (1911–78), and Zhao Hongben (1915–2000), called the *sida mingdan* ("four famous female roles") of lianhuanhua, a reference to Peking opera (Shen 2001: 105). Zhou, using Western art styles and modern themes, had many young followers; one of his major contributions was adapting Ye Qianyu's famous newspaper comic serial, "Wangxiansheng" ("Mr. Wang"), into a lianhuanhua. Shen was known for drawing opera and legendary stories, while Zhao brought progressive works to lianhuanhua.

Successful lianhuanhua, particularly twenty in a series called "Huoshao Hongliansi" ("The Burning of the Red Lotus Temple"), released between 1928 and 1931, were quickly developed into movies. Together with theater, movies became the main sources for the books (see also Jiang Weipu 1989, 2000).

Between 1933 and 1935, *lianxu tuhua* (continual pictorial novels) with "European expressionist accents"

were produced by amateur woodcut artists; these woodcut novels were artists' original works, rather than adaptations used in lianhuanhua. Lianxu tuhua also differed from lianhuanhua of the 1920s, because they increasingly were looked at as "proletarian art" and incorporated aspects of the Japanese "creative print" (*hanga*; woodblock prints of the artist's own designs) and the European "woodcut novels" of Flemish graphic artist Frans Masereel (1889–1972), whose themes ("allure and danger of the city, the misery of social inequality, and the suffering and sacrifice of the masses") and art form were adopted in China (Xiao Tie 2013).

The most accomplished of lianxu tuhua artists was Wen Tao (1907–50), a man who had more than his share of adventure and hardship. Sold by his parents to a salt merchant, Wen Tao escaped and joined the Canton National Revolutionary Army, was captured in battle with bandits who forced him to join them, escaped again, and ended up with a businessman in Southeast Asia, where he worked as a cook, carpenter, lapidary, dentist, shoemaker, and waiter. During these travels,

Wen Tao taught himself painting and music. In 1931, he became a village school teacher. He discovered woodcut inspired by Masereel's works when he gave up oil painting, because he could not afford the paint. Later in the 1930s, he directed an art school, acted and served as choreographer in the school's theater troupe, and edited the Communist *Enlightenment Daily* and *New Phase* magazine (Xiao Tie 2013). His most important work was *Her Awakening*, an account of his own suffering in "woodblock novel" form.

Summary

To summarize, Chinese comic art development was an evolutionary process that sped up in the late nineteenth and early twentieth centuries, mainly for the same reasons that cartoons took hold in many parts of the world—the introduction of faster and more efficient printing technology, and the mounting dissatisfaction with domestic governments and colonial or other foreign interfering nations. By the dawn of the twentieth century, China was in the throes of increasing anger at the ineptitude of the Qing Dynasty and at foreign powers seen by some intellectuals as scavengers waiting at the borders for an opportunity to come in and claim a part of the country. That crises breed effective cartooning is a worldwide adage, and as will be seen throughout this book, that saying applies equally to the history of Chinese comic art.

Chinese cartooning, as it exists in many countries, especially of the Southern hemisphere, took its cues from Western counterparts. For example, in China, the early humor magazines often assumed British or American names; some were published by foreign owners; and their contents had a Western "feel." This tendency to look to the West, either to emulate or to reject what it has to offer, is another recurring theme in the history of Chinese comic art.

The expansion of lianhuanhua in the 1920s and '30s was but one of the phenomena that might lead one to term those years China's "golden age of comics." The premise for such an assertion is that those two decades spawned the first successful newspaper comic strips, an avalanche of cartoon/humor magazines, the initial efforts to professionalize comic art with the creation of a cartoon association and exhibition, the nourishing of the first generation of fully dedicated cartoonists, and a more precise definition of humor and cartoons.

The unsettling and turbulent times were ripe for cartoonists, whose vitriol spewed out towards such a multitude of targets. They and other intellectuals espoused opinions meant to mobilize China against an "aggressive military tide" and to bring awareness to a single-nation concept (Kushner 2013: 57). They saw their new Republic of China plagued with territorial and political fragmentation, coups and purges, advancing fascism at home and abroad, and economic depression. They recognized the May Fourth Movement of 1919 (brought on by student objections to Japan's designs on China and frustrations concerning China's destiny relative to the Versailles Peace Conference) to be of "seismic importance" in pushing China to view a number of factors in a new light. Among these were the country's international setting, its national identity and consciousness, and its cultural traditions.

Calls for the modernization of humor, art, and language were increasingly made after May Fourth; at the same time, the commercialization of culture and media began. Kushner (2013: 52) wrote that "humour was now considered an indispensable element of modernity," even though throughout the 1920s, it was a "refuge of the intellectual classes." Between 1915 and 1937, colloquial language was encouraged to replace classically written Chinese in an effort to make humor modern; the development of a national wit was also considered necessary to place China internationally (Kushner 2013: 51). Kushner (2013: 52) wrote that in the 1920s and '30s, humorists paid attention to the "intersection of humour and politics and international relations, and thus to humour as a wellspring of national identity," simultaneously as

Chapter 2

Manhua's Golden Age

cartoons became "a new form of entertainment with some informative value—many depicted courtesan culture and tabloid stories of intrigue, or combined their social criticism with a voyeuristic attitude that titillated in ways that were not previously socially permitted or not allowed by the censors" (57).

The stirrings to orient art and cartoons towards the peasantry came out of this age, as trade unions and the Chinese Communist Party saw the need to use art for propaganda purposes. Unions took pains to illustrate their propaganda papers, especially with cartoons. Local unions issued pictorials whose illustrated pages often were removed, posted on walls, or distributed as leaflets. Supposedly, in 1926, Mao Zedong (1893–1976) introduced courses on peasant art at Nongmin yundong jianxisuo (Peasant Movement Training Institute). The twenty-four-hour curriculum included fourteen hours of teachings on "revolutionary drawings" done by cartoonist Huang Zhouhua (Huang 1943: 26). Such a claim might be challenged by a scholar such as Elizabeth Perry, who stated that Mao's role in the CCP in the 1920s was marginal. In a 1927 report made in Hunan, Mao commended cartoons, saying that "simple slogans, cartoons and speeches have produced such a widespread and speedy effect among the peasants that every one of them seems to have been through political school" (Hung 1994a: 234).

When the Central Revolutionary Base Area (CRBA) was established in Jiangxi Province in 1929, followed by the China-Soviet Republic Temporary Central Government, Mao, as president of the latter and head of the Red Army, emphasized artistic propaganda. Army divisions had newspapers with cartoons, and wall cartoons were posted everywhere in the CRBA. Cartoons in the CRBA regions praised the Communist leadership and Red Army victories, encouraged struggle against the ruling class and imperialist aggression, promoted a new life in CRBA, and propagated the Soviet Union revolution. Most of these works were crude, drawn by anonymous artists, save for Huang Yuguang and a few others (Lent 1994: 284).

Waves of nationalism—such as during the Northern Expedition (1925–26), which culminated in a 1927 bloody purge of Communists by Guomindang (GMD) leader Chiang Kai-shek, and Japan's takeover of Northeast China in 1931 and a subsequent attack on Shanghai—provided fodder for a growing group of political cartoonists. Prominent among them was Huang Wennong (1903–34), credited with pioneering political caricature and the use of an individualistic cartooning style that combined Chinese and Western drawing approaches (Liu-Lengyel 2001: 43). Huang, while one of the artists and cartoonists who served with the Red Army during the Northern Expedition and at other times, depicted the aggressive tendencies of foreign imperialists and Chinese warlords, the devastation wrought by the warlords, and the peasants' difficult lives (see Feng 1998: 2).

Newspaper and Magazine Strips

One of the contributions of cartoonists in the so-called "golden age" was the newspaper and magazine comic strip (a multi-panel cartoon, usually humor- or adventure-filled with a regular character or cast). Sporadically, strips appeared, for example, by Liao Bingxiong (1915–2006), Xu Ruoming, Huang Jiayin, Feng Di, Jin Mo, Yu Yongpeng, Chen Zhenlong, and others, but they were one-shot efforts. Pioneering in continuity strips were Ye Qianyu (1907–95), Zhang Leping (1910–92), and Huang Yao (1917–87).

Ye was twenty-one years old when he created "Wangxiansheng" ("Mr. Wang"), four to eight panels built around a "triangular-headed, middle-class philistine, proud possessor of all the typical Chinese vices" (Chen 1938: 212). The strip dealt with Mr. Wang and his family as they encountered the sensations of modern urban life—luxury, gluttony, deceit, and pleasure seeking. "Wangxiansheng" started in the premiere April 1928 issue of *Shanghai manhua* (*Shanghai Sketch*, aka *Shanghai Cartoon*) and ran for nine years.

Fig. 2.1. Ye Qianyu, famous cartoonist who began his career in 1927 and went on to develop the first successful comic strip, "Wangxiansheng," led a wartime, anti-Japanese cartoon brigade, and innovated as a guohua painter.

After *Shanghai manhua* ceased publication in 1930, "Wangxiansheng" moved to *Shidai huabao* (*Modern Miscellany*), which Ye edited. Ye spread the strip around after 1932. For *Tuhua chenbao* (*Picture Morning News*), he did the series "Wangxiansheng biezhuan" ("Biography of Mr. Wang") and later drew "Story of Mr. Wang in the South" for Guangzhou and "Story of Mr. Wang in the North" for Tientsin (Tianjin). *Tuhua chenbao* kept the series alive for 182 issues (Xie 1991: 88).

When Ye began cartoon work in 1927, he "holed up in a damp Shanghai shack, [from which] he cranked out one cartoon after another to meet editors' deadlines" ("55 years . . ." 1982: 26). Ye described his work at that time: "Although I was motivated more by need than artistic fulfillment, I learned how to pick out that tell-tale trait that gives life to a character—and how to make my audience laugh or cry over it" ("55 years . . . 1982: 26). Educated by "street-wise eclecticism," Ye went on to an illustrious career as head of the wartime anti-Japanese cartoon brigade and an innovative guohua (traditional Chinese painting) painter of landscapes, actors, dancers, and China's minority people (see also Lent 1994: 288–89).

The most popular strip in Chinese cartoon history is "Sanmao" (meaning three hairs), the product of Zhang Leping. "Sanmao" came alive November 20, 1935, in *Xiaochenbao* (*Small Morning Paper*). Farquhar (1995: 149) contended this was the first of four versions, and that its emphasis was on humor and entertainment, not social exposure (see also Bi and Huang 1983: 258). However, based on an interview with Zhang related in *Asiaweek*, the cartoonist must have had social-change motives when he began his career. According to the magazine, "As he developed an awareness of China's economic and

Fig. 2.2. "Wangxiansheng" depicted Mr. Wang and his family as they experienced urban living.

Fig. 2.3. Zhang Leping, best known for his character Sanmao, made many contributions to the strengthening of the cartoon profession.

social ills—and an empathy for the suffering he saw all around him—Zhang sought a way to express his anger at the powerful individuals who benefited from the corrupt system" (Lam 1982: 32).

In the prewar strip, Zhang expressed the feelings of abandoned street children in a style that often attacked social injustices. In one series, he portrayed the starving Sanmao trying to sell himself for 10,000 "inflated pre-war yuan, only to see a rich lady spend ten times that amount on an imported doll for her coddled child" (Lam 1983: 32). Because of such episodes, people all over China sent clothes, shoes, and other gifts to Zhang for distribution to Sanmao.

After World War II—during part of which, Zhang, like Ye, was a member of the anti-Japanese cartoon brigade, where he drew occasional Sanmao posters— the strip initially satirized greed among high officials, while showing Sanmao as a brave-beyond-belief soldier, who was often the butt of older soldiers' anger. Published in Shanghai's *Shenbao* and called *Sanmao congjunji* (*Sanmao Joins the Army*), these strips were brutally graphic at times, showing bayoneted victims, a severed hand, or a splotch of blood where once stood a fellow soldier. Zhang (1983) himself acknowledged that Sanmao's ingenuous soldiering was often absurd. How absurd? In one strip, Sanmao manages to lift his heavy gun and kill four enemy soldiers with a single bullet.

Sanmao congjunji[1] was a bridge from the "for fun" strips of the 1930s and the more serious and socially penetrating ones beginning in 1947. Farquhar (1995: 151) said several traits common to the later series *Sanmao liulangji* (*The Wanderings of Sanmao*), beginning in the newspaper *Dagongbao* (*Dagong Newspaper*) in 1947, were evident in the post-World War II strips, such as their contemporary, controversial, and educational nature and their sympathetic concern for the masses. She said a fourth characteristic added to *Sanmao liulangji* was a "clear differentiation of class" (152), where Sanmao is representative of the oppressed. Both Zhang Leping and his son, Zhang Rongrong, discussed the motivation of the strip that had restarted in 1947. As Zhang Leping wrote (1963, quoted in Farquhar 1995: 149):

[In 1948 and 1949], you could see homeless children in every street and alley you walked along in old Shanghai, then ruled by the reactionary nationalist government. Some were so exploited by landlords and capitalists that they had no clothes and food and died of illness and starvation. Others became cannon fodder, forced into the army by the reactionary Nationalist clique. Still others were killed

26

Fig. 2.4. The strip "Sanmao" had a number of reincarnations, the main character shifting from an abandoned street urchin to an unbelievably courageous child soldier, and later, a representative of the oppressed class (Zhang Leping 1983: 58).

indiscriminately by reactionary American devils. . . . Every family has countless such tragedies to tell!

Zhang's son, quoted on the seventieth anniversary of "Sanmao," told how his father "created the orphan Sanmao in tears especially when he saw the young orphans frozen to death on the streets. With his pen, he wanted to help those real life Sanmaos" (*Shanghai ribao* [*Shanghai Daily*] July 28, 2005).

Some of the episodes were reminiscent of Zhang Leping's own impoverished start in life. For example, one particularly long series (thirty-three strips) that shows Sanmao working for a printer, doing menial household and print shop duties, might have related to Zhang's childhood experience as a printer's apprentice. In other series, Sanmao tried his hand at being a shoeshine boy and a rickshaw puller, but always to no avail because of his ineptitude, misfortunes that struck him (such as being robbed), impatient bosses, or penny-pinching customers. Throughout these pre-Liberation strips, he was screamed at, kicked, scolded, slapped, and imprisoned, and though he was compassionate and well meaning, he always seemed to do the wrong thing and he never fit in. He is seen sleeping on the street blanketed by newspapers and dreaming of being part of a family with food, a bed, and a loving mother; shivering from cold as he watches a wealthy woman and her dog, both in fur coats, pass by; or thinking up survival schemes.

Although Zhang is best remembered as Sanmao's creator, he made a number of other contributions to the elevation of Chinese comic art. His drawings, beginning in the 1930s (many published in *Shidai manhua* [*Modern Sketch*]), chronicled the foibles of Shanghai society in a variety of styles, from simple line art in one- and multi-panel format to more realistic illustrations, and very striking silhouettes and woodblock prints. His subjects covered all types of Shanghainese, including rogues, common people, prostitutes, businessmen, children, and temptresses revealing considerable skin (see Ding and Yu 2011).

Like other cartoonists of the 1930s, Zhang showed disdain for artists who viewed cartooning as a "low art" meant only for the masses. He said that the reason he chose the cartoon as his medium was "because, unlike many highbrow art forms, it can get directly at the heart of the masses" (Lam 1982: 32). One writer said of Zhang that "he has fathered a style which, while remaining deceptively simple in conception and organisation, permits the artist to incorporate into his work both obnoxious and inconspicuous facets of the experience of the man in the street—thus touching viewers with the relevance of art to life" (Lam 1982: 32).

Fig. 2.5. An anti-Japanese cartoon, "Kuilei xiheduo—Niubizi Chuanyan" ("There Are So Many Puppet Shows—Played by Niubizi"), created by Huang Yao during wartime. Courtesy of Carolyn Wong and the Huang Yao Foundation.

A third early strip, "Niubizi," ("Ox Muzzle"),[2] by Huang Yao (1917–87), actually preceded "Sanmao," debuting in 1934 when Huang was seventeen years old. Huang's granddaughter, Carolyn Wong, who has renewed interest in his legacy through her exhaustive research, described "Niubizi" as a "humorous, learned Chinese gentleman filled with Chinese wisdom . . . [who] spoke for the common people and had personalities that the Chinese can be proud of" (Wong 2008: 670). She added:

> The titles of the cartoon strips appeared childlike, as they were written upside down, to capture the innocent humor. Niu Bizi could take the role of male, female, or animal, portraying current, historical, literary, or mythological characters to mock the existing social or political situations in China. Niu Bizi made the readers laugh, but sometimes

in bitter resignation as they identified with Niu Bizi's plight. (670; see also Wong 2006)

Ox Muzzle was described by Xiao Xiao-lan (2011) as "a typical Chinese gentleman in a long robe and a black coat. He has a big round face, and his ears, eyes, and nose appeared to be five tiny rings. He is pigeon-toed in a pair of black cloth shoes. This funny figure could be drawn easily with just a few simple lines."

Huang's fellow cartoonist, Jack Chen Yifan (1908–95), wrote of Niubizi's (he called him "Mr. Willie Buffoon") big-heartedness, describing a panel that showed him "walking over a snow-covered landscape. He sees a beggar lying frozen in the snow. Evidently inspired by the Biblical ethics imported into China, he gives his clothes to the beggar, sends him on his way—and lies down in the beggar's place" (Chen 1938: 311).

Fig. 2.6. "Longevity Noodles"
by Huang Yao. *Xinwen bao*,
January 31, 1935. Courtesy of
Carolyn Wong and the Huang Yao
Foundation.

According to Huang Yao, he created the figure because of 1. his "wrath over Westerners' humiliation of Chinese people," in the process, creating an "impressively energetic" character; 2. his concern about Chinese young people's fascination with the flood of Western cartoons at that time, and 3. his determination to make Ox Muzzle "emblematic of resourcefulness and perseverance" (Xiao Xiao-lan 2011).

The strip "Niubizi" was extremely popular in the 1930s; at one time, about forty print publications published the strip simultaneously. Because Niubizi was easy to draw, tempting many copiers, Huang officially registered the character in 1937. That year, he also started a magazine, *Niutou manhua* (*Ox Head Cartoon*), to publish Niubizi cartoons drawn by children nationwide. The widespread appeal of Niubizi supposedly caught the attention of Japanese military forces occupying China, which, in 1942, plagiarized the character for their own propaganda efforts in Beijing (Wong, interview, 2005).

In less than two years after its creation, the "Ox Muzzle" series had eight sets, the first five, multi-paneled, the last three, single-paneled ("Story of Blessing" and "Story of If, Parts A and B"). Themes often revealed "bitter discontent" against a "brutal society," and disappointment with the "vulgarity of human nature and of the society he lived in." At one time, Huang Yao was arrested by the Shanghai Concession police for his "progressive philosophy and revolutionary art" (Xiao Xiao-lan 2011).

Beginning with "Roar of the Nation" in March 1938, Huang Yao denounced the Japanese invaders and called for public resistance. In addition to calling for resistance, his character also fought on the battlefield. Among other wartime series Huang Yao drew are "Seventy-Two Pictures of Invasion" in April 1938, detailing that number of types of atrocities committed by the Japanese; "Comic Europe" in April 1940, decrying the Nazis; "Heroes and a Chinese Soldier" in January 1941; "Chongqing on the Home Front" in August 1941; and "The Chinese People in War" and "Comic Chongqing" both in June 1943 (Xiao Xiao-lan 2011).

Because he did not join a cartoonists team or publish cartoons in the two resistance cartoon magazines, Huang Yao's wartime cartooning was underestimated, but Xiao Xiao-lan (2011) believed he was "one of the most enthusiastic and most prolific painters in the Second Sino-Japanese War." His antiwar activities took other forms; for example, Huang worked with children to form the Children Save the Country Society, which collected money to send cartoonists to the interior of China "so that cartoons would be realistic and relevant to resist the impending Japanese invasion" (Wong 2008: 271; see also Huang Mao 1947). Because of his resistance activities, Huang was warned that he should leave Shanghai, which he did on the day the city fell to the Japanese in 1937. The following year, he set up a printing press in Chongqing, which published the many books he compiled in the 1930s and the war years—on cartoons,

Fig. 2.7. Self-caricature of China's second known woman cartoonist, Liang Baibo, who played key roles as the only female member of the First National Cartoon Exhibition in 1936 and also of the anti-Japanese cartoon brigade.

new lianhuanhua, nianhua, foreign cartoons, and cartoons of places visited, as well as instructional books featuring Niu Bizi (see Wong 2008: 673–87 for a partial list of Huang Yao's books).

Writing in 1940, the twenty-three-year-old Huang expressed his ideas about the role played by cartoons, especially pertinent for wartime China:

> Cartoons are not the same as ordinary paintings, it is a weapon, it is like a short but sharp sword. Under abnormal circumstances, cartoons have certain responsibilities; it is not a forgiving medium nor a medium that is easy to influence, it is a fair platform to attack thieves, the shameless, the oppressors who will have no place to hide.
>
> Cartoons are not polite, they are fair, like a court but with a humorous judge . . . Their form of questioning, judgment and attitude is through the use of humor. Although they are not stern like judges who would scold, reprimand or sentence the guilty to death, cartoons are cold and in a word or a sentence or without words, they can cause you to not be able to cry nor to laugh! (Huang Yao 1940)

Huang's life after he left China in 1945 was full of new adventure as he resided in Vietnam from 1945 to 1946;

Kunming, 1946 to 1947; Hong Kong, 1947 to 1951; Bangkok, 1951 to 1956; Singapore, Kuala Lumpur, and Penang, 1956 to 1987, the year he died.

Though short-lived, the daily strip "Mifeng xiaojie" ("Miss Bee"), published in 1935 on *Libao*'s (*Standing Paper*) front page, is of historical note because it was created by one of China's first female cartoonists, Liang Baibo (1911–? ca. 1970).

Liang stood out for her individualistic, romantic, and adventuresome nature. She studied oil painting in Shanghai and Hangzhou, after which she sought employment in Singapore and then, the Philippines, finally teaching fine art at a middle school for Chinese immigrants in the latter. At the dawn of her drawing career, she adopted the pen name "Bomb," but at her friends' urging, changed to "Bon," still trying to preserve the sound of an explosion (Yong 1997: 368).

Liang returned to Shanghai at the beginning of 1935, where, while submitting a cartoon at Time Book Co., she met Ye Qianyu, fell in love with him on the spot, and, according to Ye's later account, took the initiative in their becoming lovers (Wei 1998: 4). Ye recalled:

> Of course Baibo knew I had a wife and children already. But she didn't care. That was the romanticism in the 1930s. I seemed like a little bird escaping from his cage . . . ; Baibo was braver than me. She absolutely did not care about mundane remarks. She passionately had her beloved who had belonged to the other woman. (Wei 1998: 4)

The next half-year or so amounted to a daring adventure for Liang. She and Ye participated that spring in a sanitation propaganda activity sponsored by the Jinpu Railroad Bureau. The project involved Liang and Ye traveling on a train through Anhui, Shandong, and Hebei before arriving in Beijing, where the couple stayed for several days. The trip was extremely productive for Ye, who, according to Wei (1998: 4), "was very excited, like a ball full of air. He drew very quickly. He had finished several hundred sketches in about ten days [edited into the collection, 'Travel Cartoons']."

Fig. 2.8. "Mifeng Xiaojie" ("Miss Bee"), the short-lived daily newspaper strip by Liang Baibo, from 1935.

escort" back to Shanghai (Wei 1998: 4). Unable to obtain a divorce, Ye settled for a legal separation, and for a long time afterwards, Liang was labeled a "fancy woman," much to her inconvenience.

Later on, Ye recalled that period of his life fondly and Liang Baibo's talent admiringly:

> Baibo is a talented painter. She is good at transforming ideology into abstract images by psychological description. The artistic image of "Miss Bee" she drew was the concrete representation of ideology. This was consistent with the idea of life that she was seeking. She had a poet's temperament. When I lived with her, I always felt I was talking to a poet. Her influence on me made me get new imaginations while I created the strip "Mr. Wang Went to the Countryside." My thinking was not limited to an inherent observation of life, but was like it had wings. More visually speaking, maybe some accomplishments in Baibo's soul were transplanted into my soul, catalyzing and making sublime the thinking activity of my cartoon creation. (Wei 1998: 6)

Liang Baibo's known cartoon works were few, but described as of high quality. Very rarely, her cartoons appeared in cartoon magazines, such as *Shanghai manhua* (*Shanghai Sketch*) and *Duli manhua* (*Independent Cartoon*). In November 1935, she drew several sketches of the marriage that month of "Cinema Queen" Hu Die. Even before "Miss Bee," Liang drew nine illustrations for a poem collection, *Children Tower*, edited by the revolutionary poet, and Liang's friend, Yin Fu (Bai Mang). The sixty-five poems and nine illustrations did not see print at that time as Yin Fu was arrested and killed by the Guomindang the following year.[3]

Although she had not drawn much, nonetheless, in 1936, Liang Baibo had the distinction of being elected as one of thirty-one members of the Arranging Committee of the First National Cartoon Exhibition (Yong 1997: 368).

Ever the adventuress, Liang Baibo joined Ye and a few other cartoonists as the only female member of the cartoon propaganda brigade, which will be discussed more

From Beijing, the couple apparently went into hiding in Jinling, Nanjing, sparking one small Shanghai newspaper to remark that "Mr. Wang" [Ye's main character] was "missing." It was while living secretly with Ye that Liang drew "Miss Bee." The strip was described by Wei Shaochang (1998: 3) as a portrayal of "a modern girl who depicted a modern female's world. The model Liang drew was very lovely; the lines were soft and beautiful, and the themes were very interesting. It drew much attention from other cartoonists and was welcomed by readers from the beginning."

On the first day, "Miss Bee" appeared with Liang Baibo's name, but from the second day onwards, the strip was credited to Ye Qianyu and Zong Bai (Liang's alias) as the couple felt it necessary to conceal her identity (Wei 1998: 4). "Miss Bee" stopped abruptly after only twenty-five days, when Ye's wife, accompanied by her father, found Ye and "forcibly" sent him "under

31

Fig. 2.9. Issue 17 of *Shidai manhua* (*Modern Sketch*), showing golfers teeing off on a woman's body, exemplifies the eroticizing and exploiting of women that was common in cartoon magazines in the mid-1930s.

fully in the next chapter. In 1938, she broke her three-year affair with Ye, married a Guomindang fighter pilot, and accompanied him to Taiwan, where she died by suicide.

Cartoon and Humor Magazines

The big story in Chinese cartooning in the 1930s was the explosion of cartoon/humor magazines, probably unparalleled anywhere in the world at the time. In the middle of the decade, about twenty such periodicals appeared in Shanghai, the hub of the cartoon magazines, some with brief stays and virtually all designed primarily for men, because, as Chen (1938: 311) reported, they indulged in some "Elizabethan coarseness. . . . influenced to a large extent by such journals as the American *Esquire*, but with an element of quite Chinese abandon." Some were accused of being pornographic.

Bevan (2016: 30–31) took exception to the charge of pornography leveled at the main cartoon magazine

Fig. 2.10. A 1937 *Modern Sketch* cover by Zhang Ding shows cartoon magazines also dealt with serious issues; here, the results of a famine in Sichuan. Courtesy of Zhang Ding.

Fig. 2.11. *Shanghai manhua* (*Shanghai Sketch*), No. 29, November 1928.

Shanghai manhua, claiming it "forced the magazine into categories in which it had no place," and making the point that the inspiration for such content came from foreign magazines and the "diverse 'modern' European artists introduced to them by those who had studied abroad" (31). He said also that little of the content in *Shidai manhua* was sexual (256) despite what is commonly believed.

The coarseness Chen discussed may have been an influence that emanated from Japan, which during the same period (late 1920s–30s) experienced a wave of *ero guronansensu* (erotic, grotesque, nonsense) cartoons. They came about because the mood of the Japanese people at that time was "very gloomy and desperate," said Yukio Sugiura (1911–?), who drew such works in 1931 and 1932 (interview, 1993; see also Silverberg

2006). Wherever their source, *seqing manhua* (erotic cartoons) became popular in China; to meet urbanites' need for entertainment, they often displayed women's breasts and couples making love. For a while, the subject of erotic cartoons stimulated discussion in the media; some, such as Wang Dunqing (1899–1990), claimed nudity and eroticism were endemic to art (mentioning Western classics); others, such as Zhang E (1910–95), discouraged cartoonists from displaying "women's alluring thighs and soft bosoms," arguing instead that they should expose the "imperialists' conspiracy to carve up China" (Hung 1994a: 34–35; see also Zhang Yingjin 2001).

Some magazines were reincarnations of titles forced to close for political or economic reasons. For example, *Manhuajie* (*Comic Circle*) started as a successor to

Manhua's Golden Age

Fig. 2.12. Zhang Guangyu, the main figure behind *Shanghai manhua*'s survival.

Modern Sketch when the latter was suspended in 1936 (which will be discussed later), and *Manhua shenghuo* (*Cartoons and Life*) was the new version of the monthly *Cartoon Life*, closed by the government in 1935 because of its leftist viewpoints (Liu-Lengyel 1993; Lent 1994: 285). *Manhua shenghuo* also stopped after only three months because of government charges that it advocated class struggle, opposed the government, and promoted the Bolshevik Revolution.

The progenitor of these cartoon/humor magazines was *Shanghai manhua* (*Shanghai Sketch*), an eight-page mixture of cartoons, sketches, and photographs published from April 21, 1928, to June 7, 1930. A major outlet for cartoonists and sketch artists, the magazine owed much of its success to Zhang Guangyu and two sponsors he found—Shao Xunmei (1906–68), "a wealthy, charismatic, and influential writer, poet, translator, book collector, socializer, editor, and publisher" (Laing 2010; for a fuller discussion of Shao Xunmei and his "circle," see Bevan 2016: particularly Chapter 2), and Zhang's brother and fellow cartoonist, Zhang Zhengyu (1904–76). The Zhang brothers and Ye Qianyu had worked together on the small *Sanri huabao* (or *Sanri huakan, Three-Day Pictorial*), which began in 1925. When Chiang Kai-shek's forces shut down *Sanri huabao* in 1927, Ye and other cartoonists, including Huang Wennong and Lu Shaofei (1903–95), started *Shanghai manhua*, a lithograph single sheet resembling a propaganda poster that was not taken seriously and ceased publication. In December 1926, Ye, Lu, Huang, the Zhang brothers, Hu Xuguang, Ding Song, and Wang Dunqing formed

Manhuahui (Cartoon Society); after it was started, eighteen additional cartoonists joined. The society's members gathered for mutual support to discuss and critique cartooning and sketching, publish collections, and start a magazine (Bi 1982: 48; Xu 1994: 85–86; Bi 2002: 129, all cited in Laing 2010). Although it was China's first organization dedicated to cartooning, Manhuahui's existence was brief; some members, particularly Zhang Guangyu, were more interested in renewing *Shanghai manhua*[4] (for a discussion of the Zhang brothers, see Bevan 2016).

Popular, with a respectable print run of 3,000, the revived *Shanghai manhua* showcased the talents of China's first generation of cartoon masters, a substantial portion of whose works were aesthetically innovative and influenced by literature. The editorial staff kept strong connections to, and friendships with, top writers and poets. In fact, the statement of purpose in the inaugural issue was in modern blank verse reminiscent of Li Jinfa (1900–76), China's first symbolist poet (Laing 2010).

Influenced by outside artists—e.g., the British artist Aubrey Beardsley (1872–98)—*Shanghai manhua* artists opened a "new approach to depicting women and the city, and relations between men and women" (Laing 2010). Covers of the magazine were brilliantly executed, sometimes erotic, following canons of ancient Greek mythology with its approval of nakedness and depiction of Herculean physiques. *Shanghai manhua* had a bit of an unusual policy in which the front cover was explained in a subsequent issue either through a short poem or prose. *Shanghai manhua* artists liked to show men as women's toys, women as seductresses pursuing their goals, and women and death, "some epitomizing the link between the twin obsessions of money and sex, plus an added frisson—they lead to death" (Laing 2010). Some covers were sensationalist and grotesque, such as Lu Shaofei's "Human Meat Market," which showed the sale of dismembered female parts, a poignant commentary on the "horrors of prostitution" (Laing 2010).

For the most part, however, *Shanghai manhua* cartoons and illustrations dealt with what Laing (2010) termed the "normal aspects of city life: its amusements,

Fig. 2.13. *Shanghai manhua* followed Greek mythology canons with its approval of nakedness. Cartoon, "She yu furen" ("Snake and Woman") created by Ye Qianyu. *Shanghai manhua*, No. 4, May 12, 1928. Front cover.

Fig. 2.14. Yu Feng, China's first woman cartoonist. Baidu.com.

its frustrations, its street life, its contrasts of rich and poor. . . . The degrading effects of Shanghai nightlife of dance hall, night club, cabaret, and cafe" and men's attraction to pretty girls.

It was in *Shanghai manhua*, in 1929 or 1930, that Yu Feng (1916–2007), the niece of literary figure Yu Dafu (1896–1945) and probably China's first female cartoonist, began her career. Her initial cartoon, imitative of the style of Aubrey Beardsley, was accompanied by a letter of encouragement from Ye Qianyu. In 1934–35, while eighteen and nineteen years old, she drew cartoons for Hong Kong periodicals, and in 1936, for *Zhongguo zhisheng* (*Voice of China*). By 1937, Yu Feng was a cartoon

journalist for *Jiuwang ribao* (*National Salvation Daily*). She continued drawing cartoons—and participated in antiwar demonstrations—during World War II. Bevan (2016: 325) claimed she was an "active member of the cartoon brigade," but her name never came up in our interviews with five brigade members. After 1949, she was a writer, artist, and clothes designer. With her cartoonist husband, Huang Miaozi, she was imprisoned for seven years of the Cultural Revolution, during which she fashioned paintings out of such materials as toilet paper, soap, and candy wrappers. She exhibited her paintings, solo or with others, including Huang Miaozi, throughout Asia, Australia, and Europe (baike.baidu.com).

Manhua's Golden Age

Fig. 2.15. "Let the Gunfire of National Salvation Smash This Pair of Shackles" by Yu Feng had an additional meaning; it implied that women should be free. Huang Miaozi, ed., *Quanguo manhua zuojia kangzhan jiezuo xuanji* (*Selected Works of Chinese Cartoonists on the War of Resistance*). N.p.: Zhangwang shuwu, 1938.

Yu Feng's 1938 cartoon, "Let the Gunfire of National Salvation Smash This Pair of Shackles," meant liberation from all forms of suppression, "including Confucianism, which relegated women to an inferior status" (Hung 1994a: 116).

Fortunately for the sake of historical preservation, Yu Feng kept contact with cartoonist friends up to her death and wrote what Bevan (2016: 332) described as "an inspired artcle on the legacy of these artists." In her essay, Yu Feng credited Zhang Guangyu with spearheading the history of Chinese modern art (Yu Feng 2010: 180–81). Although he thought the argument was "largely accurate," Bevan (2016: 332–33) countered that, from 1926 to 1938, "a new form of Chinese art had already begun to develop, first as part of the wider discourse of modernity in Shanghai and later as a propaganda tool in the fight against Japanese militarism."

The demise of *Shanghai manhua* occurred when the Zhang brothers agreed to a deal with a Singaporean businessman to launch a pictorial magazine to compete with *Liangyou* (*A Young Companion*). The photographic partners balked, and as a result, *Shanghai manhua* folded in 1930, after publishing 110 issues. The Zhangs and the cartoon staff moved to Shidai (Modern) Publications, Ltd., which later published five magazines, including *Shidai manhua* (*Modern Sketch*). Zhang Guangyu reestablished *Shanghai manhua* in May 1936 (Crespi 2011).

Shidai manhua (*Modern Sketch*), a monthly started in January 1934, was the "centerpiece of China's golden age of cartoon art," standing out, according to Crespi (2011), because of its longevity, printing quality, eclectic content, and art by young artists who became the masters of China's cartoons and culture. More than 100 Chinese cartoonists were featured in *Modern Sketch* (Wang 1935: 3). Crespi (2011) lauded *Modern Sketch* further, saying, "Most intriguing is the sheer imagistic force with which this magazine captures the crises and contradictions that have defined China's 20th century as a quintessentially modern era."

As indicated, *Modern Sketch* was one of the five magazines published in 1934 by Shidai (Modern) Publications, Ltd., the group funded by the previously mentioned, multitalented poet Shao Xunmei. In an attempt to save his extended family from bankruptcy, Shao purchased modern printing and photography equipment from Germany, recruited graphic artists who had worked for *Shanghai Sketch*, and started the company (Crespi 2011). The other Shidai Publications periodicals—the pictorial *Shidai huabo* (*Modern Miscellany*), *Shidai dianying* (*Modern Film*), the sophisticated monthly *Van Jan*, and the humor magazine *Lun Yu* (*Analects*)—also served as outlets for cartoonists. Wong (2002: 55) wrote that cartoons were very important to the popularity of *Modern Miscellany*; for a while, Ye's "Wangxiansheng" appeared, as did cartoons by the Zhangs and Huang Wennong, and poetry by Shao Xunmei. Bevan (2016: 57) wrote that Shao's stated aim of the pictorial magazine was "to allow readers to learn whilst enjoying themselves and not for them to be made to feel that reading is a chore."

Modern Sketch's editor, Lu Shaofei, seemed to prefer images over text, giving contributors artistic carte blanche to express personal views—even if embellished and exaggerated—and welcoming photographs if they were "cartoon-like." The editorial policy in the inaugural issue stated that in such a tense era, "Our stance, our single responsibility, then, is to strive! As for the design on the cover of this first issue, it shall be our logo. Its meaning: Yield to None." Lu preferred that contributions critique "the fine points of life's problems, be they large or small," describe "every level of society," promote no ideology, and "explore the future, be it bright or dark," all to make life better (Crespi 2011). Lu set a wide geographical reach with many works coming from abroad and other parts of China, and he encouraged a variety of cartoon categories and forms. Besides the standard gag cartoons (of which *Modern Sketch* published more than 1,000), political cartoons, comic strips, and caricatures, the magazine also experimented with new types and media of comic art, such as paper cut, collage, photos, photomontages, sketching, children's art, and woodblock prints. Crespi (2011) singled out *mandiao* (cartoon sculptures) as the most unusual comic art medium seen in *Modern Sketch*.

A quirk of many single-panel gag cartoons was their frequent use of a variety of windows, leading Crespi (2011) to surmise that they "should tell us something more: that these cartoonists, by observing the world around them and emulating colleagues either in China or abroad, were developing their own iconic language of the cartoon." Particularly attractive were *Modern Sketch* covers, exquisite in full color and consistently carrying an erotic theme and featuring nude or semi-nude women.

There was also a textual aspect to *Modern Sketch*; about one-third of the contents was made up of jokes, one-act plays, erotic anecdotes, and satirical songs (Crespi 2011). A significant portion of the textual matter aimed to understand, critique, and promote the art of cartooning. Various Japanese and Western theories about the nature of the cartoon filled the pages of *Modern Sketch* (Hung 1994a: 129).

Crespi (2011) wrote that the latter half of *Modern Sketch*'s thirty-nine-issue run became a "platform for airing otherwise censored information." Lu Shaofei and his magazine paid the price for this change of direction. *Modern Sketch* was suspended and Lu detained, from March through May 1936, because of an "unflattery [*sic*]" portrayal of China's ambassador to Japan. Filling the three-month gap was *Manhuajie*, edited by Wang Dunqing; it continued independently of *Modern Sketch* through 1936.

Crespi (2011) paid tribute to *Modern Sketch*:

Modern Sketch could be incisive, bitter, shocking, and cynical. At the very same time it could be elegant, salacious, and preposterous. Its messages might be as simple as child's play, or cryptically encoded for cultural sophisticates. *Modern Sketch* was many things for its many readers. The democracy of popular artistic forms it hosted, united in the mission of fusing art and the era, made it a landmark publication.

Contemporary with *Modern Sketch* was the already mentioned *Cartoon Life*, a monthly founded in 1934 in Shanghai. Reflecting the leftist ideological perspectives of editors Zhang E, Huang Shiying, Wu Xilang, and Huang Ding, it lasted a year before being closed by the government. Its replacement, *Manhua shenghuo*, also had a short life, as noted earlier.

Most active on *Cartoon Life* and its clone were cartoonists Zhang E and Cai Ruohong (1910–2002), both members of the leftist artists' organization (Lent 1994: 285). Among other cartoon magazines of the period were *Duli manhua* (*Independent Cartoon*, 1935–36), *Golden Mean* (1933), *Breezy Chats* (1936–37), Lin Yutang's *This Human World* (1934) and *Cosmic World* (1935) (Rea 2015: 133), and *Zhongguo manhua* (*China Cartoon*), the last of which not to be confused with a magazine of the same name later published by collaborationist cartoonists. *Duli manhua*, edited by Zhang Guangyu, exemplified cartoon magazines' fascination with the "Chinese and the Parisian tradition of the erotic eye" (Zhang Yingjin 2001: 131). Often, cartoons dealt with pornography, sensuality, feminine beauty, and voyeurism; Zhang Guangyu published his own romantic and sometimes erotic serial drawings, "Folk Love Songs," in *Duli manhua*.

A few cartoon magazines came out of Guangzhou, such as *Bun-gok manhua* (*The Sketch*), in 1929 and *Banjiao manhua* (*Half-Angle Cartoons*), and Tianjin, *Tianjin manhua* (*Tianjin Cartoons*). A monthly, six issues of *Bun-gok manhua* appeared with twelve issues making a volume. The initial six-month run was printed in Hong

37

Fig. 2.16. Published beginning in 1929, *Bun-gok manhua* (*The Sketch*) was an early competitor of *Shanghai Puck*, though published in Guangzhou.

Kong. Wong (2002: 55) said the main attractions of early volumes of *Bun-gok manhua* were Ye Yinquan's stories about Brother Ho and Mister Tai-shi. From volume four onwards, *Bun-gok manhua* took on a more "cynical tone," using two types of content: realistic stories of Guangzhou life or risqué and titillating illustrations and stories about women (Wong 2002: 55).

Most of the early master cartoonists (those born in the 1910s and early '20s) started their careers on these humor magazines while they were still teenagers or college students (Huang, interview, 2001). Among them were Chen Huiling (b. 1916), Ding Cong (1916–2009), Mai Fei (1916–2007), Te Wei (1915–2010), and Liao Bingxiong. Describing cartooning for those magazines and dailies in the 1930s and '40s as "a hungry situation," Liao Bingxiong (interview, 2002) said,

> I found this Shanghai cartoon magazine in a bookstore and started sending cartoons to it. I became a Shanghai cartoonist after that. They and other periodicals could not pay. I was very poor, could not afford to take the bus. I walked to the newspaper to hand in my works, and I seldom got payment. What payments there were, were very small. My hope was to get some money so I kept sending cartoons.

(For full descriptions of Liao's life and career, see Christiansen 2015; Liao Ling-er and Zhang Hongmiao 2002; Lent and Xu 2003c, 2004, 2007)

Mai Fei (interview, 2006), whose first cartoon appeared in *Zhongguo manhua* in 1935, said he was a second-year art student at the time and became "famous" among fellow students because he was published.

In addition to humor/cartoon magazines, other magazines such as *Dongfang zazhi* (*Eastern Miscellany*), *Lun Yu* (*Analects*), and *Yuzhoufeng* (*Cosmos Wind*), and newspapers and their supplements increasingly provided outlets for cartoonists in the 1920s and '30s. For example, Shanghai-based *Zhongguo pinglun zhoubao* (*China Critic*), an English-language weekly founded in 1928, regularly promoted humor and cartoons. By the 1920s and '30s, nearly all publications solicited cartoons, knowing they attracted readers (Hung 1990: 42). Male readers were the targets in "butterfly" (a genre of romantic commercial literature) magazines that featured photos and cartoon-like illustrations of nude women. By the 1930s, some movie fan magazines, such as *Qingqing dianying* (*The Chin-Chin Screen*), also featured such erotic fare (Zhang 2001: 121).

The supplements added to Chinese dailies by the 1930s occasionally included a children's page. North China dailies, in particular, sported a children's page, starting with Tientsin's *Social Welfare*, which debuted a Sunday children's page on July 2, 1929, followed by *Dagongbao* of the same city, which featured its "Kid's Weekly" beginning in 1930. Later that year, *Dagongbao* carried a daily half-page children's section. *Peiping Press* and *Peiping Social Welfare* also devoted a weekly page to children. All of these sections were successful, attracting women and children with their photographs, illustrations, poetry, essays, and, of course, cartoons (Cheng 1931: 103).

Second-Generation Cartoonists

The 1920s and '30s saw the introduction of a generation of artists who reigned over the Chinese cartoon scene until contemporary times—besides those already discussed, these individuals included Zhang Ding (1917–2010), Liao Bingxiong, Ding Cong, and Hua Junwu (1915–2010).

Work Environments, Influences, Philosophies

Being a pioneer in the cartoon field could not have provided much in the way of financial maneuverability; in the words of one of them, the cartoonists were offered "poverty and hard knocks" for their efforts (Chen 1938: 308). Jack Chen Yifan, who followed the destinies of what he called the original group of the cartoonists (himself included), reported that one died without enough money for his own funeral, one joined the government, one "disappeared after publishing a particularly pointed anti-Guomindang cartoon, six managed to hold together, to be joined by a seventh who has been in hiding for four years" (1938: 308). When the seven remaining cartoonists met at the home of their dead friend, only three had steady jobs, making about $50 in gold a month, and another $50 for extra work. Chen said that at those rates, they were the best paid cartoonists in China.

Marking the early cartoonists as distinct were their political consciousness and their sense of realism. Describing them in 1938, Chen generalized:

They do not as a group belong to any particular political party, but represent the interests of the young nationally conscious intelligentsia, and they are typical of China's revolutionary students. Not one of them is over forty. The vast majority of them are in their teens or late twenties. They are all former or parttime students, newspaper men, teachers, commercial artists, clerks. There are surprisingly few with a natural inclination for purely salacious humor; and ninety-nine per cent are animated by a sincere desire to save their country from colonial subjugation. This I stress, because the general level of political and national consciousness of Chinese artists is low. And it is a fact that there is not one avowedly reactionary cartoonist. *En masse* they are anti-imperialist, anti-feudalist. The sympathies are all with the underdog. (1938: 308)

Chen claimed that they showed "utter disregard" for the traditions of classical Chinese art and ridiculed the "old-fashioned 'bird and bamboo' painters and those would-be Westerners who 'spent their time with nudes and apples'" (308). He added that few of them were true revolutionaries; instead, they were artists who wanted to express their feelings about the "grim reality of China" (311). In that sense, according to Chen, they *were* revolutionary because, as realists, they broke from the essence of Chinese art, which sought harmony with nature, or as Chen put it: "They take Nature (or the Established Order of Things) by the forelock and give her a good walloping in order to make her behave" (311).

Chen, like other observers of cartoonists of the day, failed to elaborate, as Bevan (2016: 51) does, on some of these cartoonists' "major contribution to the art world in the early part of their careers as fashion designers, commercial artists and most importantly, artists involved in the production of periodicals which were at the forefront of Chinese modernity." Cartoonists (before they gained stature as cartoonists) often supported themselves as fashion designers, commercial artists, and, in the case of brothers Zhang Zhengyu and Zhang Guangyu, as furniture designers. In the late 1920s and early '30s, artists Ye Qianyu, Wan Laiming, Lu Shaofei, and Zhang Guangyu contributed fashion sketches to *Liangyou huabao*, *Shanghai manhua*, and numerous other magazines, and Zhang Guangyu and Ding Song drew women in fashionable clothing for tobacco companies' posters and cigarette cards (Bevan 2016: 72). A source of income for some was Yunshang Fashion Company, founded in 1927 by Shao Xunmei and others. Ye Qianyu, whose connection to fashion continued well into the 1930s, was tied to the company as a clothes designer.

Because of the important role he played in documenting the cartoonists' lifestyles, work habits, and pitfalls—as well as his own role in China's cartoon history—Jack Chen deserves some mention here. The son of Eugene Chen, who was Sun Yat-sen's chief secretary, legal/international affairs advisor (1918–25), and foreign minister of the Wuhan government (1926–27), Jack

39

Chen received an art education in Moscow; by 1927, he was in Wuhan, where he began drawing political cartoons for the English edition of *People's Tribune*, funded by the Ministry of Foreign Affairs. His widow, Yuan-tsung Chen, said that "without knowing a thing about revolution, [he] stumbled into his first revolutionary job and accidentally launched his career as the first editorial cartoonist [*sic*] of modern China" ("The Jack Chen Archives . . ." 2013). Influenced by David Low, *New Masses* artists, Francisco de Goya, and Honoré Daumier, Chen was said to have used his art to defend the poor and oppressed masses and to push revolutionary goals ("The Jack Chen Archives . . ." 2013). However, his most significant contribution to Chinese art was the dissemination and promotion of Chinese cartoons throughout China and abroad through exhibitions he organized and essays he wrote. During the Cultural Revolution, he was sent to the countryside to toil alongside the peasants (for a fuller discussion of Chen, see Bevan 2016: particularly, Chapters 5–7).

It is likely these early cartoonists also deviated somewhat from the traditional Chinese art style because of foreign influences. Japanese and Western periodicals circulated in China, some of which (e.g., *Vanity Fair* from the US) were popular. Foreign artists' works appeared in China's daily newspapers and cartoon magazines and were imitated by local cartoonists. For example, Ye's pioneering comic strip, "Wangxiansheng" ("Mr. Wang"), is thought to have been inspired by George McManus's "Bringing Up Father," an American serial comic republished in the *China Press* (1911–41, 1945–49), of which Ye was said to be an "enthusiastic reader" (Rea 2013: 392; see also Wong 2002: 15). The aforementioned cosmopolitan cartoon magazine, *Shidai manhua* (*Modern Sketch*), regularly used foreign works, for instance, by Toba Sojo (1053–1140), Honoré Daumier (1808–79), George Grosz (1893–1959), Sir John Tenniel (1820–1914), Miguel Covarrubias (1904–57), James Thurber (1894–1961) and fellow *New Yorker* cartoonists, and others from the Philippines, Singapore, and Malaya (Crespi 2011). British historian Paul Bevan (2016: 29) wrote of the impact of foreign cartoons in *Shanghai manhua*: "Flicking

through the pages of *Shanghai manhua*, examples can be seen in styles as diverse as Art Nouveau and Art Deco; forms inspired by Cubism and Surrealism, the European Symbolists and English Decadents and even the British Arts and Crafts movement." In his 2016 *A Modern Miscellany*, Bevan felt the perceived influences of Mexican caricaturist Miguel Covarrubias in the early 1930s, followed by those of German artist George Grosz, and the counterarguments that they were not especially important, were significant enough to devote a full chapter to each artist. Putting the "Grosz-style" to use were Cai Ruohong, Lu Zhixiang (1910–92), Ding Cong, Hua Junwu, and Zhang E, while the main proponent of Covarrubias's way of drawing was Zhang Guangyu, and, to a lesser extent, Ding Cong, who was also a devotee of Mexican muralists Diego Rivera, José Clemente Orozco, and David Alfaro Siqueiros. Ding Cong also liked the humor-tinged, realistic art of the American Norman Rockwell (Ding Cong, interview, 2002).

In the 1920s and '30s, Japan also had a considerable influence on Chinese art and cartooning as artists and cartoonists absorbed Japanese visual elements and jointly exhibited with Japanese counterparts. The impact of Japanese art was particularly evident on Chinese propaganda art manifested in political cartoons. Zhang Shaoqian (2014) wrote:

> Many political posters produced during the First United Front (1922–1927) borrowed the style and content of another popular Japanese pictorial genre that had emerged around the turn of the twentieth century: manhua. Chinese political cartoons reached their height after the outbreak of the May 30 Movement in 1925, probably the most significant anti-imperialist and labor movement . . . [R]ather than being seen as a challenge to the traditional Chinese artistic canon, Japanese elements seem to have been most easily incorporated into the newly emerging art styles and genres, such as the Shanghai School, or the political cartoon.

Foreign artists who resided in Shanghai also left their mark. Hua Junwu (interview, 2005) acknowledged he was impressed as a young art student in the 1930s by the

Fig. 2.17. Wartime cartoon by Sapajou. Undated.

41

DANCE MACABRE

Fig. 2.18. Feng Zikai. Courtesy of Feng Yiyin.

works of Sapajou (Georgii Avksent'levich Sapojnikoff), staff cartoonist from 1925 to 1940 on the influential, English-language *North China Daily News*. Sapajou's tragic life sounds like a film plot. A former Russian army lieutenant, he was seriously injured in World War I, leaving him with a lifelong limp. In 1920, Sapajou came to Shanghai as a refugee and five years later, joined the *North China Daily News*, where he was known for visually capturing the sometimes decadent lifestyles of Shanghainese. After losing his position when the Japanese occupied Shanghai, Sapajou survived for a while in 1942, by cartooning for a German newspaper published by Nazis. Jobless after the war, he barely existed in a Hongkou hovel, living on handouts from friends. He ended up as a cancer-stricken man in a displaced persons camp in the Philippines, where he died[5] (see Rigby 2007: 8–10; "Sapajou, Old Shanghai's Great Cartoonist" 2002; Bevan 2016: 95–96, 114, 173–75, 214, 300).

By the late 1930s, however, Chinese cartoonists moved away from foreign influences, striving for their own styles in line with their goal to raise national consciousness. As Hung (1994a: 127) pointed out: "The concern for Sinification thus symbolized their increasing awareness that this largely Western-inspired art form would not be fully accepted by the Chinese unless it was very carefully transplanted into Chinese soil." What was being called for was a blending of traditional painting with Western forms and techniques to create a new, yet Sinicized, style, what Hung (1994a: 127) termed "creative adaptation" (see also Huang Mao 1947: 64). During the next decade, Western ideas were blended with Chinese decorative art, as in the case of Zhang Guangyu, traditional hand scrolls by Ding Cong, and folk art by Liao Bingxiong. The same tendencies appeared in the Chinese animation industry after 1955.

Earlier still, in the 1920s, Feng Zikai (1898–1975)—frequently referred to as the "father of Chinese cartooning"—exemplified "creative adaptation," mixing contemporary social settings, humor, and religious (Buddhist) messages with Chinese brush painting and poetry, and what he had been exposed to while studying for ten months in 1921 at a school of Western painting in Japan. Norwegian scholar Christoph Harbsmeier (1984: 19), who wrote that the most important thing Feng learned in Tokyo was about manga, explained:

> There was something in the Japanese *manga* tradition that corresponded very naturally to Feng's artistic and philosophical inclinations. It was basically a popular, an "unbuttoned" art form, which stood in defiant opposition to official and "respectable" art. . . . an alternative tradition, an iconoclastic subculture that valued spontaneity, not perfectionist virtuosity. Often the *manga* were provocatively vulgar. . . . mostly concerned with everyday things or with grotesque fantasies. They were full of—often crude—burlesque humor.

Feng let his deep interest in the Japanese tradition be known in one of the more than 160 books he wrote, *Manhua de miaofa* (*The Drawing of Cartoons*). Because of his attraction to manga style, when *Wenxue zhoubao* (*Literary Review*) began to use Feng's drawings in the mid-1920s, they called them *manhua*, which since has been the term for cartoons in China. Perhaps, Huang Mao (1947: 24) best summed up the hybridity of Feng's cartoons, saying, Feng started as "a representative of the Japanese school of *manga*, but later merged into the main stream of more political westernized Chinese caricaturists."

Hybrids that Feng created included the lyrical cartoon, which coupled a short poem with a simple drawing (see Cao 2010 for an analysis of his poem cartoons), and the literary comic strip, based on selected modern Chinese literature. His devoted appreciation of literature and life in general was emphasized by his daughter Feng Yiyin (b. 1929), who has spent much of her life collecting, preserving, and reprinting Feng Zikai's works,

Fig. 2.19. "La Huangbaoche" ("Pulling the Rickshaw") by Feng Zikai, 1932. Courtesy of Feng Yiyin.

writing books about him, and referencing his art in her own paintings:

> He loved traditional literature and poetry very much. Most of his cartoons came from classic poems. He observed life and activities and drew them in his cartoon works. Before I was born, he drew many everyday life experiences of his hometown. His children became ideas in his works, like my elder sister Abao, and my brother Azhan seen pretending he was riding a bicycle made of two circular fans. (Feng Yiyin, interview, 2002)

Feng Zikai believed the cartoon should not be just satirical and entertaining, but also thought-provoking and enlightening, and thus as Chang-tai Hung put it, "a highly reflective piece of art" (Hung 1990: 50–51). His thinking spawned debate among cartoonists in the 1930s about what role cartoons should play: a commercial product for mass consumption, a carrier of social meaning, a genuine art form, or a propaganda tool to resist outside aggression? Feng also insisted that his drawings

42

be based on real experiences, focusing on what he saw in the streets and the happenings around him, and that they should be plain, "humanly and morally constructive," and affordable to the working class. As Harbsmeier (1984: 9–10) explained, he was largely overlooked by Western connoisseurs because he "refused to work for the learned few. His favorite themes were not inspired poets but desperate beggars, not obedient 'young masters' but naughty children, not the harmony of nature but the subtle discords of the human predicament." As a result, like other cartoonists of his time, he sought to place himself outside traditional Chinese art, which he found "elitist, esoteric, morally irrelevant and philosophically sterile" (9).

Influenced by the 1930s-era politicization of art brought about by the Japanese invasion, Feng moved away from idyllic drawings of children to cartoons of social comment,[6] although his work was never what Harbsmeier (1984: 31) called "ephemerally political," as was the case with some of his contemporaries. In fact, his social realism was never really political, but rather artistic. Harbsmeier compared his indignation at the social injustices of his day to that of a powerless child.

Professionalism

Feng is credited with giving cartoons much-needed respect, because he contributed regularly to prestigious literary journals and influential dailies in the 1920s and, over the years, added much theory and technique to the new field through his books (at least twenty on art theory alone) and countless drawings. Additionally, he illustrated many of the early works of intellectual/writer Lu Xun (1881–1936), who himself was called the "father of the Chinese woodcut movement" in the late 1920s and early '30s.

Lu Xun played a bit part in manhua history when, in 1932, he penned an article entitled "'Lianhuantuhua' bianhu" ("In Defense of Comic Strips") for the left-wing *Wenxue yuebao* (*Literature Monthly*), proclaiming that "not only can comic strips be considered works of art, but they already reside within the 'Palace of Art'" and

exhorting young art students to "value and direct efforts towards comic strips and book and newspaper illustrations" (Macdonald 2011).[7] The following issue of *Wenxue yuebao* used the intellectual Mao Dun's (1896–1981) article, "Lianhuantuhua xiaoshuo" ("Comic Strip Novels"), which was concerned with "the readership of comics, and the potential to recuperate the form for pedagogical purposes" (Macdonald 2011). Critiques such as these by two important intellectuals gave comics a push towards acceptance and respect.

The cartoonists themselves were putting comic art in a more favorable light through professional efforts. Before World War II, in less than a generation, they had established the first cartoon associations, exhibitions, and training institutes. Already in 1927, the short-lived Shanghai Sketch Society set as its goals to define the social functions of cartoons and advocate them to society, exchange artistic ideas and improve skills through seminars, exhibitions, and publications, and organize and train cartoonists.

Other cartoonist organizations were set up before World War II, including Manhua yanjiuhui (Cartoon Study Association) and Cartoon Service, the latter in Shanghai with Wang Wenlong as its head. Commenting about the Cartoon Service in 1931, one writer said:

> In recent years, cartoons in newspapers have aroused a great deal of interest among painters and artists. A number of large papers of the port cities have used cartoons with good result. It is understood that the present organization is formed so as to make it easy for artists and newspapers to communicate with one another along the line of patronage and service. ("Cartoons Come to Stay" 1931: 101)

In the spring of 1937, the cartoonists organized a national association, Zhonghua quanguo manhua zuojia xiehui (All-China Cartoon Association of Writers and Artists), based in Shanghai and with branches in Guangzhou, Xian, Wenzhou, and Hong Kong. The association was meant to "unite all cartoonists in the nation, to promote cartoons as an art form, and to use them as an educational tool" (Hung 1994a: 34), with the specific

43

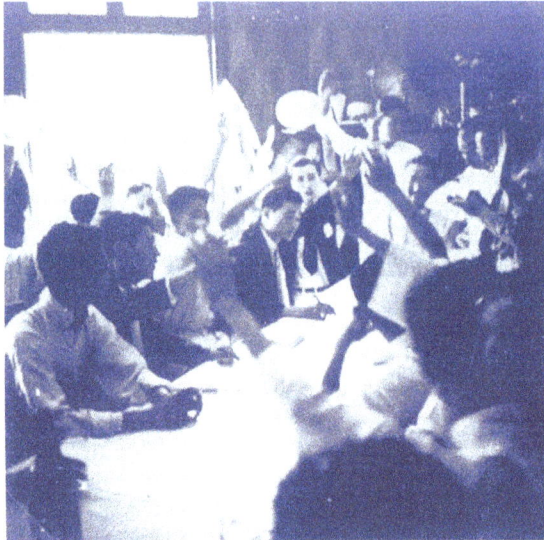

Fig. 2.20. Preparatory meeting of committee to establish the First National Cartoon Exhibition, 1936.

Fig. 2.21. Many 1930s-era cartoonists are pictured in Wang Zimei's 1936 drawing, "Manhuajie chongyang denggaotu" ("Cartoon World on a Hill in September"), published in *Shanghai manhua*, No. 6, October 10, 1936. Back row: Zhang Yingchao, Lu Zhixiang, Ding Cong, and Cai Ruohong. Middle row: Wang Zimei, Lu Fu, Zhu Jinlou, Te Wei, Huang Yao, Zhang Guangyu, Zhang Zhengyu, Hu Kao, Lu Shaofei, Gao Longsheng, and Zhang Leping. Front row: Wang Dunqing, Liang Baibo, Ye Qianyu, and Huang Miaozi. Courtesy of Li Weiwei.

goals of establishing an annual national exhibition, a seasonal professional journal (*Cartoon's Friend*), regular training sessions, an annual cartoon award, a small research library, a loan scheme for cartoonists, and tours and lodging arrangements for visiting cartoonists.

The First National Cartoon Exhibition opened in Shanghai on November 4, 1936. Initiated by Ye Qianyu and Lu Shaofei, it drew more attention than any preceding art show in the country. The critics, nevertheless, still had difficulties recognizing comic art, calling the exhibition "a small means of cutting up insects"—in other words, inconsequential art (Chen 1938: 308; also Bader 1941: 230). Other criticisms were that most of the cartoons were from Shanghai, thus negating the "national" appellation (Bevan 2016: 222), and that some were too foreign-influenced. More than 600 cartoons[8] were shown first in Shanghai, and then in Suzhou, Nanjing, Hangzhou, and southern locations such as Guangzhou. Besides many anti-Japanese cartoons, other exhibited drawings dealt with child slavery, corrupt officials, civil war, warlords, land tenure feudalism, and foreign exploitation (Bader 1941: 231). Judging from the number of cartoons with political slants shown, it seems clear that the "art for art's sake" notion was starting to shift to "art for life's sake" (Bevan 2016: 214).

Other indications of the rise of cartooning as a profession were the establishment of training and correspondence schools and the publication of anthologies. The two most famous training schools were Zhongguo diyi huashe (China First Art Society) and Zhonghua manhua hanshou xuexiao (China Cartoon Correspondence School), which, developed by Hu Kao (1912–94), consisted of junior and senior classes. The courses most often lasted six months (Hung 1990: 43). The profession was also given a boost when *Xiaopinwen he manhua* (*Personal Essays and Cartoons*), a special anthology commissioned by the important literary journal *Taibai* (*Venus*), appeared in Shanghai in 1935, under Chen Wangdao's editorship. Consisting of works by more than fifty contributors, the collection was significant, because it treated cartoons as important art alongside personal essays and attracted top writers such as Lu Xun to espouse the worthiness of cartoons (Hung 1994a: 31; see Bevan 2016: Chapter 6).

These achievements and others that signified a golden age of cartoons and comics were set aside, or adjusted to other needs, as China became embroiled in war with Japan in the 1930s and '40s, armed strife between the Communist and Guomindang parties, especially in the second half of the 1940s, and the turmoil involved in the complete restructuring of the country after 1949. Like comics' golden ages in the US, Japan, Australia, Indonesia, the Philippines, and elsewhere, China's was full of genius-like creativity as well as innovations in production and distribution. Like the others, however, it was short-lived, most likely not to return.

轟炸 嘉興所見

子愷

Early Wartime Cartooning

The September 18, 1931, Manchurian Incident and the February 1932 Japanese bombing of Shanghai have been credited with boosting the development of Chinese cartooning. As already indicated, many cartoon magazines sprang up in Shanghai, often publishing the early works of a number of cartoonists already using their pens as weapons against the Japanese, in what, by 1937, was called "cartoon warfare."

Historian/cartoonist Zheng Huagai (b. 1954) said that as early as September 25, 1931, Ding Song drew anti-Japanese cartoons; others who joined the fray were pioneer animator Wan Laiming (1899–1997), comic strip artists Ye Qianyu and Zhang Leping, master cartoonist Feng Zikai, Zhang E, Cai Ruohong, Te Wei, and Zhang Ding. Some of their depictions were shocking—Japanese using Chinese for bayonet training or feeding Chinese to dogs, or soldiers bayoneting babies; at other times, they drew Japanese as demons, ghosts, and dogs.

Feng Zikai, who had studied in Japan, had difficulty moving into cartoon warfare, not because of an affinity for Japan, but because he saw cartoons as pure art and not propaganda. Feng Zikai's cartoons were usually lyrical, graceful, and humanistic; however, after the war started, they became highly passionate and nationalistic. Hung (1994a: 136) wrote that despite the strong messages of Feng Zikai's war cartoons, he never felt comfortable doing them: "His wartime cartoons vividly reveal his ambivalence: even as he appeals to his fellow countrymen to resist the enemy's aggression, at the same time he presents a powerful indictment of the senseless waste of human lives."

When bombs destroyed his hometown of Shimenwan, burning down his beloved studio and turning his family into refugees, Feng Zikai became bitter, drawing and writing more about the need to resist. In March 1937, he became a member of the newly formed Zhonghua quanguo manhua zuojia xiehui (All-China Cartoon Association of Writers and Artists) and joined the editorial board of its *Kangzhan wenyi* (*Literature and*

Chapter 3

Cartoons as Wartime Weapons, 1930s-1949

Fig. 3.1. "Biaozhun nucai" ("A Typical Lackey") by Liao Bingxiong, 1936. Courtesy of Liao Bingxiong and Liao Ling-er.

Art of the War of Resistance), for which he drew many cartoons.

Feng Zikai's wartime cartoons concentrated on the consequences of Japan's actions, rather than the deeds themselves, and the conviction that mutual hostility must cease (Hung 1994a: 139). Before the war, his portrayals of children were as playful, innocent, and delightfully mischievous, but once the war began, they changed to patriotic little people in cruel settings (Hung 1990: 53).

Among the very young firebrand cartoonists of the early 1930s was Zhang Ding, destined to become one of China's major artists. Born in the Northeast, he and his family moved to Beijing, where he passed the examination to attend an art academy; instead, he spent a year in jail as a juvenile criminal because of his anti-Guomindang cartoons. Zhang Ding (interview, 2005) remembered:

I had a strong anti-Fascist mindset. At age fifteen, with two other youth, we organized and drew cartoons which we sent to the Chinese military in the Northeast, asking why they did not resist the Japanese. They said it is not us; we want to resist, but Chiang Kai-shek does not. We were called the three "Cs," because each of our last names started with a "C" (Zhang was Chang then). The Northeast military officer told us our title [3 Cs] was easy to be suspected as Communist. "You'd better go home," he said; "we'll resist the Japanese. Don't worry."

The following year, 1933, Zhang Ding was jailed for his cartoons, but incarceration did not deter him, as he explained: "I drew a lot of cartoons while in jail. I made friends with the guards who took them out for me. The contents of these cartoons exposed the Guomindang as refusing to resist the Japanese" (Zhang, interview, 2005).

Liao Bingxiong was also a teenager when he did his first anti-Japanese cartoons, used in a Guangzhou newspaper in 1932. His famous "Biaozhun nucai" ("A Typical Lackey"), depicting a Chinese offering his severed head on a platter and displayed at the first national cartoon exhibition in 1936, was meant to be critical of both the Japanese and the Guomindang. He said most of the 100 works by him exhibited in Guangzhou in 1938 were anti-Japanese (Liao, interview, 2002). Lin Qin was just thirteen years old when he began drawing war cartoons, published in *Guixian ribao* (*Gui County Daily*); any money he earned from these works was donated to the anti-Japanese war effort (Lin, interview, 1993).

Other young artists moved to the Communist base in Yan'an. Lianhuanhua artist Mi Gu (1918–86) joined Mao there in 1938; he was twenty years old and doing propaganda drawings for the war effort. Mi Gu's important work, *Xiaoerhei jiehun* (*Young Blacky Gets Married*), an illustrated version of Zhao Shuli's story, was drawn in a manner advocated by Mao at Yan'an—the avoidance of a Western style with shading and chiaroscuro effects that appealed to urban readers, with the use of ink outline and minimum shadow preferred (Andrews 1997: 23). Hua Junwu also went to Yan'an in 1938, after the Japanese invasion. He explained:

I was a bit to the right and then Edgar Snow's *Red Star Over China* influenced me. I discovered social problems, made some friends, and changed my ideas, gradually to progressive. When Japan invaded China in 1938, I did not want to be a slave and I went to Yan'an, the Communist Party base. Until I read Snow, I did not know the Communist Party well, but I did not like the Guomindang from the beginning. The Guomindang and Communists treated cartoonists differently. In Guomindang areas, cartoonists were active in the British concession in Shanghai, and therefore, we should appreciate imperialism. There were few cartoonists outside Shanghai, certainly not in Guomindang regions which were heavily controlled. (Hua, interview, 2005)

Cartoonist/filmmaker Han Shangyi (1917–98) was inspired to draw because of his admiration for Guomindang General Cai Tingkai, who, Han Shangyi said, "fought alone against Japan." As a Boy Scout, Han Shangyi went to pay his respect to the general, after which, he started drawing anti-Japanese cartoons (Han, interview, 1993). Like other cartoonists, he believed Chinese cartooning got its start during the anti-Japanese campaign as a reflection of "patriotic feeling," mainly in the numerous cartoon periodicals, which he said he treated as "my best friends."

New Art Movement

By 1938, Chinese cartooning had changed significantly in style, format, and techniques. Previously, the cartoons were usually (but not always) on the symbolic and indirect side, with many abiding by Chinese government strictures. But this changed after 1937.

Zheng Huagai (interview, 2005) said of cartooning in the late 1930s:

As the country united against the Japanese, anti-Japanese cartoons were boldly drawn with dark lines and lots of black. One cartoonist drew US soldiers as door guards protecting China, another of an old lady biting a Japanese soldier's fingers, others on perfect Chinese families, all members of which fight the Japanese at home and abroad. Liao Bingxiong did a comic strip book, *Resist the War: Must Fight*, with the cover in strips and other strips inside, a number showing the Guomindang and Communist parties cooperating to fight Japan. Some cartoons were drawn to be sent to Japanese soldiers—perhaps by cannon—to get them to surrender.

What cartoonists innovated through their daring work during wartime became known as the "Xinmeishu yundong" (New Art Movement), characterized as appealing to the masses, more realistic, and socially and/or politically oriented in content. Woodcut artist Lai Shaoqi (1915–2000) said three changes brought about the movement: realism, the unprecedented unity of Chinese artists, and an end to "vulgar, erotic" art which he called

49

"art of women's butts" (quoted in Hung 1994a: 124). Historian and cartoonist Huang Yuanlin (interview, 2001) said these "unhealthy" [erotic] cartoons in the humor magazines gave way to the more serious political and propagandistic works after the 1937 invasion of Shanghai.

Their works called "lowbrow," "vulgar," "imitative of the West," and "shoddy" by traditional painters, cartoonists from the mid-1930s onward tried to find a sound theoretical framework for their profession. Cartoonists believed traditional artists were detached from the people—even snobbish and aloof—and once engaged in cartoon warfare, the cartoonists sought "liberation from the prevailing academic constraints, seeking instead a more open, bold, realistic, mass art geared not to a select few but to the common people at large" (Hung 1994a: 124). Some of the cartoonists' theoretical conceptions appeared in a series of articles in *Shidai manhua* (*Modern Sketch*) between 1934 and 1937, and later in 1943, were compiled into wartime cartoon theory books, including Huang Mao's *Manhua yishu jianghua* (*Cartoon Art Speech*) and Feng Zikai's *Manhua de miaofa* (*Cartoon Drawing Skill*).

The tasks of wartime cartoonists were daunting: they had to bring the cartoon to the people, not just art galleries; make it reflect life; use it as a propaganda vehicle; and keep it both Chinese and genuinely artistic. Various suggestions were made and implemented to effect these changes. Cartoonist Hu Kao prescribed *baodaohua* (reportage picture), an easily printed drawing using simple brush strokes and describing real events. Having begun his career at age twenty on *Shidai manhua* and *Lun Yu*, Hu Kao used an "art deco" style, described by Pan (2008: 155) as "more consistent than that of most other contemporary cartoonists and, its strong tendency towards stylization, more consciously modern." Other cartoonists explored wartime propaganda techniques. Liao Bingxiong (interview, 2002) implored fellow cartoonists to use simple, direct language, storytelling techniques, and easy-to-understand titles and proverbs to avoid ambiguity, and Huang Mao (1942: 18–19) proposed reaching more people by having cartoons appear in different forms (huge banners across streets, signboards,

wall posters, magazines, packaging, postcards, touring cars) and in every conceivable place (exhibitions and street, mobile, and window displays). Cartoonists were encouraged to go to front lines and record battles and to depict the war as witnessed by the rural peasants. Realizing the countryside was an untapped source of resistance force, some cartoonists shifted from the urban middle class to the peasants as a target of their propaganda.

The Sinicizing of cartoons drew mixed reactions from the cartoonists, but they seemed to want a distinctly Chinese style with Western elements, such as fuller, more realistic figure drawing. Huang Mao (1947: 64) described a Sinicized cartoon:

The Sinicized cartoon . . . does not disregard the merits in Chinese traditional painting. . . . We must retain the marvels of brush and ink in Chinese art. But we also lack a scientific approach to drawings and are short of basic sketching techniques. By combining these with Western perspective devices and the art of human anatomy, we can create a new style. In brief, Western techniques must be expressed through our national forms. . . . If we can blend Chinese reality with our national forms, Sinicized cartoons [*zhongguohua de manhua*] will emerge.

Later, in 1942, some of these ideas about mass appeal and the use of Chinese traditional modes of expression in cartoons were codified at the Yan'an Forum on Literature and the Arts. The talks at Yan'an elaborated upon decisions made at the Gutian Conference of 1929, such as shifting propaganda from the army to the Chinese Communist Party (CCP). In his introductory remarks at Yan'an, Mao Zedong objected to "wholesale, uncritical importation of foreign images, as well as their use in Chinese art"; rejected art for art's sake as being bourgeois; advocated the "rich, lively language of the masses"; and implored art and artists to serve politics by following the demands of the CCP (Landsberger 2001: 35). Furthermore, art was primarily needed to show people how to act and behave and not merely to reveal enemies, and to present positive aspects of peasant life. Mao Zedong's Yan'an Talks, according to Farquhar (1999: 192), "provide the framework for understanding the theory of comics as revolutionary, popular art after 1949," emphasizing comics' use as ideological weapons as in World War II, aimed at ordinary Chinese, against internal and external enemies, and accessible to illiterate masses. The talks also called for use of traditional art forms, a category to which comics belonged.

Landsberger (2001: 33) discussed the evolution of a Chinese style of cartoon warfare in the CCP base areas:

> Large numbers of artists, who were more motivated by idealism and antipathy to the feeble Guomindang resistance against the Japanese, rather than staunch communists, traveled to the base areas. There, they usually followed short courses at the Lu Xun Academy of Literature and Art (*Luyi*), established in Yan'an in 1938 to teach drawing, propaganda painting, caricature, printmaking and art history. Posters, serial stories and cartoons were used to maintain the anti-Japanese sentiments among the peasant population, to mobilize popular resistance against the invaders, and to educate the masses. To counter the lack of peasant interest in the Western-inspired woodcuts and the Japanese use of traditional elements of popular culture, a search was undertaken for a new style that was to parallel the forms of art popular among the people. In 1940, during the New Year's Propaganda Movement, the decision to use traditional Chinese New Year prints was made.

The National Salvation Cartoon Propaganda Corps

An important offspring of the cartoonists' efforts to unify was the National Salvation Cartoon Propaganda Corps (*Jiuwang manhua xuanchuandui*), a group initially made up of eight cartoonists led by Ye Qianyu, whose mission was to persuade the people to resist and to raise soldiers' morale at the front. They did this by any means possible—publishing magazines and journals such as *Jiuwang manhua* (*National Salvation Cartoons*) and *Kangzhan manhua* (*Resistance of War Cartoons*),

Fig. 3.2. National Salvation Cartoon Propaganda Corps members, 1938. Starting from front, third from left: Zhang Leping, Ye Qianyu, Mai Fei, and Te Wei.

holding more than 100 exhibitions, and producing thousands of cartoons on billboards, banners, murals, vehicles, and large posters.

Hung (1994a: 94) said the Corps was formed by Shanghai manhuajie jiuwang xiehui (National Salvation Cartoon Association), itself established after the Marco Polo Bridge Incident in July 1937.

Jiuwang manhua, published every five days and containing between forty-five and fifty cartoons per issue, became a very influential magazine in 1937, showcasing some of the most artistic and vehemently propagandistic cartoons. It lasted twelve issues in Shanghai, folding in December 1937 when the Japanese occupied the city. Other issues appeared later in Hankou, Guangzhou, and Hong Kong (Shen 2001: 116). *Kangzhan manhua* was started by the Corps in January 1938, while it was in Wuhan. It also carried many anti-Japanese cartoons and, like *Jiuwang manhua*, lasted twelve issues, closing when the Japanese invaded Wuhan. Three additional issues appeared while the Corps was in Chongqing. Bi Weimin, son of cartoon historian Bi Keguan and a researcher himself, implied they succeeded each other but were basically the same periodical, using the same editors and artists but with different titles (interview, 2014).

Starting in Shanghai in 1937, the National Salvation Cartoon Propaganda Corps moved frequently, staying ahead of advancing Japanese troops. In September 1937, the Corps left for Nanjing, then Wuhan in December 1937, Changsha in Fall 1938, and Guilin shortly after. In Guilin, the Corps split into two groups, one headed by Te Wei which stayed in Guilin, the other by Zhang

Fig. 3.3. Front cover, *Kangzhan manhua*, No. 2, 1938.

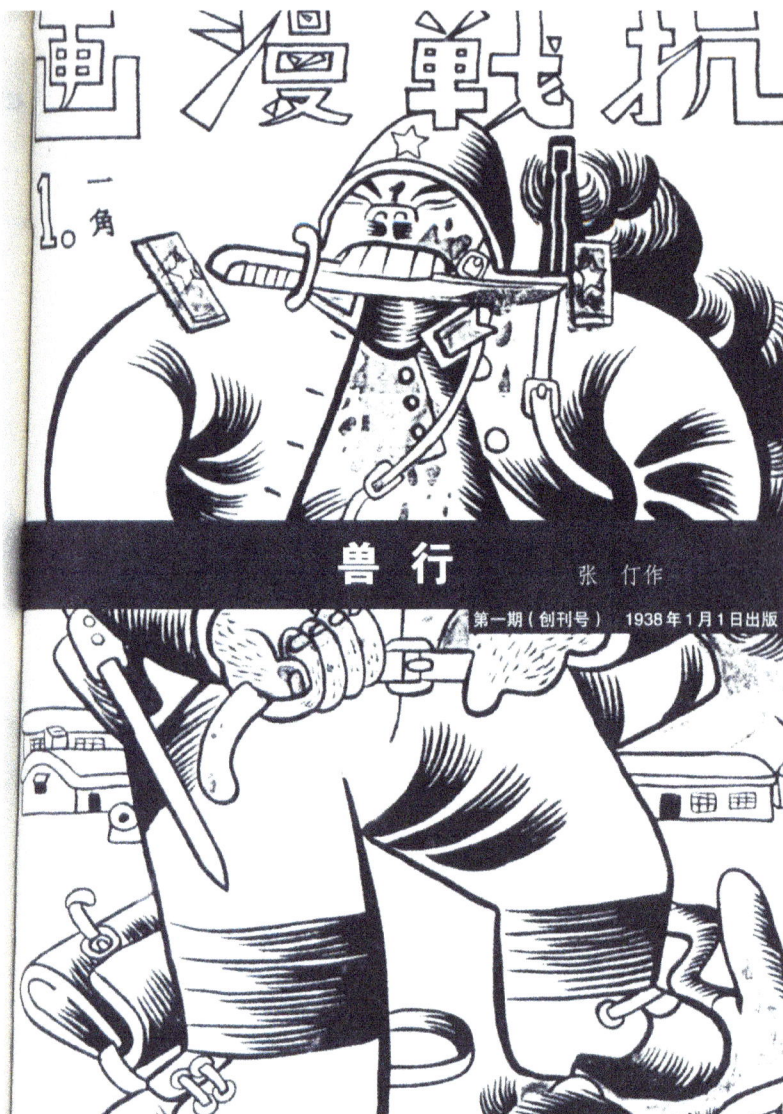

Fig. 3.4. "Shouxing" ("Beastly Behavior") by Zhang Ding. *Kangzhan manhua* back cover, 1938. Courtesy of Zhang Ding.

Leping, which left for the southeastern battlefields. Te Wei's team went to Chongqing in early 1939. The following year, the Guomindang discontinued funds for the Corps and it disbanded. As will be read later in this chapter, Corps member Mai Fei said censorship was the cause of the dissolution.

While the Corps existed, its cartoons were very conspicuous, as Chu (1938: 72) reported:

> Every city in China is plastered with war cartoons. Some give highly satirical portrayals of all aspects of Japanese aggression in the Far East, but the majorities are aimed at keeping China's all-front resistance at a high pitch of patriotism.
>
> On the walls along the streets, on posts, on banners carried by the numerous war service groups[,] in newspapers and magazines are seen these cleverly conceived cartoons.

Although the names of only seven cartoonists are listed on the original manifesto of the Corps, others joined the group as it meandered throughout southeastern China. Some of them left a record of their wartime activities, including five interviewed by the authors of this book—Te Wei, Zhang Ding, Liao Bingxiong, Han Shangyi, and Mai Fei. In these and other accounts, the cartoonists emphasized the perils and harsh conditions they faced, the tasks they tried to carry out, and the enthusiastic response they received from ordinary Chinese people.

For example, Xuan Wenjie (1979: 37–38) told of the Corps creating a "furor" in Zhenjiang after joining hands with the drama corps to stage street propaganda shows; of being tailed by Japanese planes as they "bombed trains and people, leaving seas of fire and a land of

Fig. 3.5. Zhang Leping drawing a huge anti-Japanese cartoon poster, 1938.

moaning"; of working ceaselessly to draw propaganda cartoons on "pieces of huge cloth, recording enemy brutality that we had just witnessed"; and of staging anti-Japanese cartoon exhibitions "despite constant air raid sirens." Xuan Wenjie said audiences were "engrossed in each and every cartoon on display," reflecting their "confidence [in us]." After the Corps moved to Wuhan in December 1937, Xuan Wenjie said its mission was to draw many large propaganda cartoon posters to display in neighboring cities, design other "printed material for anti-enemy propaganda," and edit *Kangzhan manhua*. The contents of the magazine and other printed works mobilized citizens to donate gold and money for the war effort, paid "tribute to the people's heroic resistance effort," reported on resistance movements elsewhere in China, and hammered away at enemy brutality (Xuan 1979: 38).

Another Corps member—and later the leader of one of its branches—was Te Wei, who went on to become one of China's most important animators. He headed the Shanghai Animation Film Studio from 1949 to 1988, during which time he directed some of the studio's classics. Te Wei began his cartooning career in 1933, and said that after 1935, he increasingly drew international news cartoons, some about the Japanese. He was twenty-two or twenty-three years old while a member of the Corps. Te Wei remembered: "We did everything by ourselves at a time when conditions were very difficult, especially economic. We managed to find ways to survive" (Te Wei, interview, 2001).

Corps member Zhang Ding said that he originally learned traditional Chinese painting, but when he realized the Guomindang was not resisting the Japanese, he

became "very angry" and switched to doing cartoons. He added:

I was very angry with the Guomindang as I saw so many Chinese people suffer. I used my cartoons to wake up people. I joined the propaganda corps as one of its first members. Ye Qianyu as leader sent me to the west to awaken the Chinese people. I carried many cartoons by others to show, exhibit. I also trained local people on how to draw. [I avoided capture by the Japanese] because I was active in areas not occupied. I survived by sending my work to newspapers and magazines to receive payment. (Zhang Ding, interview, 2005)

After the Corps was dissolved, Zhang Ding went to Yan'an, quit drawing cartoons, and began teaching at Lu Xun Art Academy.

Liao Bingxiong (interview, 2002), who had become the top cartoonist in China years before his death in 2006, recalled how he joined the Corps:

When Shanghai was occupied, they [the Corps] went to Wuhan. I heard about them, but I did not have the money to get a ticket to go to them. A cameraman sold his camera to buy two tickets and we joined the group in Wuhan. The Corps lasted four years. Ye Qianyu was the leader and Zhang Leping the vice leader at the beginning. I followed Leping from Wuhan to Anhui to Guilin to Chongqing and then I went to Hong Kong.

Filmmaker/cartoonist Han Shangyi, who joined at the beginning of 1938, talked about his work with the Corps:

I was creating very large-scale cartoons as posters that propagandized anti-Japanese feeling. After Wuhan was lost to the Japanese, I was with many cartoonists and artists and we did a large wall mural in a street of Hankou—mobilization against the Japanese. I was in charge of one part; this wall painting was 100 meters high and 200 meters long. It described the whole perspective—from front-line fighting the Japanese to the rear, and how citizens there supported the front line to fight. In the Corps, the Communist Party

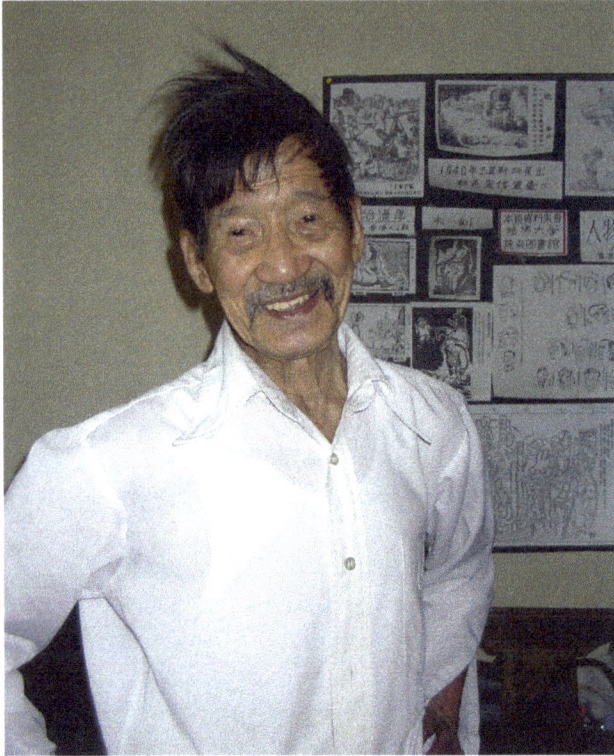

Fig. 3.6. Mai Fei, deputy leader of the Corps, pictured in his New York City apartment, June 16, 2006. Photo by Xu Ying. Courtesy of Mai Fei.

organized the murals well; leaders within the Party in charge of propaganda were good organizers. The big murals were put up before the Japanese arrived. The Japanese knew of the big wall painting before they got to Hankou. They published in a magazine that the mural was done by Guomindang and we (Communists) kicked them out. Actually, the Japanese did good propaganda for us who had made the mural. (Han, interview, 1993)

Like other Corps cartoonists, Han Shangyi left Wuhan and Hankou as the Japanese arrived. In Han Shangyi's case, he went to Chongqing, where he began to work in the film-making department; others escaped to Hong Kong.

Mai Fei, who lived in New York City from the 1980s until his death in 2007, working in various mediums, including Chinese painting, joined the Corps in 1938. He was finishing his fourth year of studies at the Guangzhou art academy when Ye Qianyu, who knew of his cartoons published in the Guangzhou newspaper *Dongyuan huabao* (*Mobilizing Pictorial*), edited by Te Wei, wrote a letter inviting him to become a member of the Corps. Mai Fei wrote to Ye Qianyu, delaying joining the Corps until he received his certificate from the academy. Once that was accomplished, he "bought train tickets to go join the corps in Wuhan but a bridge on the way had been bombed by the Japanese and I could not get through so I went to Guilin. I joined the Corps in Guilin at the end of 1938. I should have joined earlier after my graduation, but could not because of the bridge being bombed" (Mai Fei, interview, 2006). Mai Fei (interview, 2006) said his classmate Huang Mao went with him to join the Corps, invited by Te Wei because they needed someone to write articles (which Huang Mao could do). According to Mai Fei, not everyone could join the Corps; "it depended on whether they wanted you or not." He said that the Corps was under the Guomindang military committee leadership of Chiang Kai-shek and that committee had a political department with Zhang Zhizhong as director and Zhou Enlai (1898–1976) as deputy director. Under the political department, the Third Office, with Guo Moruo as director, was in charge of propaganda. The Third Office had several groups, including a performance (drama) corps and the cartoon propaganda corps.

Corps members, most of whom hailed from the cities, quickly learned how to make do with sparse materials and inadequate facilities. Mai Fei (interview, 2006) recounted experiences in which the Corps

> stayed in civilians' houses in villages as there were no military buildings. Civilians were very cooperative; the local governments arranged everything for us. Local people emptied rooms for us; there were rental fees. We did not eat with the locals as we had our own food and supplies. We were also advantageous to the local people, because we had a medical clinic with us and we could help them.

He said that by the time the Corps reached Guilin, in 1939 and early 1940, conditions were "very difficult, and we had no printing equipment." He said that at that point, the Corps split; he and Zhang Xiya, Ye Gang (Ye Qianyu's brother), and Zhang Leping stayed in the third battle region in Jiangxi Province, while the other group, including Te Wei, Liao Bingxiong, and others, went to Chongqing. The latter group, according to Mai Fei (2005), folded first, unable to survive in the more expensive Chongqing area on their half of the 600 yuan allotted the cartoon Corps. He said, "300 yuan for the Chongqing group meant nothing, as prices were very high there, so that group was dissolved. Its members had to survive by themselves, find their own way to live."

Mai Fei moved up to deputy leader of the remaining section by appointment of Zhang Leping, who left to recover from a lung disease. With Ye Gang and Zhang Xiya, Mai Fei continued to bring out the one-page "Manhua zhoubao" ("Weekly Cartoon"), which was part of the eight-page tabloid *Qianxian ribao* (*Frontline Daily*). The fifty-two numbers of "Manhua zhoubao" were produced in very trying times, as Mai Fei (interview, 2006) remembered:

> There was no electricity some days, so we could not use the printing machine. We took photographs, and when there were rainy days, we could not take photos either. So, we sometimes had to cut woodcuts. Zhang Xiya was an etcher; I also knew how to do woodcuts. We did the woodcuts at night. Ye Gang wrote articles to fill spaces around the woodcut cartoons. We printed in daytime and were never delayed. We worked day and night.

Mai Fei (interview, 2006) delineated the events leading up to the dissolution of the Jiangxi cartoon corps, stating, "In 1941, the Guomindang government attacked the New Fourth Army led by the Communist Party in what was called the 'Wannan shibian' (Southern Anhui Incident). Most of the New Fourth Army were killed. After that, the Guomindang changed its policy to be anti-Communist first and then anti-Japanese." Mai Fei said that the Guomindang believed the Corps was led by the Communist Party, despite the fact that neither he nor the other cartoonists, with the possible exception of Te Wei, had been affiliated with the Communist Party. He said, "The rest of us swore allegiance to the Guomindang as the Corps was under the Guomindang political department. After Liberation, the Communist Party criticized me because I worked for the Guomindang."

Guomindang leaders were suspicious of the political loyalties of the wartime artists, correctly suspecting a number of Communists among them. Partially in reaction to this concern about Communist infiltration, the Guomindang in 1940 curtailed funds for the propaganda corps and removed Guo Moruo as head of the Third Section of the Political Department, responsible for propaganda.

When Zhang Leping turned over the Corps and the "Manhua zhoubao" page to Mai Fei in 1941, he was told that he could publish what he wanted. Therefore, Mai Fei said that he was dismayed by the Guomindang's restrictive actions after the Southern Anhui Incident, explaining,

> Someone from the Guomindang political department told me I had to send works to them first to be censored. In fact, the Guomindang once censored *Qianxian ribao* "Manhua zhoubao" and removed a cartoon and said we should replace it with another. I said it is not easy to do any cartoon to fill the space. So I wrote a report to the Guomindang political department and said the Corps is dissolved. The Guomindang said, how can you be finished? I said because the Guomindang is not anti-Japanese and so we are finished. The Corps title is Anti-Japanese War Cartoon Corps; the Corps did not belong to the formal office of Guomindang; we did not get wages—just 600 yuan subsidy for support of our activities. And the Corps leaders were not selected by the Guomindang, but by the Corps members' vote. So, none of us was formally with the Guomindang. We had no payment from the government, so when I said it was finished, it was finished, as I was the deputy leader. I had the equivalent of the rank of a major in the Guomindang military, but I never received payment. (Mai Fei, interview, 2006)

Previously, in 1941, Mai Fei said he had a run-in with the Guomindang when fellow Crops member Zhang Xiya was arrested because he was suspected of being a Communist. According to Mai Fei (interview, 2006), when he heard about the arrest,

> I got angry and said I have one less Corps member now. I went to the Guomindang political department and talked

Fig. 3.7. Corps cartoonists displayed their anti-Japanese drawings in every possible venue, including on the sides of trucks.

Hu Kao (n.d.), writing in the 1940s, gave a different set of figures, stating that in 1936, China had about 200 cartoonists and during the war of the 1940s, between 500 and 800; he did not say how many were drawing cartoons denouncing Japan. Most importantly, as Zheng Huagai (interview, 2005) and others emphasized, the cartoons played an important role in areas where illiteracy was high and availability of newspapers low.

Corps member Xuan Wenjie (1979: 39) summed up the group's activities: "In its more than three years of existence [1937–40] the Corps traveled to places like Nanjing, Wuhan, Changsha, Guilin, Chongqing, Tunxi, Shangrao, held more than 100 exhibits, edited numerous magazines and journals and produced thousands of cartoons."

There were other cartoon propaganda crews, for example, in Guangzhou and Xian. In Wuhan, the National Association of Chinese Cartoonists (formerly of Shanghai) established a committee for propaganda coordination throughout China. Hung (1994a: 96) discussed the "flurry of activities" that followed:

> Cartoonists established training classes in Guilin and Xi'an, held individual exhibitions (such as those of Ding Cong [b. 1916] in Chengdu and Zhang Wenyuan [b. 1910] in Kunming), and launched various magazines, including *Cartoon and Woodcut* (*Manhua yu muke*) in Guilin and *Anti-Enemy Pictorial* (*Kangdi huabao*) in Xi'an. In south China, Guangzhou became an active cartoon center; a host of talents gathered there to form a regional branch of the National Association of Chinese Cartoonists, with Yu Feng (b. 1916), Zhang E, and Huang Mao as its leading members. When the city fell into the hands of the Japanese troops in late 1938, Hong Kong replaced Guangzhou as the leading cartoon center in the south.

to the leaders to get Zhang released. The political department leaders negotiated with the intelligence agency leaders, because I said that if you don't release Zhang, I'll stop the cartoon page. The Guomindang political department thought the cartoons were important propaganda, so they forced the intelligence people to release Zhang. But we needed two people to sign the form that said he was not a Communist. I and the editor of *Qianxian ribao* [*Frontline Daily*] signed. I was in charge of the Corps and was responsible for my people, so I used the threat that I would stop the page. I did something very dangerous for no one dared protect a Communist Party member.

The National Salvation Cartoon Propaganda Corps left an indelible impact, certainly on those artists who participated but also on the cartooning profession and the public who saw the cartoons. Bi Keguan (Various speakers 2005) said Te Wei and Liao Bingxiong cried when the Corps had to be dissolved. He also reported that at the beginning of the war, only ten [*sic*] cartoonists were in the Corps, but by the end of the war, about 100 cartoonists were drawing anti-Japanese cartoons.

These cartoon propaganda teams were extremely resourceful under the dire circumstances. For example, they used a mode called *jiehua* (picture storytelling). These were large white cloth banners with painted propaganda cartoons, displayed in any space available and orally explained by the cartoonists (Hung 1994a: 96–97).

Other Wartime Cartooning Activities

Besides those connected with the National Salvation Cartoon Propaganda Corps, many other cartoonists opposed the Japanese, working for various institutions (including studios, newspapers, and magazines), serving with military units, or acting independently.

Newspapers and magazines in which cartoonists' works appeared were plentiful in China, particularly at the outset of the war. In April 1937, the total number of dailies was 1,031; Shanghai, with fifty newspapers, led the pack, followed by Beijing, with forty-four, Tianjin, twenty-nine, and Nanjing and Hankou, twenty-one each. Illustrated material was an important part of newspapers, some of which issued pictorial supplements (e.g., *Shenbao*, *Xinwenbao*, etc.).

Communist newspapers appreciated the need for a variety of art forms, in contrast to Guomindang papers such as *Zhongyang ribao* (*Central Daily*), with its "unappealing layout and poor use of visual effects" (Hung 1994a: 234). Hung (1994a: 235) elaborated on the use of cartoons by the Communist press:

> Cartoons began to appear everywhere. They could be found in pictorials such as Yan'an's *Resistance Pictorial* (*Kangdi huabao*) and Jin-Cha-Ji Border Region's *Shanxi-Chahar-Hebei Pictorial* (*Jin-Cha-Ji huabao*). The work of Hua Junwu, Zhang E, and Cai Ruohong also became a constant feature in Yan'an's *Liberation Daily*, the CCP's official newspaper. The *New China Daily*, which was published in Guomindang-controlled Hankou and later in Chongqing, gave this powerful art even more prominence, frequently devoting its front page to biting cartoons. . . . In addition to promoting cartoons, Zhang E, art editor of the *New China Daily*, also labored hard to bring a variety of other art forms like woodcuts and comic strips to this influential newspaper, blending forceful messages with simple images.

As indicated elsewhere in this chapter, Mao Zedong early on had a clear vision of the capabilities of cartoons, and he knew what he expected from them. One point he stressed over dinner with Hua Junwu, Zhang E,

and Cai Ruohong in Yan'an, after viewing their February 1942 exhibition, was that cartoons should not be too focused on problems within the Chinese Communist Party, but should dwell on the CCP's political struggle with external foes. He told the artists that they should not concentrate on the demerits without showing the merits, and that the targets of exposure cannot be the masses, but the "aggressors, exploiters and oppressors and the evil influence they have on the people" (Hung 1994a: 236).

The Yan'an cartoon campaign was better structured and more innovative in styles and formats than that of the Guomindang. At Yan'an, an art workshop to promote cartoons was set up by Hua Junwu and Jiang Feng (1910–82) in 1941; simultaneously, woodcut cartoons, drawn from local experiences and using simple themes to portray China's bright future under Communism and strong antagonism against the Japanese, enhanced Communist art. The woodcuts fit well with Communist art in wartime, having been dominated by left-wing artists for years and using a material (wood) readily available in the Yan'an region, especially since zinc printing plates were in short supply. As Hung (1994a: 239) wrote, "For Communist artists, the cartoon and woodcut were twin developments that provided mutual nourishment and affirmation in a period of crisis."

On the other hand, Guomindang cartoons suffered from the "fairly disorganized and poorly managed" propaganda efforts of the Party. For a while in late 1938, the Guomindang Propaganda Bureau seemed to be getting the knack of propaganda, publishing two manual-like books, as well as printing leaflets and safe-passage surrender passes for Japanese soldiers. However, as Kushner (2006: 143) related, "obstacles continued to plague KMT [Guomindang] propaganda efforts."

Guomindang newspapers were also hesitant to attack the Japanese in cartoons. For example, Liao Bingxiong (interview, 2002) said that in the 1940s, only one Guangzhou newspaper in which his work appeared published anti-Japanese cartoons, and it was run as a personal propaganda tool by warlords wanting to establish "another Guangdong Kingdom against Chiang Kai-shek."

Wartime journalists, acknowledging the urban nature of their newspapers and magazines and the largely illiterate population, were concerned about the urgency to popularize the press. Leftist journalist Liu Shi (1903–68), for example, proposed including popular songs and ballads and using more cartoons and pictures; Zou Taofen (1895–1944), in his wartime magazines (especially *Kangzhan* and *Quanmin kangzhan* [*United Resistance*]), emphasized the use of graphics, including cartoons (Hung 1994a: 178–79). In other instances, moves were made to set up *difang baozhi* (local newspapers) to further the national efforts.

In addition to general interest periodicals, there were the cartoon magazines and literary journals that attracted cartoonists' works. Wartime cartoon magazines were few in number (about a dozen) and limited in circulation (Bi and Huang 1986: 152, 160, 176–77), but those that existed were determined to provide anti-Japanese propaganda to the rural masses. Writing about one of them—*Guojia zongdongyuan huabao* (*National Mobilizers Pictorial*), edited by Lu Shaofei and Zhang E in Guangzhou in 1938—Huang Miaozi (1913–2012) (1938: Preface) said:

> Unlike previous cartoon publications published in the cities and geared to the taste of the petty bourgeoisie and intelligentsia, this pictorial was launched to bring pictures to the masses as propaganda messages. It concerned practical topics, and its styles are both realistic and easily comprehended. And because of its unique distribution network, the whole endeavor was such a big success that it had to change from publishing every five days to every three. It circulated throughout Guangdong province and developed a cordial bond with the people. Total sales ran as high as fifty to sixty thousand copies. It was truly unprecedented!

Similarly, some of the literary journals offered space to wartime cartoons. One in particular was *Kangdaodi*

Fig. 3.8. Xu Ling of the Eighth Route Army drawing a propaganda cartoon mural, 1942.

Fig. 3.9. Jiang Yousheng, cartoonist for the New Fourth Army, in his Beijing apartment, December 17, 2002. Photo by Xu Ying. Courtesy of Jiang Yousheng.

(*Resisting Till the End*), which lasted for twenty-six issues, from January 1938 to November 1939. Edited by Lao Xiang, who vowed to "use ink as blood and to turn words into weapons," the semi-monthly published many cartoons, especially those by Zhao Wangyun (1906–77) (Hung 1994a: 203).

Military units (both Guomindang and Communist) had their own periodicals, in which cartoons against the Japanese were regularly published. The Eighth Route

Army, under the Communist Party, had a team of cartoonists drawing propaganda cartoons used on cartoon wall newspapers, murals, leaflets, and as parts of street exhibitions. Some of the artists involved were etchers Li Shaoyan (1918–2002) and Shen Yiqian (1908–44), Xu Xiaobing (1916–2009), and Xu Ling (1918–92). Zheng Huagai (interview, 2005), himself a cartoonist, as well as a military colonel and an historian, told of the difficult conditions under which they published:

> Conditions were bad and some published using oil ink. Some of the newspapers and cartoons done in the mountains were carved into wood by pen, or into wax paper stretched over steel board, then inked, rolled, and printed. A special issue in 1939 of *Kangdi sanri kan* (*Resistance Enemy Semi-Weekly*) was done in the latter way. Its title was in the form of a cartoon; all issues of this newspaper had cartoons.

One military cartoonist, Jiang Yousheng (1921–2015) (interviews, 2002, 2006), described the organization, functions, and hardships of cartooning in battle regions. Jiang Yousheng started working in a Shanghai medical facility when he was eighteen (in 1939), but decided to create cartoons after reading a book on woodcut etching. At the same time, he began participating in the activities of a progressive group in the British and French Concessions and publishing his cartoons in newspapers. In 1942, after the Japanese had invaded the Shanghai foreign concessions in December 1941, he went to the Subei Anti-Japanese Base and became a New Fourth Army (N4A) soldier. (The N4A was a Guomindang outfit in the South, but like other Guomindang armies, had Communist soldiers. Jiang Yousheng described himself as a Communist at the time.) Soon, he was leader of the cartoon woodcut etching group of artists.

Jiang Yousheng (interview, 2002) said that the N4A had seven units, each between 10,000 and 20,000 soldiers, and each unit had a pictorial periodical and six or seven cartoonists. The periodicals, which Jiang Yousheng (interview, 2002) said were sent to the

Guomindang to get them to unite with the CCP to fight Japan, were pamphlet- (digest-) size with about eight to ten pages. One such periodical was *Suzhong huabao* (*Central Jiangsu Pictorial*). Jiang Yousheng (interview, 2002) explained that the N4A had this many cartoonists because "there was no base for N4A; they traveled from area to area almost like a guerrilla army," and the cartoonists, who worked like soldiers, also had no home base (as did other units). He said, "If a unit had a home base, it could draw upon local cartoonists stationed there to draw for it."

Besides publishing the periodicals, the N4A cartoonists also drew posters, wall murals, and woodcut prints, all done under the harshest wartime conditions. In one battle, Jiang Yousheng said, he saw about a third of his fellow soldiers killed, adding,

> Conditions were very difficult; people could not imagine now. We stayed in the suburbs of Shanghai and Nanjing; once, we moved three times in one night. In between, we tried to find chances to draw cartoons and woodcuts. It is very difficult to do woodcuts as it takes time. We did oil prints where we used black oil as a printing substance. We used simple machinery like hand presses. (Jiang, interview, 2002)

In 1944, N4A sent Jiang Yousheng to the Anti-Japanese Military and Politics University, where he worked at the Ninth Branch Political Brigade. He said that the brigade moved with the army everywhere and when there was a lull in the fighting, brigade members seized the time to draw slides, which would be shown in villages to army personnel and local people. Based on an interview with Jiang Yousheng, Zheng (2007) described the crude machinery and materials used in these "domestic movies":

> They were painted on glass. The colors red and purple were made by medical liquids; yellow by plant seeds mixed with water; blue directly from pen ink. The outside of the slide machine was a box of wood and iron nailed together. The lens used was a magnifying glass and the light source

59

was a gas lantern. When they showed the slides, they had to shout out captions loudly. When necessary, they added drums and Erhu music. These colorful slides and similar operas were dubbed "domestic movies" and drew masses of local people. The contents of the slides mostly blasted the Japanese and Guomindang militaries' evil behaviors and the landlords' exploitative crimes, and were titled "Rijun baoxing" (Japanese Military Evil Behaviors) and "Xue lei chou" (Blood and Tears Hatred). (Zheng 2007)

Hua Junwu, who was in Yan'an from December 1938 to August 1945, related the hardships of getting to that military camp and working as a cartoonist:

After Japan invaded Shanghai in August 1938, most cartoonists had to escape. As they knew nothing about Yan'an, few cartoonists went there. Hu Kao was the first, I the second. It was a rural area; we went there because the Communist Party made it famous. There were no buses, no cars; we walked. We ate as the local people did or worse. Conditions were primitive at Yan'an as the Guomindang cut off everything. I had to hide to do woodcuts and then print them. Their quality was low; that is why I did not draw many. In Yan'an, we had a Communist newspaper, but it had very few cartoons. When I arrived, they knew I was a cartoonist, so they asked me to draw. I drew a cartoon on wood but I said I did not know how to do woodcut. They said, "That's the way." It was very difficult work. We also drew cartoons on school walls and on huge sheets of paper and put them on the walls. (Hua, interview, 2006)

Hua Junwu's claim to be the second cartoonist, after Hu Kao, to join Mao at Yan'an is inaccurate as Trinidadian-born journalist Jack Chen Yifan, who considered himself a Chinese cartoonist, accompanied Hu Kao. Chen actually went to Yan'an in September 1938, after he had been at the front. Author Freda Utley (1878–1978), who had known Chen in Moscow, and also reported from China's front lines, wrote of Chen's activities there. "We were to find his [Chen's] drawings scattered about all over the front, on walls, in notebooks of officers, and even in a cave within range of the Japanese guns" (Utley 1939:

Fig. 3.10. Cai Ruohong, Hua Junwu, and Zhang E at Yan'an, 1942.

171–72, quoted in Bevan 2016: 293). While in Yan'an, Chen held an exhibition of British and American artists entrusted to him by leftist fundraising organizations abroad. Hu Kao taught at Luyi (the Lu Xun Academy), but after a couple of years, moved to Hong Kong (Bevan 2010: 67–68; see also Chen 1939).

In Yan'an, Hua Junwu, with Zhang E and Cai Ruohong, held the "Sanren fengci manhuazhan" (Three Man Satirical Cartoon Show) exhibition in February 1942, which gained them praise from viewers and an invitation to dine with Mao Zedong, whereupon he critiqued the trio's works and told them what he expected from cartooning (Hua, interview, 2006). Hua Junwu said that his cartooning changed after listening to Mao's 1942 speech on art, in which he called for the nationalizing and popularizing of culture. Hua Junwu (interview, 2006) said:

I followed Mao's words that Chinese culture should be nationalized and popularized. Chinese cartoons did not look that way before Mao's talk. I explored ways to nationalize and popularize cartoons, and after that, I got things figured out little by little—like the Chinese style of humor. People said the Chinese don't know humor, but that's not true. It is just different from Western humor.

As for nationalization and popularization, only Mao talked about that. No one had talked about that before, so you had to think about it yourself. You had to think, as I did, that what is nationalized has to be popularized. But

Fig. 3.11. Lu Xun Art Academy cartoon wall newspapers in Yan'an, 1942. Courtesy of Zheng Huagai. *Zhongguo manhua* (*Chinese Cartoon*), May 2005. http://www.ndcnc.gov.cn/jingpinzy/manhua.

nationalized does not equal popularized. You have to think about it.

Some cartoonists moved about with the drama propaganda corps, drawing anti-Japanese posters that were displayed where a troupe performed or designing sets and costumes for performers. The cartoons contributed much to the success of the drama troupes' performances, according to Li Qun (1937: 8), a member of the Sixth National Salvation Drama Propaganda Team, who wrote, "no matter where we were, the only thing that could draw a large peasant crowd and really arouse their interest was the huge drawings we brought along." Li Qun added that the drawings were more effective than the songs, dramas, and speeches.

Liao Bingxiong (interview, 2002) used a drama troupe to display his works. In 1938, he said, "I had read Mao's book on waging war against the Japanese. I drew eight cartoons, one for each of the chapters in that book. I took rope and hung those large cartoons on trees. I followed a drama troupe and before the troupe performed, I'd show my anti-Japanese cartoons."

Ding Cong was also tied to drama. After serving as art editor of *Liangyou huabao* (*Young Companion Pictorial*) and drawing for *Dadi* (*The Earth*) and *Jinri zhongguo* (*China Today*) in Hong Kong, he was invited in the

autumn of 1941, to work at the "China Film Studio" in Chongqing, where, he said, he designed costumes and stages and became known enough that other famous Chinese playwrights asked him to do stage art design (Ding, interview, 2002).

Like so many other wartime cartoonists, Liao Bingxiong and Ding Cong often depended upon exhibitions to get their cartoons seen. There were many exhibitions, often in the streets for lack of venues; they were necessary because, at times, printing cartoons was nearly impossible. Cartoonists were constantly looking for alternative ways to print: when zinc plates were unavailable, they used woodblocks to produce cartoons in newspapers, resulting in the genre called *muke manhua* (see Ji 1942: 4; Liao 1940: 4); when ink was in short supply, they used black oil. And, as Ding Cong (interview, 2006) related about Chongqing later in the war, when "there was no place to print our work, we had to do exhibitions." He elaborated:

I did many wartime cartoons for exhibitions. Printing was in short supply so I did them as woodcuts. I'd draw a cartoon and exhibit it several times. There was no payment, but we felt very comfortable doing these anti-Japanese cartoons. In the 1940s, there were many of these exhibitions. Inside [subtly], the cartoons were anti-Guomindang; the outside enemy was the Japanese. These works were long, scroll-like drawings, very realistic. There was no other way; you drew the painting and exhibited it.

Other cartoonists went their independent ways. Te Wei, who had fled to Hong Kong after his work with the cartoon propaganda corps, returned to Chongqing in 1942, at which time he changed his tactics. He said:

It was difficult to publish cartoons as the Guomindang controlled culture closely. I changed my idea. I went to the mines, factories, military bases to collect subject materials, to do sketches. I drew big water/ink sketches to reflect poor people's problems. I would stay with friends in those areas. I went into the mines to sketch for one day; drew two paintings about factories, two about mines, others about

61

Cartoons as Wartime Weapons, 1930s–1949

people's lives. They were paintings, not cartoons, meant for exhibition. (Te Wei, interview, 2001)

Whatever their medium—newspapers, magazines, posters, huge white cloth banners, signboards, leaflets, pamphlets, slides, books, or exhibitions—the Chinese cartoonists of the War of Resistance against Japan were steadfast in their determination to wear down the enemy by cartoon warfare. They carried out their tasks at great risk and sacrifice, and as Bi Keguan (Various speakers 2005) explained, in the spirit of cooperation, support, and resilience. According to Bi Keguan, cartoonists belonging to older generations gave up publishing opportunities to allow younger cartoonists to make money to support their families.

Cartoon Leaflets

Leaflets as a distinctive form of propaganda were published and dispersed in profusion during the conflicts with Japanese invaders, some as early as 1931. By 1937, they became a part of the previously mentioned "cartoon warfare" Wang Dungqing had called for, notably utilized in the anti-Japanese propaganda dispensed by the National Salvation Cartoon Propaganda Corps. Some of the Corps' leaflets were drawn for the Guomindang and the US Air Force to drop on Japanese soldiers, imploring them to surrender.

Other resisters secretly printed leaflets, especially after the Imperial Army committed atrocities on the Chinese; they distributed them in schools, movie houses, and buses. For example, messages that followed the Nanking Massacre included, "Show your conscience, fellow countrymen" and "The National Army will attack Nanking in a few days and kill all the Japanese devils and [Chinese] traitors" ("Psychological Warfare" 2000).

Interestingly, cartoon leaflets, rather than bombs, made up the payload of the China Air Force's first transoceanic "bombing" attack on Japan. On May 19, 1938, Chinese bombers took off from Hankou (a part of Wuhan) with the mission to drop leaflets over major cities of Japan, "calling up the consciousness of the

Japanese people" (Dunn 2006). This decision was made after the Japanese bombarded Wuhan (China's political center) in early 1938, when the China Air Force, with Chiang Kai-shek's approval, planned to bomb Japan as an act of vengeance. However, the secretary general of the Guomindang Aviation Committee, Song Meiling,[1] suggested throwing leaflets (also called pamphlets) as an alternate weapon. Bi Keguan (2008: 138) related what happened next:

> After the decision was made, Jiang Jieshi (Chiang Kai-shek) ordered the Political Division of the Military Affairs Committee to make pamphlets as soon as possible, which task were [sic] to be shouldered by the Caricature Propaganda Taskforce led by Ye Qianyu, who was an officer in the third political hall. When the pamphlets were read, the director of the third political hall, Guo Muruo, delivered the pamphlets in person to the Aviation Committee. In the evening of 19th May, 1938, a team of planes led by Captain Xu Huangshen flew to Nagasaki, Fukuoka and Saga and threw millions of pamphlets.

The reaction was one of shock worldwide and pride and excitement in China, according to Bi (2008); Chinese military and government officials sent many congratulatory messages to the crew, and Feng Zikai drew a cartoon, "A Million Pamphlets Are Like a Million Seeds of Bombs," to honor the event. Bi called the cartoon the "only graphic record of the 'event'" (139).

There were conflicting reports about the leaflets' messages, delivery method, and targets, according to Dunn (2006), who wrote that Chinese press reports asserted that the leaflets carried a "message of goodwill to the Japanese people . . . [and] told of Japanese atrocities committed against Chinese civilians and solicited moral solidarity from the Japanese people." On the other hand, the Japanese press reported that only one plane was involved, that it did not fly over any major city, and that the leaflets were "violently anti-Japanese in content" (Dunn 2006).

Although military units of both the Guomindang and Communist parties made use of cartoon leaflets, the

Fig. 3.12. Eighth Route Army cartoon leaflet boasting of Chinese military accomplishments. Courtesy of Zheng Huagai. *Zhongguo man-hua* (*Chinese Cartoon*), May 2005. http://www.ndcnc.gov.cn/jingpinzy/manhua.

Guomindang initially had difficulties implementing an effective leaflet campaign, because, "it proved exceedingly difficult to get other KMT [Guomindang] offices, both military and government agencies, to coordinate their efforts, especially to organize planes to drop the leaflets" (Kushner 2006: 143).

On the other hand, Communist-created, anti-Japanese cartoon leaflets were carefully fashioned, often aided by Japanese prisoners of war. Nosaka Sanzō (1892–1993), founder of the Communist Party of Japan, who went to Yan'an in March 1940, shaped the prisoners of war into effective propagandists in a school set up to re-educate them and through his propaganda strategy for "Chinese-sponsored anti-Japanese propaganda" (Kushner 2006: 135). Among the many instructions he gave to POWs working in propaganda was that cartoons and pictures should be used very often and leaflets should contain fewer than 500 Japanese characters and focus on one theme.

A US military report in late summer 1945, recognizing lessons learned from the prisoners of war, stated:

Jap [*sic*] bodies have been found with morale leaflets on them. Chinese compete to pick up news leaflets despite drastic counter measures by the Japanese authorities, downed airmen attribute their rescues to leaflet instructions to the Chinese, Japanese work projects have been abandoned, communications clogged, active resistance

encouraged and brought about, and interrogation of prisoners has revealed numerous instances of morale leaflets having a marked discouraging effect on the Jap soldiers who read them. (quoted in Kushner 2006: 154)

Most of the thirty-one anti-Japanese cartoon leaflets discussed in this chapter were drawn by artists of the Eighth Route Army, the reformulated Red Army after 1937; a few were drawn by the New Fourth Army, the Communist force south of the Yangzi River.

A considerable number of the drawings were directed at *hanjian* (traitors). Traitors were told through leaflets to go home to their waiting families (especially at New Year), to not steal from Chinese farmers to help Japanese soldiers, to join the Eighth Route Army, and to not hurt their own people. Images depicted a Japanese soldier raping a traitor's wife while he has to watch, and the contrast between what traitors could expect when they aided the Japanese or supported the Chinese. One leaflet, issued by the Eighth Route Army, warned traitors that the Soviet Union, claiming that the Japanese helped Germany invade the USSR, would not allow Japanese "fascist criminals" to go free now that the war in Europe was over. Another leaflet of unknown origin proclaimed that in the following year, all of the Allies would be fighting the Japanese.

Two cartoon leaflets proudly boasted of summer achievements of the Eighth Route Army, Bohai District, including the return of 2,587 traitors to the Eighth Route Army and the liberation of two million people. Another leaflet, listing the "glorious achievements" in 1944 of the Eighth Route Army, Shandong Luzong, Fourth Military District Political Department, included 657 Japanese and traitors killed, 1,411 enemies captured, thirty bases occupied, and 6,446 square kilometers liberated. It took credit for being involved in 179 small battles, where it captured 1,204 short and long guns, eighteen machine guns, as well as 124 animals, 3,915 pieces of clothing, and 95,000 kilograms of grain. Worthless Japanese military money was also the subject of Eighth Route Army cartoon leaflets; one claimed that the Japanese purchased Chinese materials with the bogus currency and then bombed the Chinese people, while another reported that the enemy traded its money with that of China to buy arms in foreign countries.

Other flyers not directly attributed to the Eighth Route Army included a series showing ways (at least seven) that the Japanese utilized to steal grain from peasants and a five-panel strip informing traitors of the consequence of joining the Japanese. Pointing out that the Japanese lost or were losing battles in Taiwan and The Philippines and that its navy had been devastated, one leaflet portrayed a Japanese official kneeling in defeat, his hope being that Buddha would bless him. Another leaflet was addressed to Guomindang soldiers, telling them that victory news appeared regularly and urging them to fight in the coming year, because smart people know the right way. Despite having committed crimes, the Guomindang soldier was given a way out in the leaflet—if he did good things in the future, he would gain fame and save his life. A New Fourth Army leaflet, aimed at Mongolian soldiers under Japanese control, tried to persuade them to turn their weapons against the Imperial Army.

The format of these leaflets was one sheet, one side only, with splotches of color. With a few exceptions, the majority were one panel; however, some of the multi-panel leaflets were not sequential. The drawings were crude and seem difficult to grasp quickly, especially by rural people with very little visual literacy. Sad, tearful

mothers, wives, and children were depicted as victims of depravation and rape; also portrayed was the desertion of loved ones to the side of the enemy. Japanese soldiers were shown as rough, with a few stereotypically portrayed with glasses and mustaches. Comparing Chinese cartoon leaflets with those of Japan in this sample, the latter appear more sophisticated in drawing style, message, and design.

Themes of Cartoons

The themes of wartime cartoons varied wildly, depending, of course, on the targeted audiences and the side (Communist or Guomindang) from which they came.

Already in the aforementioned 1936 cartoon exhibition, Japan figured prominently as a theme; about half of the works displayed were anti-Japanese. Because the Chinese government was "still pursuing its policy of appeasement," cartoonists and other artists were not permitted to show a "recognizable face" or the words "Japan" and "Japanese"; instead, they resorted to symbols, such as a snake swerving its way through the Great Wall as in Mu Yilong's "A Viper Wriggles Southward" (Bader 1941: 230).

Bader, writing during the war, said that subtlety gave way to increasingly Western-style direct attacks in August 1937, after war broke out and Shanghai fell. He described the "new caricature" as "much more realistic and powerful as an educative agent" with "a violence, a grotesquely terrible quality about some of it, indicative of the strong feeling of both artists and audience" (1941: 233). The chief themes, according to Bader (1941: 233), were "Japanese brutality, Japanese imperialistic greed and *Han Chien* [sic] or Chinese traitors."

Differences can be discerned between how these three themes were expressed: brutality by "grimly realistic pictures of death by bayonet, sword, bullet and bomb," reminiscent of Goya's etchings of the Spanish Civil War; imperialism by symbolism in "greater measure"; and treason by linking present traitors with famous traitors of the past (Benedict Arnold, Shi Jingtang, Qin Hui, or Wu Sangui),[2] attacking Chinese

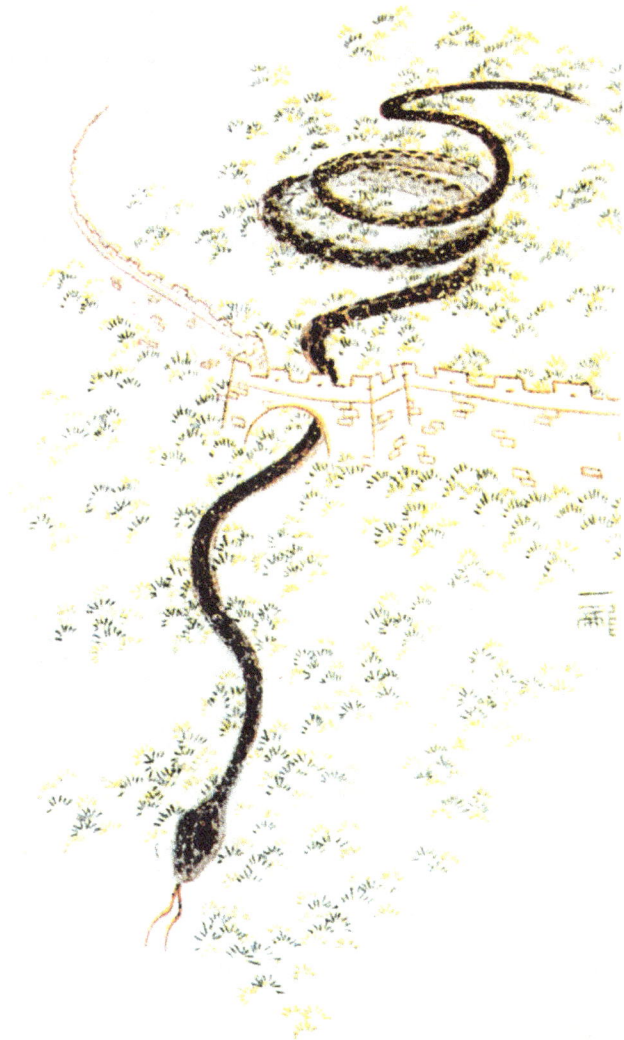

Fig. 3.13. "A Viper Wriggles Southward" by Mu Yilong.

Fig. 3.14. A Japanese soldier portrayed as a killer of multiple children. Zhang Leping, 1938.

who served as officials in Japanese-established puppet regimes, ridiculing the "Japanese propensity for elaborate and senseless espionage," and pointing out what happens to Chinese civilians who welcome the invaders (Bader 1941: 233–37). Heart-wrenching stories about the consequences faced by the Chinese bribed to help the Japanese appeared—such as one by Liang Baibo, showing a Chinese man taking money from a Japanese man as payment for poisoning the village well; lying nearby is the first victim, the Chinese man's own son. A full page of caricatures, Bader (1941: 237) described, portrayed such traitorous activity as:

Pretending to be patriotic, profiteering, grafting on relief funds, contributing to relief funds but selling Japanese goods, taking refuge in foreign concessions, maltreating the poor, evading military duty, compromising, creating rumors to inspire fear, spending money on luxuries, conserving rice for the Japanese, defeatism. Chinese social stratification is interestingly revealed in the pictures. It is a merchant who profiteers, grafts and sells Japanese goods. It is a peasant who evades military conscription. And it is Chinese in Western-type clothing—the modern educated class—who put their money in foreign banks, flee to foreign concessions, live luxuriously and give up defeatism.

Hung (1994a: 97–124) elaborated on images portrayed in wartime cartoons, concluding that they depended upon directness and simple common imagery, focused on the "physical concreteness of the crisis," and pinpointed who the enemy was (97–98). As Hung wrote, "What they lacked in artistic subtlety and refinement, however, they more than made up for in their robust vitality and compelling images" (99). The theme of Japanese brutality was hammered home, usually depicting an actual happening, as in Li Keran's (1907–89) "Killing Contest," which showed two Japanese soldiers in a contest to decapitate 150 Chinese, or Feng Zikai's capturing of a woman's head being blown off while she

Fig. 3.15. "Hongzha" ("Bombing") by Feng Zikai, 1937. Courtesy of Feng Yiyin.

妇女共同起来歼恶仇！

Fig. 3.16. "Funü gongtong qilai jianechou" ("Women Stand Together to Kill the Enemy") by Lu Shaofei.

is nursing her baby. Feng Zikai used a *ci* poem with the drawing:

> In this aerial raid,
> On whom do the bombs drop?
> A baby is sucking at its mother's breast
> But the loving mother's head has suddenly been severed.
> Blood and milk flow together.

Japanese bestiality of other types (looting, raping, reducing villages to ashes) were often shown, but, according to Hung (1994a: 101), the cartoonists were most distressed by the "indiscriminate killings." In a number of cases, the gruesomeness was such that it could be displayed only as characteristics of beastly and unsavory animals, such as monstrous apes, snakes, or pigs. Chinese cartoonists distinguished between the Japanese people and their military, laying the blame for the war onto militarism and the country's lack of respect for international law. Threats within China were also featured in cartoons, such as the role of traitors (*hanjianmen*) willing to do anything for their foreign masters

and the weak will to resist among Chinese (110–11). On the other hand, cartoonists also praised the unified will of patriotic soldiers and heroic civilians who fought the Japanese. Hung (1994a: 116) wrote that soldiers were depicted as nondescript, "selfless and valorous" men ready to die a "heroic death." Women and intellectuals were also subjects of cartoons, the former shown in the many roles in which they served their country and as latter-day Hua Mulans; the intellectuals as "guardians of moral rectitude" with duties to "assume a greater burden of responsibility in time of war" (116).

Claiming caricature as "one of the most effective agents in educating the masses and keeping up their spirit," Bader (1941: 228) described how Chinese cartoonists caricatured the Japanese during the war:

Everybody knows what a Japanese looks like. In particular, everybody knows what a Japanese soldier looks like. He has become stylized throughout free China. He is a squat, runty little man with a rising sun arm band and a strut that indicates a large sense of his own importance. He has huge projecting teeth, a scrubbing-brush mustache and large

Cartoons as Wartime Weapons, 1930s–1949

goggles. In fact, he looks like an Oriental version of old caricatures of Teddy Roosevelt. Sometimes he is depicted as brutal, sometimes as merely stupid, but he is always ridiculous.

Summing up, Hung (1994a: 120) wrote that the themes and images of wartime cartooning were

nationalistic, emotional, and idealistic. Using visual rhetoric, they portrayed a besieged nation fighting not merely for survival, but for justice and peace. The majority of cartoons were strong and spirited political statements, resting on the simple assumption that the current conflict was caused by Japan's unbridled imperialism—a theme designed to rekindle the bitter memories of repeated foreign encroachment on China in the past century. To repel the invaders and to rebuild China, nothing short of total unity was required. Unity was thus the cartoonists' battle cry.

Collaborationist Cartooning[3]

Early on, visual propaganda—mainly in the form of posters, broadsides, and handbills, and to lesser degrees, books and pamphlets—was considered vital to Japanese invasion and occupation tactics (Rowe 1939: 579). Bader (1941: 240) wrote that Japanese propaganda cartoons were meant to convince the Chinese that the Japanese conquest was beneficial to them and that they should embrace the Greater East Asian Co-Prosperity Sphere.

Characteristics of early cartooning in Japanese-occupied regions included: 1. cartoons were authorless, though very likely drawn by Japanese artists within the Japanese army (Okamoto 1997); 2. a secondary purpose of cartoons, besides their propaganda use, was to fill the augmented number of newspapers taken over or started by the Japanese, with "quotidian images" (of "female celebrities" and "amusing sketches of urban life") (Taylor 2014: 2); 3. many early occupation cartoons were plagiarized, an example of which was Huang Yao's "Niubizi" strip (Wong 2007: 27; see

Fig. 3.17. "Youjun weiwu sucheng shijie duyi" ("Friend's Military Power Claimed Unique in World") by collaborationist cartoonist Tian Qingquan, 1943.

also Wong 2006; Wong 2008); 4. recruiting Chinese artists to draw pro-Japanese cartoons was facilitated by the desire of some cartoonists to continue working or to break into the field (Taylor 2014: 5); and 5. children were also targeted, especially in brightly colored picture books drawn in a "bold and lively style." Concerning the latter, the books' drawings depicted Chinese children friendly with Japanese soldiers as well as Chinese children waving Chinese and Japanese flags, shouting, "Welcome! Welcome! Here comes an airplane. Truly is an angel of happiness," as a Japanese plane flies over. Another picture shows a mere infant appreciating that the "illusion of prosperity" offered to the Chinese by the "Communist bandit" cannot compare to the actual "prosperity" offered by the Japanese soldier ("Chinese Children . . ." 1938).

Taylor makes reference several times to the considerable space new and old newspapers (e.g., *Guomin xinwen* and *Zhonghua ribao* [*Central China Daily News*]) and magazines (notably *Xindongya* [*New East Asia*]) made available for cartoons (2014: 5, 7). *Zhonghua ribao*, closely aligned to Wang Jingwei, head of the Reorganized National Government (RNG), carried cartoons on its front page and in its weekly pictorial supplement. The abundance of publication space and the "exodus of intellectuals westward or into the Shanghai International Settlement," according to Taylor (2014: 6), opened up opportunities to young cartoonists who previously had not published in large newspapers or magazines. Most of the Chinese collaborationist cartoonists have been erased from the history of cartoonists, but a few are known: Chen Xiaozuo (pen name, Mu Wu) of *Xin dongya*; Huang Yebai, both a journalist and illustrator; Jiang Dongliang and Dong Tianye, both of whom had been anti-Japanese cartoonists before contributing cartoons to collaborationist periodicals (Taylor 2014: 14), and Tian Qingquan (1906–?), who drew cartoons with titles such as "Mighty Friendship Military" and "Make Contribution Again and Again."

Both in the north and south occupation zones, propaganda via cartooning was emphasized by 1939 and 1940. For the Beijing and Tianjin collaborationist cartoonists, there was Huabei manhua xiehui (North China Cartoon Association), funded by the Beijing Propaganda Office, and its magazine, *Beijing manhua* (*Beijing Cartoons*—started in 1940), published by the collaborationist-inclined daily *Wudebao*.

The scenario was similar in the Shanghai-Nanjing zone. As Wang Jingwei formed the RNG by 1939, propaganda (particularly visual) took on added importance and his government formally mobilized cartoonists under a Bureau of Propaganda; its primary goal was to present the RNG as the "only legitimate 'bearer of national identity'" (Brook 2007: 39, quoted in Taylor 2014: 8). That cartooning was a vital vehicle of this propaganda was indicated by the formation of Zhongguo manhua xiehui (Chinese Cartoon Association [CCA]) in late 1942 and its magazine, *Zhongguo manhua* (*Chinese Cartoons*), in October 1942.

Zhongguo manhua, like *Beijing manhua* (and the anti-Japanese cartoon periodicals), declared it was time to bring cartooning to the masses, continuously extolling the virtues and techniques of the profession through exhibitions, parades, and seminars.

Taylor (2014: 10–11) described the contents of *Zhongguo manhua*:

The magazine was, from the start, an outlet for overt propaganda, ranging from hagiographic portraits of Wang Jingwei to calls for the building of a "new China" under RNG guidance. In such depictions (often containing images of China's "toiling masses" that looked strikingly similar to those emanating from Yan'an), CCA artists made visual references to the "light" that the Wang regime promised to bring to the country once the clouds of war and communism had been dispersed, with cartoon Chinese pagodas radiating brightness like the walls of Manchukuo had done in visual propaganda a decade earlier.

Nonetheless, the bulk of the images it pushed depicted urban Chinese streetscapes (the Bund being particularly popular), attractive cheongsam- and suit-clad men and women [*sic*], and advertisements of a decidedly middle-class nature (i.e., for restaurants, theaters, and photo studios). It included . . . inspirational texts about the merits of cartooning—much of it crossing into travelogues, reviews of recent films, and topical but often mundane essays [and] . . . commentary on happenings in the world of film and popular music, and comic, though sympathetic, images of attractive movie stars on its covers.

Urban women featured prominently in occupation cartoonists' works, especially those by Chen Xiaozuo, Jiang Dongliang, Dong Tianye, Japanese Army cartoonist Miura Yoshio (pen name, Miura Noa), and Huang Yebai. Researchers, including Taylor (2014), Henriot and Yeh (2004), and Huang (2005), felt the portrayal of the "modern girl" in all of her charm, beauty, and gracefulness, decked out in a cheongsam and high heels, served a political, though complex, purpose. Chen Xiaozuo showed women as victims of policemen of the International Settlement, thus invoking an anti-British feeling in line with that of the RNG, or as distractions from the "mundane realities of war" (Taylor 2014: 19), while Jiang Dongliang and Dong Tianye's depictions of the modern girl waxed nostalgic for prewar Shanghai (17). Miura Yoshio's drawings were often "inter-textual Japanese representations of Chinese women," sometimes featuring attractive Chinese women coupled with kind Japanese men (20), and Huang Yebai derided the inequities apparent in fur-wrapped Shanghai women supported by rich businessmen when contrasted with the many barely clothed war refugees (22).

As said at the outset of this section, the collaborationist cartoonists made extensive use of posters and leaflets to disseminate messages to the Chinese to surrender, collaborate, and unite with the Japanese. Ding Cong told how he and his friends took care of such propaganda: "We would sneak out at night, rip down posters put up by the Japanese troops, change them subtly so they poked fun at the Japanese, and then stick them up again" (Wu Dunn 1990: 2).

Taylor's conclusion, reacting strongly against the "binary reductionism" common in scholarship on the wartime period, merits repeating:

> The ease with which cartoonists crossed political boundaries throughout the 1930s, 1940s, and 1950s, the multiplicity of meanings that can be read into the work that many produced late in the occupation, and the diversity of careers that many went on to explore after 1945 suggests a far more complicated picture. (2014: 25)

Civil War, 1945–1949

Except for time out to fight the invading Japanese, the Communist and Guomindang parties had been warring against each other since the 1920s. With the Pacific War out of the way, it was inevitable that collisions between the two sides would erupt. Popular disillusionment with the Guomindang-controlled government under Chiang Kai-shek was prevalent by the early 1940s, related to issues of extreme inequality, economic dislocation, corrupt politicians and businessmen, and penniless intellectuals (Hung 1994a: 97). Liao Bingxiong's 1945 "A Professor's Meal" was a classic focusing on the latter, showing a down-and-out professor and his family with empty bowls as they eat a Western book. Cartoonists

Fig. 3.18. "Jiaoshou zhican" ("A Professor's Meal") by Liao Bingxiong, 1945. Courtesy of Liao Bingxiong and Liao Ling-er.

aimed their barbs against Guomindang bureaucracy and its corruption in these "veiled and allegorical" drawings (Hung 1994a: 97).

As Hung (1994b: 125) described, during the post-World War II era China experienced a shift from external to internal affairs, from patriotic and anti-imperialistic to political and anti-government. He explained that the Guomindang had been badly wounded after the war and the country was enduring inept leadership, impoverished masses, Chiang Kai-shek's authoritarianism, mismanagement of the economy (including US aid), corruption, incompetent military leadership, intra-party fights, and, then, Chiang's decision to wage war against the Communists in December 1945.

Cartoonists certainly did not lack subject matter. Those who had left China during the latter years of the war returned to Shanghai, and some started magazines. They faced many hardships, including a lack of materials and the oppressive control of the government. In Guomindang-occupied areas, the artists had to resort to exhibitions and underground publications for outlets and were forced to be subtle in getting their messages across. In Shanghai, an underground Cartoon Worker

Student Group (CWSG) was secretly set up in 1946 to train young people in cartooning skills. Shen Tongheng, Ding Cong, Mi Gu, Hong Huang, and other famous cartoonists instructed between forty and 100 teachers, art students, workers, and salespeople each month. The group published a small periodical of the students' work.

When the Guomindang government closed all periodicals with Communist Party leanings in the spring of 1948, the CWSG organized an "underground" Cartoon Monthly Exhibition which toured the country with "Picture of Spring Dreams" in April and "The Song of the Funeral Procession" and "Baptized in the Fire" in May. While the exhibition was at the Shanghai Law School, the Guomindang "broke into the exhibition room, stole four drawings and injured visitors. Three students were arrested and sentenced to one and a half years of imprisonment. This was the first bloody political event caused by cartoons in Chinese history" (Liu-Lengyel 2001: 45). The CWSG exhibitions ended after six weeks.

A young member of CWSG, Hong Huang (interview, 1993) said that because there was "no place to publish as newspapers were suspended, we thought to use exhibitions, touring exhibitions." After the incident when the exhibition works were stolen and the students arrested, "the mayor held a press conference and held up the stolen cartoons to show how reactionary these were," according to Hong (interview, 1993).

Because the Guomindang scrutinized printed media more carefully than exhibitions, the latter became a preferred cartoon outlet. Group and individual exhibitions became popular. A collected exhibition was mounted as early as March 1945 by Ye Qianyu, Liao Bingxiong, Ding Cong, Zhang Guangyu, and others. First shown in Chongqing at the Sino-Soviet Cultural Association, the exhibition moved on to other cities (Bi and Huang 1986: 180–82). Hung (1994b: 139) wrote about the exhibitions: "All of these works reiterated the charge that the present political system was flawed and that the continuing dictatorship of the Guomindang threatened to undermine the fragile democracy and to plunge the country into chaos, and they were all warmly embraced by the general public."

It was generally agreed that visual art was more impactful than text during the domestic war period. As Hung (1994b: 137) pointed out, "No written word seems adequate to encompass the forcefulness and emotional range of the cartoon." Contending that politics also embrace "feelings, opinions, and images," Hung (1994b: 238) wrote that

> cartoonists created political images which offer a new avenue to the study of political culture and created a contentious and explosive public opinion which can hardly be overlooked. . . . For historians looking for answers for the rapid collapse of the Guomindang regime in the late 1940s, cartoons contribute a fresh assessment of this tumultuous period. . . . They [cartoons] fueled opposition to a government mired in political malaise . . . [and] galvanized popular discontentment and grievances against Jiang Jieshi [Chiang Kai-shek] and his policies and ultimately hastened his demise.

Despite being very political, the Chinese cartoons were not without high aesthetic values; particularly, Liao Bingxiong and Ding Cong's works declared that cartooning was an "artistic activity with an element of irreducible playfulness in it" (Hung 1994b: 132). Art generally, in the late 1940s, according to Westad (2003: 96), was "realist in tone and critical in attitude." He added, "In a more effective way than any Communist propaganda, these artists exposed to the middle class the increasing hollowness of the government's claim to represent all of China."

What is amazing is that the cartoonists could retain the impactful and aesthetic qualities of their works during highly stressful wartime conditions. The cartoonists we interviewed related the trying times and dangers they faced. For example, Ding Cong (interview, 2006) said:

> In the Civil War, drawing anti-Guomindang cartoons in those regions was more dangerous than drawing anti-Japanese ones. I drew many. People in the streets held up large signs of my cartoons that were anti-Guomindang. In the Civil War, the Guomindang did not dare to do me harm as I

Fig. 3.19. Ding Cong in his Beijing apartment, December 20, 2002. Photo by Xu Ying. Courtesy of Ding Cong and Shen Jun.

was famous. The Guomindang told the people they wanted democracy, so, if they did me harm, it would not look good for them.

Before the Communists left Shanghai, Zhou Enlai told us not to draw cartoons that would bring us problems. The Communist Party would call us every day at the same time to see if we were okay. If they could not reach us [no answer when they called], they would look for us. To answer the phone meant you were all right, safe. All the cartoonists were anti-Guomindang, so gradually we had to escape to Hong Kong.

Ding Cong (interview, 2006) said that the cartoonists "volunteered" to negatively depict the Guomindang and that they drew freely without "any guidance from Zhou Enlai." He added,

As long as someone published it, we would draw it. It was very hard at that time. We had to draw advertisements and illustrations to make a living, because the Communist Party did not pay us. To live, I found a part-time job as editor of newspapers or books. I published in progressive magazines, which the Guomindang sometimes confiscated; when they forbid the publications of these magazines, I had to leave Shanghai. After the Communists left, there was no one to protect us so we eventually went to Hong Kong. It [the Civil War period] was the most meaningful time of my life.

He summed up his cartooning as a "rich experience—anti-Japanese, anti-Guomindang, and then followed by the Communist Party, and beaten by it too" (Ding Cong, interview, 2006).

Ding Cong was self-taught, his famed cartoonist father Ding Song refusing to give him instruction because of the hard life an artist had to endure. He learned from life's hard knocks, usually showing sympathy for the poor and ignorant in his illustrations. While with a repertory company, Ding Cong observed the social outcasts and drew "The Red Light District" and other works on the difficult lives of prostitutes in Chengdu and China's rampant corruption (Yang and Yang 1992: 5–7). Some of his best work came after World War II, when he criticized Chiang's government. He liked to play on contradictions, had a "keen sense of the ridiculous," and "achieved his bite by concentrating on facial expression," according to Hung (1994b: 127).

Hong Huang's cartooning began while he was in Chongqing "about 1945 or 1946"; his cartoons were published in the *Weekly Pictorial* supplement of the daily *Business News*. Hong (interview, 1993) remembered that he published as an amateur, his livelihood depending upon his work in the social services office, "doing ads, movie posters, and decorating the office reading room" (Hong, interview, 1993). His cartoons were predominantly about hardships that refugees faced when trying to return to China after the war, obstacles he blamed on the Guomindang's poor transportation system.

Returning to Shanghai in 1946, Hong became a middle-school teacher, simultaneously publishing his cartoons in the newspapers *Xinmin Evening* and *Wenhui News* and the magazines *Time and Essays* and *Outlook*. He described the political situation as a continuous protest against the Guomindang's rotten leadership, especially its lack of food for the masses. I did a cartoon in 1948 called "Sharp Contrast" that contrasted the Guomindang taking from the people and the Communists giving to the people. I drew cartoons on the big political issues, such as the movement calling on Chinese people to use Chinese goods. (Hong, interview, 1993)

In 1947, when the periodicals to which he contributed were suspended by the Guomindang as "too leftist," Hong narrowly escaped arrest on two occasions. He said:

> In one episode, two agents were waiting at my door. I said to them, I know that fellow (meaning myself, which they were asking about) and I was able to escape. Two men came again and waited till midnight. I was not home. They took away my clippings and works. (Hong, interview, 1993)

Hong (interview, 1993) proudly recalled that just before Liberation in 1949, his cartoons were republished and hung on walls by students to "welcome Liberation. By then, we knew the Guomindang was defeated. They were also to attack the Guomindang further. For Liberation, I and five other cartoonists made a large cartoon. When the Communist troops arrived in Shanghai, it was visible on the wall."

Other budding cartoonists were involved in anti-Guomindang activities. Famed artist/animator Zhan Tong (Zhan Tongxuan, 1932–95) was a teenager in 1947–48, when he was asked by "the underground Communist Party" to draw cartoons to attack the Guomindang. He said, "I and two classmates made cartoons, and wherever we went, we put them up as exhibitions. They were destroyed by the Guomindang. The situation was such that everyone was involved in this type of activity" (Zhan, interview, 1993).

Working "underground" when he returned to Shanghai in 1945, Han Shangyi also covertly produced a film that indirectly lashed out at the Guomindang by showing the hard lives led by the people. Han (interview, 1993) drew "some cartoons under government control that went through censorship; others published

by patriotic forces with social messages." As with Zhang Leping and his "Sanmao," Han had a four-panel strip, "Miss Shanghai," describing the "miserable life in Shanghai," which was published from 1945 to 1947 in *Federation Pictorial*. The strip sidestepped Guomindang censorship because *Federation Pictorial* was owned by an American publisher, which the Chiang government did not wish to offend because of the financial and other support it received from the United States (Han, interview, 1993). Han (interview, 1993) said,

> The way I used cartoons, sometimes, they would make a big score, but usually, they were on a small scale, subtle-like. Once, I drew a cartoon that even other newspapers [besides *Federation Pictorial*] were afraid to use. It was a drawing of a crab, implying that the Guomindang would not last long, because, as with a crab, it was walking the wrong way. Sideways.

The most important newspaper strip of this period was Zhang Leping's revived "Sanmao" in *Dagongbao*, which dwelled on the deplorable conditions under which urban poor children managed to survive. Hung (1994b: 129) said of Zhang Leping that he might "lack the sarcastic tone of a Liao Bingxiong or a Ding Cong, but his San Mao [*sic*] drawings nevertheless raised many more troubling questions for the authorities." Farquhar (2001: 152) described this stage of Sanmao's life as that of an

> orphan boy eking out a lonely, miserable existence in Shanghai's streets. No family, no food, no shelter, no clothes. The illustrator made him a fictional symbol of the hundreds of thousands of orphaned children around the city before 1949. . . . Throughout the text, Sanmao's orphaned state is emphasized by comparing him to the powerful, the well-connected, the well-fed and the well-clothed.

As some of the above cartoonists indicated, subtlety was a necessary ingredient of Civil War cartooning. The Guomindang had strong censorship laws, confiscated

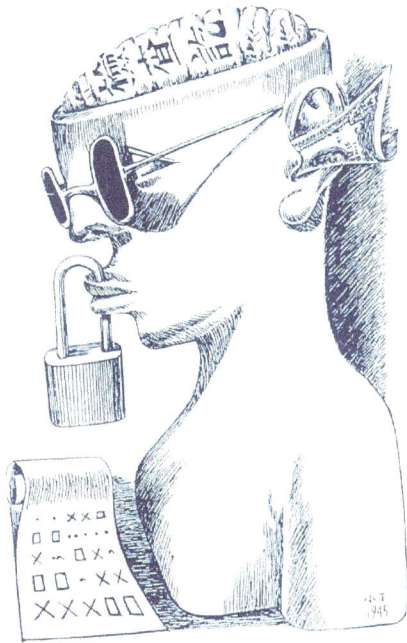

Fig. 3.20 "'Liangmin' suxiang" ("Portrait of a Model Citizen") by Ding Cong, 1945. Courtesy of Ding Cong and Shen Jun.

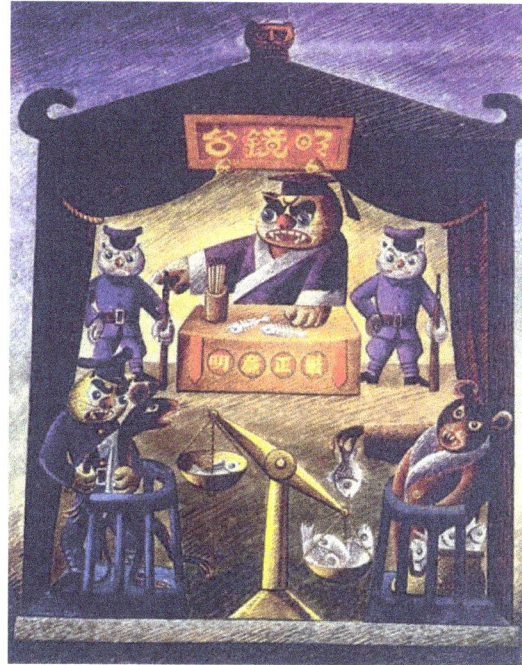

Fig. 3.21. "Maopan" ("Cat Judge"), part of Liao Bingxiong's "Maoguo chun-qiu" ("Annals of the Cat Kingdom"). Courtesy of Liao Bingxiong and Liao Ling-er.

and banned periodicals (e.g., *Zhoubao* [*Weekly*] in August 1946 and *Minzhu* [*Democracy*] two months later), and harassed cartoonists. Blank spaces (*tian-chuang* or "skylights") brought on by censorship were common in periodicals. To avoid persecution, famous cartoonists were forced to flee to Hong Kong (e.g., Ding Cong, Liao Bingxiong in 1947).[4]

Despite what Chinese cartoonists told us about Guomindang censorship of art and journalism, Westad (2003: 97) reached a different conclusion:

Artistic expression was probably freer during the last part of the 1940s than at any other period of Chinese history up to the 1990s. Although official censorship was reinstated in 1947, until the last months of GMD rule their censors did little beyond banning journalism that told the truth from the battlefields. . . . And in an increasing number of cases, the publishing houses and film studios did not care much about the government's wishes.

The discrepancy in perspectives might have occurred because Westad discussed art generally and neglected cartooning, which, more than likely, fell under journalism and the press, or because our sources did not delineate the specific time of the war they were describing.[5]

The subtlety claimed by some cartoonists came in various forms, such as layers of meanings, allegorical depictions, and juxtapositions of reality with fantasy. For example, Ding Cong's "Portrait of a Model Citizen" (1945) sarcastically showed an ideal Guomindang citizen as one with padlocked lips, unseeing eyes, money-stuffed ears, and a thoroughly scrutinized mind.

Masterpieces in their use of veiled characters and meanings were Liao Bingxiong's "Maoguo chunqiu" ("Annals of the Cat Kingdom") and Zhang Guangyu's "Xiyou manji" ("Journey to the West"), both individual exhibitions. Liao's work was shown at the Sino-Soviet Cultural Association in Chongqing in March 1946, and in Chengdu and Kunming, but was canceled by the

Cartoons as Wartime Weapons, 1930s–1949

authorities in Guangzhou in July 1946 and in Shanghai later that year. Five sets of works totaling more than 100 drawings, and using cats and mice in place of people to depict the brutality and corruption of the Guomindang, "Annals of the Cat Kingdom" took Liao six months to complete, from September 1945 to February 1946. Hung (1994b: 126) called Liao's exhibition "an artistic tour de force blended with unmistakable anger and frustration," "a consummate piece of political art which never raises the topic of politics," and described Liao as "relentless in lashing out at the Guomindang government, but he did it indirectly and ingeniously."

Zhang Guangyu resorted to telling a Chinese traditional story, "Journey to the West," employing four pilgrims who encounter, on their journey westward, spying, bribery, economic collapse, and government demoralization, all of which are allusions to Chiang's government. The show first appeared in Chongqing in 1945; it included sixty color images.

Unlike previously, comic art activities existed in places outside Shanghai, e.g., Chongqing, Kunming, and Guangzhou. Much Communist Party cartooning was in northeastern China. Among cartoonists there were Hua Junwu, Cai Ruohong, Zhong Ling (1921–2007), Jiang Yousheng, and Zhang Ding, the latter, editor of *Dongbei manhua* (*Northeast Cartoons*). As the Guomindang tightened control, some of the most active cartoonists fled to Hong Kong. Liao Bingxiong (interview, 2002), who stayed in Hong Kong from 1947 to 1950, related his work there and what led to his leaving the mainland:

> Chiang Kai-shek arrested many progressive intellectuals, killed them. Friends helped me to go from Chongqing to Kunming and arranged for me to be a primary school teacher.
>
> After several years, I found that the Communists protected me and arranged some work for me. They had arranged for me to escape the Guomindang's killing of intellectuals. In 1947, I went back to Guangzhou and then to Hong Kong. I was forced to leave for Hong Kong under the intensifying white terror in the area ruled by Chiang's

Fig. 3.22. "Muohaodao zaisha" ("Sharpen the Knife First, and Then Kill") by Hua Junwu, 1947. Written on the shield is "Peace Agreement." Chiang Kai-shek is ready to launch an attack, shielded by a peace agreement. Courtesy of Hua Junwu.

regime. In Hong Kong, I satirized politics and culture in cartoons. At the end of 1950, I went back to Guangzhou.

I published more than 3,000 in Hong Kong; I drew too many daily. I had more than ten pen names. Hong Kong was a cultural desert and enjoyed a low cartoon level. I followed them; I drew the way they liked. But, in Chongqing, I drew high-quality cartoons.

In addition to the Guomindang and Chiang Kai-shek, the United States was the other target of the cartoons, mainly because of the financial and moral support it extended to the ruling government and the rude and disrespectful behavior of some American soldiers employed to police China's Civil War. Anti-American feelings, especially among the students, began to well up immediately after World War II, but especially after the rape of Peking University student Shen Chong (Shen Jun, later the wife of Ding Cong) by two US soldiers on Christmas Eve, 1946 (Lent 2015b: 611–15).[6] During this time, cartoons depicted materialistic "Jeep girls" (Chinese women cavorting with US soldiers), the influence of US popular culture, drunken, American military men brutalizing rickshaw drivers and pedestrians, and the setting up of red-light districts to service American soldiers and the resultant spread of venereal diseases. The cartoons strongly suggested that the Guomindang was incapable of exerting control over the behavior of US soldiers. For the Communist Party, American troops in China "served as a shorthand for the era of national humiliation at the hands of militarily stronger Western powers" (Cathcart 2008: 151), and this belief was expressed in the cartoons.

Defeated Japan came in for limited cartoon criticism. The magazine *Guancha* (*Observer*, 1946–48) carried occasional anti-Japanese cartoons, and a few others popped up elsewhere from time to time, but the main focus was on China's miserable conditions under the Guomindang and its sponsor, the US (see Kushner 2013).

Though fewer in number, there were cartoonists loyal to the Guomindang and Chiang Kai-shek as far back as the Northern Expedition of 1925–26, when Chiang rose to power, and the following year, when he purged Communists from the Nationalist Party and Guomingemingjun (National Revolutionary Army or NRA). The Northern Expedition was marked by an abundance of political artwork, much of it modeled after Soviet propaganda and carried out by Communist artists working within the NRA, who were the first to "regularly caricature foreign imperialists and capitalists in a systematic way" (Taylor n.d.). At the same time, a small group of artists who remained at Chiang's side throughout his career created favorable portraits of him that were published in NRA publications such as *Geming huabao* (*Revolutionary Pictorial*). When Nanjing was established as the new capital city of Republican China in 1927, Chiang, through groups such as Lizhishe (the Officers' Moral Endeavour Association, or OMEA), set up the foundation as a personality cult that glorified his leadership and promoted him as the natural heir to Sun Yixian's (Sun Yat-sen) Republican revolution (Taylor n.d.). During the Nanjing Decade, symbols (e.g., Chiang's cape and cropped haircut) used by partisan cartoonists to "build a canon of Chiangiana" were used also by Communists and urban intellectuals to poke fun at Chiang (Taylor n.d.).

Fig. 3.23. Liang Dingming and fiancée, Li Roulan. *Shanghai manhua*, March 9, 1929, 6.

Among cartoonists who stood by Chiang Kai-shek beginning in the 1920s were the Liang brothers—Zhongming (1907–82), Yiuming (1906–84), and Dingming (1898–1959), who used their art to express patriotism, deal with contemporary issues, and attack the landlords. Known as the "Liang Family's Three Heavyweighters,"[7] they carried out written orders from Chiang Kai-shek to work on the front lines during World War II to create drawings concerning Japanese atrocities, the bravery of, and sacrifices by, Chinese soldiers and civilians, and enemy weaknesses. They did much of this through *Army Graphic*, which they published.

It is likely the elder brother Liang Dingming took the lead in joining with Chiang Kai-shek. A very successful artist for British American Tobacco Company, especially adept at producing colorful cigarette calendar posters, Liang Dingming first met the Nationalist leader in 1925, after which his "artistic career would hereafter be entwined with Chiang's Nationalist Party" (Laing 2004: 176; for more information on Liang Yiuming, see Yuan Quan 2015).

Another periodical, *Soldier Weekly*, started in 1940 by the Guomindang Political Department of National Defense, also provided space for cartoonists, such as Ting Kuang, Chou Cheng, Yang Hsien-ming, and Hsu Hai-chin, to draw comics. After the weekly moved to Taiwan, it became known as *Youth Warrior Daily* (Yang 1988).

Many mainland cartoonists moved to Taiwan in 1949 and immediately after, and continued their anti-Communist crusades in both newspaper editorial cartoons and/or comics. Among them were the Liang brothers, Chang Ying-chao, Ching Ho (real name, Chen Ching-ho) and Niu Ko (real name, Li Fei-meng). In Taiwan, Liang Zhongming and brother Liang Yiuming established *Graphic Journal* in 1949, to carry international political cartoons, domestic editorial cartoons, social satire, humor comics, and comics serials. Liang Zhongming also organized and taught arts training classes to military personnel who, in turn, contributed cartoons to *Graphic Journal*. When *Graphic Journal* folded after one year, Liang Yiuming and Liang Zhongming were invited by *Central Daily News* to become editor-in-chief and arts editor, respectively, of the newspaper's cartoon page, where they continued to attack the Communist Party and especially its leaders. Yiuming's "Bumpkin Goes to the South" and "Doctor Mo" and Zhongming's "Huang Hsing Autobiography" cartoons were very popular.

The tendency in Taiwan initially was for the transplanted mainlander cartoonists to draw political cartoons that attacked the Communists and for indigenous Taiwanese cartoonists to draw comics. A notable exception was Niu Ko, especially famous for his newspaper comic strip "Uncle Niu Fights as a Guerrilla."

Summary

Cartoonists worldwide point out that their jobs are made easier by crises, whether they be societal, political, or economical. Chinese cartoonists throughout the country's comic art history would likely agree, and they would probably pinpoint the 1930s and '40s as a cartoonist's paradise in that regard. For a time, they (both Communist and Guomindang cartoonists) had a common enemy (Japan) to attack; after the war, they certainly did not lack topics to satirize as China was seriously affected by political divisiveness and economic blight.

As is so often the case with China, changes in how art connected with society underlined cartooning at the time. In the late 1930s, the New Art Movement set the parameters for cartoonists; i.e., art should be appealing to the masses, more realistic, socially and politically oriented, propagandistic, and marked by a distinctly Chinese style with Western elements. Some of these characteristics were codified by Mao at Yan'an in 1942.

Throughout the war with Japan, cartoonists concentrated on the themes of Japanese brutality and imperialistic greed and Chinese traitors, spreading their messages through print media, exhibitions, murals, leaflets, banners, and woodblock prints. They joined together in the mobile National Salvation Cartoon Propaganda Corps, at Mao's Communist base in Yan'an, as soldier cartoonists with the New Fourth Army and Eighth Route Army, and as participants in drama troupes.

The resumption of the Civil War in late 1945 saw a widening split in the cartoonists' ranks, the positions they took, and the methods they used. Much of the Communist propaganda focused on the ineptitude and corruption of the government while the Guomindang heaped praise on Chiang Kai-shek and called for patriotism. The Communist cartoonists also depicted the misconduct of US military personnel stationed in China, usually blaming it on Chiang Kai-shek's pandering to Washington, DC. Communist cartoon campaigns generally were more structured and innovative than those of the Guomindang; the Communist cartoonists were flexible, for example, depending on exhibitions which were less scrutinized by the authorities than print media.

The concept of comics as revolutionary popular literature was developed before the Communist victory in 1949, and subsequently applied with constant shifts and re-interpretations after 1949. In practice, popular but "counter-revolutionary" works were criticized or purged while exemplary "revolutionary" works were held up for emulation. (Farquhar 1999: 192)

The Seventeen-Year Period, 1949–1966

Theory, Practice, and Control

As discussed in Chapter 3, Mao Zedong in his talks at Yan'an in 1942, already prescribed a theory for art—and thus cartoons—that was implemented in post-Liberation China; art was to be an ideological weapon promoting the Communist and nationalist cause, made accessible to and understandable for the illiterate masses.

In July 1949, ways to implement Mao's policies were discussed at the first China National Literature and Arts Worker Representatives Congress, attended by Mao, Zhou Enlai, and Zhu De, all of whom spoke. The Congress was often used to signify the "end of the New Democratic literary and art movement and the beginning of socialist culture" (DuYing 2014: 90). The fundamental purpose of the Congress was to set up national associations to provide a united front in culture and the arts for both the "old liberated areas" and those regions which were newly Communist. Cartoonist Ye Qianyu played an important part, serving as chairman of the Congress. In his address, he said that he and others of the progressive art movement had shortcomings that could be remedied by studying Mao's thoughts and policies on art. The shortcomings, as listed by Galikowski (1998: 13), were "factionalism, a lack of strong leadership, and incorrect or superficial understanding of Party policy towards the arts, divisiveness, individualism, remoteness from the masses and social life, and excessive reliance on 'western bourgeois artistic methods and aesthetic values.'" Ye and fellow cartoonist Cai Ruohong were appointed vice chairmen of the newly formed Artists' Association, and Zhang Ding, who had fiercely

Chapter 4

Liberation, Maoist Campaigns, and Cartoons, 1949-1976

attacked the Japanese with his World War II cartoons, became one of five Party members in charge of the very influential Central Academy of Fine Art.

The official line on cartooning after 1949 was spelled out by leading art theoretician Wang Chaowen (1909–2004) (1980, Vol. 1: 37–41) in a series of articles in the early 1950s. In a *People's Daily* article in 1950, he advocated that cartoons be varied in style and lively; he complained bitterly about the trend towards standardization of all cartoonists' styles. In 1951, Wang wrote "We Need Children's Cartoons," an article that held up Feng Zikai's work as a model but cautioned that not all of Feng's cartooning should be imitated, because some of it was escapist, pessimistic "old-fashioned humanism" (Harbsmeier 1984: 36–38).

Much of the thinking about what art (and comic art) should be was influenced by Soviet socialist realism—in other words, art as it looks in the real world with an emphasis on fine drawing. During the early 1950s, Soviet artists and theorists were invited to China, and, in return, Chinese artists, including cartoonist Cai Ruohong, went to the Soviet bloc nations to learn. Furthermore, exhibitions of Soviet and Eastern European art were held in China, and Soviet art books, including ones on political cartooning, were translated into Chinese. Imitation of Soviet works was so pervasive that when the Chinese animation short, *Why the Crow Is Black*, won a major award at a European festival, it was announced as a Soviet work (Te Wei, interview, 2001).

The thinking concerning the role of art in the Communist system after 1949 wavered; it was sometimes imprecise and contradictory. The major issue was the place, if any, that *guohua* (traditional Chinese painting) should have in the new China. But, first, there had to be agreement on what the imprecise term "guohua" entailed. As Andrews (1990: 557) wrote, "It [guohua] excludes work in Western media, even if painted by Chinese artists, but in recent usage its relationship to Chinese painting of the past may be tenuous." For some artists, guohua referred only to medium; for others, to medium and style. There was also the dilemma of fitting traditional Chinese painting into, or eradicating it from,

a new system whose main purpose was to destroy the old social order. As Andrews (1990: 559) phrased it:

> The fundamental question [from 1949 to 1957] was whether traditional painting should be preserved, reformed or simply eradicated. One sign of this ambivalence was the decision made soon after liberation to retrain artists in Shanghai to become illustrators of books that would appeal to and edify the masses. An oddly-mixed group of comic book artists, calendar print designers, and traditional Chinese painters was assembled for Marxist-Leninist thought reform, instruction in the principles of the new art, and practical training in techniques, especially in Western figure drawing.

Gradually, guohua was reformed to be realistic and socially useful with tinges of Western influence, exemplified by paintings by cartoonists Ye Qianyu and Zhang Ding (for more on guohua, see Andrews 1994: 169–78).

With the basic Mao theory in place, the Communists after 1949 "turned their attention to 'practice,' namely organization and action" (Schurmann 1968: iii). Policies and organizations designed to control the print media and their content, including cartoons, were put into effect immediately after the founding of the PRC. In particular, the Shanghai press and publishing and distribution industries, considered key purveyors of government policies, were kept in check by Shanghaishi junshi guanzhi weiyuanhui wenhua jiaoyu guanli weiyuanhui xinwen chubanchu (Shanghai Military Control Commission Culture and Education Management Committee Press and Publication Bureau, shortened to Shanghai Press and Publication Bureau, or SPPB). Especially important to SPPB were *xiaobao* (tabloids), designated by the government as "sugar-coated medicine" (*tangyi liangyao)* "to educate backward petty urbanites" (Du Ying 2014: 94). In 1949, the SPPB, responsible for the takeover of publishing and distribution sectors from 1949 until the end of 1953, issued three reports on tabloids, criticizing tabloid writers for writing "in the service of cultural hooliganism," recommending new tabloids, and suggesting that most old tabloid writers be dismissed, that content be revised, and that new tabloid journalists be subjected to self-criticism (Du Ying 2014: 96). Before the end of 1949, all old tabloids had been banned, replaced by *Yibao* and *Dabao*. New tabloids were free to publish commercial and entertainment fare denied to literary magazines and supplements, and were not subjected to the same rigorous censorship applied to Shanghai broadsheets and literary magazines. A shift also took place when it came to tabloid content, which became more diversified, including highbrow writing along with traditional mass-appeal stories. However, these perks proved to be short-lived for the tabloids when the state took over all Chinese mass media.

The reorganization, collectivization, and specialization of the Shanghai newspapers was swift; by 1953, no private newspapers existed in Shanghai. State ownership of publishing and distribution companies took until 1956 to be implemented; in that year, only thirteen private firms remained, all tied to religion (Du Ying 2014: 116). Tight organizing and regimenting of private publications nationwide meant that the state now owned these industries, giving it the power to organize them by structure and function and to decide the topics they could cover. As this occurred after 1955, Beijing became the center of the press, publishing, and distribution industries.

The transformation was not smooth, according to Du Ying (2014: 126–28) in his analysis of the Shanghai press, publishing, and distribution industries. It was characterized by frequent adjustments by three government agencies that gradually moved from "supportive to restrictive" (126), the lack of a "clear and fixed blueprint for the so-called 'new culture' or 'socialist culture' that government cultural agencies, publishers, and writers in Shanghai could follow" (127), and an inability in the early 1950s of traditional literati and private publishers to "totally free themselves from their old tastes and old mind-sets in the production of popular publications" (127).

Du Ying (2014: 127–28) concluded that,

in the print and publishing world of the early 1950s, a process of negotiation occurred among political, commercial, and cultural forces, between new content and old forms, and between new topics and old frameworks in the various forms of popular publications in circulation. Old-fashioned or mixed popular publications appealed to the masses because they borrowed from established forms of popular culture; meanwhile, radical new thoughts, presented with some old-fashioned flavor, helped the new government explain itself to its people. However, authors with old taste and using old frameworks tended to vulgarize the subject so as to grab the masses' attention, and this vulgarization and popularization could also disturb, confuse, or subvert the supposedly serious and sublime new ideology. In 1951 and 1952, SPPB began to give up its policy of using private tabloids and the broadcasting industry as "sugar-coated medicine" to indoctrinate backward petty urbanites, quickly transitioning to a policy of socialization and regimentation of the press and publishing industry, which was almost completed nationwide by 1956. In this sense, the policy adjustment was not so much the product of an omnipotent state apparatus and its well-defined plan as it was a response to the thriving private publishing entities and the popularity of their publications.

Among the mass media, according to Farquhar (1999: 201–2), the "comic book" (lianhuanhua) was one of the "first targets for organization and ideological control" because of its immense popularity and potential as an educational medium and its already-in-place "dispersed and powerful publishing and distribution network." Controlling the lianhuanhua industry meant that some major publishers came under the Communist domain.

Control was affected organizationally and critically, comparing pre-1949 comics with those following Liberation. A Shanghai report at the time, according to Farquhar (1999: 213–14), showed that the "grassroots bureaucracy set up to control the publication of comics was inseparable from the stated aim of an 'attack' by new comics on the territory of the old." When a resolution on the reform of pre-Liberation literature passed at an important July 24, 1949, conference, some lianhuanhua publishers did what comic book publishers in the United States and at least twenty other countries were

81

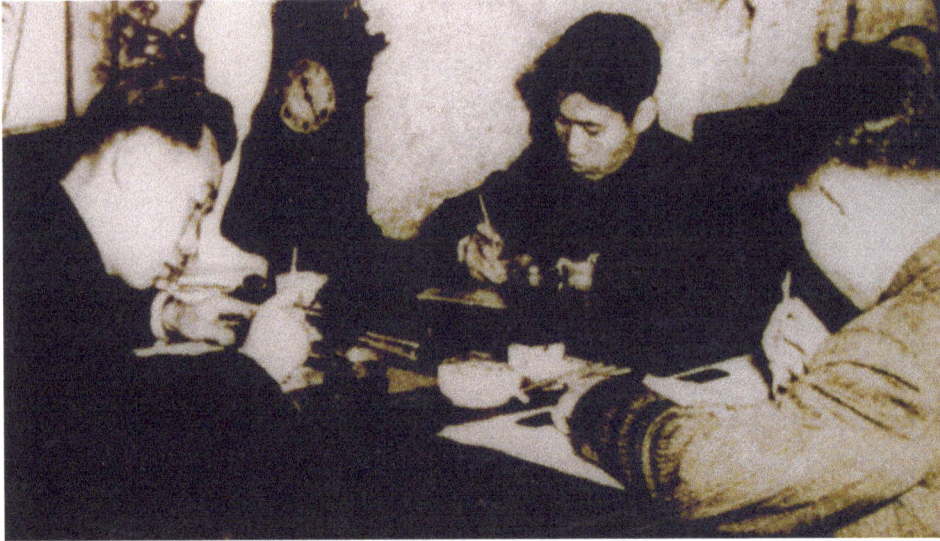

Fig. 4.1. Lianhuanhua artists working in cramped space, late 1940s. On the left is famous lianhuanhua artist Zhao Hongben.

to do during the anti-comics campaign in the early 1950s (see Lent 1999b, for a discussion of these campaigns); they created their own organization—Shanghaishi Lianhuantuhua Chuban Xiehui Bianshen Weiyuanhui (The Censorship Committee of the Shanghai Association of Lianhuanhua Publishers). The committee was tasked with approving or rejecting all lianhuanhua titles according to these rules established at the July 24 conference:

1. Stocks of all pre-Liberation publications were to be investigated by each publisher or bookshop and a list of these titles, together with a sample of each for filing, were to be sent to the Publishers' Association. The entire stock of any works found to have serious errors was to be sent to the Public Security Bureau for burning.
2. A sample of all comics published after Liberation and before 1 August 1949 were to be sent to the Censorship Committee before distribution, and those with errors could either be revised or sent to the Public Security Bureau for burning.
3. A sample of all manuscripts ready for printing after 1 August was to be sent to the Censorship Committee for publication approval or rejection.

The Committee classified works into three categories according to ideological correctness:

1. Works with minor mistakes could be corrected and then printed.

2. Works with major, but not serious, mistakes could be corrected and resubmitted.
3. Works with serious and irreparable errors would not be published. (Farquhar 1999: 214)

Numerous problems plagued the committee; most significantly, many publishers resented this bureaucratic intrusion into their businesses and therefore ignored the rules. Other restraints were audiences' preferences for the old comics and the lack of government leadership; however, the latter was solved when the Party took over all publishing in 1953.

Organizational control was also exercised through cartoon groups and periodicals launched shortly after 1949, and functioning under the Ministry of Propaganda. The first Cartoonists Club appeared in Shanghai; chaired by Shen Tongheng, it boasted more than 100 participants, including traditional Chinese and oil painters, etchers, and lianhuanhua and cartoon artists. Already on June 1, 1950, the group brought out *Manhua* (*Cartoon*) magazine, staffed by Mi Gu, Zhang Leping, Shen Tongheng, Te Wei, and Zhang Wenyuan (1910–92). It lasted for 163 issues, closing in 1960 because of economic problems. Among other associations during succeeding years were Two Knives, consisting of Central Art Academy graduates, Beijing Workers Cultural Palace Cartoon Group (1956), a Shanxi cartoonists group (1956), as well as one in Wuhan (1961). Cathcart (2004: 53) said that the associations "set production goals and encouraged collective work, but they also functioned as a forum for self-criticism and criticism from the

82

Fig. 4.2. Cover of *Manhua*, No. 14, 1951.

Party, one's colleagues and superiors." He added that as cartoonists realized they could not work outside of Party supervision, they "adapted and aligned as best" they could with principles laid down by Mao at Yan'an.

Critical control came through "public denunciation of 'bad' works and approbation of 'good' works," examples of the latter, given by Farquhar (1999: 203–12, 218–23), being *Sanmao*, *Jimaoxin* (*Feather Letter*), and *Dongguo xiansheng* (*Master Dongguo*), characterized by "'a correct political orientation,' an artistry capable of 'moving the reader,' and capacity to deliver 'lasting ideological education'" (Farquhar 1999: 217). Unacceptable were themes relying on sensationalism, political naiveté (especially relating to the class struggle), deceit (e.g., a comics cover suggesting correct political content while the actual story inside praised feudal concepts), and "textual oxymorons" (Chen Xiao 1952: 21).

From the early 1950s, some cartoonists had opportunities to draw satirical cartoons inspired by Chinese domestic life. Li Binsheng (b. 1925), after joining the *Beijing Daily* in 1952, introduced one- and four-panel cartoons that poked fun at daily happenings, while attempting to change situations for the public benefit. Li gave examples:

> A hospital had mice; a patient brought in a cat. I drew about this and immediately the hospital improved its conditions. A woman came to my office and showed me her hair was burned off by a barber. After my cartoons, the barber apologized and paid her. Other cartoons showed a lightless street, a bike rider with no light, and more. Those

cartoons were well received; they solved many social problems, and other papers throughout China had their own versions. (Li, interview, 2013)

Because of his cartoons, in 1955, Li Binsheng was selected as a Beijing people's delegate to the National People's Congress.[1]

Much of the content of post-Liberation propaganda art—particularly cartoons and lianhuanhua, and to slightly lesser extent, nianhua and woodcuts, all key components of the Communist propaganda arsenal—portrayed and demonized enemies of the new regime. Hung (2011: 158–59) wrote that

> a familiar technique Chinese artists used in attacking their enemies was a sharp distinction between "us" and "them," between friends and foes, heroes and villains. Such a clear contrast comes primarily from the Marxist conception of class struggle, which, in theory, divides the world into two antagonistic camps: oppressed versus oppressors, socialism versus capitalism, and proletariat versus capitalist.

Considered the major enemy, the United States and its leaders were viciously portrayed through allegory (represented as a snake or wolf), name-calling (General Douglas MacArthur renamed "Mac the Madman" or "Mac the Devil"), and satire. The Soviet Union influenced Chinese cartoons that attacked the US; works by the Kukryniksky (the collective name of cartoonists Porfirii Krylov, Mikhail Kuprilianov, and Nikolai Sokolov) and Boris Efimov were reprinted in both official Beijing and regional dailies, and works in the Soviet cartoon magazine *Krokodil* (*Crocodile*) were emulated by Chinese cartoonists. Besides the US, other enemies figuring in Chinese cartoons at the birth of the PRC were Chiang Kai-shek and the Guomindang, "counterrevolutionaries at home: spies, saboteurs, and others," "class enemies: capitalists and landlords," and "bourgeois intellectuals," chief of whom was Hu Feng (Hung 2011: 166–77).

Political cartoons, known as *shishi manhua* (current affairs cartoons), and lianhuanhua were the main

83

vehicles for reflecting government policies in the 1950s: shishi manhua because of their immediacy, lianhuanhua because of their ability to tell coherent stories, either as books or serialized installments in newspapers, and their immense readership, and both for their appeal to the large illiterate population, using direct, simple, and recognizable images. The reach of this comic art was wide-ranging, according to Hung (2011: 180), who wrote, "But if cartoons of news events were created more for urban consumption, then lianhuanhua such as *Aunt Yao Apprehends the Spy*, with peasant women as protagonists, were intended to reach a broader audience, appealing both to peasants and urbanites alike."

Korean War, 1950–1953

Mao's dispatching of more than 300,000 Chinese soldiers early in the Korean War, in support of Korean Communism and the resultant mass movement against American "imperialism," were taken seriously by cartoonists, who followed the Party line that Americans were "foreign devils whose hollow bravado was best portrayed as a 'paper tiger'" (Cathcart 2004: 43).

Early on, the anti-Americanism campaign found many followers in the art community. Theoretician Wang Chaowen, in a 1950 *Guangming ribao* article, proclaimed that it was the sacred duty of cartoonists to use cartoons as propaganda, and that this responsibility included invoking hatred for the enemy in the Korean War and strengthening the determination for victory. Titles of some lianhuanhua definitely reflect this anti-American animosity: e.g., *Meiguobing shouxing* (*The Animal Behavior of American Soldiers*) and *Jizhu meidi xuezhai* (*Remember the Blood Debt of American Imperialism*).

One propaganda tactic employed by cartoonists, particularly Zhang Ding and Mi Gu, was to pull out World War II images showing the Japanese as bloodthirsty, drunken war criminals and to apply them to the United States. They followed the official line that the US was rearming Japan "to storm the Asian mainland" (44). This assertion, popularized by Zhang Ding, was the basis of a series of pamphlets, *Cartoon Propaganda Reference Materials*, produced by the Central Academy for the Fine Arts in Beijing and authorized by the Ministry of Propaganda, beginning in November 1950. The pamphlets served as stimuli for the expansion of cartoon outlets (wall posters, cartoon newspapers, etc.), guided cartoonists concerning the Party's policies, and provided cartoonists with source material (45). Concerning the latter point, Edward Hunter (1953: 213) wrote:

> Source material is difficult to obtain, particularly for amateurs, and here [in the handbooks] was a plentiful supply of it for amateur cartoonists and artists, showing the way every important personality should be drawn, in simplified fashion, and showing how every important political issue of the day should be represented pictorially. The Party, with its usual skill in exploiting the indomitable, finer qualities in any people, assumed correctly that once a cartoonist or artist had followed the models shown in the propaganda sketch book, he would be inclined to believe that they were true, and even to argue that they were, for weren't his own creations and honor at stake?

The wide dispersal of the *Cartoon Propaganda Reference Materials* and their use of "Japan bashing" to induce hatred for the US "lent momentum to the outcry for a just war" and spread the message "never again" (Cathcart 2004: 49). Adam Cathcart (2004: 52–53) concluded that by "replacing Japan with the U.S., cartoon mediums were of inestimable help for the Party" (52); however, as the war wore on, cartoonists probably lost their spontaneity and wit (MacConaughy 1951, quoted in Cathcart 2004), and, according to Cathcart (2004: 53), "anti-Japanese themes become mandated and ritualized; pure hatred and hagiography dominated the cartoon medium, serving only to inflame the Chinese people and raise the bile of past humiliation in the service of a questionable war."

Maoist Campaigns

The Seventeen-Year Period was a time of criticism and contradiction, tied to a series of campaigns mounted by

Fig. 4.3. "Haopengyou" ("Good Friends") by Hua Junwu, June 1955. Hu Feng wears a mask as if a friend, at the same time he is leaking secrets as a spy. Courtesy of Hua Junwu.

Mao and the Party as they sought to throw out the old and introduce and firm up the new. These were unsettling years for cartoonists, as well as other artists and intellectuals, resulting in many arrests, imprisonments, and banishments to the countryside, as they failed to comprehend or were accused (often wrongly) of not heeding the official policies.

The first campaign (besides the Korean War) cartoonists were called upon to support with their scathing drawings was that against the celebrated writer and critic Hu Feng (Zhang Mingzhen) (1902–85), a member of the executive board of the Writers' Union. At first, the critical attacks against Hu and his followers were confined to literary and artistic circles, but by 1955, what the group espoused was seen as political and they as counter-revolutionaries.

From the 1930s to 1948, Hu had written theoretical essays on literature, a chief point of which was that writers should adopt a subjective viewpoint, contrary to other members of the left-wing literary group and the Party, who felt literature should serve political causes by depicting class struggle. As early as 1952, a report by the Ministry of Propaganda, intended for the Central Committee and Zhou Enlai, spelled out "major mistakes" of Hu. Among them were that his ideas "obliterate the world view and class stance," and that he "replaces socialist realism with old realism, actually replaces proletarian literature and arts with that of the bourgeoisie and petit bourgeoisie," "stresses the abstract 'objective fighting spirit,'" and "worships western European bourgeoisie literature and art" (Hong Zicheng 2007: 52–53).

In 1954, Hu presented a report to the Central Committee, blaming the country's intellectual sterility on the Party's literary watchdogs. Occasionally, during this period, Hu lamented the "sameness in public opinion" (*yulun yilü*) and cultural discourse, which Mao countered, saying that for people who wanted to use freedom of speech to push counter-revolutionary messages, they surely would only have "sameness in public opinion." In his 1954 speech, Hu also criticized the Party for its imposed political indoctrination and its restriction on freedom of expression. The following year (1955), the press and its cartoonists mounted a campaign of criticism against Hu; that year, the *Literary and Art Gazette* was filled with criticisms of Hu and his politics and aesthetics. Particularly, when old accusations that Hu Feng had been a spy arose, cartoonists such as Hua Junwu and Mi Gu had a "field day" (Andrews 1994: 178). The July 1955 issue of *Literary and Art Gazette* mentioned the role of cartoons, reporting that artists were active in criticizing Hu by producing cartoons. Galikowski (1998: 46) wrote:

> Cartoons appeared more regularly in official publications during this campaign than any other art form because they were considered to be the best vehicle for satirical attacks, particularly on "enemies of the people", who were conventionally depicted as being wicked and, at the same time, laughably foolish. The message conveyed was that counter-revolutionaries might be cunning and evil, but they were no match for "the people."

Also, in 1955, Beijing's Municipal Party put up an anti-Hu Feng cartoon show.

Galikowski (1998: 47) concluded that, while artists were not the targets during the Hu Feng campaign, the criticism politicized art discourse, brought artists into "line by purging any signs of dissent," and "turned the cultural and artistic field into a periodical political background." As for Hu Feng, he was arrested in mid-1955 and imprisoned until 1979.

Uncertainty marked the next decade (1956–66) for Chinese artists and intellectuals, brought on by "the shifting nature of the relationship between art and politics as the authorities alternated between relatively liberal policies and tight ideological control" (Galikowski 1998: 55).

In May 1956, Mao, for reasons still debated, set into motion a more liberal direction when he proclaimed, "Let a hundred flowers bloom; let a hundred schools of thought contend." The Hundred Flowers campaign that followed was, according to Mao, "designed to promote the flourishing of the arts and the progress of science." At first, not much criticism was generated and the issues discussed were not very important, but when Zhou Enlai suggested to Mao that the central government should encourage intellectuals and artists to criticize, and Mao responded that criticism was preferred, the floodgates of disapproval were opened wide, especially in May 1957. In July 1957, Mao stopped the campaign, because it had become uncontrollable with what he viewed as too much hateful and destructive, rather than constructive, criticism.

Cartooning figured prominently in this brief atmosphere of relaxed standards. For example, Hua Junwu and several others edited one of the new art magazines, *Multi-Image*, that sprouted; there was a call for the lifting of all restrictions on cartoons; and a National Exhibition of Cartoons was held in January 1957, satirizing "Party bureaucratism and the wastefulness of the state" (Galikowski 1998: 63). In fact, Galikowski (63) claimed that "in the art world, overt criticism came mainly in the form of cartoons," explaining the evolution of their uses:

> Cartoons had previously been used for the purpose of criticism both at Yan'an and since the founding of the People's Republic, but their function had been to expose and satirize external enemies, or encourage a more radical outlook amongst ideological waverers. During the Hundred Flowers movement, however, the cartoons focused much more on criticizing the Party itself and the bureaucratic practices generated by its policies.

Mao halted the Hundred Flowers campaign with a *People's Daily* editorial on July 1, 1957, criticizing

Rightists (those voicing dissenting views) and thereby starting the Anti-Rightist campaign. A probable effect of Hundred Flowers was to identify the critics of the Party and Mao; as Mao himself said, it "enticed the snakes out of their caves." At least 500,000 people were purged, most sent to prison and labor camps, as all opposition was silenced. Many had not challenged Party principles and were arrested for personal reasons.

Among cartoonists who were classified as Rightists, lost their positions, and were sent to prison or the countryside for re-education and to do menial work were Liao Bingxiong, executive member of the Chinese Artists' Association and deputy president of its Guangzhou branch; Wang Zimei of Sichuan; Shen Tongheng; Ding Cong; and Li Binsheng (see the section "The Plight of Cartoonists" later in this chapter for a fuller treatment). The cartoonist who was most heavily involved in accusing artists of being Rightists was Hua Junwu, who did so in a July 1957 *Fine Art* article and again during the following two months. Nearly fifty years later, the cartoonists we interviewed, with much vehemence, told how Hua and Ying Tao ruined the careers of fellow artists by pointing them out as enemies of the state (Zhu Genhua, interview, 2009). Also, during the summer of 1957, Cai Ruohong participated in the Anti-Rightist campaign on the side of the authorities.

On the heels of the Anti-Rightist campaign, in early 1958, Mao instituted the Great Leap Forward movement, designed to rapidly expand industrialization and agricultural collectivization in an effort to rival the Soviet Union and United Kingdom. The Great Leap Forward took two forms—a mass steel campaign using 600,000 backyard furnaces and the creation of 26,578 people's communes, each of the latter consisting of 5,000 households. The guiding principle of the campaign was: "Go all out, aim high and achieve greater, faster and better and more economical results in building socialism" (Galikowski 1998: 79). The fierce rivalry that resulted led to grossly inflated steel and grain production figures, not to mention a mostly unusable grade of steel and terrible famines brought on by the diversion of farm workers from the fields to the backyard furnaces. By early 1959,

Fig. 4.4. "Damaisui dayumi yundao Beijing qujian Maozhuxi" ("Big Wheat and Big Corn Sent to Beijing for Chairman Mao's Viewing") by Jiang Chaoling, 1958. Promotional cartoon for the Great Leap Forward.

it became evident that the campaign was in serious trouble; from 1959 to 1961, the Great Leap Forward turned into a disaster as China was hit by natural disasters and tens of thousands of people perished in famines.

From the outset of the Great Leap Forward, the art and cultural communities were expected to forego private work and fully support the movement. The Artists' Association rather quickly proposed an agenda for all artists in China that included:

1. A work plan in art for the Great Leap Forward.
2. Artists must pay attention to ideological and artistic aspects and not let quality decrease.
3. Artists must give "utmost support to the popularization of art works, which meant producing more New Year pictures, picture-story books, cartoons, propaganda posters and illustrations."
4. More emphasis must be placed on training the masses in technical aspects of art and encouraging amateur works.
5. Artists must go to the countryside and factories at least once yearly. (Galikowski 1998: 81)

As with other endeavors of the Great Leap Forward, absurd competition resulted, and high (often impossible) targets were set. During a series of meetings of artists in Beijing in 1958, thirty-nine cartoonists pledged to draw 5,800 cartoons in 1958, "meet the needs of amateur-cartoonists," and organize a Great Leap Forward cartoon exhibition (81). Many of the cartoons of the period illustrated commune life and iron and steel production, in keeping with the priorities of the Great Leap Forward.

In 1958, amateur cartoons by workers, peasants, and soldiers appeared in profusion in magazines, newspapers, cartoon albums, and exhibitions; however, newspaper columns devoted to workers' cartoons already existed in the previous decade (see fuller discussion in Chapter 5).

Artists continued to be closely watched during the Great Leap Forward, expected not to deviate from the "imposed orthodoxy" or to show any sign of "independent expression" (Galikowski 1998: 107). When Defense Minister Peng Dehuai wrote a letter to Mao in mid-1959, criticizing how the Great Leap Forward was being implemented, the fallout was severe; on August 7, the Party stated that Rightist Deviation (meaning criticism of the Great Leap Forward) had become a serious problem. In the ensuing months, about 6.6 million people were singled out and criticized as Rightist Deviation Opportunists; some artists were among them.

The vacillating atmosphere of the 1950s continued into the 1960s. Recognizing the disastrous results of the Great Leap Forward, the Party and Central Committee shifted to more pragmatic and realistic policies. New documents were issued on science, higher education, and culture; victims of the Anti-Rightist Deviation movement were rehabilitated; and top-level leadership changes took place. The 1962 culture document called for, in Galikowski's words,

the encouragement of artistic work which provided enjoyment and satisfied the people's needs, as well as educating them in socialist ideology. . . . [it] stated that themes should be rich and varied, that there should be a variety of styles and schools, and that individuality in creative work was to be supported. . . . the policy of sending those involved in cultural activities to the countryside should be drastically modified. (1998: 110–11)

In sharp contrast to the "strong political overtones" of the late 1950s, cartoons in the early 1960s played on the poetic, "the formal aspects of art which appealed to the artist's and viewer's aesthetic sensibilities," and form (Galikowski 1998: 116).

Cartoonists such as Mi Gu and Hua Junwu, who in the 1950s denounced non-political art, revised their opinions. Hua Junwu wrote that he always inserted poetic elements into his cartoons, contending, "there is much that it [the cartoon] can learn from poetry" (Hua Junwu 1963: 86). This deviated widely from his earlier articles that stridently pushed for art in the service of proletarianism. Another Yan'an veteran, Mi Gu, praised paintings that had been denigrated since the early 1950s and was now mute on art serving workers, peasants, soldiers, and social construction (Galikowski 1998: 117).

But the relaxation period was brief. In an effort to re-establish his political control, Mao, on two important official occasions in 1962, reaffirmed the importance of class struggle and helped foment movement away from the realistic approach. In 1963, another Mao-created campaign, Socialist Education ("Four Clean-ups"), was started, whereby, in culture, Mao, "sought to reverse the trend toward 'revisionism' or ideological erosion and the re-emergence of an intellectual elite that had resulted from the party's effort to win the cooperation of the intellectuals" (Goldman 1981: 88). Mao's attacks had a strong impact as ideological control was tightened again as a prelude to the Cultural Revolution.

Cultural Revolution, 1966–1976

The Cultural Revolution was officially set into motion with the "May 16th Circular" in 1966, in which Mao emphatically let it be known that the start of the Cultural Revolution, which was meant to shake up all aspects of Chinese society, had to be in the cultural arena. According to Mao's radical wing of the Party, the culture was dominated by bourgeois intellectuals whose reactionary thinking had to be "thoroughly" criticized, at the same time that the power of cultural leaders was to be seized (Wang Nianyi 1988: 13–14). Unofficially, the genesis for the Cultural Revolution was in Jiang Qing's (wife of Mao) reforms to purge Peking opera of bourgeois and feudalistic influences, an effort that began in 1961 and hit its stride in 1965.

In effect, the Cultural Revolution was a continuation of the radical line of Mao and his followers and the conflict between the radical and pragmatic elements in the Party. It was designed to shore up Mao's diminished power during the Great Leap Forward and to implement the ideas for a new society contained in his Yan'an Talks.

The movement unleashed monstrous forces that seriously altered Chinese society, as well as millions of people's personal lives. It is estimated that one million people died in the first three years; of these, 239,100 were executed on false charges, and the rest died by torture, beating, suicide, and mass killing (Lu Xing 2004: 16).

Implemented by the Red Guards, the Cultural Revolution aimed for mass persuasion and behavioral change through confession, self-criticism, and political study. In their propaganda, the Red Guards used the rhetorical themes of moral/ethical appeals, Mao cultism, and conspiracy theories. Slogans were their main strategy; these were broken down into the following categories: 1. never forget the class struggle; 2. to rebel is justified; 3. sweeping away all the monsters and demons; 4. destroy the four olds and establish the four news, 5. Eulogize Mao Zedong; and 6. frequent quoting of Mao. Simple, provocative, violent, and profane language was standard, as were metaphors of objectification and dehumanization ("cow ghosts and snake spirits") (Lu Xing 2004: 53–66 and 77–84 passim).

With culture as the springboard of the Cultural Revolution, the Red Guard propaganda targeted artists and intellectuals, the results of which were that traditional teachings were tossed out; all art education institutions stopped recruiting for four years; all art periodicals ceased publishing; much artistic and cultural production stopped; and artists and intellectuals were severely punished and stripped of their independence and creativity. Simultaneously, the main figures in the Propaganda Department, Ministry of Culture, and Beijing Party Committee were criticized, purged, and replaced by the Cultural Revolution Small Group, made up of radical followers of Mao.

In fact, the art, and by extension, cartooning worlds felt the impact of the Cultural Revolution before the

"May 16th Circular." Three prominent cartoonists—Ye Qianyu, Hua Junwu, and Cai Ruohong—were singled out for criticism in mid-1965 and January 1966. Hua and Cai, who had been with Mao in Yan'an, and Wang Chaowen were the most powerful leaders in the Artists' Association. In June 1965, Hua, Cai, and Wang were asked to "stop work and reflect on their mistakes," and large meetings were held to criticize Hua (Galikowski 1998: 141). Then, on January 11, 1966, Hua and Cai were attacked in *People's Daily*, *PLA Daily*, and *Guangming Daily* as counter-revolutionary revisionists. An illustrative news cartoon was carried in the *People's Daily* edition that day that depicted Hua and Cai being carried up by a "powerful revolutionary huge pen" (Liu Yiding 2004: 262–62). Among the various criticisms leveled against them, the major one concerned a 1962 exhibition they organized, which the accusers said did not have political content and was full of "feudal dregs or bourgeois junk which should have been consigned to the rubbish heap of history and which in no sense supported the Talks" (quoted in Galikowski 1998: 141). Hua and Cai, according to the Red Guards, toured China inviting "black artists to exhibit black works" and then allowed Ye Qianyu, the "cultural spy" known for his "reactionary and lewd cartoons," to have the most works exhibited (142).

Additionally, Cai was "vehemently condemned" for his role in drafting the "Ten Points on Literature and Art" in 1961, while Hua was labeled "an old hand at producing black, anti-Party cartoons," his "crimes" going as far back as the late 1930s and his time at Yan'an in the early 1940s. Also brought up was the dinner that Hua (and Cai and Zhang E) had with Mao in Yan'an (see Chapter 3), at which, according to the Red Guards, Mao severely chastised Hua for drawing negative aspects of life at Yan'an for an exhibition the three held. Hua remembered the meeting differently—as cordial, not hostile. The exhibition, which basically made fun of the local farmers' laid-back disposition, was very successful, according to Hua (interview, 2005), and Mao was told about it. The day Mao attended, Hua was taking his turn to oversee the event. Hua accompanied Mao to the door after his visit, and as was usual procedure in Yan'an

at the time, asked Mao for feedback. Hua (interview, 2005) said, "Chairman Mao only said cartoons should be developed. I wondered what that meant but I dared not ask him." In August 1942, Mao asked a *Liberation Daily News* writer to invite the three cartoonists to visit him. Hua (interview, 2005) said,

> We went to Mao's place, faraway; we walked half a day. We wondered what Mao would ask us. We were a bit nervous; Mao found we were nervous and joked with us. . . . Mao gave me advice: In the future, if you draw cartoons, the one on top should satirize, the one on bottom, praise. I did not listen. During the Cultural Revolution, Gu Yuan criticized me; he said I never listened to Mao. I said I listened but not always. Mao said cartoons should be popularized and I listened to that concept and followed it my whole life.

Hua (interview, 2005) added that some people were dissatisfied with the exhibitions he and his colleagues had organized and criticized them sharply, especially during the Cultural Revolution. To the charge that Mao personally berated them in 1942, Hua (interview, 2005) said,

> They [the accusers] never knew how happy we were that day. Mao was happy too; he invited us to lunch. I asked Mao if it was true he ate hot peppers with watermelons. He said it was true. During the Long March, he had gone to a small town and had lunch. There were hot peppers on the table. Someone brought in watermelons. With one hand, he said, he ate hot peppers, with the other, watermelon. If Mao had criticized us, how could I have asked him that question? I would have been too nervous.

Nevertheless, Hua continued to receive flak for what was claimed to be his anti-Party stance after 1949 in

cartoons such as *The Weathercock* (which portrayed a Party cadre as half man and half weathercock—the implication being that cadres having no firm principles of their own, simply follow whichever way the political wind blows), *Something Wrong* (which depicted a dragon dance with the leader leading the dragon by the tail instead of the head.

光明日報

凡是错误的思想，凡是毒草，凡是牛鬼蛇神，都应该进行批判，决不能让它们自由泛滥。

毛泽东

穆欣和华君武合谋在《光明日报》上抛出"内部讽刺画"是反党反社会主义反毛泽东思想的黑画

Fig. 4.5. The August 29, 1967, front page of *Guangming Daily* which mocked Hua Junwu by printing his cartoons upside down. Courtesy of Hua Junwu.

This supposedly "Criticizes our Party leadership as giving orders at random and losing sight of the general direction"), and a whole series of cartoons directed against the Great Leap Forward. All of these were taken as evidences of a "long, thick, malodorous black line" running "through all his [Hua's] so-called cartoons . . . from the thirties to the sixties." (Hung Yu 1967: 133, quoted in Galikowski 1998: 142–43)

Hua was criticized at other times; for example, on August 29, 1967, *Guangming Daily* carried an article that displayed three Hua cartoons upside down as an act of disrespect.

Other actions that occurred prior to the "May 16th Circular" did not bode well for artists. On January 3, 1966, a rebel group loyal to Mao took control of the Artists' Association, which left the group in shambles and probably set the stage for what was to follow: Red Guards breaking into artists' homes and galleries and burning art works and books, artists being physically attacked, and a new Cultural Revolution artistic style coming into play. One of the main purposes of that style was the deification of Mao; others were the alteration of history through art, the denigration of pre-1966 work as "products of feudalism, revisionism and bourgeois thinking" or as "poisonous weeds," (145) and, as in the Great Leap Forward, the elevation of the amateur worker and peasant art. Art played a key role during the

Cultural Revolution with the creation of propaganda paintings and the "many cartoons designed to ridicule and attack 'Black Factionalists' and other targets" (145).

In July 1969, all members of various cultural groups, including the Artists' Association, were sent to "May 7th" cadre schools (named for Mao's "May 7th Directive" of 1966, which set forth his vision for a new society) to be re-educated and to farms to labor. The rationale for the shake-up of the Artists' Association was that the group was made up of "bourgeois intellectuals, Rightists and feudal remnants" (143); in fact, only 3.2 percent of the 1,116 Artists' Association members were peasants, workers, or soldiers. Galikowski (1998: 144) described the Cultural Revolution as, "perhaps, the darkest days for artists since 1949. They were faced with a wave of cultural nihilism that denied the importance of China's traditional high culture, and denigrated many of the works of art produced since 1949."

Mistaken notions about the Cultural Revolution were that the country's culture was insular, totally cut off from the world, and that there were no Chinese cartoons published. Intellectuals who lived through the period told Barbara Mittler (2012: 18–21) that cultural life was varied, containing a mixture of Chinese and foreign components, leading her to form an alternative perspective to that of the "exclusively negative understanding of 'propaganda'" (27). Among Mittler's arguments were:

There was quite a lot out there, then, apart from the official propaganda art, and furthermore, official propaganda art served to introduce both popular and high art forms to those who had never been exposed to them before. . . . (21)

[A]lmost everyone was involved with creating and thus embodying this cultural experience (in reenacting the model operas, singing songs, painting portraits of Mao, or drawing comics, etc.), while not necessarily accepting the propaganda messages outright but reformulating them within his or her own context. (21) A large portion of this art and the cultural experience of the Cultural Revolution generally, I would argue, was in fact based on self-organized, self-initiated grassroots activity, not simply following top-down decrees. People and artists are and were on productive and receiving ends of cultural processes: Cultural Revolution Culture is popular culture. (22)

Mittler (2012: 30) also contended that Cultural Revolution Culture was not "exceptional," "particularly xenophobic nor iconoclassic, and, most importantly, that it was [not] without historical precedents." Although they talked about the deprivation and repression they endured during the Cultural Revolution, the cartoonists we interviewed also discussed creative projects they were involved in, sometimes with peasants (such as Liao Bingxiong's poster-making, Ding Cong's occasional "cartoons" for a provincial newspaper, Mi Gu's sculpting of ducks out of earth, or Zhu Genhua's carving figures on bamboo), and things they learned from rural folk later to be incorporated in their cartoons and animation (see "The Plight of the Cartoonists").

Contradictory and complicated, the Cultural Revolution, according to Mittler and some of our interviewees, was a time of "destruction and restriction" and of "continuous practice and development in the arts" (Mittler 2012: 385). However, the destruction exceeded the construction by a rather large margin.

As for the myth that there were no cartoons published during the Cultural Revolution, perhaps the confusion was related to what constitutes a cartoon. Of course, cartoons critical of officialdom, or those purely of a humorous nature, were virtually nonexistent. But cartoon-like drawings appeared, criticizing counter-revolutionaries and revisionists, mocking innocent people under attack, illustrating stories propagating Maoist doctrine, or praising workers, peasants, and soldiers as heroes (for an analysis of how Japanese cartoonists portrayed the early years of the Cultural Revolution, see Esselstrom 2015: 953–76).

Poster-like "rebel cartoons" appeared everywhere—e.g., in "rebel booklets" or on street walls—and served the functions of "uglifying" top officials out of favor with Mao and the Red Guards and attacking innocent people at every level. Distributed widely, these poster cartoons focused on both higher and lower level officials who were accused of "going on the capitalist road." Especially

targeted were Liu Shaoqi, Deng Xiaoping (1904–97), Peng Zhen, Luo Ruiqing, Lu Dingyi, and Yang Shangkun. The most powerful and influential of the "rebel posters" was "Qunchoutu" ("Parade of Clowns"), published February 22, 1967, in *Dongfanghong* (*The East Is Red*), an important newspaper sponsored by the Capital College's Red Guards Revolutionary Rebel Liaison Office. Signed as being "distributed by the Arranging Office Against Peng, Lu, Luo, and Yang Counter-Revolutionary Revisionist Group," the cartoon depicted in negative terms 100 leaders of the Party, state, art, and literature using the following slogans: "Always keep in mind the class struggle" and "Clear away all cow evils and snake spirits unrestrainedly." Apparently, Mao was angered by the cartoon, telling Beijing security commander Fu Chongbi that it was a "curse to us" and could not be allowed to circulate. Mao continued: "We just have 163 Chinese Communist Party committee members. On this were drawn more than 100. As the Chairman of the Central Committee, I should stand by most of them." Inquiring who authored the cartoon, Mao was told Kuai Dafu.[2] Angrily, Mao said,

> I heard of this person. He is a commander of students, very arrogant, and thinks he is number one in the world. You tell him, this is uglifying the Communist Party and is reactionary. He can send it to Jiang Jieshi (Chiang Kai-shek), send it to the American imperialists and Soviet revisionists to get an award. (quoted in Wu Jijin 2003: 57–61)

Cartoons were also published in *Little Red Guards News* (later called *Good Children* magazine), sanctioned by the authorities who thought there should be a publication for young people. Founded in 1969, and continuing as one of the few available periodicals, *Little Red Guards News* published the work of many important cartoonists. Du Jianguo (interview, 1993) said, "Many good cartoonists published here as there was nowhere else to do so. Almost every issue had top cartoonists. The contents usually related to children's lives, and contained some political items that satirized Soviet revisionism and some political bad guys. Jokes from other countries were

Fig. 4.6. "Qunchoutu" ("Group Ugliness Picture") of 1967, which reportedly upset Mao Zedong.

Fig. 4.7. *Liu Hu-lan*, a serialized lianhuanhua about a Chinese girl who became a martyr in her attempt to save villagers from the Guomindang military.

Liberation, Maoist Campaigns, and Cartoons, 1949–1976

also illustrated with cartoons." Renamed *Good Children*, the magazine attained a circulation of 300,000 by 1993, when it was made up primarily of cartoons aimed at early primary school children (Du, interview, 1993).

Lianhuanhua continued on and off during the Cultural Revolution, although they never achieved the popularity they had from 1949 to 1963, when 12,700 different titles with a combined circulation of 560 million appeared. The numbers had increased quickly during those years, from 670 titles and twenty-one million copies in 1952, to 2,300 titles and more than 100 million copies in 1957 (Chiang 1959). The themes of these books changed from those concerning gods, ghosts, kings, ministers, scholars, and beauties to those "praising the Party, Chairman Mao, socialism, heroes of the new era, workers, peasants, and soldiers" (Ma Ke 1963).

Yet, when the Cultural Revolution began, the lianhuanhua of the seventeen years since Liberation were criticized as being feudalist, capitalist, and revisionist, and many were burned as "poisoned weeds," their artists and editors criticized, censored, and sent to the countryside to be reformed. An article in *Shanghai Art World Criticized Material Collection No. 9* during the Cultural Revolution promoted lianhuanhua as important propaganda agents for Maoist thought, but lamented that for seventeen years, their artists neglected the class struggle, spread "poisoned" ideas, and pushed for the revival of capitalism in China. The article reported that in 1962, Minister of Culture Zhou Yang gave the Shanghai Peoples Art Press paper to print more than twenty-seven million copies of the lianhuanhua, *Sanguo Yanyi* (*Three Kingdoms Stories*), blamed for spreading feudalism in China, as well as in Hong Kong, India, Macao, and elsewhere through exportation. (Jie 2004: 37)

For five years (1966–71), seldom were any lianhuanhua published, but, then, on September 11, 1971, Zhou Enlai called leaders of publishing companies together and told them to revive lianhuanhua as soon as possible to solve the next generation's lack of spiritual nutrition. On April 12, he met some publishers again and re-emphasized the idea. Because art and literature policy was controlled by the "Gang of Four" (Jiang

Qing [1914–91], Zhang Chunqiao [1917–2005], Yao Wenyuan [1931–2005], and Wang Hongwen [1935–92][3]), lianhuanhua contents were what they ordered—*yangbanxi* or model operas (eight operas ordered by Jiang Qing),[4] heroes' stories, and criticisms of Lin Biao and Confucius.

The model operas were the standard for all creative work in China and were meant to emphasize four points: 1. each individual work can stand alone but is connected with other pieces to form a complete system; 2. the main figures are proletarian heroes and heroines; 3. technical innovations are introduced; and 4. simplicity and clarity are necessary. Ch'i Cheng (1974: 112), while analyzing a favored lianhuanhua story, showed how its artistic techniques came directly from revolutionary operas. He said, "Contrasts between light and shade, between solid objects and space, between different angles, characters and scenes are used to portray heroic characters." Farquhar (1999: 238) elaborated on the effects of the opera style on lianhuanhua:

> The medium lost its distinctive character. It was subsumed by revolutionary operas into pale sycophants of their dramatic action; the unabated emphasis on stereotyped proletarian heroes with prescribed rules for portrayal reduced the arts to a continued glorification of a disembodied triumphant Marxist "truth"; and the "three prominences" commonly led to a pedestal effect with heroes elevated like well-lit statues while reactionaries skulked in the shadows.

Jie Ziping (2004: 38) simply said these works had no artistic merit.

During the decade of the Cultural Revolution, 1,500 lianhuanhua titles, with more than 700 million copies, were printed all over China. They were most popular in Heilongjiang Province (354 titles) and Shanghai (200 titles). Moritz (1973: 9) reported that in the early 1970s, as many as seven million copies sold in Heilongjiang Province, and the Beijing and Shanghai art institutes were responsible for yearly outputs of thirty and sixteen million copies, respectively. Among the types were those based on real people's lives; although they were seldom

93

Fig. 4.8. *Baimaonü* (*White-Haired Girl*), revolutionary ballet lianhuanhua.

signed, they all came from the pens of famous artists. Some important representative titles were "Harbor Workers Create a Miracle," "Mao Zedong Thoughts Propaganda Maker Guan Guangfu," and "Chairman Mao's Red Guard Jin Xunhua's Story." Another genre made by mass groups was called "criticize movement lianhuanhua," reflecting the status of a place or company's movement. They used very serious words, mixing satire of contemporary situations with ancient stories. Their language consisted of slogans used as criticism; their images drawn in an orderly fashion but appearing as quickly-drawn cartoons. A total of ten sample opera lianhuanhua were published, the popular "Hongdengji" ("The Red Lantern") and "White-Haired Girl" among the initial six.

Cultural Revolution lianhuanhua, such as the model operas, both criticized Party and state enemies and lauded heroes of the Revolution to the extreme. They emphasized stories the Red Guards wanted praised. Of varying sizes, they came in two versions—one illustrative and "cartoonized," used to criticize their subjects;

the other photographic, meant to espouse the achievements of heroes (Jie 2004: 42).

All lianhuanhua started with a page of Mao's words; though not a rule, it became a customary, widely used practice. Additionally, some others published the words of Marx, Lenin, Engels, or Stalin; the content determined who was to be quoted. When, in October 1972, the Shanghai Peoples Press published a film-inspired lianhuanhua, *A Fu*, based on the Vietnamese movie of the same title, Ho Chi Minh's sayings appeared on the first page (Jie 2004: 42).

Series of lianhuanhua favored several themes, such as the two class/two roads struggle, Little Red Guards and Red Guards, criticism of the Lin Biao, Confucius struggle, intellectual youth going to the countryside, industrial learning from the Daqing oil wells, and farming learned from Dazhai (village) revolutionary struggle stories (Jie 2004: 43). If a study situation was depicted, many of Mao's books would be on bookshelves, and all those seen in the lianhuanhua would be holding Mao's books. If a farm harvest was shown, many bags and piles of grains and fertilizers were visible, as were farming machines, all of which were neatly lined up.

The popularity of lianhuanhua has been attributed to their readability (Nebiolo 1973) and contents. Concerning the latter, Moritz (1973: 9) wrote that the stories showed "the same fearless action, the same simple morality play—with the triumph of virtue over all odds and a near magical aura of invincibility in the virtuous hero—that seems always to have delighted and intrigued Chinese audiences."

Nebiolo (1973: n.p.), while traveling by train in China, observed Chinese adults engrossed in their lianhuanhua, which prompted him to write:

> All through the night we exchanged comic books, without even speaking. . . .
>
> I observed my companions—workers, petty officials, and peasants. Only two women and one old man laid aside their comic books and fell asleep. Among the others, no one paid attention to the cold or to the repeated stops; they were all completely absorbed in their reading. And if one of them finished his comic book before the others, he looked around him with restrained impatience, and then, when he got the next one, plunged into it without delay. Several times the stewardess came into the compartment with more hot water for the tea, but no one noticed, and the conductor had to knock his ticket puncher against the metal rim of the baggage rack, as if to arouse sleepers, in order to get any attention. At dawn, just a few minutes before arrival at the central station of Shanghai, one of the passengers collected the comics, smoothed frayed corners, and turned them over to the stewardess, who wrapped them in a plastic case.

Mittler (2012) tried to fathom why Cultural Revolution lianhuanhua, despite their "trite and predictable structure and content," engaged readers so intently and were successful enough to leave lifelong impressions on people. She concluded that this was the case because

> they could build on the "Socialist Internationale," which served as a powerful and systematic backdrop to the story;

they made use of a "popular entertainment rationale"; and . . . they took on the functions of popular religion. (263)

> The most talented artists [were] employed by the Chinese Communist Party to visualize the political trends of the day. Artists like [Ye Qianyu and Zhao Hongben[5] (1915–2000)] were quickly co-opted and incorporated in the various governmental and party organizations set up to produce propaganda images precisely because of their skills in the commercial arts. (265)

> [T]hey combine and repeat, as a composite, the most important and typical aspects of this culture. They present themselves as stories of the ordinary and the everyday for all to consume, and they draw on all the different elements important to Cultural Revolution Culture. . . . (331–32)

Exemplifying their emphasis on messages of loyalty, humble self-sacrifice, and attendance to duty, Moritz (1973: 9) cited *Twenty-Four Tales of Filial Piety*, a picture storybook about a young boy who lowers his body onto the ice to melt a hole so that his starving father can fish. Generally, according to Hwang (1978: 58–59), the subject matter of lianhuanhua were categorized as "serial pictures which mold the heroic image of the proletariat," "serial pictures dealing with Chinese Communist revolutionary history and contemporary reconstruction campaigns," those based on traditional folklore (not very popular during the Cultural Revolution), and those "dealing with the history of the international Communist movements and struggles." Writing during the Cultural Revolution, Nebiolo (1973: n.p.) gave an example of loyalty and the "heroic image of the proletariat" in a book entitled *A Pailful of Manure*:

> [The] peasant heroine, Qien [*sic*] Er-xiao, was, to be sure, a conscientious worker, but was corroded by the subtle poison of bourgeois selfishness. From her personal latrine she removed a pailful of potential manure for use in her own vegetable garden. Fortunately her husband was a good citizen, ready to give up the manure for the good of the community and, indeed, to scatter it over the collective field. . . . Around the smelly pail the entire village took part in a doctrinal dispute, and, social considerations, quite

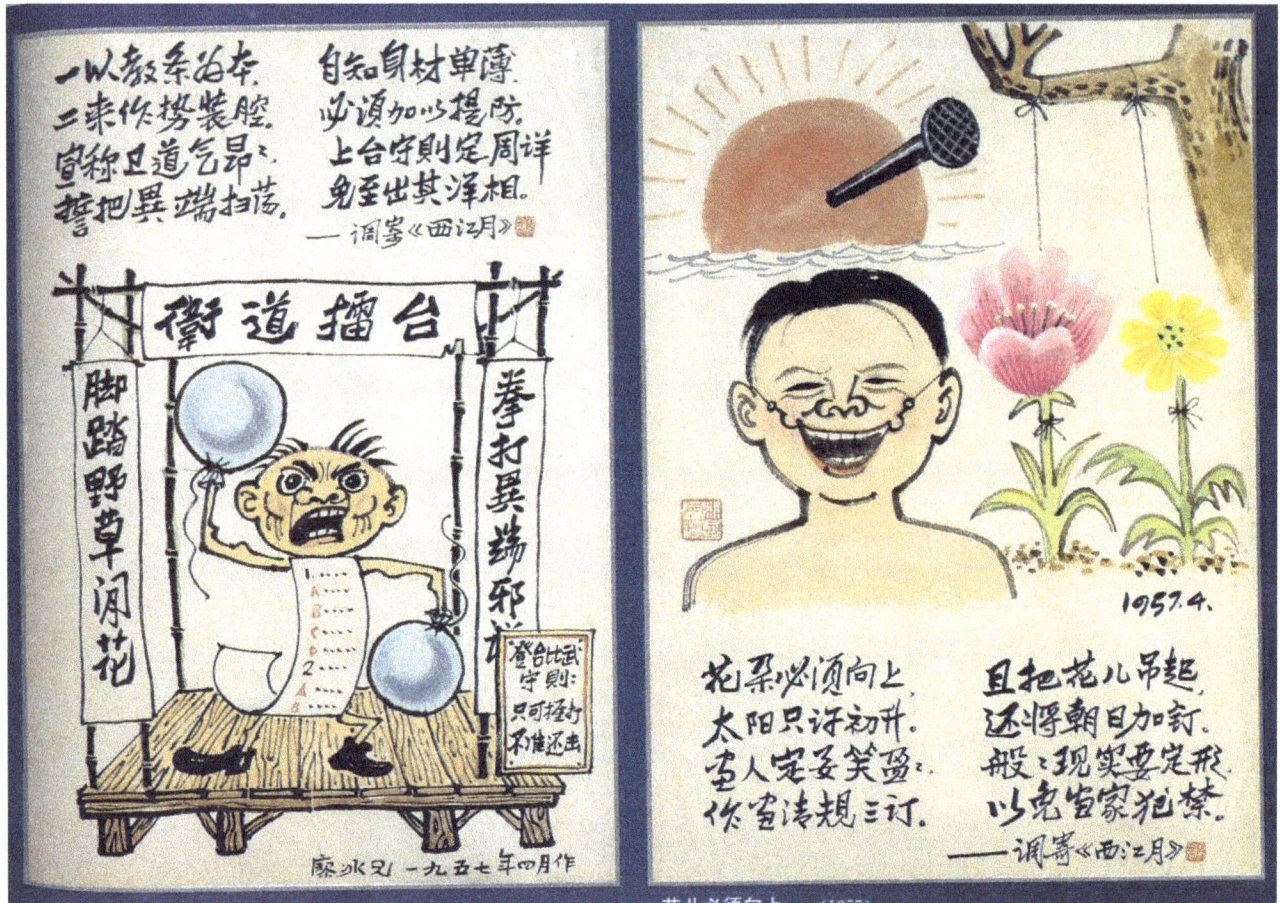

Fig. 4.9. "Huaduo bixu xiangshang" ("Flower Blossoms Must Face Upward") by Liao Bingxiong, 1957. Liao's criticism of dogmatism. Courtesy of Liao Bingxiong and Liao Ling-er.

rightly won. Qien [sic] Er-xiao understood what she was supposed to [do], happily gave in to her altruistic husband, and thanked the villagers for opening her eyes.

According to Hwang (1978: 66–67), lianhuanhua artists worked under strict guidelines that stipulated the use of captions rather than balloons (because captions allow for more narrative information, while balloons are less aesthetic), an emphasis on a multitude of close-ups of heroes/heroines, and the centering of the main character in the pictures. Making clear that the heroes/ heroines were paramount in lianhuanhua, Jie (2004: 44), describing the "three prominences" (santuchu) of lianhuanhua, said: all positive characters must look outstanding; among positive characters, heroes must look outstanding; among heroes, the major hero must look outstanding. Other rules required portraying enemies of the masses with sinister looks, drawing scenes and minor characters to serve the main proletarian hero/

heroine, and employing graphic devices of contrast to reflect the relationship between the hero/heroine and the enemy. Colors were effectively used: enemy and ugly characters were drawn in cold greys; heroes were rendered in bright colors (Jie 2004: 45).

The Plight of the Cartoonists

As alluded to above, many cartoonists' fates were already sealed with the Anti-Rightist campaign in the late 1950s; the Cultural Revolution severely exacerbated their situation. Cartoon historian Huang Yuanlin (interview, 2001) termed 1957 through 1966 as the most complex period in cartooning history. He and fellow cartoonists—including Wang Fuyang (1935–2008), Ding Cong, and Liao Bingxiong—felt the cartoon society was dealt a death blow during those years. Those artists catergorized as anti-socialist (usually for drawing cartoons on the bad behavior of government officials) sometimes lost their publishing outlets, were removed from their positions, and began long stays in prison and/or remote countryside locations. Wang Dazhuang (b. 1936) was cut off from his income source, with no newspaper daring to publish his cartoons after one of them was criticized as being "satirical of the socialist system" in 1957; Shen Tongheng was removed as editor of *People's Daily*, working as night-shift clerk at the archives from 1957 to 1966, before being deported to Xinjiang; Zhang Wenyuan was sent to the far northwest for more than twenty years, where, according to his account, he shared with other bachelors a broken table, broken chair, and broken bed (Liu-Lengyel 1993: 144).

Because of cartoons he drew for *Manhua* magazine in 1957 that mocked "dogmatism," Liao Bingxiong was regarded as being anti-Communist Party and anti-socialism and, the following year, was sent to Baiyunshan (White Cloud Mountain Farm) for labor. Liao (interview, 2002) said he did not have to do farm labor, because the local leader knew of his fame as a cartoonist and decided to assign him to make posters for the collective farm. In 1968, he was jailed as a reactionary; for more than twenty years, until 1979 when he was sixty-four, he said he was not permitted to draw cartoons (interview, 2002). Another cartoonist, Chen Huiling (interview, 2009), who was an art editor of a Nanjing youth newspaper in the 1950s and '60s, claimed he published a Liao cartoon at the time, saying, "When Liao was declared a rightist, he sent his work to me. Liao used Cao Zhongxian as his pen name. I recognized his style immediately and published his cartoon."

Both Wang Fuyang and Ding Cong had similarly harrowing experiences. Wang's "crime" was that he tried to protect one of the country's best cartoonists [Li Binsheng] who was wrongly labeled a rightist. Wang (interview, 2002) said,

I was not yet twenty-three when I was exiled to a deserted place in the West. I fed cattle, did hard work on farms. I hardly could draw cartoons. I was twenty-two years in the province. I did draw some cartoons for a paper, but because

there were no cartoons then, so hardly were they cartoons. I drew for my children. My whole family went to that province. Actually, one of my children stayed with my mother in Beijing; one came with us.

In a eulogy upon the death of Wang in 2008, fellow cartoonist and friend Zheng Huagai (2008: 550) wrote:

In 1966, the political storm of the "Cultural Revolution" made him have one disaster after another. The days were harder; he had duties such as clearing human excrement and working as a farmer. Recently, when we had a chat, he revealed that, "there were several times when I had almost death experiences."

In Wang's view, "Chinese cartoons were stopped during the Cultural Revolution, but decayed from 1957 onwards with the political movements" (Wang, interview, 2002).

Ding Cong, punished for what were called Anti-Rightist cartoons and also banished to the countryside for twenty-two years, agreed that the blight of the profession began with the political movements that came after 1957. He divided cartoons of the time into two types:

Political satire cartoons on the imperialism of the United States and China's enemies. These used a strict, direct way to depict characters and followed the Soviet way. The other kind was satire of the domestic situation. These you could not draw very sharp or directly. They were like a surgeon's knife, not meant to kill but to help one live. You could criticize, but you could not kill. Chairman Mao decided that with domestic problems, one could not use sharp weapons. (Ding Cong, interview, 2002)

Uncertainty leading to extreme caution marked cartooning, Ding said:

After movements one after another, you could not control which line was correct for such domestic cartoons. If you satirized the Party, it was interpreted as you were against

Fig. 4.10. "Jiandongqing lianxiang." Feng Zikai's 1949 cartoon associating cutting hedges with trimming people to one size was criticized during the Cultural Revolution for meaning that Communist Party art policies resemble scissors. Courtesy of Feng Yiyin.

the Party. After Liberation, only the Communist Party was recognized as the leader of the country; so, if you criticized the Communist Party, you were against it and that brought you problems. So, only one type of cartoon existed—those against the US. At the beginning of the 1960s, these cartoons too could not exist as the government wanted to establish foreign relationships. Cartoonists did not know what to draw. So, they seldom drew cartoons any more. In newspapers, there was no international, no domestic satire. The leaders never said you could not draw cartoons, but where could you publish them? (interview, 2002)

Because of China's close ties with the Soviet Union, Chinese cartoons of the 1950s often followed ideas found in Soviet publications (Lin Qin, interview, 1993; Hong Huang, interview, 1993; Zhan Tong, interview, 1993), usually those with an anti-American bent. Few dared to draw cartoons on domestic issues, and those who did, opted to praise the Party and state.

Cartoon master Feng Zikai stopped drawing and penning his literary works even before the Anti-Rightist campaigns. His daughter, Feng Yiyin, said that prior to Liberation, Feng Zikai thrived on doing satire. But, after he was criticized in post-1949 China, he moved into safer areas, translating Japanese and Russian works. "If he translated, then it was not his work," Feng Yiyin

(interview, 2002) said. She said critics used any pretense to chastise him:

If he did a work showing only the dark side of socialism, he would be criticized. If Father saw a ladder locked against a wall and drew it, he'd be criticized. They would say he was saying China has many thieves. Thus, he translated most of the time. He seldom did any cartoons or drawings even privately after 1949. He traveled a lot, liked to read Japanese literature very much.

Also, Father seldom talked publicly after 1950. At one conference, someone criticized him, and he never said anything publicly after that. After Liberation, he seldom wrote. He did some articles—one on a lovely cat, for which he was criticized and told to write about soldiers and workers. During the Cultural Revolution, Red Guards said the cat referred to Chairman Mao as the Chinese call a cat, "mao." About three-fourths of his articles are before 1949, a tiny portion during the Cultural Revolution, when he would get up at 4 a.m. so no one knew he was writing. Most of these were about traveling; he did not dare to write other articles. (Feng Yiyin, interview, 2002)

Te Wei, cartoonist-turned-animator, whose leadership of the Shanghai Animation Film Studio between 1949 and 1984, fostered China's two golden ages of animation, told of his plight during the Anti-Rightist movements. He said his second ink-washed animated film, *The Cowherd's Flute*, completed in 1963, was criticized as not reflecting the class struggle and was banned in China. After that, he said,

They demanded that I write self-criticism, not only pertaining to my own film, but all the films they thought were not right, because I was, after all, the director of the Studio at that time. I really did not understand what they were after and why. I wrote the self-criticism I felt I could justifiably write, but they were not satisfied. They asked me to write it again and again, and I grew sick, with a stomach disease. In the end they wrote it instead of me. All this happened even before the Cultural Revolution. When they were finished with their criticism of me, they sent me to work

Fig. 4.11. Li Binsheng's "Meizui de ren" ("The Man without a Mouth") in *Beijing Daily* played a role in his being labeled a rightist, 1957. Courtesy of Li Binsheng.

Fig. 4.12. Li Binsheng displaying a Peking opera move (Li considers himself a better actor than cartoonist), Beijing, June 16, 2016. Photo by Xu Ying. Courtesy of Li Binsheng.

in a factory. I was out of the Studio until 1966, when I was called back due to the Cultural Revolution. When I came back, I was "welcomed" by a multitude of banners spread over the walls of the Studio, all of which were criticizing me. My crimes were named, "The person who walked on the Capitalist Road" and "Reactionary intellectual." (quoted in Ehrlich 2001: 14–15)

Like fellow cartoonists, Li Binsheng took Mao at his word and drew critical cartoons during the Hundred Flowers campaign. As a result, he was called a rightist, lost his people's delegate post, and in 1957, was labeled one of the top three rightists in art, along with Jiang Feng and Liao Bingxiong (Li Binsheng, interview, 2013).

The main cartoon that made trouble for Li Binsheng showed a man without a mouth, meant to reflect that freedom of expression did not exist in China. Li Binsheng (interview, 2016) described the genesis of this cartoon:

The newspaper *Red Flag* asked me to draw a cartoon. The newspaper's officials took me to dinner, at which they showed me clippings of democratic people who did not have freedom of the press. They asked me to do a drawing on this topic. It was at a time when the Communist Party called for criticism.

Though not as severely, he was also criticized for a cartoon depicting a Chinese family crammed into a room, each person stacked in beds, one on top of another, with a baby sleeping in a basket suspended from the ceiling. *The Times of London* picked up the cartoon and

reprinted it, bringing Li Binsheng much criticism in 1957; he was labeled a British spy trying to make China look bad, shooting a "cannon bullet against China" (Li Binsheng, interview, 2016).

In a conversation with Xu Ying in 2015, Li Binsheng, then ninety years old, said he was still strong, because he worked strenuously over long periods of the 1940s through mid-'70s. His first forced labor experience was when, at age nineteen, he avoided compulsory military service by bribing a recruiting officer with 100 yuan. Instead, he was sent to a Japanese labor camp in Manchukuo to work alongside "disabled or retarded" people who also were deferred from serving as soldiers. Li said he and other deferees were beaten regularly by the Japanese while they worked. After he was labeled a top rightist in 1957, he was sent to West Mountain, where he planted trees and quarried stones, and subsequently to a Beijing suburb to help build houses and scaffolds. He was "pardoned" in 1979 (Li Binsheng, interview, 2015).

The one cartoonist who continued to draw domestic satirical cartoons in the late 1950s and early '60s was Hua Junwu, although much of that work returned to haunt him during the Cultural Revolution. As cartoon historian Huang Yuanlin (interview, 2001) said, "Hua was the only one so brave; did not get into trouble. In the Cultural Revolution, however, his cartoons were used as proof he was anti-socialist. Hua became the biggest anti-socialist as a result." Hua did hundreds of internal satirical cartoons—against the government's bureaucratic red tape, long and meaningless political meetings, those who pretended to work hard while doing little, cadres occupying key positions while possessing limited brain power, etc. Liu-Lengyel (1993: 154) attributed Hua's ability to avoid Party/state interference in the pre-Cultural Revolution era to these factors: 1. Hua was established since the 1940s and was well-known; 2. editors supported him because they were close friends; 3. Hua had been president since 1953 of the Chinese Artists' Association, a position officially accepted by the Communist Party and state; 4. he had been instructed about satirical cartoons by Mao in a February 1942 meeting; and 5. Hua's targets were low-ranking officials, not the Communist Party or socialism itself.

Hua's own interpretation implied that he sensed the mood of the period to his advantage. He (interview, 2005) said:

> From 1959 to 1964, I drew a lot of domestic satire cartoons that brought me problems in the Cultural Revolution. But I believe many others who were not cartoonists also suffered a lot. . . . In 1957, some cartoonists were criticized as right wing. Why could I continue? I have my opinions on why they were criticized. After the establishment of the new government, not all of the old society disappeared. Feudalism, superstitions still exist till today. The old ideas could not disappear immediately. New and old struggles continued and still exist. The new advanced knowledge against old knowledge struggled for a long time. Contradictions existed for a long time. I drew much domestic satire on people's contradictions. Even Mao admitted these contradictions were present. That's why I continued to do my cartoons on these.

The stories of Chinese cartoonists during the Cultural Revolution decade have common characteristics; they are tales of cruelty and illogical and irrational treatment by the Red Guards, and they are often told with a touch of humor to show the ridiculousness of the times and perhaps ease the pain of remembrance. What differs in

Fig. 4.13. Cartoonists and other artists publicly humiliated and criticized in 1966, their names X-ed out as they are made to stand in the airplane position. Among the art critics and cartoonists are Wang Chaowen, Hua Junwu, Cai Ruohong, Mi Gu, Zhang Ding, and Jiang Yousheng.

these stories are the severity of the punishments and the degree of cleverness the artists used in coping with them.

Besides suffering humiliation and vilification (e.g., labeled "stinking number nine,"[6] "black cartoonists," or worse) and being deprived of opportunities to remain creative, many cartoonists had irreparable damage done to their health and spirit. The person mainly responsible for advancing cartooning in China, Feng Zikai, died of lung cancer in 1975, an unhappy man. His daughter Feng Yiyin (interview, 2002) said,

> What hurt most was the Cultural Revolution. Father liked to drink yellow wine, but during the Cultural Revolution, he drank from early morning as he felt confused. He was sent to the countryside south of Shanghai. In winter, he slept on rice straw. I visited him and there was snow around his pillow as there was a leak in the roof. He was sent to the fields to pick cotton; that was considered light work.

Chen Jinyan (1925–77), a multitalented artist who was probably China's third female cartoonist, died prematurely at the age of fifty-three after suffering a heart attack, "possibly caused by the years of mental depression and suffering during the Cultural Revolution" (Liu-Lengyel 1999: 266). Her famous cartoonist husband, Fang Cheng, believed this, saying,

> My wife died in the Cultural Revolution, because of it. She used to be an active athlete in basketball, volleyball, and table tennis; she used to come home singing opera. After the Cultural Revolution, she had no words. She had been a strong personality; number one in the university. She had been with the underground Communist movement before Liberation. During the Cultural Revolution, she was sent to a cow farm [as Fang was]. She was hit, cursed at; our house

Fig. 4.14. Chen Jinyan, the first woman cartoonist of the New China, a victim of the Cultural Revolution. Courtesy of Fang Cheng.

was ransacked; she was exiled from the Party. She could not endure this. She had no disease but, after so many things happened to her, she died of a heart attack. In twenty-five years of marriage, she was never hospitalized. (Fang Cheng, interview, 2001)

From the founding of the PRC, Chen Jinyan worked on newspapers, where she found time to draw strips, cartoons, and woodcuts (Fang Cheng 1980: preface). Most of her cartoons appeared in *Beijing ribao* (*Beijing Daily*), where she was vice chief of the art department (see Chinese Modern Arts Volumes Committee 1988: 10–11, 44, 61).

Wang Dazhuang, Mi Gu, and others were detained under "mass dictatorship," meaning they were put in prison camps guarded by the organized masses, not the official police. Wang, whose cartoons were called "reactionary," and he, "a Rightist who slipped through the net (in 1957)" and "an active counter-revolutionary," was under "mass dictatorship" for nine months in 1969, during which time he was physically beaten and tortured on twenty-eight occasions. His head was so swollen by the beatings that he could not lie on his back (personal communication to HongYing Liu-Lengyel, 1991). Mi Gu was forced to engage in labor ten hours daily while under "mass dictatorship." At the age of sixty, he lost his speech, and for eight years, he was bedridden, unable to move (personal communication, Shen Tongheng to HongYing Liu-Lengyel 1991).

The husband-wife founders of the Frog Cartoonists Group (to be discussed later) of Hebei province, Chen Yuli (b. 1934) and Li Qingai (b. 1938), suffered immeasurable pain during the Cultural Revolution, as they were labeled Guomindang members or "spies." Li (interview, 2009) said she was tortured with forty kinds

of punishment, including with sticks, fire, water, and bricks, and on three occasions, she lost consciousness. She said: "They knew I loved my baby, so they burned my nipples. Also my buttocks, breasts, and back. The rebels would make my baby cry and make me listen." Chen (interview, 2009) said the rebels told him to make bricks into sharp-edged triangles and then forced him to watch his wife kneeling on them in the hot sun.

Others had horrific stories. Animator Te Wei told of being confined to a small room, where he said he actually felt peaceful:

I practiced Tai-Chi, but when they saw that, they wouldn't allow even that because they said I was not permitted to speak and act freely. I sang, but was not allowed to sing loudly. I just tried to recall the old songs and sang them softly. Once they made me stay awake for three days with no sleep, and they kept forcing me to "tell the truth." I could not tell them nothing different from what I had already told them, so they demanded I kneel down. When I refused to do so, they hit me in the knees. I fell down, my teeth struck the ground and fell out and my mouth bled. Another time, they put a chair on my neck and head and leaned on it until I lost my breath. One person laughed and sat on the chair. I fought to stand up. More people came in to watch and they said this old man was fierce. Then they left, laughing among themselves. I could not even think of ever drawing a film. I only wished I could become a bird to be able to fly freely out.

I was confined to the room for a year. Then they sent me to the 7 May "School" in the countryside to learn from the peasants. I carried garbage and manure and dug a river. At first, I could carry only 15 kilos, but later I could carry 70. Then I raised pigs with A Da. I worked and sang with him, and we caught some cats to cook and eat. (Ehrlich 2001: 15)

The usual procedure was to be sent to May 7 cadre schools, followed by hard labor among the farmers. Individuals were assigned to groups (cows, pigs, sheep, etc.) which specified their duties (feed the pigs, tend to sheep, etc.); the higher they were in their professions prior to the Cultural Revolution, the worse their assigned jobs on the farms. Some of the cartoonists have since joked

101

about their places in the hierarchy. Jiang Yousheng (interview, 2002) said Hua Junwu "was a big name so he got to feed the pigs two extra more years than me"; Miao Yintang (b. 1935) (interview, 2002) explained that, because he was young, he was considered "small grass" and did not suffer as much as Hua, Ding Cong, or Wang Fuyang. Hua (interview, 2005), looking at his total seventy years of cartooning, said he did not suffer as much as people have claimed he did—"just during the Cultural Revolution but not because I was a cartoonist." His duties during the Cultural Revolution were as follows: "I carried shit to the fields, ten thousand kilograms, for a year; planted cabbages two years, and fed pigs four years." Ye Qianyu was considered at a level that did not even allow him to work; he was imprisoned for seven years (Hong Huang, interview, 1993). Ironically, Zhang Leping, elderly and in frail health, was assigned the same job (picking up waste paper) that his famous character "Sanmao" had in his own comic strip.

Discussing the Cultural Revolution in the presence of fellow cartoonist detainees Zhan Tong, Hong Huang, and Lin Qin, Han Shangyi (interview, 1993) explained how they ranked in the groups:

> The big shots were considered more criminal; they were under the bull division. Zhan and I were in bull; Lin and Hong were not so high; they were in the goat division. Lin and Hong could wear Mao pins; Zhan and I could not. But those who carried Mao's pins were angry because they would rather not wear them.

Other policies and instructions meted out by the cadres were both ridiculous and a waste of time. For example, the one cartoon Hong Huang drew during the Cultural Revolution, criticizing young people for sleeping on the job, resulted in a thorough investigation of him. He said, "Because of this cartoon, one of the 'Gang of Four,' Zhang Chunqiao, ordered a check of my family background, back to my great-grandparents. Wanted to know why I'd criticize the working class. Maybe one of my grandparents was from a family of non-working class" (Hong Huang, interview, 1993). Zhan Tong

(interview, 1993) gave an example where the leaders encouraged dishonesty; he said, "We bulls were told to steal grass for the pigs from the goat group, and if we did, then our task would be fulfilled."

It did not take much to incur the hatred of the Cultural Revolution leaders. In the case of Wang Dazhuang, even the cartoons he drew praising the Revolution were suspected and labeled: "While holding the 'red flag' in his hands, he was attacking the 'red flag.'" The Red Guards scrutinized cartoons with great suspicion and a sense of paranoia, reading meanings into them that were far removed from the creators' intentions.

Ye Qianyu, charged with seven "crimes" and imprisoned for the same number of years, discussed the deliberate misinterpretation of some of his drawings over a sustained period of time:

> Most ridiculous thing was they regarded my painting "Chinese Nationalities United Greatly" in 1953 as bull ghosts and snake spirits surrounding Chairman Mao; the female farmer in "Qin Chuan Wheat Harvest" in 1962 was regarded as some "sanxiangu" (witch); the fisherman in "Sketching Scenery of Shenjiamen" was regarded as an "airborne spy" from Taiwan. In 1962, Chinese and Indians fought a border war. My painting "Illustration of Indians Presenting Flowers" was regarded as full of the enemies' emotions because I printed a jiqing (placing one's emotions) stamp on it. Thus, the rebels made a far-fetched interpretation; no wonder the "Gang of Four" slandered a number of beautiful Chinese paintings as politically-implied "black paintings" and put Chinese artists into the 18th layer (deepest) of hell in 1975. (Wu Jijin 2003)

Feng Zikai's cartoons and articles were similarly misunderstood as "ducao" ("poisonous weeds"), as were those of other artists. Zhang Ding was made to suffer during the Cultural Revolution for a 1958 exhibition he and his graduate students held. A number of fabricated crimes were attributed to him after the Red Guards posed a series of questions about individual works exhibited and then gave their wrong interpretations: Why did you draw the Dai girl's feet so fat? No, they are swollen with water.

That implies Dai people's lives are very difficult. Why is the oil lamp without oil? That means socialism is almost finished. Why did you draw the cock as so saber rattling? Is that an echo of Khrushchev? Because Khrushchev used to call Mao Zedong a "fight-like cock" (Wu Jijin 2003).

In other cases, cartoonists were punished for actions or associations not related to their artwork. Han Shangyi (interview, 1993), who said he was treated as a "political criminal, the scum of the Earth, anything but a human being," remembered how, during the Cultural Revolution, "you could be criticized for drinking a little wine or eating pork. You could not enjoy yourself." Trying to understand why her husband was criticized as a rightist, Ding Cong's wife (Shen Jun [1927–2014]) surmised, "if you looked like a rightist, you were a rightist." She continued:

Ding used several scenery pictures in *Pictorial*; some thought he was doing things like an imperialist, not like a proletariat. Another example—some of his friends had a drinking party. Someone said they were conspiring to form a group against the Communist Party. The front page of *People's Daily* criticized them for having a drinking party.

At the same time, some Soviet experts worked at *Pictorial*; their views were not Chinese and Ding criticized them. He was accused of not being a friend of the Soviets.

Also, Ding had served in the United States OSS. in World War II; he drew some cartoons for OSS. So, he was accused of being a US spy. (interview, 2002)

Ding (interview, 2002) added that the Party found a picture of him with Edgar Snow[7] and based on that, accused him of being a US spy. "They did not know who Snow was. They just came to the house, took my books, papers, etc.; took everything away."

Ding and other cartoonists found ways to keep their creative spirits alive, imagining drawings in their heads or secretly sketching at great risk. In Ding's case, he did drawings and then hid them under the bed covers. He said he even helped a local leader publish a small periodical, *Beidahuang* (*Great Northern Wilderness*) (Ding, interview, 2002). Mi Gu, to give himself some comfort,

sculpted ducks out of earth and humorously referred to his small room as "Thousand Ducks Hall." Animator A Da (Xu Jingda, [1934–87]) hid under his mosquito net at night, drawing from memory and imagination the unflattering caricatures of the "Gang of Four" which he later used in print and animated cartoons, and Te Wei (interview, 2001) used the pen the guards gave him to write self-criticism to sketch on a pane of glass that was on his table. When he would hear the guard approaching, he would erase the glass with a cloth and proceed to read Mao's thoughts. Zhu Genhua (b. 1932), who later drew cartoons for *People's Daily*, spent part of his ten years in the countryside, doing carvings on bamboo and cartoon characters on cups. He said:

That was the way I survived. I would find interesting bamboo when I gathered wood to cook food for the pigs. If you love art, it is hard for that to die. The authorities did not allow cartoons, so I changed to other art. Sometimes I felt happy inside when the rebels criticized me as I would think of a cartoon I could draw of the situation. When slogans were shouted, I smiled as I thought about a possible cartoon. They thought I was crazy. (Zhu, interview, 2009)

Zhu was quick to admit he was frustrated and frightened while detained, and angry that he had been forced to forfeit the "best creative period" of his life to feeding pigs. He said:

Everyone censored me. I often looked at the sky and cried and cried. I suffered a lot, more than others. The rebels scared me. When they killed criminals, they made me kneel down next to these dead people. One time, I picked up a watch and turned it in to the rebels who criticized me as a watch thief. I'd have to get water at the well. Rebels would kick my barrels into the well and then shout at me for damaging property. (Zhu, interview, 2009)

Despite having experienced these cruelties, some cartoonists saw benefits deriving from their countryside stays. Wang Fuyang (interview, 2002) felt that he learned much about rural people, stating, "Before, I could not

103

draw farmer cartoons; I would not have been able to do it without contact with them." Miao Yintang (interview, 2002), who lived in the countryside for ten years, watched his relationships with farmers metamorphosize from a good to a bad situation. He said:

> I know farmers very well. I ate with them, slept with them, and had fleas on my body like they did. . . . At the beginning, when I went in 1959, I felt very good as I could eat and work with the farmers. We respected the farmers and they respected us. After the Cultural Revolution, it changed from a studying to a punishing situation as we were lower than the farmers. My first year in the countryside, I felt very good; I was enriched by the farmers; I experienced a different life that was good for my creating. That suffering was a treasure for us in some ways.

At the same time, Jiang Yousheng (interview, 2002) disagreed, saying the Cultural Revolution wasted the productive years of most famous cartoonists' lives. "Some cartoonists may feel the experience helped them, gave them a chance to be with the farmers, but, even without the Cultural Revolution, artists can learn about the rural areas," Jiang said.

Remarkable is the spirit in which many of the cartoonists and animators coped with being robbed of years of creativity, not to mention family life and decent living conditions. The general feeling was that their lives must go on and, in order to compensate for the lost time, they had to work even harder and longer. Fang Cheng, for example, into his nineties, had a work schedule that would exhaust most people half his age. He has his work planned out until he reaches the age of 100 (interview, 2001). According to Wang Fuyang (interview, 2002), when he was freed, he thought he had to make up some of the lost twenty-two years, helping Chinese cartoonists revive the profession and encouraging young people to publish their works. He added:

> I remembered a French writer who said of life's suffering, that if you view it from a distance, you can find some elements of

humor and drama. Can you find something useful for the rest of your life? The arduous work made us experience different things, a smoother life with the people. Not only were we doing hard work, but our spirit suffered a lot. This made us mature and affected our lives afterwards. We tried to think of things in different ways. But the hard work destroyed our health, did harm to the physical, to the spirit. These losses cannot be compensated for. Another good result, however, is that because we suffered a lot, we don't want to have it done to others in the future. We will fight against that. For so long, we could not draw art and cartoons and, when we could do this again, we have been very diligent and do our best.

Ding Cong (interview, 2002) expressed similar sentiments, saying,

> You must live on. How can you have anger for twenty-two years? You just work on; there is no other choice. Most of my friends were put in prison; compared to them, I was lucky. After 1980, I was free so I kept all my energy. I wanted to make up for lost time. Not many cartoons were published after 1980, so I drew illustrations for books and did costume and stage design.

He said that after 1980, he drew more cartoons and illustrations than in the previous sixty-three years of his life.

Others, such as He Wei (1934–2012) (interview, 2002) and Miao Yintang (interview, 2002), said they too believed overcompensation was part of the solution. Miao Yintang said, "I came back to work and wanted to account for the lost time. I was thirty-forty years old at the time of the Cultural Revolution; the best years to be a cartoonist, and I was in the countryside."

Husband-wife animators Yan Dingxian (b. 1936) and Lin Wenxiao (b. 1935) experienced contrasting emotions at the end of the Cultural Revolution. Yan said he just wanted to work again; "[W]e were angry but we couldn't talk about it. It was normal for everyone at that time. We were always afraid when we returned to the studio in the early 1970s, and were very careful" (Ehrlich 2001: 14). His wife said:

104

We could even begin to dance again at that time. In our studio! . . . When we began [*One Night in an Art Gallery*], we were not afraid. We thought the Gang of Four were in prison and we didn't believe they could rise again. After all that happened to us in the Cultural Revolution, we were not afraid. Nothing could have been worse than that. (Ehrlich 2001: 14)

Te Wei, in trying to understand those who perpetuated the cruel circumstances under which he survived, said:

The Cultural Revolution made me see clearly what kinds of people there really were. They were simply actors on the stage of history. I didn't hate them afterwards and do not bear them ill will now. They were ignorant, cheated, merely used by others. I think it's better to look forward instead. The most important thing is to make better and better films and to make my artistic life persist. (Ehrlich 2001: 16)

Summary

As in other periods of modern Chinese history—but not to the same extreme and for such an extended length of time—the era from Liberation through Mao Zedong's death in 1976 was marked by major adjustments in how culture (and art, including cartoons, more specifically) was to be defined, organized, and controlled, and the policies it needed to promote in the building of a new nation.

Maoist thought on art, some of it going back to Yan'an in 1942, was key to this transformation, as was, in the beginning, but to a lesser degree, Soviet art influences. Cartoonists played major roles in the ensuing reorganization, collectivization, and specialization of the art and press communities; two of them, Ye Qianyu and Cai Ruohong, assumed top leadership roles in the newly formed Artists' Association, and Zhang Ding became one of the five heads of the Central Academy of Fine Art. A main task of cartoonists was to portray and demonize state and Party enemies, chief of which was the United States, especially during the Korean War.

Fig. 4.15. Red Guards drawing cartoons critical of anti-revolutionaries, 1966.

105

During much of the Seventeen-Year Period (1949–66), a series of Maoist campaigns (the Hundred Flowers, Anti-Rightists, and Great Leap Forward) were orchestrated successively to allow for the expression of many different ideas and criticisms, to weed out domestic intellectuals and artists thought (often wrongly) to be strong critics of Mao and his doctrines, and to rapidly build up China's agricultural and industrial collectivization. These campaigns were strongly promoted by both lianhuanhua and newspaper cartoonists.

The shifting relationship between art and politics led to much confusion, ambiguity, and apprehension among cartoonists, a number of whom were labeled as rightists, arrested, imprisoned, and sent to the countryside. After a brief relaxation time in the early 1960s, traditional Chinese culture was harshly dealt with during the Cultural Revolution (1966–76), as the old institutions and periodicals were halted, and artists (including many cartoonists) were arrested and sent to the countryside to work with the peasants. The new policy was based on principles of deification of Mao, alteration of history through art, denigration of pre-Cultural Revolution art, and elevation of the amateur worker and peasant art. Despite the upheaval of culture, cartoons, lianhuanhua, and other creative endeavors managed to appear, though not as profusely as before.

When the "Gang of Four," who were blamed for the Cultural Revolution, were toppled in 1976, cartoonists obviously were joyful, but still cautious. Their exhilaration was dampened by feelings of fear and suspicion that, as at other times in the 1950s and '60s, their worst nightmares would return.

翁晨 ○

（日童话）

（□童话）

□童话

们迎来了新伙伴……

TOY B

刘军 ○

Background

The deaths of Mao Zedong and Zhou Enlai in 1976 and the subsequent arrests of the "Gang of Four" made for much uncertainty. At the same time, these events ushered in a reform era that was initially regarded with deep suspicion by intellectuals and artists, despite the Party's assurance of what was to become the highest level of freedom since 1949. A cartoon by Liao Bingxiong, "Zichao" ("Self Mockery," 1979), his first work in twenty years, best represented the hesitancy of the Chinese to take the authorities at their word; Liao drew himself outside a cracked jar, arms folded, afraid to move although he was free. Liao (interview, 2002) said that drawing represented a whole generation of Chinese people.[1] In line with Liao's statement, cartoonist Jiang Yousheng (interview, 2002) said that he also did not draw in the immediate aftermath of the Cultural Revolution. "I was fearful; I waited a year, observed if it was safe, and then I drew."

The art community, generally, came out of its shell rather quickly, recovering (actually, progressing) in the first half dozen post-Cultural Revolution years, as it rallied against political interference, organized into new art groups independent of the Artists' Association, mounted exhibitions featuring art from the US, Japan, and Western Europe and by unofficial Chinese art groups, resumed *Fine Art* in March 1976 and launched other periodicals, including *Satire and Humor* in 1979, and produced Samizdat publications for a short period in the late 1970s.

With the new art groups, including one for lianhuanhua, artists could exercise greater freedom and develop their own styles. As for the official Artists' Association, it was restructured during the Fourth National Congress of Literary and Art Workers in October 1979, at which its pre-Cultural Revolution leaders were reinstated, including cartoonists Hua Junwu, Ye Qianyu, and Cai Ruohong, who were among its ten vice chairmen.

Fine Art remained the major vehicle for artists, though, for a period after it was revived in 1976, the contents of the magazine were "barely distinguishable from

Chapter 5

Reform, Modernization, Market Economy, and Cartooning

Fig. 5.1. "Zichao" ("Self Mockery") by Liao Bingxiong. Courtesy of Liao Bingxiong and Liao Ling-er.

communication to HongYing Liu-Lengyel, 1991), the show drew an average of 6,700 visitors daily for 100 days. Fellow cartoonist Hong Huang (interview, 1993), who edited two cartoon collections from the exhibition, added, "The exhibition was held in cold weather, yet so many people jammed in, they had to use fans to cool off the Shanghai hall."

What cartoonists endured during the Cultural Revolution defined some of their works in the late 1970s. Hua Junwu's penchant for drawing pigs was inspired by his having to feed pigs as punishment for four years (interview, Hua, 2005; interview, Zheng, 2002; interview, Wang Fuyang, 2002). Caricatures that A Da had secretly sketched of the "Gang of Four" while he was in the labor camp were featured in a 1979 cartoon exhibition and many newspapers; they were also the basis of the animated *One Night in an Art Gallery*, co-directed in 1978 with Lin Wenxiao. Ehrlich (2001: 17) said that this film "reduced the four ["Gang of Four"] to ridiculous figures who censored and turned upside down the most innocent of paintings, only to be driven off by children in the end. It signaled to the Chinese audience that the bad times were over." A Da used what he observed in the countryside in other animation masterpieces he directed. For *Monkeys Fish for the Moon* (1980), he adapted a peasant harvest dance he had watched, having the monkeys dance with a sense of "spontaneous freedom" after "harvesting" the moon (Ehrlich 2001: 19). A Da's *Three Monks* (1980), and the division among them, was, in the words of Ehrlich (2001: 19), his "special cry that the split in China caused by the Cultural Revolution, the split that turned one family member against another, would result only in destruction and should never be repeated."

[those] during the most radical period of the Cultural Revolution" (Galikowski 1998: 187). Soon after, *Fine Art*, as well as other art periodicals, "regularly featured picture stories, woodblock prints and especially cartoons (the favorite medium for attacking political opponents) to denigrate aspects of the Cultural Revolution and to discredit 'the Gang of Four'" (187).

"The Gang of Four" and Cultural Revolution experiences were featured in many cartoons in the late 1970s and early '80s. These works were popular, attested to by the first post-Cultural Revolution cartoon exhibition, "Overthrow of 'Gang of Four,'" held in Shanghai in early 1977. According to cartoonist Han Shangyi (personal

Fig. 5.2. Liao Bingxiong presenting a model of "Self-Mockery" to John A. Lent, Guangzhou, January 4, 2002. Photo by Xu Ying.

Fig. 5.3. "Zeitizi" ("Thieves Ladder") by Ying Tao, 1977. Anti-"Gang of Four." Courtesy of Ying Tao.

These three works ushered in China's second golden age of animation, which Te Wei said was "much higher than the first because of the terribleness of the Cultural Revolution":

> Because all of the artists were oppressed during the Cultural Revolution and collected much energy and wanted to do something, the level was much higher. All of them wanted to make their best works and worked hard during that time. After the Cultural Revolution, animation films were revived; it was the best period. (Te Wei, interview, 2001)

Singling out 1979 as an important year in the transformation of Chinese art, Julia F. Andrews (1994: 390) listed three trends common among young and middle-aged artists that year: 1. an Art Deco style for ornamental purposes; 2. a "new sympathetic realism identified with 'Scar' literature, which lamented the personal tragedies of the Cultural Revolution"; and 3. the "politically engaged modernism of the Stars." Cartoons or cartoonists figured prominently in each.

Concerning the first trend, in early 1979, it was the painter/cartoonist Zhang Ding who led a group of artists commissioned by the Ministry of Light Industry to decorate the new airport with painted and ceramic murals. No doubt, some cartoonists' works were subsumed under "Scar" art (the second trend), which gave them vehicles through which to release their strong emotions about the Cultural Revolution (Galikowski 1998: 193). Lianhuanhua figured prominently in this genre, as some of these picture books drew on "Scar" literature stories (e.g., Lu Xinhua's short story "Scar").

One lianhuanhua, *Feng* (*Maple*, written by Zheng Yi and drawn by Chen Liming, Liu Yulian, and Li Bing), sparked a controversial discussion about how historical figures ought to be depicted. The story tells of two classmates who fall in love, join opposing Red Guard groups, and die in separate tragic situations. The main character, Feng, is the female Red Guard. After the story appeared in the August 1979 *Lianhuanhua bao*, (*Serial Pictures Gazette*), the Bureau of Publications ordered that sales cease, stating that Lin Biao and Jiang Qing were portrayed as "positive" in *Maple*. The order was ignored by the editors and no action was taken. The standard procedure for depicting "enemies of the state" was distortion, and as Galikowski (1998: 197) wrote, "The favoured vehicle for such representations remained the cartoon, with its powerful, biting satire and its ability to distort and exaggerate. The ugly and evil-looking cartoons of Lin Biao and 'the Gang of Four' thus became their standard public images." *Maple* artists were vilified for presenting Lin Biao and Jiang Qing without distortion, in line with their consistent policy of not exaggerating any characters in the lianhuanhua.

"Scar" art had a profound impact on cartoonists; it not only provided them an opportunity to vent their anger about the Cultural Revolution, but it also introduced the propositions that the individual (not just heroic workers, soldiers, and peasants) was important and that the audience was active, capable of deciding whether a cartoon was positive or negative, good or bad.

Andrews (1994: 394) wrote of "Scar" art: "Never before had artists been permitted to express their criticism of any aspect of the communist experience in paint." She also labeled the "Stars" (Xingxing) exhibition of unofficial dissident art as the "most notorious artistic event" of 1979, leading to many calls for "artistic democracy" in the press (Andrews 1994: 396). Describing the liberalization of cartoons in the late 1970s, one outside source said that they were sensationalistic, "occasionally slipping into a sexual ribaldry that seemingly had little to do with the crimes or political issues then at hand" (Lam 1983: 52). Such content likely reflected what Galikowski (1998: 191) called the failure of the authorities "to address the ambiguous nature of the relationship between themselves and writers and artists, and between politics and the arts." She elaborated that, while the "dominance of political considerations" was necessary, "undue official interference was not to be tolerated; writers and artists were encouraged to be more adventurous in their creative work, though it was also stressed that their work should meet the needs of the workers, peasants and soldiers" (Galikowski 1998: 190–91).

The pragmatic Deng Xiaoping, speaking at the Fourth Congress of Writers and Artists, May–June 1978, was equally imprecise in outlining a policy on art; he acknowledged that the "political restraints" on art remained, but much leeway existed for work that was "helpful" to reforms. Deng said:

Geared to reach the common goal of realizing the Four Modernizations [proposed in 1963 by Zhou Enlai and officially launched in December 1978 by Deng], writers and artists should broaden the horizons of their work; their creative thinking, themes, and techniques should change and adapt to the changing times, and they should be able to plough new ground. (quoted in Galikowski 1998: 189)

New ground was plowed as Findlay (1984: 108) related: "In the past eight years [1976–84] the concerns of Chinese cartoonists have been surprisingly broad, drawing from a wide range of sources for their political and social humour." But, he added, much of the inspiration came from officially sponsored political, social, and economic campaigns. Among cartoonists' topics were corrupt and lazy bureaucrats, rude, Westernized youth, consumerism, and materialism. Although some of these issues existed pre-1976, they were rarely satirized. "Since 1978, however," according to Findlay (1984: 108), "in campaigns to warn people about the error of their ways and to indicate some of the reasons for the lack of progress, the CCP has allowed cartoonists greater freedom to expose such problems."

Some cartoonists of the 1980s tried to explain the widening of the boundaries of satire: Bi Keguan, at the time the director of the Institute of Fine Arts in Beijing, said that the major task of satirists at that time was to "castigate various social ills"; Ding Cong explained that the emphasis had moved from satirizing the "contradictions between the enemy and ourselves" to exploring contradictions within Chinese society; and Hua Junwu said that, despite changes, the purposes of cartoons remained unchanged. That purpose was to serve the "purposes of education, both ideologically and aesthetically" ("China Draws upon Humour" 1987: 53). A one-time breakthrough in 1986 was the publication of caricatures of Deng Xiaoping as a bridge player, and CCP general secretary Hu Yaobang as a music conductor, in *Liberation Daily* (for examples of cartoons in 1980, see L. Chen 1980: a, b, c).

Just as agriculture, industry, national defense, and science and technology (the Four Modernizations) were to be modernized, so was art. This was to be implemented by allowing *ziwo biaoxian* (the individual expression of the artist), specifically, to shift from emphasis on the collective to the ordinary individual, accepting Western ideas, and first interlinking form and content and then recognizing form over content. These notions undermined many of the concepts about art that had been in effect since 1949.

A backlash occurred from October to December 1983, when the Party's Central Committee called for an end to what it termed "spiritual pollution," perhaps defined by the Artists' Association in its late 1983 meeting when it attacked art theory and works that had "bourgeois ideas of humanism, freedom and individualism" (Galikowski 1998: 233, 235). Deng Xiaoping and others warned against "cultural contamination" from foreign (especially Western) sources, *shangpinhua* (commodification of cultural products), growing tendencies to focus on humanism (labeled "un-Marxist" by Deng), and excessive individualism. Unlike other post-1949 campaigns, "Anti-Spiritual Pollution" was canceled after just twenty-eight days (Wren 1984).

A dissident type of art was renewed in the "new wave" or "avant-garde" movements of the late 1980s, when artists again looked to the "Stars" as models. In the process, they rejected official art and expressed enthusiasm for Western modernism and postmodernism, and as they had a decade before, stirred up much controversy (Andrews 1994: 399).

The changing of policies and practices in the Chinese art world, as well as, to some degree, the infrastructure, and the opening of the country to a market economy had profound impacts on cartooning from the 1980s to the present. New professional and other cartoon-centric groups appeared, as did cartoon/humor magazines; old forms of comic art, such as lianhuanhua, made room for Japanese manga and xinmanhua, and the comics and animation industries increasingly fended for themselves. Other significant changes occurred in the realms of education and other areas of professionalism, exposure of Chinese cartoonists to the outside world, the role of women, and the emergence of a new breed of outward-looking, sometimes entrepreneurial cartoonists. These phenomena did not occur overnight, and most came about after the late 1990s.

The cartooning community was shored up during the 1980s by the establishment of professional committees and groups such as the Cartoon Art Committee of the China Artists' Association (CAA) (Zhongguo meishujia xiehui manhua yishu weiyuanhui) and China Journalistic Caricature Society (CJCS) (Zhongguo xinwen manhua yanjiuhui). Other groups specified for workers, farmers, and soldiers either continued to thrive, or were established, in the 1980s.

Professional Organizations

The Cartoon Art Committee was set up as one of about ten such bodies under the Artists' Association. It is administered by twenty famous cartoonists (Wang Fuyang, interview, 2001). For twenty years after its 1986 inception, the backbone of the Cartoon Art Committee was Wang Fuyang, a cartoonist who faced the wrath of authorities from 1958 to 1978. First as vice director and then as director after 1999, Wang kept the committee active, organizing exhibitions, training sessions, and other events, and bringing out *Manhua yiweihui tongxun* (*Cartoon Art Committee's News Report*), edited for a time by Zheng Huagai. The committee, under the China Artists' Association personnel system, was not given funding or an office by CAA. As later Cartoon Art Committee secretary Zheng Huagai (2008: 548) wrote:

Master Wang's house actually became the Cartoon Art Committee's office. His wife [painter Cui Zhenguo] and son took on the role of his "secretary." His son, who always helped him at the expense of his own career, was regularly paid from Master Wang Fuyang's pocket. He made long-distance phone calls from home to cartoonists all over China and paid phone bills with his own money. He also bought a fax machine and a copy machine using his own money to serve the Cartoon Art Committee.

Fig. 5.4. Wang Fuyang, Beijing, December 16, 2002. Photo by Xu Ying. Courtesy of Wang Fuyang.

Because of illnesses which ultimately claimed his life in 2008, Wang Fuyang stepped down as director in 2006, replaced by Xu Pengfei (b. 1949), then editor of *Satire and Humor*. The Cartoon Art Committee remains active.

With the major aims of connecting news cartoonists and art editors nationwide and improving "professional competencies," the China Journalistic Caricature Society (CJCS) was founded in Beijing in 1987; its first president was Shen Tongheng. The organization is registered by the national Ministry of Civil Affairs and supervised by the China National Journalists' Association. CJCS has fifty subgroups of central, provincial, and municipal newspapers and local journalistic caricature societies. Originally, a province could have only one group member (Zhang, interview, 2001).

CJCS lists its scope of activities as to:

1. Intensify the academic study of journalistic caricature, improve the quality as well as increase the quantity of journalistic caricatures.
2. Systematically organize various kinds of journalistic caricature exhibitions and publicity campaigns.
3. Carry out programs for exchanging experience in journalistic caricature business and for foreign exchange.
4. Provide academic papers and news reports on journalistic caricature and arrange contests

to select outstanding journalistic caricature workers.
5. Annually arrange contests and other activities with China Journalists' Association, including the China Journalistic Caricature Prize and other national prizes in the field. (International Cartoon Competition . . . 2014: 239)

Among events sponsored by CJCS are the annual Environmental Protection competition/exhibition and the ink-wash painting exhibition, and a 2005 seminar of remembrances of wartime cartooning on the sixtieth anniversary of the end of World War II. (The authors were guests at these events.)

The director of CJCS, Zhang Yaoning (b. 1951) (interview, 2014), said that, among all of the group's activities (training, exhibitions, exchanges, symposia, and awards), the most important are the two prizes given for best cartoon and best page layout at the annual China National Journalists' Association awards ceremony. Zhang likened the twenty-nine total awards for news and editorials to the Pulitzer Prize in the United States. The awards were initiated in 1990. CJCS is also proud of its news cartoon website, the largest in China.

Worker-Specific Cartooning Groups

Unique worldwide are worker-specific organizations, such as the Qiu County Farmers Frog Cartoon Group, the Beijing Workers Cartoon Group (and its imitators), and the Military Camp Humor Group of an artillery brigade of Beijing Military Region, all of which have given village farmers, working-class urbanites, and soldiers opportunities to learn cartooning skills. These groups also provide such people a voice, as well as some prestige and money.

Qiu County, Hebei Province is predominantly agrarian, and many in its population of 220,000 are engaged in farming cotton and various vegetables. It would seem an unlikely place to start a cartoon group, but not to octogenarian Chen Yuli and his wife, Li Qingai, who did just that more than thirty years ago.

Fig. 5.5. Qiu County Farmers Frog Cartoon Group founders/leaders Chen Yuli and Li Qingai. Courtesy of Chen Yuli and Li Qingai.

Now the "banner of the county," in the words of Dong Mingguo, director of Qiu County Propaganda Department (interview, 2009), the Frog Cartoon Group has attracted the attention of China's leading cartoonists and its main newspapers and television channels, as well as the *New York Times*, ABC News, and other foreign media outlets. The government and Communist Party have been very much aware of the Frog Cartoon Group, lending support on numerous occasions.

At least 2,000 farmers and other workers have been Frog Cartoon Group members over the years, many starting out at early ages in what is called the Tadpole Cartoon Class. Chen (interview, 2009) explained the group's name: "Because I was a farmer, I thought the frog is an animal that protects grain from insects and then sings at harvest." He made an analogy; like the frog, the cartoonist also safeguards, in this case, society.

Chen and Li laid the foundation for the Frog Cartoon Group in the early 1980s. Li (interview, 2009) attributed the origins of the group partly to a provincial leader who told the couple, "You are artists and you should go out and see the mountains and the scenery." The leader then pledged 2,000 yuan for such an excursion. However, only 200 yuan filtered through the county leadership and reached Chen and Li. Not deterred, they met a Hebei newspaper editor, who provided them a list of cartoonists to meet in Beijing. For their visit to the capital, Chen drew what Li (interview, 2009) termed as an "art beggars' map," indicating cartoonists from whom they would beg for help. Two famous cartoonists were particularly encouraging: Hua Junwu, who said, "You are farmers; draw farm life, not urban," and Fang Cheng, who told them, "Seldom do farmers draw cartoons and because China has a large farmer population, you should train farmer cartoonists" (Li, interview, 2009).

The Frog Cartoon Group's beginnings in 1983 were modest in the extreme. The original seven members met in two small rooms of an old building, on "one side of which was a long bed and kitchen; on the other side, a cupboard of five small shelves," with each member assigned living and work tools, such as books and cooking utensils (Li, interview, 2009). Students, teachers, and visitors slept on straw spread on the floor. Li (interview, 2009) said that as newspaper stories appeared about the Frog Cartoon Group, visitors came: "Some walked long distances to get here, and they came from all over China [in 1985 and 1986] to study cartooning."

Besides teaching budding cartoonists drawing skills, Chen and Li also found outlets for their works. Originally, Frog Cartoon Group works were placed in the newspaper display windows on the streets, such exhibition meaning that the cartoonist had been "published" (Li, interview, 2009). Also constituting publication were wall drawings. Li (interview, 2009) elaborated:

Also in the town, we had a whole wall where people could draw. Every one of the 218 villages of Qiu County has a street where people can draw on the walls. We [Chen and Li] and four others began to draw on walls in 1958. If the government had a propaganda task, we would draw it. Rain would damage the drawings and we repainted them.

From 1983 to 2006, some Frog Cartoon Group drawings were carried in the "Handan Cartoon" column in *Handan Daily*, the newspaper of the nearest city. By the late 1980s, with the help of the provincial deputy director, Chen and Li compiled books of collected Frog Cartoon Group drawings; these were published. Beginning in 1984, Frog Cartoon Group members participated in exhibitions all over China, frequently winning awards.

With the unstoppable determination and energy of Chen and Li, financial assistance from government agencies, and the generous instructional and other support of important cartoonists/artists, the Frog and Tadpole groups prospered. Beginning in 1990, they shared space with the culture museum and library; when the latter moved out in 1999, the Frog Cartoon Group

113

occupied the entire forty-room building. The building badly needed repairs, funds for which came from provincial, county, and city governments. Chen and Li have been meticulous in collecting, preserving, and cataloguing the many drawings, calligraphies, and scrolls done by visiting artists that decorate the walls of two large galleries, and exhibiting, each in a separate room, the many awards received by Frog Cartoon Group artists, works for sale of famous painters and cartoonists, cartoons by the Tadpoles, Frog Cartoon Group cartoons about the countryside and modernization, and signature drawings by some of the group's more prominent artists. The building also has conference and lecture rooms, an office, and a well-stocked library, all of which noticeably function well without a single computer.

Among the hundreds of current group members, Li, Chen, Ren Guangqiang, and Hu Yantin remain from the original 1983 contingent. Ren left farming years ago, and since graduating from art school, has been a teacher and then an official in the local government's culture and art association. Trained formally in art, Ren (interview, 2009) prefers farmers' drawings, which he described as more exaggerated and freer; "they [the farmers] draw what they want."

Most current Frog Cartoon Group members remain farmers, a fact appreciated by Chen (interview, 2009), because, in his view, they are the best cartoonists, explaining that, "After they become clerks, seldom do they draw cartoons." He singled out one Frog Cartoon Group and former Tadpole Cartoon Class member, Zhang Aixue, as a successful professional cartoonist. Zhang makes his living doing four to five four-panel strips daily, which keeps him working until 2 a.m., even with his wife's help in coloring. As Zhang (interview, 2009) lamented, "What I pay in hours worked does not match what I get."

Membership regulations for the two groups are not stringent, as Li (interview, 2009) explained: "We never pay attention to age or the village they come from. We don't ask them to show work to join the Frog Cartoon Group, and we don't stop them if they want to leave." The youngest Tadpole when the authors visited was a

Fig. 5.6. Li Qingai instructing young cartoonists of the Frog Cartoon Group in its early days, 1985. Courtesy of Li Qingai.

four-and-a-half-year-old child. Considered by some to be too active to teach, she represented a challenge to Chen, who, upon meeting her, asked her to draw snow. The little girl drew a snowman with a Japanese flag, and in a second panel, the melted snowman. The cartoon impressed Chen, because the assignment was to depict something about the "anti-Japanese war." Frog Cartoon Group teachers usually stimulate the youngsters by giving them topics to illustrate, such as the environment, anti-Japanese war, conservation of water, use of water for the fields, "civilized villages," etc. The Tadpole cartoons exhibited were sharp, insightful, meaningful, and creative. With both the Frogs and Tadpoles, Chen is merciless in his critiques, making members redo their works repeatedly.

Frog Cartoon Group members also benefited from useful external criticism of their work, given by many of China's art, cartooning, and caricature masters, including Te Wei, Hua Junwu, He Wei, Fang Cheng, Wang Fuyang, Xu Pengfei, Wang Shuchen, and Zhan Tong. Some of them and others made multiple trips to Qiu County to instruct farmer cartoonists. The professional cartoonists' expertise and support, and occasional government funds, went a long way in making the Frog Cartoon Group viable. Still, their efforts paled in

Fig. 5.7. He Wei as a perspiring hard worker. Self-caricature. Courtesy of He Wei.

Fig. 5.8. First issue of "Workers' Drawings," *Workers Daily*, May 1, 1949. Courtesy of He Wei.

comparison to those of Chen Yuli and Li Qingai, who devoted almost all of their time and wages to the betterment of the Frog Cartoon Group and its members. At various times, they assumed roles of teacher, parent, agent, and promoter.

Chen and Li have remained busy with a myriad of activities, including turning the Frog Cartoon Group building into a museum, partly to satisfy the county government's desire to generate revenue, and fending off county and city government's offers to support animation production under the group's roof. Chen is also hard at work creating a book he calls *Nongmin Li Si* (*Peasant Li Si*), which will relate, using four-panel strips, the harsh conditions the couple has endured during their lives.

Similar to what Chen and Li did for farmers, Beijing cartoonist He Wei did for other types of workers. For about forty-six years (1953–99), he supervised a column in *Gongren ribao* (*Workers Daily*) made up of cartoons and other drawings by workers. Named "Gongren de hua" ("Workers' Drawings") by a laborer, the column debuted on May 1, 1949, in *Dazhong ribao* (*Masses Daily*), appearing irregularly, "roughly and on poor paper" (He Wei 1989). One of the founders of *Dazhong ribao*, Zhang Rong, had noticed a worker's drawings and asked art editors Wang Hong and Tian Ling to gather a page of such art for May Day. They edited several issues after that, reflecting workers' ideas and displaying their talents (He Wei 1989). In July 1949, *Dazhong ribao* changed to become *Gongren ribao* (*Workers Daily*).

Upon moving to *Workers Daily* in 1953, nineteen-year-old He Wei was assigned the task of editing "Workers' Drawings" on a regular schedule. The workers' art in the early 1950s, according to He Wei, was "just a bud,"

with only a few workers who drew very infrequently. To remedy this shortcoming, he and colleagues established a workers cartoon group at the Labor People's Culture Palace (Laodong renmin wenhuagong) and he began teaching at the Beijing Art Vocation School (Beijing meishu zhuanke xuexiao) and at Drum Tower Cultural Hall (Gulou wenhuaguan) with the goal of upgrading aspiring artists' skills. Additionally, he solicited cartoons and paintings through the mail and during trips to factories in other cities. In 1955, he edited *The First Workers Art Exhibition Collection* (*Diyijie zhigong meishuzhan huace*), a catalogue of the First National Workers Art Exhibition (Diyijie quanguo zhigong meishuzhan), of which he was a judge. This experience enabled him to meet worker artists from other cities.

Imitators of the column followed: "Labor Art Column" ("Laodong yishu zhuanlan") in *Shanghai Labor Daily* (*Shanghai laodong ribao*); "Everyone's Drawings" ("Dajia de hua") in *Tianjin Workers Paper* (*Tianjin gongren bao*); and "Workers' Art Column" ("Gongren meishu zhuanlan") in *Northeast Labor Paper* (*Dongbei laodong bao*). He Wei edited the latter, beginning in 1952, which he said was influenced by "Workers' Drawings."

From 1949 to 2009, more than 1,300 "Workers' Drawings" columns appeared in *Workers Daily*, consisting of cartoons and oil, watercolor, and ink-wash paintings drawn by thousands of workers, some of whom later gained fame as artists. Twice monthly, *Workers Daily* devoted one page each to cartoons and other types of drawings. At other times, the general editors drew from the pool of worker cartoons to illustrate other pages of the newspaper. He Wei (interview, 2009) said the workers preferred doing cartoons because they "reflected workers' lives"; they were called "echoes or noises of the workers." Many were satirical.

He Wei credited much help given by his art editor colleagues at *Workers Daily*, Xu Jin and Ye Chunyang. The workers also drew collectively, as was explained by He Wei (interview, 2009): "Several workers would discuss co-workers' cartoons and help each other to perfect ideas or to decide if an idea had been used before."

The initial goals of the column were to provide workers an outlet to show off their talent and engage them in eye-opening activities to hone their skills. He Wei prided himself in paying close attention to artists' first works.

Activities were oriented around a theme for the column. He Wei (1989) wrote, "We used to organize visits to open artists' eyes, then, we would discuss together the works we saw, and select some for the column." There were numerous visits in the 1950s and '60s to rural villages, factories, and large stores, after which "Workers' Drawings" columns appeared with titles such as "Small Factory, Big Ambition," "Commercial Newcomers," and "Dedicating to People Who Work on Holiday." During a visit He Wei made to Shanghai in 1955, "Workers' Drawings" for the first time was co-edited with another newspaper, *Labor Newspaper* (*Laodong bao*). While in Shanghai, He Wei pulled together the works of business workers and store clerks which were sent back to Beijing for publication in the column.

Much of the activity of "Workers' Drawings" artists was done jointly with the Beijing Workers Cartoon Group, which He Wei and fellow *Workers Daily* editors started in 1958. The group was credited with educating editors and new cartoonists and giving the latter outlets to publish their works.

"Workers' Drawings" reflected the artistic and sociopolitical life of China; in the mid-1950s, domestic satire cartoons were favored after the Chinese Communist Party called for criticism and self-criticism. The criticism came back to haunt cartoonists during the Anti-Rightist campaign of the late-1950s and the Cultural Revolution. Art editors, during the Anti-Rightist times, He Wei (1989) recounted, were "walking like on a wire; they did not know when something would happen. Cartoonists were confused; the newspaper leaders were very careful." Workers' cartoons alone survived nearly unscathed the repression of the Anti-Rightist movement. He Wei (interviews, 2006, 2009) explained, "The reason workers' cartoons survived in the 1950s campaigns is because they were done by workers and workers were considered first class in the CCP chain of command. Censorship was not so severe for workers." Also, the column continued, because it reflected workers' lives and published works illustrating approved political concepts and propaganda (He Wei 1989). He Wei (interview, 2009) said that, as head of the *Workers Daily* Art and Photograph Department, "I followed the CCP instruction that self-criticism should continue. I kept up self-criticism through the workers' cartoons. Later, in the Cultural Revolution, I was warned and put on probation by the CCP." In another interview, He Wei said that in 1959, he was accused of being a "middle-rightist" and was sent to work in a Shenyang bronze factory for a year, but, upon his release, he was encouraged to keep the "Workers' Drawings" page alive. Because the column was the only one in existence during those difficult times, many cartoonists other than workers contributed their drawings (He Wei, interview, 2006).

The column was not so fortunate during the Cultural Revolution. Criticized as "full of poison grass," the "Workers' Drawings" column and the newspaper in which it appeared were closed on New Year, 1967. Some of the column's cartoonists were jailed; on several occasions, rebels came to the *Workers Daily* editorial office seeking original works as proof of crimes. He Wei protected the

Fig. 5.9. "Workers' Drawings," 1000th issue, Oct. 1, 1999. Courtesy of He Wei.

worker cartoonists, always falsely telling investigators that *Workers Daily* did not keep original works.

Upon the reopening of *Workers Daily* in October 1978, the newspaper's editorial committee asked He Wei and other editors to restart "Workers' Drawings" on page four. The Beijing Workers Cartoon Group also was revived, and many old (and some new) cartoon contributors in other cities drew again. Major tasks included contemplating the role of art in the news, establishing other worker cartoon groups around the country (post-1980, workers' art developed immensely, partly because of these hundreds of active worker art groups), and choosing topics to satirize. A favorite topic was bureaucracy; others were waste and youth problems.

Worker cartoonists have been very active since 1978. Young artists progressed quickly with instruction from comic art masters Hua Junwu, Ye Qianyu, Fang Cheng, Zhang Ding, Wu Guanzhong, and Hou Baolin, better known as the master of *xiangsheng* (comic dialogue); other famous cartoonists, such as Ding Cong, Ying Tao, Jiang Fan, and Wang Fuyang, also met with workers to critique their drawings and hold symposia (He Wei 1989).

Beginning in 1985 and continuing every two years through 1989, when funding was no longer available,

workers' cartoon competitions were held. The first of the competitions, held with the Second Automobile Company and five other enterprises, drew 1,700 works, from which 204 were selected for recognition. An exhibition of the winning cartoons was held at the National Art Museum, and Japanese cartoonists were invited to exchange ideas with the awardees. The second contest in 1987 was held in conjunction with workers' periodicals from five other cities. Out of 14,895 entries, 209 were awarded prizes. Besides publishing a catalogue, He Wei also organized an exhibition at the National Art Museum of China and in seven cities of China (He Wei 1989).

Because cartoons are an "international language, not requiring interpreters," in 1985, He Wei and *Workers Daily* organized the "Ambassador of Laughter—China and Japan Workers Cartoon Exchange Exhibition" with the Japan Union Cartoon Group. Each country contributed fifty works. He Wei (1989) said that this was China's first cartoon exchange exhibition. On establishing an Ambassador of Laughter award, He Wei (1989) remembered:

I had no money for the award so I bought small gifts from the culture market to give winners. I asked the Hungarian

117

118

Fig. 5.10. Selection of *Junying youmo* (*Military Camp Humor*) cartoons published in *Satire and Humor*, September 20, 1986. Courtesy of Zheng Huagai.

and German embassies in Beijing and a Russian labor paper and Ukraine cartoon magazine to have works sent for an exhibition. Afterwards, I sent the small gifts to the cartoonists. The award winners were happy to get the gifts but I was embarrassed that I could not buy something nicer.

The exhibitions became training grounds for young cartoonists as they introduced new works and skills. Other exhibitions included one on national minority art work (1979), a five-city worker cartoon exhibition and the Guilin workers landscape (*shanshui*) painting exhibition (both 1982), and a seven-cities workers' etching exhibition (1986).

Training was part of other projects throughout the 1980s as He Wei and Xu Jin went to towns and villages, military bases, and other locales to support local cartooning. As examples, in 1982, He and Xu promoted the establishment of a cartoon workshop in Shan Ying (Mountain Eagle) to teach cartoon skills to automobile and machinery factory workers; in 1985, they organized forty cartoonists/reporters from all over China for a symposium at Shanxi Baoji Changling Machinery Factory.

Both "Workers' Drawings" and the Beijing Workers Cartoon Group are still active and He Wei's involvement in their development is remembered appreciably (Miao, interview, 2002; Bi 1988; Luo 1995). Xu Jin, who helped edit the "Workers' Drawings" from 1978 until he retired in 2005, said the style of the page and means of soliciting cartoons have changed. Previously, the editors asked workers directly, going to their homes and factories for cartoons. He said now they are sent in via the internet (Xu Jin, interview, 2013).

Over the years, the column and *Workers Daily* have been called "the cradle of cartoonists" and "a good teacher and friend," and praised by top cartoonists. But, to fully appreciate the accomplishments of *Workers Daily*, He Wei, and the column, one must take notice of the immense number of quality cartoons produced by thousands of worker cartoonists, a number of whom reached the higher echelons of the profession.

As an aside, He Wei also encouraged women to draw cartoons, at a time when few female cartoonists existed. He started a column in *Workers Daily* called "Rosebush" ("Qiangwei"), which lasted two years beginning in 1991. He Wei talked about the genesis of "Rosebush":

> I had seen a TV drama, "Longing" ("Kewang"), about a very kind woman who devoted everything to helping others. I thought we should not encourage this type of behavior. Women should do what they like and not live for others. So, I insisted on having this column for more than two years. [Cartoon works by] more than twenty-four women were published on this page. But, most of them had lots of chores at home, got married, and so they gave up. The column was an unsuccessful experience. (He Wei, interview, 2002)

Of course, the military was involved in cartooning even before Liberation in 1949, producing cartoon periodicals, leaflets, and other propagandistic visual art during World War II and China's Civil War (see Chapter 3 for fuller discussion of that period). However, most of those cartoons aimed to build morale among the public, denounce the enemy, and persuade the other side to surrender.

The first evidence of something similar to the farmers' and workers' cartooning activities among soldiers occurred in 1986, when, on January 31, *Junying youmo* (*Military Camp Humor*) appeared. Serving the People's Liberation Army's Artillery Brigade No. 51392 (Xuanhua) of the Beijing Military Region, *Military Camp Humor* grew out of a "Soldiers Cartoon Study Class," set up that month by military leaders, the most passionate of whom was Zheng Huagai, himself a cartoonist who was the periodical's editor. Thirty soldier students, all under twenty years of age, participated, none of whom had drawn cartoons previously, and some of whom were not even familiar with the term "manhua." Zheng Huagai (1987b) recalled:

> So, we edited cartoon teaching materials based on soldiers' characteristics—generalized as "Cartoon Three Character Primer" and "Cartoon Four Character Table"—and easy for them to memorize. We adopted methods similar to those for military training, explaining, demonstrating, getting students to ask questions in class, and evaluating them with comments. After some study, soldiers deeply loved cartooning and continuously submitted their work for comments.

Feeling a need for an outlet for the soldiers' cartoons, Zheng, with approval from the military higher-ups, started *Military Camp Humor* in mimeographed form; after two issues, the tabloid was photocopied. Published biweekly, *Military Camp Humor* was full of soldiers' cartoons of every stripe—humor, satire, fantasy, social life, and "praising" (rewarding good deeds and behavior) (Mao 1986). With the cartooning activities, the brigade aimed to educate and build spirit among soldiers. During the periodical's first two months, the thirty soldiers brought out fourteen issues and created several hundred cartoons (Mao 1986; see also Shi 1986). Within a year, about 100 works by fifteen soldiers were accepted by important national periodicals, such as *Workers Daily* and *Satire and Humor*, as well as *Jiefangjun bao* (*PLA Daily*) and *Zhanyou bao* (*Fellow Army Daily*).

Soldiers' cartoons had their own style—usually optimistic, simple, and honest, whose characters were "modest, with a smile, fat, with little snobby noses and a sense of humor" (Mao 1986). The characters and themes came from everyday life, and while the drawings were "childish," "rough and clumsy," they did have "deep meaning" and were "humorous" (Mao 1986).

Also in 1986, ten top students of the cartoon class started the Military Camp Humor Cartoon Group, which spurred soldiers to exchange cartooning experiences with one another, to submit works to *Military Camp Humor* and other publications, and, in August of that year, to hold "The First Military Camp Humor Cartoon Exhibition" at the China Revolutionary Military Museum. Coordinated by Zheng Huagai, the show featured 212 cartoons drawn by the brigade's soldiers. Cartoonists and art editors from ten major Beijing and Tianjin newspapers and magazines showed up to critique the works (Lihu n.d.).

A strong outside supporter of the soldiers' group and magazine was Hua Junwu, who wrote a letter of encouragement upon receiving a copy of the first issue of *Military Camp Humor*. In the ensuing months of 1986, he wrote several more letters, occasionally offering advice, evaluated thirty works mailed to him by individual soldiers, designed the magazine's logo, and, in December, visited the camp to deliver a lecture. In his six-hour presentation, Hua emphasized the need for cartoonists to serve the people, read vociferously, observe the life around them, and strengthen political culture. He said, "Many of my cartoon themes came from life [experiences] as I expressed my feelings. I hope all of you draw something you are familiar with; thus, it will not be so easy for you to crash" (Hu, Zhao Z., Zhao W. 1986; see also Zheng 1987a). When an anthology of selected *Military Camp Humor* cartoons was published in 1990, Hua wrote the preface, in which he praised Zheng Huagai, the military leaders, and soldier cartoonists for their persistence, and optimistically stated, "Obviously, nothing is difficult; things can certainly be done. I use such a feeling to enjoy this cartoon selection book" (Hua 1990). In a later article, Hua (1998) singled out a few military men who found success in cartooning—namely, Wang Yu, Du Chongcai, Zhang Bin, Jin Ma, and Zheng Huagai.

Zheng Huagai continued teaching cartooning to soldiers, drawing his own cartoons about camp life, setting up soldiers' cartoon pages and columns in various military newspapers, and publishing collections of military cartoons in book form. In 1992, he was transferred to the editorial office of *Zhanyou bao* (*Fellow Army Daily*) as its art editor. During the following years, until his retirement in 2015, Zheng compiled and published at least nine collections of soldiers' cartoons, including his own, with titles such as *Junying youmo manhuaxuan* (*Military Camp Humor Cartoon Selection*), *Junlu youmo* (*Army Humor*), and *Manhua shishi: Zhongguo renmin jiefangjun* (*Cartoon Epic: The People's Liberation Army of China*). He categorized his own cartoons (and many of those by other soldiers) as "praising," or positive. An example Zheng gave was his "Shibing de zuji" ("Soldiers' Footprints") showing that where soldiers left footprints, green sprouts and lush trees grew, a reference to the military's forestation endeavors (Zheng n.d.).

Zheng took pride in the work he and fellow soldiers accomplished. His own creative streak was demonstrated in 2007, when he converted 100,000 words of *Zhongguo renmin jiefangjun jianjunshi* (*The History of the People's Liberation Army of China Establishment*) into fifty sentences by summarizing and abstracting them as "Four Characters Ballads" with rhythm. He then changed the ballads into the above-mentioned series of cartoons, "Manhua shishi: Zhongguo renmin jiefangjun" ("Cartoon Epic: The People's Liberation Army of China"), that were first serialized in *Fellow Army Daily*, before becoming the book (Zheng n.d.).

In recent years, according to Zheng (n.d.), various services, branches, departments, and units of the PLA requested cartoons as propaganda and instructive tools, including "Manhua baomi shouze" ("Cartoons of the Rule of Confidentiality"), "Manhua jingwei gongzuo guifan" ("Cartoons of Security Specification"), "Manhua junshi cangku anquan" ("Cartoons of Military Warehouse Security"), "Manhua shitang weisheng" ("Cartoons of Food Service Sanitation"), and others. The forms of these cartoons varied, including poker cards, pocket books, electronic slides, small labels, cartoon light boxes, etc.

Cartoon/Humor Magazines

The main outlet for cartoonists after 1979 was *Satire and Humor*, established by Hua Junwu, Jiang Fan, Ying Tao, Miao Di, and Jiang Yousheng as a supplement of the national daily, *Renmin ribao* (*People's Daily*). Jiang Yousheng (interview, 2002) gave the reason for its start: "During the Cultural Revolution, no one could draw satire. After those ten years, there were many cartoons on the 'Gang of Four,' but no place to publish them." *Satire and Humor* provided that place; in 1986, Ying Tao said, the magazine received more than 100 cartoons daily from amateur cartoonists (ZhangYu 2015).

In the very first number of *Satire and Humor*, the editor made his intentions clear, writing that cartoons are for revolution "to be used for enhancement of unity, self-education, and exposure of as well as dealing of blows of enemies" (Chen 1980a: 3). In the beginning, *Satire and Humor* had a circulation of 1,300,000; its later editor, Xu Pengfei, claimed that people in the early period queued to be sure to receive a copy (Xu, interview, 2001). By the late 1980s, the fortnightly became one of China's most popular periodicals. By then, it had also led, through its example, to the start of at least six other cartoon magazines, including *Children's Cartoon*, *Selected Cartoons*, *Laugh*, *Humor Master*, *The World of Cartoons*, and *Cartoon Monthly* (Hebei Province, 1985); about ten cartoon newspapers (e.g., *Thorny Roses*, *Little Hot Peppers*, and *Gag Cartoon Paper*), and at least twenty cartoon columns in various newspapers and magazines. Their vitriolic or contrasting sweet and sour aims were apparent from their names: "Thorny Plum" in *Beijing Evening News*, "Red and Green Lights" in *Beijing Daily*, "Flower and Thorn" in *Shenyang Daily*, "Honey and Sting" in *Yantai Daily*, and "Cactus" in *Encounter Monthly*.

The World of Cartoons, a sixteen-page cartoon magazine started in 1985 by animator/cartoonist A Da,

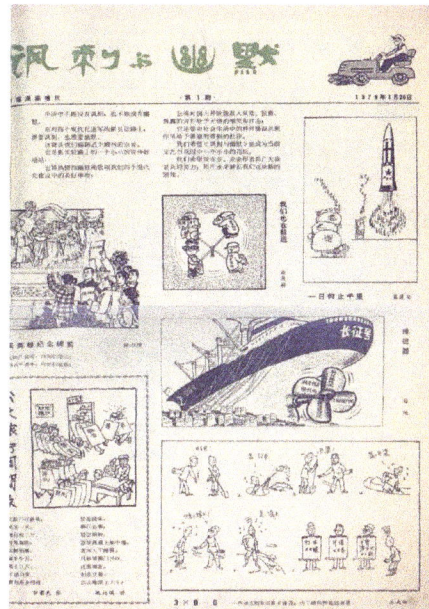

Fig. 5.11. Inaugural issue, *Fengci yu youmo* (*Satire and Humor*), January 20, 1979.

Fig. 5.12. *Manhua shijie* (*The World of Cartoons*), No. 6, 1992.

in Shanghai, was perhaps *Satire and Humor*'s major competitor in the 1990s. The first chief editor and deputy chief editor were Zhang Leping and Te Wei, respectively; other editorial board members were A Da, Wang Shuchen, Zhan Tong, Xu Keren, Du Jianguo, and Zheng Xinyao (Zheng Xinyao, interview, 2001). Initially designed for cartoonists and cartoon lovers, *The World of Cartoons* was part of the Xinminwanbao group, whose main daily, *Xinmin Evening News*, founded in Nanjing in 1929, was known for its extensive use of cartoons (Zhang Linlan, interview, 1993). Originally published monthly, *The World of Cartoons* became a semi-monthly by 1993, steeped in political cartoons, and for a while in the 1980s, even featuring "portrait cartoons" (caricatures) of politicians and other newsworthy people on its cover. Zhan Tong (interview, 1993) said that *The World of Cartoons* succeeded because its "format was very simple, the price was very low (the equivalent of $.02 in 1993), and it introduced foreign cartoons" before other post-1949 cartoon/humor magazines. A managing editor, Sun Shaobo (interview, 1993), gave the criteria for selecting those to use from the forty to fifty cartoons received daily:

> Every day, we face the big task of selecting cartoons from the well-known and newly-born [*sic*] cartoonists who send in work. The criteria is based on content and artistic presentation. If we find cartoons with good content and the skill suffers, we send them back to the cartoonists with comments so as to educate them. We keep good relationships with about 100 cartoonists in every corner of China. Besides freelance cartoons, there are regular columns for special cartoonists.

Although, when interviewed in 1993, the staff of *The World of Cartoons* praised the relative freedom the magazine and its parent company enjoyed, the former deputy editor-in-chief of *Xinmin Evening News*, Xu Keren, was dismissed in 1990, because, as he said, he "attended a street demonstration" in June 1989 (Xu Keren, interview, 1993). He said he was "lucky" to be asked later to be director in charge of selecting special articles for *The World of Cartoons*.

Due to a loss of revenue, *The World of Cartoons* died as a separate publication in 1999. In its reincarnation as a page in *Xinmin Evening News* in 2000, it appealed to all types of readers, according to its editor, Zheng Xinyao (interview, 2001).

Some cartoon magazines—e.g., *Zhongguo manhua* and *Cartoon Monthly*—took on additional commercial

Fig. 5.13. *Zhongguo manhua* (*China Cartoons*), No. 3, 1989.

characteristics, such as replacing front cover cartoons with photographs of entertainment stars and local cartoons with Japanese manga (Wang Fuyang, interview, 2001).

In regions devoid of cartoon magazines, such as Nanjing, local branches of the Artists' Association sometimes carried out activities for cartoonists in the post-Mao period. At the end of the 1970s, the Jiangsu branch of the Artists' Association started cartoon exhibitions which went by the name of Big Turnip. Chen Huiling (interview, 2009) said the exhibitions featured self-ridiculing works and were called "turnips" because that vegetable represents idiocy to Nanjingers. But, he added, "turnips are also good for one's health so cartoons are good for society."

Satire and Humor remains as one of *Renmin ribao*'s many supplements, all designed to offset the seriousness of the government daily with content to meet readers' needs. (Xu, interview, 2001) As with most types of print media, *Satire and Humor* has suffered severe losses in circulation, attributable to stiff competition for readers from electronic media, the internet, and Japanese comics. By 2001, the sixteen-page magazine printed 300,000 copies fortnightly (Xu, interview, 2001). Just four years later, *Satire and Humor*, by then a weekly, dropped to 110,000 copies (Xu, interview, 2005). In 2015, the periodical's managing editor-in-chief, Xiao Chengsen, gave the circulation as 80,000 (Zhang Yu 2015). Other differences were evident, according to Xu (interview, 2005);

Fig. 5.14. Lianhuanhua used diverse styles, including photo-comics in the 1980s. *Shiliuhao bingfang (Ward #16)* explores the views on life of hospitalized young people.

the magazine was more market-inclined, selling mainly at newsstands; more open to the use of foreign-originated cartoons; less artistically motivated; and more concentrated on news and politics, rather than "humor and funny things" (Xu, interview, 2005).

Whereas other newspapers and magazines pay cartoonists according to their rank in the profession, *Satire and Humor* compensates them by the quality of their work; thus, amateur cartoonists have been known to receive space on page one. Xu (interview, 2001) said that cartoonists are asked to draw on specific topics—timely themes, government policy, and, especially the common people's concerns. Every sixteen-page issue includes a page of comic strips, very popular with readers. Despite being an appendage of the government newspaper, *Satire and Humor* has "no limitations, as we can control everything ourselves," Xu (interview, 2001) said.

Xu (interview, 2001) proudly stated that *Satire and Humor* cultivated a new generation(s) of cartoonists, who "get more and more famous publishing in *Satire and Humor*, for which they are grateful." He also pointed out *Satire and Humor* has the longest run in the history of Chinese cartoon/humor magazines.

The Accelerated Metamorphosis of Comics

When China began its evolution from the cocoon of Maoism in the late 1970s, the only semblance of a comic book was the lianhuanhua, which, in the eyes of some critics, was more a picture book than a bona fide comic book. By the advent of the twenty-first century, comic books incorporating Japanese and Western features to create a hybrid with Chinese characteristics were in vogue. Lianhuanhua still exist but play a diminished role among readers.

The Peaking and Bottoming-Out of Lianhuanhua

After Mao's death in 1976, lianhuanhua publishing was reorganized yet again. Exiled older artists returned to the studios, joined by young draftsmen; room was made for freelance artists' works; strident propaganda was replaced by very subtle messages; styles of art became more diverse; and, with Deng Xiaoping's rule after 1979, rigid controls were abandoned (Andrews 1997: 31). The popularity of the miniature books resulted in huge profits for publishing houses between 1978 and 1984; in 1983 alone, 2,100 titles appeared, surmounting 630 million copies, or about one-fourth of China's total book production that year (Jie 2004: 33, quoted in Pan 2008: 706). The number rose to 800 million the following year. Martin (2014) reported that in the early 1980s, lianhuanhua made up one-fourth of all publishing in China; in the peak year, 1985, more than seven lianhuanhua were printed for each Chinese citizen.

Lianhuanhua experienced its final golden age in the 1980s, not only in sales, but also in the diversity of subject matter, goals, and art styles. According to Menjie Chen (quoted in Martin 2014), as many prohibitions were relaxed,

> traditional stories set in ancient China, criticized in the 1960s for featuring royal and upper-class protagonists rather than contemporary proletarians, reappeared in lianhuanhua works. Folktales, fantasy, and fables—genres suppressed during the Cultural Revolution for reasons ranging from superstition to preaching feudalism, capitalism, and revisionism—came back to entertain young readers.

Also, explicit love and sex, "sometimes almost pornographic," made up lianhuanhua scenes (Mittler 2012: 368). Foreign works from Europe and the US, including films such as *Star Wars*,[2] were adapted to lianhuanhua, as were examples of Chinese "Scar" art. Mittler (2012: 368) reported that a 1988 *Lianhuanhuabao* issue contained French, Russian, and Turkish comics stories. And, in the 1980s, the goals of lianhuanhua were expanded, including "intellectual development and education in science and culture for young people" (Martin 2014).

Unlike in previous periods, lianhuanhua in the 1980s used many artistic styles (modernist, gouache, oil, classical painting), employing innovative influences and experimental designs. Martin (2014) explained:

> The lianhuanhua illustrators employ a tremendous range of styles. Some are clearly inspired by Japanese and Western comics, while others adapt the stylized *gong bi* line from traditional Chinese ink painting. This diversity of technique reflects the diversity of backgrounds among the illustrators. Some specialized in lianhuanhua, while others were painters who found paying employment by illustrating comics. Artist and curator Luo Fei notes lianhuanhua illustration was a well-paid day job for artists before China developed a contemporary art market.

As to who were the young lianhuanhua artists of the early 1980s, Andrews (1997: 3) said that they were men "who spent their adolescences laboring on collective farms or factories. In spite of xenophobic rhetoric of the

Cultural Revolution period, the emphasis on propaganda painting led to a generation of young people who were thoroughly trained in Western drawing." Shanghai People's Art Publishing House and other publishers hired young men who were factory-worker artists during the Cultural Revolution, and the high profitability of lianhuanhua led to publishers seeking freelancers' works. Andrews (1997: 32) wrote that lianhuanhua were so "extraordinarily profitable" that publishers were able to attract "first rate artistic talent with the high fees and instant fame they could offer their artists."

Prominent painter Wang Wei agreed that drawing lianhuanhua in the early 1980s was profitable and that he was free to use a wide range of drawing styles. Claiming it was an honor to draw lianhuanhua at the time, Wang Wei said that for his work with a drama troupe, he was paid thirty-nine to forty-one yuan monthly, but he received 120 yuan to draw one lianhuanhua (Wang Wei, interview, 2012). Discussing his lianhuanhua experiences, Wang Wei (interview, 2012) recalled:

> I used different styles (brush, pen, etching, etc.), depending on the content. If I drew ancient stories, I used brush and long lines. For war stories, I used pen. Stories were given to us by the publishers. I did much research on the subjects, people's dress, customs, etc. I'd design everything—conceptualize, sketch, and ink the story. A draft then would be drawn for the editor's approval. He corrected the work, we would discuss it, and I would do a new version. The whole process was taken very seriously. All lianhuanhua artists were very serious; there were different values then. Every detail and style was carefully done; versions were drawn over and over.

The seriousness for which lianhuanhua were known came through in 1980, when the Chinese Central Fine Art Institute established the Department of Lianhuanhua and New Year's Paintings, officially acknowledging lianhuanhua as a fine art (Pan 2008: 706).

Wang Wei (interview, 2012) showed how his lianhuanhua (and the industry generally) dwindled in circulation by the mid-1980s; in 1980, his first title, *36*

Strategies, sold 1.8 million copies; a second, *Xuezhan shahe*, in 1984, 850,000 copies; and a third, in 1985, 340,000 copies. He blamed the entry of Japanese manga into China in 1984 as the main reason for lessened interest in lianhuanhua.

But others said that the 1986–87 crash of the lianhuanhua market was a result of the widespread availability of television sets and videocassette players; the diminished quality of books as publishers and artists quickened their production pace to meet reader demands (Cao 2002; Yu 2000; Lin 1997; Hong 1995); increased content censorship that rendered lianhuanhua irrelevant in a rapidly changing society; and the replacement of the government-secured distribution system with one for which publishing houses were responsible. The market reforms also affected bookstores, which would not buy unprofitable or marginal profit books without a government subsidy (Xu 1999: 53, quoted in Pan 2008: 706–7).

State publication bureaus attempted to save the industry by regulating publishing houses and the books' quality, but to little avail. In 1987, total sales of lianhuanhua amounted to fewer than eighty million copies (Jiang 1989: 8). Sales dropped considerably more in the 1990s, and lianhuanhua began to be collectables, rather than rich reading material. Collecting lianhuanhua for profit escalated, encouraging some renowned presses to republish old versions. In 2014, a set of *Romance of the Three Kingdoms* lianhuanhua sold for $32,000. Part of the reason for collecting lianhuanhua is nostalgia for the years before the open economy when government social welfare was a guarantee for everyone.

In recent times, the line between lianhuanhua and comics blurred, leading to the coinage of the term "cartoon-lianhuanhua." As Pan (2008: 713) explained:

> Several implications underlie the mixture of usage. First, it shows the compromise of traditional lianhuanhua with overseas comic art. Since the tastes of Chinese children and youth have been shaped largely by imported cartoons or comic books lately, the publishers tried to win back readers by catering to their preferences. Second, it signals the innovations within the lianhuanhua, which aims at competing

with the imported cartoons or comic books by learning from their artistic style and marketing strategy. Lastly, the term "cartoon-lianhuanhua" disclosed the direction that the pictorial book industry works toward in boosting the domestic market, i.e., while learning from overseas counterparts, certain elements of the traditional lianhuanhua would be maintained.

The dominant foreign influence after the late 1980s was the Japanese manga.

The Hybridization of Manga and Xinmanhua

By the end of the twentieth century, the influence of Japanese comics (manga) had spread across the globe, playing havoc with domestic markets, homogenizing, and sometimes hybridizing, drawing styles and ways of storytelling, transforming leisure-time activities, and occasionally nourishing a new interest in comics at a time when their popularity was waning (or was nearly nonexistent) because of competition from television, videocassettes, and the internet, and overused writing/drawing formulas (such as those of Disney and superhero publishers).

In East Asia, including China, the increased traffic in manga came during the mid-1990s, when Japan's "economic bubble" burst and its cultural image needed a boost; thus, the country was forced to search for foreign markets, to acknowledge the importance of cultural products such as manga, and to use comics and anime (animation) as cultural ambassadors. In fact, in 2007, Japan's then-foreign minister, Taro Aso, himself a manga devotee, said there should be a Nobel Prize for Japanese comics and established the International Manga Award, given yearly to a foreign cartoonist for his/her Japanese style comics. When Chinese artist Xiao Bai won the 2011 award for her "So Far, So Close," a tale of a university student who meets a boy who ends up being her son from the future, Taro Aso said that he hoped the awardees "will convey to others in their home countries what is interesting about manga, and will also look to expand the circle of friendship" (Meyers 2011).

125

Explanations for the widespread acceptance of manga around the world, including in China, were: the freshness and diversity of the style of drawings and stories, developing story plots that allow for involvement with complex and vulnerable characters; the alternative they offer to the worn-out Disney and US superhero formulas; their appeal to a generation that grew up playing video games and using the internet; their inexpensiveness (despite their huge size) relative to some other comics; their origins in a different, unknown culture; and their plentiful supply of sex of all forms and violence. The attraction to manga by Chinese youth also appealed to their new tastes in fashion, lifestyle, and entertainment, imported from Japan and the West, and their attempt to find an identity in the open market economy.[3] Still another explanation is that because of the one-child policy, today's youth is a demanding—yet a pressurized—generation; to release some of the pressure to succeed and adjust, they let their imaginations escape through manga and anime ("A Second Cultural Revolution" 2008). Also responsible for the widespread acceptance of manga was the creation of audiences through anime, which had strong connections to manga and which had been seen on television screens a decade or two earlier. The phenomenon was certainly prevalent in China.

However, China's tie-ins to manga preceded television by at least a half-century, beginning in 1921, when Feng Zikai was impressed with the "poetic resonance" and "casual essays executed in paintings [manga]" while studying in Tokyo (see fuller discussion in Chapter 2). Although manga as comic books did not yet exist, the term denoting cartoons or caricatures became widely used (Barmé 2002: 93).

Astro Boy and *Doraemon* comic books entered China on a small scale in the 1980s, but it was in the early 1990s that manga took root in the country, with *Saint Seiya*, *Dragon Ball*, *City Hunter*, and *Ranma ½*. *Saint Seiya* is credited with making the greatest impact when it was published and televised in 1990. Within a year, more than six million copies of *Saint Seiya* were sold. The continuous order demands exhausted its state-owned printing company, Hainan Publishing

Company of Photography and Fine Art, which could not keep up despite operating its machines twenty-four hours every day, overloading them until some broke down, and outsourcing work to smaller printeries (Wang Yang 2005: 19).

Piracy rampant throughout Asia helped to meet the augmented demand for manga and anime, offsetting disadvantages to audiences of copyrighted original materials that were costly, inaccessible, and in Japanese. Also, as Chew and Chen (2010: 173) wrote, Japanese publishers "did not have incentives to expand operations, distribute products, and glocalize contents for any anime and manga markets outside Japan. Moreover, the Chinese state was still unaware of the potential social impact of anime and manga and hence did not try to regulate their circulation in China."

This set of circumstances was ready-made for the pirates, who consequently produced large quantities of manga; constructed an elaborate distribution system of informal bookstores, stalls, and street vendors, a mail-order system, and rental facilities in pirated manga stores; and lowered the prices of manga for Chinese young people with limited amounts of money. Small cities and towns were provided pirated manga by large city book wholesalers, resulting in quickly made manga rental sheds that sprang up everywhere (Chew and Chen 2010: 173–74). Manga dissemination in China was also enhanced by new technology, especially the internet.

The most successful pirate publisher was Sichuan xiwang shudian (Sichuan Hope Book Store), which published the comics magazine, *Huashu dawang* (*Comic King*), initially very popular for its pirated manga series. Shortly, *Huashu dawang* filled some pages with traditional lianhuanhua stories and asked Chinese artists to draw their own manga-styled comics. As the latter became huge successes, other comics and youth magazines followed suit, leading to a new form, *xinmanhua*.

Matthew Chew and Lu Chen, whose article about xinmanhua is rare and welcome (2010: 174–75), offered a number of differences between traditional lianhuanhua and this hybrid; their named characteristics that make xinmanhua distinctive are:

Fig. 5.15. Yao Feila, an early xinmanhua artist.

Xinmanhua artists of this early period were mainly manga fans, white-collar workers, and students without any education in fine arts or professional training in the comic arts. These young artists took comic drawings as a part-time hobby; they were not organized into work units or professional workshops. . . . Because most of the xinmanhua artists took popular manga as their models, they tended to produce fictional stories, love fantasies, and fairy tale-like contents; their drawing style tended to be less realistic and more embellished than that of lianhuanhua. The images of characters in xinmanhua were as exaggerated as those of manga—e.g., female characters with huge starry eyes and extra long legs. Xinmanhua's use of camera style motion and filmic perspectives also distinguishes it from the static lianhuanhua perspective. In lianhuanhua and manhua, being sarcastic was a commonly used way to create comical effects, but in xinmanhua, artists adopted the symbols, facial expression, and gestures used in manga to achieve comical effects.

Being a hybrid, xinmanhua incorporated aspects of lianhuanhua and manga to create a new comics form drawn by Chinese artists, many with "unique personal touches in drawing, plots, and character design" (Chew and Chen 2010: 176). Although a few of the artists copied manga to the verge of plagiarism, others, such as Jiang Ling and Yao Feila, after a while veered off to create their own localized manga or xinmanhua.

Chinese government actions in 1994 and 1995 attempted to alleviate piracy and spur on a local comics industry. After legal Japanese manga publishers, in 1993 and 1994, filed complaints about piracy, the Chinese authorities forcefully shuttered Sichuan Xiwang Shudian, banned *Huashu dawang*, and temporarily subdued piracy, though some activity was carried out underground, but with limited success. On the positive side, they implemented the 5–15–5 Project under the General Administration of Press and Publication (GAPP), designed to establish "five major comics publishers within three years to publish fifteen series of comic books and establish five comics magazines" (Chew and Chen 2010: 176–77).

The five comics magazines had many of their set-up tasks already taken care of, inheriting production capabilities and markets established by the pirates and recruiting xinmanhua artists nurtured by *Huashu dawang* and its contemporaries. With the government crackdown, there was an unoccupied comics market to be filled. (*Huashu dawang*'s circulation alone had been 600,000 copies per issue.) The five magazines used their government sponsorship and funding to legally acquire copyrighted manga, but made sure to also fill pages with xinmanhua, something other than "dull [lianhuanhua?] historical stories of thousands of years ago" ("China Challenges . . ." 1996: 4).

Shaonian manhua (*Youth Comics*) and *Beijing katong* (*Beijing Comics*) were the longest-lived and most influential magazines; others were *Katong wang* (*King of Cartoon*) and *King of Popular Science Comics*. Stories in these magazines often had Chinese characters, ideological messages, and some weird twists; examples of the latter in *Beijing katong* include "Handsome Boy," who cheats in a singing competition, and still gets the girl; and "Nie Shuer," about a teenage "accident-prone martial-arts ingénue" ("China Challenges . . ." 1996: 4).

127

Reform, Modernization, Market Economy, and Cartooning

Fig. 5.16. Cover of *Beijing katong* (*Beijing Comics*), No. 6, 2001.

Named by one Western writer as an example of an ideologically or politically motivated comic book was the 1996 favorite, *Soccer Boy*, sixty episodes about a boy who makes China's national soccer team under a coach working to "overcome the laziness and lack of discipline that plagues the spoiled kids . . . growing up in the era of China's one-child policy" (Mufson 1996: A31). Published by the Sichuan Children's Publication Press and chosen by the government to lead the way in developing Chinese comics for children, *Soccer Boy* was a reaction to government and public outcries about the cultural "malnutrition" caused by children's reading of foreign comics, and a partial answer to President Jiang Zemin's request that animators "foster the lofty idea of working hard to invigorate China and train its youth into a new generation with lofty ideals, moral integrity, a good education and a strong sense of discipline" (A31).

Chew and Chen (2010: 177–78) contended that fans, not just the state, tried to regulate the spread of Japanese manga and promote xinmanhua for ideological and political reasons. They wrote:

A controversial aspect [for fans] was the prevalence of teenage love affairs in Japanese manga story lines . . . because of its breaches of contemporary Chinese social norms. Also controversial was the frequent depiction of sex in Japanese manga. . . . Fans with feminist sensibilities objected that teenage love scenes in manga discursively reinforced the inferior status of women, propagated conservative values,

Fig. 5.17. Tang Weiqing's *Nüchuangwang* took as its protagonist's model a famous Taiwanese film star.

and undermined the career ambition of Chinese young girls. (Ningmeng 1996)

These objections led to a modified second stage of xinmanhua development, where the stories had moral educational aspects, featured paragons and heroes, emphasized values opposing the sex and violence in manga, expressed love in "either a covert or moralistic mode" through ancient historical characters, mixing "romance with a magical fantasy context," and treated teenage love in an "edifying" manner (Chew and Chen 2010: 178).

To carry out campaigns against the negative influences of manga, artists and parents were asked to give talks at the magazines on ways to keep the deleterious contents out of children's hands, and artists sometimes informed students at leading universities on how to keep their studying and comics-reading in a manageable balance. Also, to reduce the impact of manga, the magazines called for non-Japanese diversified styles and contents. Some xinmanhua artists, such as Zheng Xusheng, Yao Feila, and Tang Weiqing, looked to Hong Kong and Taiwan popular culture for inspiration; others, like Nie Jun, borrowed from American and European characters and images; and still others reverted to traditional Chinese painting skills, including ink-wash painters such as Zhao Jia, Wang Ziyang, and Quan Yingsheng.

Near the end of the 1990s, xinmanhua did well, sprouting from the five magazines into single books circulated throughout China, making famous artists such as Jiang Ling, Xiao Yanfei, Hu Rong, and Yao Feila, who won prizes in Japan and Hong Kong, and becoming "mature, localized, and diversified" (Chew and Chen 2010: 180).

Then, by 2000 and 2001, China's comic scene changed as the official magazines suffered financially;

Reform, Modernization, Market Economy, and Cartooning

not able to meet payrolls and, in the process, losing artists and other staff members, all five had died by 2005. Chew and Chen (2010: 180) pointed out the factors that led to this reversal of fortune:

1. Technological advancements in digital media allowed pirate publishers to make available large quantities of CDs, VCDs, and DVDs at extremely low costs, thus greatly lowering the purchasing price of pirated Japanese animation, while pirated Japanese manga prices escalated. The result: Chinese audiences shifted from printed (pirated and legal) manga to pirated Japanese anime.

2. The pirated manga of this period were unauthorized Chinese translations of Japanese manga published in Taiwan and Hong Kong. These versions were half the size of China's comic books and they were expensive. A new version of pirated printed comics, *si-pin-yi* (four pages in one page), minimalized the page size and then printed four pages on a thirty-two-fold page. Though printed on bad quality paper, and using faded ink and a difficult reading order, these books still were also out of the price range of Chinese readers. (181)

3. The five official magazines were adversely affected by the revival of pirated manga. Also, "as direct affiliates to the state bureaucracy, these magazines were hardly motivated to respond to market forces or labor demands." (181–82)

Alongside these changes, a new platform for xinmanhua was created, the semi-legal info-magazines brought out by non-government personnel. Prevalent also in other parts of Asia (particularly in Malaysia), info-magazines collect, translate, and publish information on manga and anime from Japanese print magazines and the internet. Typically, an issue includes information on Japanese manga and anime publications, reviews by Chinese fans or editors, and a Japanese anime VCD. In China, info-magazines (e.g., *Dongman shidai*

[*Animation and Comic Times*], *Xinganxian* [*Comics and Ani's Reports*], and *Manyou* [*Comic Fans*]), from 1998 to 2006, published various adaptations of xinmanhua, one example being the combining of oil painting techniques with Japanese manga style. According to Chew and Chen (2010: 183–84), *Manyou* was most active, devoting the most space to xinmanhua, from artists who had been previously with the official magazines—Yao Feila, Qi Xiao, Xia Da, Yao Wei, Ruan Junting, Yan Kai, and Zhang Bin—and holding annual comics contests and festivals. When the internet sucked the life out of other info-magazines, *Manyou* survived by targeting teenage girls with original xinmanhua works that played to their love fantasies, and by securing government financial help in 2008.

Both the bane of, and a boost for comics, the internet offered new possibilities for xinmanhua to thrive, most especially through *oekaki* bulletin board systems (BBS), beginning in 2002. A few artists had applied computer technology to their drawing of comics in the late 1990s, but the oekaki BBS helped anyone with the desire to draw comics to use computer graphics and post their works. Many online forums were created in the early years of the twenty-first century, accommodating manga, anime, and xinmanhua fans and creators with reviews, technical knowledge, interviews, and spaces to share opinions.

The "anonymity and decentralized circumstance" offered by the internet enabled Chinese comics artists to dispense alternative views and stories, whether they be "distasteful" manga or "politically sensitive or socio-morally unacceptable contents" (Chew and Chen 2010: 186). Many comics artists post such alternative perspectives on the social media site Douban, begun in 2005. As R. Orion Martin (2015) indicated after interviewing Douban-user cartoonists, "Scarlet-Faced Dog" and "Bu Er Miao," much of the content of these comics is purposely weird, nonsensical, or bizarre. "Scarlet-Faced Dog" sometimes makes use of "horrifying violence," while remaining "undeniably funny" (Martin 2015). "Bu Er Miao" draws sci-fi escapism in brilliant colors, with her work usually taking on a

130

"one-thing-leads-to-another sense of discovery" (Martin 2015). She tries to put all of her "weird" ideas into the comics that often feature the characters Electric Cat and Lightning Dog.

One common, potentially sensitive topic of online comics is the upheaval of Chinese society caused by the race to "modernization." As the senior author of this book wrote elsewhere:

> One such popular online work in the late 2000s was Liu Gang's "Suicide Rabbit," portrayed with "gentle humor the million little abuses suffered by Chinese people as their society endures a bumpy transformation" (Cody 2007). Another strip by Luo Yonghao, published online and in a literary magazine, followed a fly character trapped in a glass bottle trying to escape, an allusion to the dilemma of Chinese people trying to follow their heart, truth, and honesty, instead of the increasingly materialistic Chinese society (Xing 2010). As another example, Benjamin Zhang Bin's comic books push the belief that materialism and money are not the best paths to happiness. (Lent 2015a: 39)

A comic book created in 2015 by a Chinese lecturer and his students in Australia for exportation to China's rural areas, addressed the issue of the "left-behind children." Called *Rural Super Kids*, the manga-style comic was meant to inspire and entertain some of the sixty-one million children left in the countryside when their parents moved to urban areas to seek work.

Some of these alternative comic books are brought out by self-publishing collectives, either in China or abroad, that produce underground comics. These mini-groups, such as Cult Youth and Special Comics, usually consist of young artists who make a modest living in the video game or animation industries, and spend their free time drawing comics to be critiqued by others in the collective. Some of this work makes it to book form, but most goes unnoticed because its subject matter is frowned upon by the state and/or has no commercial value. Cult Youth is an independent Beijing collective formed to make and redefine manhua. From 2007 to 2011, Cult Youth artists self-published three collections

of works which they sold online. Founded by "Chairman Cai," the community is a "group of friends having fun on the side of their day-jobs, not a potential career path" (Damluji 2011). An online documentary about Cult Youth starts with the narration: "If you were not born in the '80s and couldn't decode the plots, then give up! This is not for you! This is a new generation free of the reasons and worries of the past" (Damluji 2011).

One comics genre that has blossomed in China since the late 1990s, despite threats from the state, educational institutions, and the mass media, is the boys' love (aka *danmei* in China) manga. Depicting boy-to-boy love, danmei is very popular among Chinese female students and heavy internet users, as it generally is elsewhere. Early on, press coverage of danmei alternated between hot and cold; sometimes the media credited the comics with promoting gender equality, other times, they blamed them for stimulating sexual deviance—converting readers into homosexuals. One must remember that homosexuality in China was not decriminalized until 1999 and not de-categorized as a mental illness until 2001. After the Anti-Danmei Campaign of 2007, any publication and distribution of boys' love manga was deemed illegal. There were protests against the ruling that implemented protest postings, moved content to offshore servers, eventually revived content in cyberspace, and displayed supportive slogans at comics conventions (Liu 2009).

Besides the lianhuanhua, manga, xinmanhua, and online comics, newspaper comic strips provide another outlet for China's cartoonists and a source of enjoyment for readers. Most are humor-based and offer a gag a day. The tabloid *Beijing wanbao* (*Beijing Evening Newspaper*), for instance, uses a mixture of one- and multiple-panel strips in color each day.

The authors of this book have not seen other genres (adventure, love, mystery, etc.) among the strips, nor serialized stories. An exception to the latter was Sun Xiaogang's (b. 1962) "Lang Que" ("Sparrow Lang"), serialized full-page weekly in color in *Zhongguo shaonian bao* (*China Youth*) for three years at the turn of the millennium, and continuing to be published in a set of fifty-five books. The strip is built around the character Lang Que, whose story links together with those of other characters. Sun Xiaogang (interview, 2016) described "Lang Que" as:

> like a soap opera; it lasts very long. A story looks to be independent, but it fits with the previous and next episodes. I use humor and art to tell stories about the sources of societal problems. All of the strips deal with real issues or what I have experienced in life.

New Breed of Cartoonists

Regularly—though not rapidly—comics are gaining a foothold in China, and, in the process, some cartoonists have gained fame and commercial success. No doubt the internet, with its capacity for cartoonists to network and to help them in producing and distributing their works more speedily and efficiently, has been a major boon. Perhaps equally important has been the business acumen some artists have gained, allowing them to promote their works more widely, spin-off episodes into television shows and movies, and sell their characters for merchandising and licensing purposes.

Recently, a coterie of clever and enterprising cartoonists has put China on the international comic art stage through their participation in exhibitions, cooperative projects, and competitions. They hail from all types of comics (manga, webtoons, alternative, and underground) and exhibit a variety of drawing styles, ranging from cinematic-type manga to traditional Chinese ink-wash paintings. Their common trait is their youthfulness and the sense of adventure and excitement that comes with it. Among them are some successful women cartoonists, breaking the stranglehold males had had on the profession.

Among China's most prominent female comics creators are Rain (Ru An), Yishan Li, Coco Wang, Xia Da, A Geng, and Zhang Xiaobai, all in their mid-thirties at the time of this writing and nearly all with study and/or work experiences in Europe, North America, or Japan.

They are part of the "turn-of-the-century" generation of women cartoonists, the first of its kind in the long history of Chinese comic art; previously, the total number of female comics artists could be counted on one or two hands. Manga contributed to this gender change of personnel (A Geng, interview, 2013).

Rain (Ru An) (b. 1980) has many of the characteristics of the "turn-of-the-century" women artists—youth, foreign study in US, publishing experience abroad (two collections in Canada), stories with much emotion and a "strong Chinese feeling," and drawings that "play on the romance and whimsy of captured moments" (Cha 2007). She usually does handmade comics in watercolor and sometimes with the aid of computer software. Her first comic books were *Ethereal Wings* (2004), *Midnight Ink* (2005), and *Silent Rainbow* (2007), all published by Comicfans Culture. Rain has also produced animation and has contributed to cartoon magazines, such as *Katong wang* (*Cartoon King*), *Katong xianfeng* (*Cartoon Vanguard*), *Manyou* (*Comic Fans*), and *Shaonian manhua* (*Youth Cartoon*).

Born in Tianjin, Yishan Li (b. 1981) now lives in Edinburgh, Scotland, with her British husband. Her first manhua and her own favorite, *Our Dormitory*, was influenced by manga and based on her experiences while studying at Nankai University. First serialized in *Katong wang* (December 2001–February 2002), *Our Dormitory* was converted to a graphic novel in 2003. Both *Our Dormitory* and *My Memory* (in *Shaonian manhua*, 2002) were drawn while Li was a Nankai student, sometimes during lectures. Between 2005 and 2008, the very prolific Li published or prepared for publication twelve other comic books with publishers in the US, England, and France. Comfortable working with all genres, Li prefers drawing "girly stuff" (Hooper 2007). Her work shows a strong manga influence.

Coco Wang has left an indelible mark on the promotion of manhua in China and abroad. Straddling Beijing, Hong Kong, and London, Wang has represented her generation of experimental and underground Chinese creators well, publishing a *tu wen*[4] (diary comic), *Coco Goes to Study in England* (2007); a series of moving documentary webcomics about the 2008 Sichuan earthquake; the graphic novel *Meet William*; and a strip, "Old and New," for *ArtReview Asia*; as well as assisting on a musical production and developing animation and children's book projects. Perhaps most innovative was the conversion of her traditional Beijing courtyard house into a private comics/manga club, "Coco's Yard Story," a type of café which requires advance booking and has a trove of "comics, manga, illustration, graphic design, fine art books, pop-up books, children's illustration and movies," the latter shown in an underground home theater on the premises. "Coco's Yard Story" is unique in China in that it is developing a comics community and providing its members a comfortable place to gather (Gravett 2008).

While still in high school, Xia Da (b. 1981) published her first comic, *Chengzhang* (*Growing Up*) in *Beijing manhua* (*Beijing Cartoon*). Her doll-like characters and bold strokes made her popular both in China and Japan. Her 2009 comic book, *Zi buyu* (*You Keep Silence*), was serialized in Japan's top comics magazine, *Ultra Jump*. While still in her twenties, she had created other favorites, including *Siyue wuyu* (*April Story*), *Midelande chenxing* (*Midland Stars*), and *Luoxue wusheng* (*Silent Falling Snow*), the latter adapted for television. Xia Da said she is inspired by ancient Chinese culture, and her first comic book started from traditional poems (see *Huaxi City Newspaper*, zhidao.baidu.com and wenwen. soso.com).

Manga also plays a role in the career of painter/cartoonist A Geng (b. 1979). When manga found their way into China in the 1990s, teenager A Geng became interested in them, impressed with their "sketch, style" (A Geng, interview, 2013). Her first comics story, "Blue Sky," was published in a magazine in 2000, after which the editor wanted her to expand it into a book. She declined the offer to pursue her studies at art school, which she financed by the voluminous amount of illustration work she did. In 2008, A Geng turned to drawing comics, initially doing a magazine comic called "Appointment Drawing." The continuing story, "Tiptoe Looking," about young people facing issues of love, friendship, and

societal tensions has appeared in five volumes; the sales of the first four reached a total of 200,000 copies. Additionally, A Geng teaches in the Guangxi Art College and works as an illustrator and painter.

A Geng does not find gender to be an inhibiting factor in her career as a cartoonist. She said that before 2000, societal constraints about the role of women in society handicapped their chances to become cartoonists. Today, however, publishers are eager to publish comic books, including those by women; according to A Geng (interview, 2013), Chinese women's comics have not fully made their mark because they have a limited domestic audience of primarily young girls and are not published abroad.

Other young women drawing comic books include Zhu Letao, influenced by manga in titles such as *Ma ta, Gaozhong 5 ban riji* (*The Diary of Class Five in High School*), *Yingzi* (*Shadow*), and *Pugongying* (*Dandelion*), and Qian Haiyan, whose works are characterized by their humor and a deep awareness of humanity and literature.

Stalwarts among the new generation of Chinese male comics creators and entrepreneurs are Quan Yingsheng and Chen Weidong, founders and owners of the two largest comics companies in China, Beijing Heavycomics Culture & Media Co, Ltd., and Shenjie manhua gongsi, respectively.

Quan Yingsheng has the creative traits of a multitalented artist while also exhibiting that rare quality among cartoonists: the ability to make money. Quan draws and publishes manga, xinmanhua, and manhua. His manhua are distinctly Chinese in aesthetics and storytelling, applying traditional ink-wash painting techniques to stories such as *Chenjisihan* (*Genghis Khan*, 1999), *Chanlai chanqu* (*Buddhahood Twines*, 2002), eighty paintings describing a little monk's story, *Qigai anzai* (*Beggar Boy*, 2003), an adaptation of a popular Taiwanese homonymy, and *Geshaer Wang* (*King of Gesar*, 2011), an account of the world's longest historical epic (more than a million verses) relating the ancient history of Tibet. *Chenjisihan* (*Genghis Khan*), which Quan drew, wrote, and produced, is his major work because of its detailed, strong,

Fig. 5.18. Quan Yingsheng's *Gesaerwang* (*King of Gesar*), 2011, 10–11. Courtesy of Quan Yingsheng.

and subtle drawings, as well as a plot described by the company as "deep and dignified, simple and implicit" (Beijing Heavycomics brochure).

Quan (interview, 2011) intertwines comics and traditional painting to disprove people's perception that "if you draw comics, you cannot draw as an artist." He also found through the years that his ink-wash painting comics do better financially than his manga titles. Because the manga-style comics market is already gorged, there is very little room for expansion, while the company's ink-wash painting manhua, because of their uniqueness and very limited talent pool, are popular and have potential for overseas sales (Lent and Xu 2012).

Reducing its manga production in favor of Chinese-style manhua, Beijing Heavycomics publishes a long line of manhua (many in multi-volume collections) devoted to Chinese adventure, history, love, sports, detective, and other genres. Among them are *Zhongguo gudai shenhua* (*Chinese Ancient Fairy Tales*), ten volumes,

each of 200 pages, all in color with seven pages of ink-wash painting illustrations as an insert; *Hongloumeng* (*Dream of Red Chamber*, 2004), twelve volumes of love comics; *Manhua zhongguo gongfu* (*Chinese Kungfu Comics*), recounting the history of this martial art form, and the Entertainment and Teaching Comics series, consisting of manhua about Chinese idioms, world inventors, basketball boys, Chinese fables, diaries, a biography about Yishou Liu, and others. Besides educational manhua for children from kindergarten through high school, Quan had also published ten graphic novels and other adult manhua by 2012.

Keeping abreast of the field, in June 2013, Quan Yingsheng created an online comics series, "Zhongguo jingqi xiansheng ("Chinese Thriller"), with QQ.com; within a year, it was the server's top site with one billion hits. After its first three months, "Chinese Thriller" was turned into an animated work by QQ.com. Quan incorporated ink-wash painting, Buddhist painting, comics, animation, and oil painting, all of which he is adept at, into the series, as well as a Daoist perspective and content which mix current events and "social hot issues," including corruption, with humorous and ridiculing portrayals of people's characteristics. Readers and viewers are mainly white-collar workers (Quan Yingsheng, correspondence, 2015).

Quan uses a variety of styles to meet audience preferences. His company is extremely prolific, having published by late 2011, more than 1,000 weekly or monthly series and single books in China, Hong Kong, South Korea, the United States, Taiwan, and Thailand. He said he allows two or three internet companies to have his company's books (Quan, interview, 2011). The titles that spurred Beijing Heavycomics' development are *Genghis Khan*; *Zhongguo shenhua* (*China Myth*, 2004), a twelve-volume series simultaneously published in China and South Korea (first on the internet), which became one of the top three bestselling Korean comics; *Chaoji baobao* (*Super Baby*, 2007), a children's drama published with a South Korean partner, and *State Ranger*, a Sino-United States comics series.

If any one cartoonist and comics company epitomizes the hybridization of comics in China, it is Quan Yingsheng and Beijing Heavycomics. In about sixteen years, Quan has shown how it is possible to create aesthetically outstanding xinmanhua and manhua, while also publishing audience satisfying manga.

Chen Weidong is also an influential cartoonist, recognized for the strong literary value of his comics, and, like Quan, he is a creative businessman willing to risk taking different approaches. Chen established Shenjie manhua gongsi (aka Creator World Cartoon Co.) in Tianjin in 1997, and as the company faced the prospect of closing by 2001, he reversed traditional market strategies with much success. Usually original comics seek domestic markets before going international; in Shenjie's case, successful deals with South Korean and Japanese companies acting as international copyright agencies spurred domestic publishers to join Shenjie's ventures. In another atypical move, when Shenjie received funding as the company faced bankruptcy, its owners

immediately bought houses for its artists and significantly increased their incomes (Zhao 2014). Chen also quickened the pace of reaching international markets by setting up a joint venture, Cunren Cartoon Co., Ltd. (aka Villagers [Tianjin] Manga Co.), of which he owns 70 percent of the shares (the other 30 percent is owned by Korean capital) and completely controls management, finance, and personnel (Zhao 2014).

Shenjie's comic books combine Chinese painting techniques with literary classics, such as *Romance of the Three Kingdoms*, *Dream of the Red Chamber*, *The Water Margin*, and *The Journey to the West*. Chen, with Liang Xiaolong, were the first PRC cartoonists whose works entered the extremely competitive Japanese market ("Comic Books of Chinese . . ." 2006). Chen, nevertheless, felt that Chinese comics had to differ from manga in form, style, and language.

The model used by Shenjie to recreate Chinese literary classics in a comics format depends on: "First, applying Chinese painting elements adds value; second, innovative funding and distribution models assist the generation of content; and third, attracting and retaining talent is crucial" (Zhao 2014).

Perhaps, a fourth factor should be added: promoting works and the company through innovative campaigns and contests. In 2014, Shenjie launched a comic design competition in South Korea open to cartoonists worldwide, to find a cartoon character, "Spring Wawa," to represent Chinese culture during Spring Festival 2014. The contest, whose winner was to receive $48,900, was designed to "promote China's traditional festival culture overseas and stimulate related economy," much like Christmas has done globally (Xinhua 2014).

Though not owners or chief executives of comics companies, cartoonists such as Zheng Jun, Benjamin Zhang Bin, and Nie Jun added immeasurably to the new comics revolution. A rock star, Zheng Jun was also adept at the business side of comics. He used his musical profession to create a story about a dog that grew up in a Buddhist temple and his travails en route to becoming a rock star in Beijing. The first edition of this manhua sold all of its 100,000 copies, was made into a movie, and spawned dolls and other merchandise ("Tibetan Rock Dog Rocks On" 2009).

Benjamin Zhang Bin, more commonly known as Benjamin, is an exemplar of a growing phenomenon across Asia—a local cartoonist sidelining for the American comics company Marvel, for which he draws book covers. Working from Beijing, Benjamin is unusual among his peers, painting his manhua in bright colors instead of the usual black-and-white. Because of this extra step and making his characters very realistic, Benjamin produces limited numbers of manhua. His first work published in the West, *Orange*, (in France by Xiao Pan and the US by TokyoPop), reportedly took three years to finish. Other early Benjamin books were *Remember* and *One Day*, both with Spanish, German, and English editions, and *Flash*. Benjamin's stories revolve around everyday people in their late teens and adolescence. He has admitted that his characters, like himself, are "a bit withdrawn," in a "doubting, lonely" mood, and that madness, suicide, and mental disturbance are themes of his manhua. His explanation was that these negative thoughts are on the minds of many Chinese youth, who are under

> enormous pressure, psychologically and professionally, as a result of the dazzling development of China. There is also the paradox which affects these young people's moods a lot, between what they got from early on through an education centred round devotion to your country, and the logic they adopted later on of personal profit and individualism now ruling our society. (interview by Rebecca Fernandez, in Gravett 2008)

"Young wanderers, a naughty boy who flees his comic book, a blind girl seeking her eyes with the help of a magic dog" typify the themes of Nie Jun's comics stories, the first of which was published in a Beijing magazine in 1995. His most famous strip is "My Street," serialized in *Beijing Cartoon* from 2001 to 2003, about two youth looking for love and life's meaning while living abroad. Nie Jun's "Electronic Bus" strip, also containing a warm feeling based on love, won an important Japanese award in 2003. Early on, he published two books of comics, *Fox*

Diudiu and *Don't Want to Grow Up*, the latter a nostalgic account of his childhood; he described his works as "very Chinese" ("Cartoonist: Nie Jun" 2005).

China's reform, modernization, and open market economy have had varying degrees of impact on the development of this new breed of cartoonists and their manhua and xinmanhua. Certainly, most are exposed to comics outside China, from which they learn and benefit by having their works published and exhibited abroad. Also, though cartoonists are still restrained, they are freer under post-Mao reforms to experiment with new formats and contents than at any time since perhaps the 1930s. Furthermore, these artists have options to work with modern technology, such as computers, as well as traditional tools. These three factors have allowed artists to work outside the mainstream in venues that lend themselves to experimental, challenging comics.

At the same time, the cartoonists and critics show that the new era is encumbered with problems, some tied to the opening of China to a market economy and modernity. For one thing, some critics observe, China has become a "big post-production" country where top Chinese cartoonists are used as tools of US or European production houses; the incentive is mainly monetary. The most severe problem—one that afflicts Chinese society at large—pertains to cartoonists chasing quantity strictly for profits, rather than quality of workmanship. Benjamin said of adapting one's art to what the market demands:

> As for young artists, or the most talented ones, the excessive fierce pursuit of things with nothing to do with art (things about business, for example) can't help but pollute their artistic free will, affecting the quality of their work, as well as stifling their chances for their art to evolve in the future. (Gravett 2008)

Coco Wang minced no words in discussing the effects of China as a "fast-profit world":

> Oh yes it's good to see there are opportunities and profits everywhere now, but if you are slow, someone else will

snatch the profit away from under your noses. You must be quick. You don't want to do this job for 5 Euros? Someone will be happy to do this for 3 Euros. OK, I will do it for 5 Euros, and I was only given two hours to do the job, so I will do it fast and the quality won't be good, but the "good" part is that my client doesn't care about the quality, they just want the thing done quickly and throw it into the market to grab that [sic] quick profits. Why doesn't the client care? Because the customers don't care! Why don't the customers care? Because there are too many bad quality things in the market that they wouldn't appreciate the difference of good and bad quality things. (Gravett 2008)

She felt such a "vicious cycle" adversely affected Chinese cartoonists' own comics, not just what they were commissioned to do for foreign companies.

Yishan Li said that because of doing work for overseas companies, and incessantly reading Japanese, European, and American comics imports all their lives, Chinese cartoonists scarcely have a distinctly Chinese drawing style. In her view, "it is hard to tell what is a Chinese comic just by looking at the pictures. . . . It is only easier to tell which one is Chinese Manhua when it comes to the story" (Oliver 2008). But, as is the case with Chinese cinema, comics and animation stories and scripts are weak; they are also short, not in series form as with manga. Coco Wang said that contemporary comics stories cannot stand the test of time; that is why "you see relics like San Mao [sic] and Monkey King being dressed up again for big screen now." Her explanation is that artists focus on techniques of drawing because it is safe: "You are not breaking any rules or regulations, so it's a surer way to get things published" (Gravett 2008).

Perhaps the dilemma faced by respected underground comics artist Lu Ming speaks to what is happening to manhua production: her works are unsuitable for the state but not commercial enough for investors (Vincent 2009).

President Xi Jinping was very much aware of nearly all of the shortcomings mentioned here when he addressed the Beijing Forum on Literature and Art on October 15, 2014. Quoting Mao, Marx, and Lenin,

President Xi emphasized "rejuvenation" or "restoration" of Chinese culture, recognizing globalization of the arts will continue, but in China, the arts can and should be managed and controlled, despite the freedoms achieved through market reform. Because of the president's blanket indictment of the direction of Chinese culture, some of which has been addressed in these pages, large segments of his speech are quoted here under eight categories:

Striking out at vulgar popular culture

Since reform and opening, our nation's arts have ushered in a new springtime, with the creation of a great many acclaimed works. At the same time, it cannot be denied that, from the perspective of artistic creation, we have quantity over quality . . . and problems of plagiarism, imitation, stereotypes and repetition, assembly-line production, and fast-food consumption. Some works ridicule the sublime, warp the classics, subvert history, or defile the masses and heroic characters. In others good and evil cannot be distinguished, ugliness replaces beauty, and the dark side of society is over-emphasized. Still others blindly chase and cater to public tastes, vulgar interests, chase financial gain, and provoke the "ecstasy" of the senses. Others churn out baseless works of shoddy quality and make irrelevant comparisons, creating a kind of cultural "garbage," while others pursue luxury . . . flaunt wealth and ostentation, and emphasize external appearance over content. There are also those obsessed with the so-called "art for art's sake" . . . who remove themselves from the masses and reality. All of these should be a warning to us: the arts must not lose their direction within the trend of the market economy, they must not deviate on the question of whom they are for, otherwise art will have no vitality.

On the fickleness of contemporary culture

In discussions with several people in the arts, I asked what was the most obvious problem in the arts. Without prior discussion, all brought up the same word: fickleness. Some feel, that if you cannot realize a pragmatic value in a work of art or make money out of it . . . it's not worth it. This type of attitude can not only mislead the creative process, it can also allow vulgar works to become very popular, letting the bad money drive out the good. As the history of human artistic endeavors makes clear, shortsightedness . . . and creating shoddy works is not only a kind of injury to the arts, but also a kind of injury to the moral life of society. Entertaining the simply sense organs will not equate to a happy spirit. The arts must win the people's approval, fancy but ineffectual work is not acceptable and egotistical self-promotion is not acceptable. . . .

The market value of the arts is secondary to social value

Compared to social benefits, economic benefits are secondary. If a conflict arises between the two . . . , economic benefit must be subservient to the social benefit, and market value must be subservient to social value. The arts cannot be a slave to the market, they must not be covered in filthy lucre. When it comes to outstanding works of art, it is best if they first achieve success in terms of ideology and art, and subsequently are welcomed by the market. The ideals of aesthetics and the independent value of art must be maintained, and while we cannot neglect and ignore indicators such as distribution, ratings, click-through rates, box office gross and others, we also cannot prioritize these indicators and be led by the market.

A conservative and patriotic view of arts

Contemporary arts must also take patriotism as a theme, leading the people to establish and maintain correct views of history, nationality, statehood, and culture while firmly building up the integrity and confidence of the Chinese people.

Arts must not chase after the foreign

If we treat the foreign with reverence, treat the foreign as beautiful, only follow the foreign, take overseas prize-seeking as the highest goal, blindly following and unsuccessfully impersonating others . . . there is absolutely no future! In

fact, foreigners have also come to us seeking inspiration and source materials, with Hollywood making *Kung Fu Panda*, *Mulan*, and other films using our cultural resources.

On the need to sanitize foreign art forms

After reform and opening, our country widely studied and borrowed from the world's arts. Nowadays, circumstances are still the same, and many art forms arise from overseas, such as hip-hop, breakdance, etc., but we should only adopt them if the masses approve of them, while also endowing them with healthy, progressive content.

Foreign films stimulate the domestic industry

Nowadays the world is an open world, and the arts must also compete in the global marketplace, and without competition there is not vitality. For example, in the realm of film, which is experiencing market competition, foreign films have not defeated our domestically produced films, but have stimulated our domestic film production to raise its quality and standards, to develop in the midst of market competition, and possess even greater competitive power.

On the need for greater control of new art forms

When it comes to the production and distribution of traditional arts and culture, we have a set of relatively mature organizational systems and management measures in place, but for new art forms, we still lack effective management methods and techniques. In this matter, we must catch up and work hard to come to a resolution. We must deepen reforms, improve policies, and establish robust systems in order to create quality products and develop talent. (Canaves 2015)

The State's Roles in Cartooning

Governments normally deal with mass media—and by extension comic art forms—in facilitating, regulating, and restricting capacities; all too often, the latter two dominate. In China, since the mid-2000s, the state has facilitated the development of comics and animation at a level perhaps equaled only by the government of South Korea.

The Government as Supporter
of Comics and Animation

Very likely following the model set up by the South Korean government beginning in 1994, Chinese authorities about a decade later recognized the benefits of pumping up animation and comics as important cultural products. Two significant changes birthed primarily in the 1990s led to this official acknowledgment—the conversion from a planned economy to a socialist market economy and the technological revolution led by the internet. Also catching the authorities' eyes was the prevalence of foreign-produced and culturally irrelevant and even damaging animation on China television, and Japanese, American, and other countries' comic books in bookstores, and the possibility of the domestic production of these creative industries becoming the third pillar of the economy with the potential to achieve more than 10 percent of the gross domestic product.

Efforts to offset the strong foreign influences were partially stimulated by the findings of a nationwide survey that revealed the most popular comics and animation in China were from Japan and South Korea, at 60 percent, US and Europe, 29 percent, and China/Hong Kong/Taiwan, 11 percent. Another survey conducted in Beijing, Shanghai, and Guangzhou, reported in 2006 (Cai 2006), showed that foreign-made comic books, animation movies, and TV series took 90 percent of the Chinese market. We saw the same thing when we visited a comic book/internet café near Shanghai University in 2005; we were not able to find even one mainland China product, as the books and comics-related merchandise were manga-related with a smattering of Korean and Hong Kong works.

After some expensively produced animated works flopped in the late 1990s and early 2000s, and as many Chinese economists claimed that China was entering a post-industrialization age, government officials began seeing animation and comics as soft industries that could help to sustain the country's rapid growth. (For a discussion of animation's economic status during this time, see Chapter 6.)

Although the comics and animation industries were expanding prior to 2006, and the government was already announcing its supportive plans (see Chapter 6), it was during the 11th Five-Year Projection for Social and Economic Development (2006–2010) that this sector was listed as a key cultural industry to be developed at the national level. In short order, the central government provided technological innovation funds, preferential income, and value-added tax policies to small- and medium-sized enterprises. Local governments encouraged the establishment of new animation and comics companies by subsidizing office leases and giving tax breaks and "outright payments for finished products" ("Drawing on Creative Enterprise" 2014). In late 2009, the Ministry of Culture began overseeing the development of animation and comics.

Even by 2006, more than twenty provinces had listed animation and comics as a new industry; nine cities had established their own production bases with preferential policies; and many animation/comics extravaganzas, such as festivals, competitions, and conferences, had taken place. Between 2006 and 2010, the industry's financial value grew at an average of 30 percent annually, and at the end of the 11th Five-Year Projection in 2010, the combined worth of the animation and comics industries was more than 47 billion yuan ($7.7 billion) ("Drawing on Creative Enterprise" 2014). The number of government-supported animation base cities rose to forty during this period. This rapid development resulted from the largesse given by central and provincial governments. Some provincial governments were more generous in dishing out incentives than others; for instance, Shenzhen's Yijin Animation and Comics Base, which upon its inauguration in May 2006, provided low-interest loans, waived rent for three years, and gave cash awards to companies whose works were broadcast on national CCTV or local stations (Cai 2006).

Much support came through preferential tax policies to support the comics and animation industries, issued by the State Administration of Taxation (SAT) and the Ministry of Finance (MoF) in July 2009. Categories of preferential tax policies named by SAT and MoF to aid comics and animation were VAT, enterprise income tax, business tax, and import duties and import VAT.

The availability of this strong financial support has had negative results in many instances, according to some sources (including President Xi Jinping, as already discussed), who claim that making money is of primary importance, rather than providing creative entertainment for the public. Jin Peng, deputy chief for animation in the Ministry of Culture's Department of Cultural Industries, blamed some companies for not researching the markets or profits but instead "diligently" researching local governments' policies. The subsidies have been so plentiful that it is possible for an animation company to win sufficient government funds to cover the entire cost of a production (Wang Xiaoqing and Mei Ke 2012).

In some cases, the government largesse has been siphoned off for personal uses. As an example, a recent Yubao municipal government-funded production budgeted at 12 million yuan was the subject of an inquiry by thirteen industry experts who thought the film was allocated at least 10 million yuan more than was used in its making (Wang Xiaoqing and Mei Ke 2012).

Although most of the emphasis is placed on helping animation businesses—which is understandable, because of the export possibilities of animation and the role it plays in filling time on the burgeoning number of television stations—comic book companies benefit, too, notably through state support in promoting manhua in China and abroad. Financial backing, mainly from provincial and municipal governments, led to the creation of scores (perhaps as high as 100) of extravagant festivals and competitions scattered across China, most meant to draw attention to manhua and animation, recognize artists, exhibit Chinese cartoons, comics, games, and comics-related merchandise, and garner international recognition. The festivals are key to developing an industrial chain in which derivative products—such

as comics, clothing, candy, toys, and stationery—are popular and lucrative, to such an extent that adaptability of plots and characters to merchandise is considered when scripts are written (Zheng 2013). Even so, a major problem in making huge profits from ancillary products is rampant piracy.

The senior author of this book lectured at comics and animation festivals in Guiyang, Beijing, Hangzhou, Changzhou, Changchun, Wuhan, and Fuzhou, and is co-founder and co-chair of the Asian Youth Animation and Comics Competition, held annually beginning in 2007. These festivals typically include talks by academic and comic art professionals, forums, numerous exhibitions, animation and comics competitions with substantial money awards, cosplay, marketing spaces, and an elaborate, televised award ceremony with performances by Chinese entertainers. Attendance rivals (and, in some cases, far exceeds) that of the largest such festivals in Europe and the United States, drawing hundreds of thousands of visitors. The State Administration of Radio, Film, and Television (SARFT)-sponsored First China International Cartoon and Animation Festival (CICAF) in Hangzhou (started in 2005) had 1.23 million attendees at its 2013 event, and generated 13.62 billion yuan ($2.6 billion) in contract signings. By 2015, when some local governments and their business partners failed to see the results they expected in attracting international clients to join their comics/animation production zones, funding was considerably decreased. One criticism of the allocation of government funding is that most of it goes into the construction of too many animation industry parks (Raugust 2008).

Also tied to this government support is the planning/building of comics and animation museums/centers. While not directly funded by the state, the first non-artist-specific museum/center was the Asian Research Center for Animation and Comic Art (ARCACA), founded in 2005 at Communication University of China (CUC) by the senior author, with strong support of CUC President Liu Jinan and the School of Animation. A much larger center (to include a museum, archives, library, auditorium, exhibition and screening rooms, etc.), also proposed by Lent, in 2008, and backed by the government and corporations, has not come to fruition, and is not likely to, despite being designed architecturally and allocated considerable government land in Guiyang to a real estate firm. Already completed are the China Comic and Animation Museum in Hangzhou, brilliantly designed by a Dutch firm as a set of huge speech balloons; the Shanghai Animation and Comics Museum; and the Jilin Animation Museum.

The Hangzhou museum is the largest in China, with an area of 30,000 meters spread over eight interconnecting balloon-shaped buildings that allow text images to be projected on the balloons' exteriors as if they are speaking. Included in the museum are a cartoon exhibition hall, IMAX cinema, and shops. One billion yuan ($150 million) was projected as the cost of the construction. Hangzhou is a key animation center, often leading China in number of minutes of animation and number of quality animated television series produced annually.

Individual cartoonists are honored with museums or pavilions named after them and collecting their works, usually located in the city of their birth. Among them are Fang Cheng in Zhongshan City, Ding Cong in Fengjing, Feng Zikai in Tongxiang, Bi Keguan in Weihai, Liao Bingxiong in Guangzhou, and Ye Qianyu in Tonglu County. Hua Junwu and Ying Tao's works are featured in the Frog Group cartoon museum in Hebei.

In recent years, the Chinese and provincial governments, along with some animation and comics companies, have jointly sponsored pavilions at festivals abroad, with the twin goals of exposing Chinese talent to the world and having top-notch manhua reprinted in other languages. For example, at the 42nd Angoulême International Comics Festival (France, January 29–February 1, 2015), the city of Guangzhou had the place of guest of honor and was granted a spacious exhibition area dedicated to Chinese cartoonists and their works. Supported by provincial and city governments, a large Chinese delegation traveled to France to present the comic books of seven featured cartoonists (Li Kunwu, Yao Wei, Yao Feila, Gui Huazheng, Jin Cheng, Nie Jun, and Xia Da), the first three of whom already had published their

works in France. The permanent Chinese pavilion also included a heritage section featuring masters of old (Zhang Leping, He Youzhi, and Wang Hongli). During the festival, Guangdong Province and Guangzhou city officials presided over the signing of a contract between the Chinese Comiclans Company and the Franco-Belgian Média Participations group (program, 42nd Angoulême International Comics Festival 2015: 12–3). China and its manhua creators also were the guests of honor at the 61st Frankfurt Book Fair in 2009, where ten Chinese cartoonists gave their impressions of Beijing through fifty enlarged comics. Through the book fair, a few manhua artists have had their comics published in German.

The Government as Regulator and Censor of Comic Art

Confusion and overlap of duties have marked the regulation of Chinese mass media, including comics, cartoons, and animation. This tendency was exacerbated by the introduction of the internet. Before March 24, 2013, the key regulators were the State Administration of Radio, Film, and Television (SARFT, formed in 1998), which oversaw broadcast media, and the General Administration of Press and Publication of the People's Republic of China (GAPP, founded 2001), which regulated books, newspapers, and magazines. As a result of the 2013 State Council Organizational Reform and Functional Changes Plan, adopted during the twelfth National People's Congress, the two agencies merged to form the State Administration of Press, Publication, Radio, Film, and Television (SAPPRFT), seemingly to resolve the lack of a clear demarcation of roles. Nonetheless, the presence of other key media regulators, particularly the Ministry of Culture (MoC), and to lesser degrees, the Ministry of Industry and Information Technology and the Press Office of the State Council, hampered a clean-cut solution.

Before the merger, the areas of responsibility of these agencies were:

GAPP: responsible for drafting and enforcing prior restraint regulations; screening books; approving new publishing units and publication distributors; investigating and prosecuting illegal publications, and examining/approving applications for Internet sites to engage in information. Based on its draft provisions of December 18, 2012, GAPP intended to take authority over online publication of games (a major bone of contention), cartoons, and audio-visual products. GAPP also had the legal authority to screen, censor, and ban print, electronic, or Internet publications and to deny licenses to publish.

SARFT: in control of all radio, television, satellite, and Internet broadcasts in China with censorship powers concerning materials offensive to Chinese government or cultural values.

Ministry of Culture: among other duties, supervises Internet cultural products, including online games, "online cartoons produced solely for the Internet . . . , cartoons and so forth reproduced or disseminated through the Internet." (Hogan Lovells 2013)

To point out the frustration businesses experience in obtaining licenses, the animation industry has been jointly administered by all three regulators—MoC, responsible for animation industry planning, industry base planning, project construction, exhibition and training activities, and market supervision; SARFT, overseeing the administration of film and television animation, online animated films and TV shows, and online audio-visual animation programs; and GAPP, taking care of the approval and publication of animation books, newspapers, periodicals, and video products.

Some sources were dubious about the capability of the merger to result in a significant overhaul. According to an advisory by the international legal firm Hogan Lovells (2013), there "seems to be little evidence of any genuine integration" between SARFT and GAPP, and, therefore, it is

anyone's guess as to whether the merger has made any real impact on the rationalisation of regulation within China's Internet media and entertainment content industry. Perhaps the key issue is whether we should read anything into the fact that MoC has been excluded from this round

of institutional reform, and whether, as a ministerial level of authority, this should be taken to mean that a question mark is being raised over its role going forward. It seems that despite the merger, there remains a lot more work to be done in order to bring some semblance of order to this hugely over-regulated space and provide some respite for businesses both foreign and domestic struggling to make sense of it all and comply with the requirements of each of the regulators.

A communications professor at Beijing Foreign Studies University, Qiao Mu, felt the merger fell short, as there had been talk of establishing a super-ministry of SARFT, GAPP, and MoC. He questioned how willing SAPPRFT was to deregulate itself, especially concerning licensing, and thought the merged agency would come under more control of the Publicity Department of the Communist Party, which is not accountable to the State Council and top legislature (Raymond Li 2013). The merger was not expected to lead to liberalization or deregulation.

Outright censorship of cartoons, comics, and animation by the authorities occurs, but probably not as often as suspected by China-watchers in the West. The reason for this is that official censorship is not necessary in many cases, for one or more of the following reasons: 1. cartoonists know the precise boundary between what is and is not permissible, and do not cross it; 2. the dividing line is fuzzy and not clear enough for the cartoonists to chance stepping over it; 3. the editors specify the contents of cartoons, and when there is deviation from these specifications, they either ask the artists to alter the drawings or they delete them; 4. the cartoonists follow traditional customs common elsewhere in Asia, that leaders and elders deserve respect and should not be held up to ridicule; and 5. the long history of censorship and punitive repercussions keep editors and cartoonists on their toes.

In reported instances where outright censorship occurred, it resulted because of content considered violent, lewd, sexual, or pornographic and not considerate of government and political sensitivities. Liew (2009)

142

wrote that everything can be published except sex, the Tibetan situation, and that of Xinjiang (the Uighur region where there has been ethnic unrest). In late 2011, these reasons were seemingly lumped together by the president at the time, Hu Jintao, who denounced the West's "assault" on China's culture and ideology. As he warned in his speech, which was published in *Seeking Truth*:

> We must clearly see that international hostile forces are intensifying the strategic plot of Westernizing and dividing China, and ideological and cultural fields are the focal areas of their long-term infiltration. . . . We should deeply understand the seriousness and complexity of the ideological struggle, always sound the alarms and remain vigilant, and take forceful measures to be on guard and respond. (quoted in Wong 2012)

Hu felt one response was to develop Chinese cultural products that would attract the interests of the Chinese public. By the time of Hu's remarks, China had been bolstering local culture, including Chinese comics and animation, for at least a half-dozen years, through all types of preferential treatment. Ironically, often, the government, through its emissaries, sought Western "expertise" for advice on implementing domestic policy and practices.

The types of comics/cartoons censored in China for cultural and moral reasons are those that raise the ire of arbitrators of public taste everywhere—even in more liberal environments: that is, content that is considered morally inappropriate and offensive or potentially unsafe for the physical well-being of humans—in other words, basically sex and violence.

China has no rating system for cartoons; instead, it uses the universal guidelines for children's cartoons and a relatively new SAPPRFT mandate on standards for TV animation content, among which are to:

> "promote good and lash out at evil," "advocate socially [*sic*] morality and family virtues," and resist "egoism, money worship, hedonism, superstition, pseudoscience and content

containing harmful thoughts and bad habits." It also said cartoons should avoid violent scenes, including depictions of attacks that children could easily imitate, and should not use daily necessities for dangerous purposes (blog post in *Wall Street Journal*, reported in Hoekstra 2013)

About the same time as this directive, SAPPRFT censored China's most popular animated work, *Pleasant Goat and Big Big Wolf*, for violent content after three young boys tragically imitated a gruesome episode. The series was filled with violent scenes: e.g., of the 500 episodes examined, the wolf had been struck by a frying pan at least 9,544 times and the goat had been boiled 839 times and electrically shocked on 1,755 occasions. A studio official assured authorities that the more than 1,000-episode cartoon would be changed. Other animators followed suit, altering names of characters and their activities. An animated series, *Boonie Bears*, about two bear brothers who thwart the tree-cutting work of a lumberjack, was changed; the "smelly black bear" was renamed "little bear," and scenes of the bears entering homes when the occupants were away were avoided (Denyer 2013).

Inappropriate content was cited again in December 2014, when the Ministry of Culture censored twenty-one comics and animation websites belonging to Tencent and China Telecom. The ministry said several domestically made cartoons on these sites contained "severe violence, horror and sexual content inappropriate for young viewers" (Hung 2014). Similar crackdowns preceded SAPPRFT's revision and implementation of new guidelines in 2013. A few examples will suffice; one involving a manga, the other, a domestically produced xinmanhua. In mid-2007, Chinese authorities inspected book and stationery stores nationwide to confiscate pirated print and electronic versions of *Death Note*, a manga popular among Chinese middle school students. The main character in the story has a magical notebook with powers to kill people whose names are written in it. The officials also shut down a website tied to the manga, claiming *Death Note* promoted death fantasies (Saeki 2007; Coonan 2007). Even so, *Death Note* continued to be a top trending manga in China; by mid-2015, "posts containing the hashtag #DeathNote have been read more than 100 million times on Weibo," according to a BBC report (Allen and Rowntree 2015). In April 2015, China announced still another crackdown on violent and pornographic content.

In 2008, a xinmanhua about a rabbit that finds itself in assorted bizarre suicidal situations was pulled from Shanghai bookstore shelves after a spate of suicides and suicide attempts by children. Created by local cartoonist, Liu Gang, the book was inspired by a British cartoonist ("'Bunny Suicides' Cartoon Book . . ." 2008). Very popular on the internet, Suicide Rabbit was a hapless, well-meaning character who dared "to suggest, even faintly through tiptoe satire, that the society created by China's economic boom has its comical drawbacks" (Cody 2007: A12). Although Liu claimed to have no interest in politics (just social themes), he did have Suicide Rabbit mock George W. Bush's warmongering as well as Japanese cars, and comment on a rough-handed, anti-government demonstration in Taiwan, but he steered the character away from taboo subjects (such as China's leaders, party politics, and corrupt party officials). Liu's rabbit did encounter Chinese social problems, including

> low-level Beijing officials who don't want people to stop spitting because it would cut down on the income they get by imposing fines on spitters.
>
> . . . the frustrations of many Chinese at the money-grasping attitude that has emerged since the country started moving toward a free market system 25 years ago. (Cody 2007: A12)

Sexual content still raises a bright red flag for Chinese censors of comics and animation; however, some liberalization, however shaky, has happened this century, due to, as stated by Jiang Leiwen of the Institute of Population Research at Beijing University, the "shift in values towards greater individualism and a recognition of the right to seek self fulfilment," which he said led to increasing tolerance of so-called "deviant" behavior (homosexuality, extramarital sex, single mothers, or non-marital cohabitation) (Liew 2009). As discussed earlier relative to boys' love comics in China, tolerance at any given time cannot be relied on, and comics and animation producers are well aware of that. They also know very well that the line between "acceptable satire and detainable offense" is fuzzy, always moving, and seldom perceptible (Larmer 2011).

Chinese cartoonists have been quick to point out that they can criticize some social problems but restrict themselves from dealing with political matters. Veteran cartoonist Fang Cheng (interview, 2001) said that cartoonists cannot play the watchdog role relative to government and politicians, and that they avoid many serious social problems and refrain from caricaturing or naming officials in their cartoons. He thought cartoons without people's names were beneficial, because, "I can use the same cartoon next year or five years from now." Having written a number of books on humor and cartoons, Fang advocates an indirect approach to cartooning, using metaphors and references to literary and historical people and events (see Fang 2006, 2007). Other cartoonists, such as Liao Bingxiong (interview, 2002), Fang Tang (interview, 2002), He Wei (interview, 2001), lamented the current drought of courageous cartoonists, who had been so plentiful in the past.

"Politically sensitive content" covers a wide swath of topics in China; for example, Chinese printers used this reason in 2010 to reject a foreign graphic novel, *Titanium Rain*, in which a future civil war in China was depicted. Besides the obvious, such as attacks against party and state officials or policies, among other off-limit topics to have afflicted cartoonists in recent years are the Tiananmen Square massacre of June 4, 1989, and the Communist Party-outlawed religious group Falun Gong. In June 2010, the *Southern Metropolis Daily* attempted to commemorate the Tiananmen Square incident (where tanks and troops squashed a call for a democracy movement, resulting in hundreds of deaths) by publishing a cartoon of a boy drawing a person standing in front of tanks, an image thought to reference the iconic photograph of a protester who stopped a

144

column of tanks in 1989. The drawing was removed from the Guangzhou newspaper's website; it was unclear by whom (Bristow 2010).

Veteran cartoonist Zhu Genhua (interview, 2009) spoke of how a cartoon he drew shortly after the Tiananmen Square incident got him into trouble with the authorities:

> I drew a cartoon on an efficient way to lose weight for which I was criticized. 1989 was the year of the horse. I drew a horse with a girl on it. When the horse lost weight, the girl didn't and weighed the horse down. The officials said the horse represented China and the girl was the Western world. They said the cartoon meant the West was punishing China for human rights violations.
>
> This was very ridiculous; I did not think that when I drew the cartoon. *People's Daily* [for which he drew] did not use satire, so I drew humor cartoons for them to fill space. At that time, everyone wanted to lose weight. I did not think political. Some censors are very smart, too smart.

Two cartoonists who were members of the banned Falun Gong religious group felt compelled to leave China before the 2008 Olympics for fear of being further "persecuted" by the authorities. Guo Jingxiong, founder of the Flag Cartoon Creation Alliance and an award-winning animator, had published a series of cartoons to counteract the CCP's accusations against the Falun Gong and, along with others in the sect, had advised people to quit the CCP. Guo said that he was tortured while in custody in 2007 and 2008, accused of creating a cartoon that damaged the CCP's image and other charges. He and his assistant, Wang Haibo, had published cartoons for the historical work *Nine Commentaries on the Communist Party*. According to Wang, he was also jailed and tortured before he too fled to the United States (Wei 2008; Zhu 2008). In 1999, when Falun Gong was outlawed, Chinese authorities published several comic books demonizing Li Hongzhi, founder of Falun Gong, in a manner similar to cartoons drawn about the Gang of Four from post-Maoist times (Faison 1999).

An incident in October and November 2015, involving political cartoonist Jiang Yefei, may have enshrined a July 2015 Beijing national security law that allowed Chinese law to be enforceable abroad. Jiang Yefei had fled China in 2008 after he was detained and tortured for criticizing to the foreign press the CCP's handling of the aftermath of the Sichuan earthquake. He had been living in Bangkok, where he chaired the Thai branch of the Federation for a Democratic China and recently drew cartoons which mocked President Xi Jinping. Because of the cartoons, he was cited for inciting subversion of state power. In April 2015, he was granted refugee status by the United Nations High Commissioner for Human Rights and given a UN "protection letter" as he waited to be resettled in Canada. On October 28, Jiang Yefei was placed into custody by Thai immigration police on grounds he had entered Thailand illegally. He pleaded guilty and was fined $167, which the Chinese authorities paid after "tricking" him into signing a document in Thai, which he did not understand, and which he was told would speed his way to Canada. Instead, the document granted the authorities permission to deport him to China. He was sent back to China on November 12 (Mcauliffe 2015; Xin 2015; Wen and Ho 2015).

The dreary picture veteran Chinese cartoonists painted of political satire in interviews with the authors from 2001 and 2002 had worsened by 2015. This is not surprising; stability has not characterized the level of tolerance in China, a country motivated and plagued by many campaigns and movements. Exacerbating this factor are a decline in reader interest of print media (in favor of internet), the play-it-safe attitude of publishers and editors, and, of course, stringent restrictions by the media. Not only have cartoon/humor magazines folded or suffered deep drops in circulation during the past decade, but regularly published cartoon columns in newspapers became almost extinct, too. Managing editor-in-chief of *Satire and Humor*, Xiao Chengsen (quoted in Zhang 2015), said that, whereas nearly every local-level CCP newspaper had its own cartoon column in the 1980s, today, he estimated that a mere twenty newspapers nationwide regularly publish editorial cartoons. Cartoonists quoted by Zhang (2015) weighed in on reasons behind these trends. Gouben, a contributor to three major newspapers, said, "The essence of a political cartoon is satire. Politicians in China are used to praises and applause. It's natural that they have no appetite for thorny satire, especially in publications they view as their publicity tools." He added that some newspapers required that "officials involved in news scandals should not be caricatured" or "painted as fatter than they really are" (Zhang 2015). While Gouben made these statements, the Chinese authorities permitted cartoon depictions of national leaders (e.g., Jiang Zemin, Xi Jinping, First Lady Peng Liyuan) to appear in mass media for the first time since the 1980s. Kuang Biao, the former cartoon page editor at *Southern Metropolis Daily*, told Zhang (2015) that in 2008—a year before authorities ordered him to terminate his paper's cartoon page and not to start a new one—he had to prepare two to three "back-up works each week in case a cartoon had to be revised or pulled completely." Because of cartoonists' relative youthfulness and their lack of sufficient social and life experiences, Kuang said, "It's hard for artists to draw powerful and trenchant political cartoons" (Zhang 2015).

A number of Chinese cartoonists are increasingly pinning their hopes on social media to spread their political messages, despite the government's stringent control of the internet. They follow in the footsteps of earlier generations of Chinese cartoonists, masking their messages in "protective layers of irony and satire" (Larmer 2011). Coded language is so much a part of Chinese subculture that the name *egao* ("evils works" or "mischievous mockery") has been applied to it. Larmer (2011) gave an example of egao: "President Hu Jintao's favorite buzz word, 'harmony,' which he deploys constantly when urging social stability, is hijacked to signify censorship itself, as in, 'My blog has been harmonized.'" Another explanation was given by Xiao (2007) for the association of the word "harmonize" with censorship: in Chinese, "harmonize" (*hexie*) is a homonym of the word for 'river crab,' and a crab in folk language also refers to bullies with violent power." Xiao (2007) continued:

So the image of a crab has become a new satirical, politically charged icon for the netizens who are fed up with government censorship and who now call themselves the River Crab Society. Photos of a malicious crab are traveling through the blogosphere as a silent protest under the virtual eyes of the new cyber-police officers.

One anonymous cartoonist adopted "Crazy Crab" as his pen name and "Hexie Farm" (Crab Farm) as the title of his political cartoons about the dictatorship, censorship, and propaganda of the CCP. "Crazy Crab" has described himself as an "anonymous cartoonist who doesn't know how to draw" ("Criticizing Everything . . ." 2012). He started "Hexie Farm" as a "series of political cartoons depicting a 'great, glorious and correct' era of 'harmony.'" "Hexie Farm" was inspired by George Orwell's *Animal Farm* (Magistad 2012). No doubt, "Crazy Crab" worried about repercussions even before he started, questioning himself, "Am I crazy enough to draw such political satire for nothing but a nightmare?" ("Criticizing Everything . . ." 2012). The series lasted from 2009 to October 2011, when it was placed on the "banned search terms" list and therefore, completely stopped in China (Royaards 2012). For a while, another anonymous internet cartoonist, pen name "Wang Zuozhongyou," found ways around the censors with what he called "character news." "Zuozhongyou" created this layered meaning system to tell news stories "by deconstructing characters and numbers, replacing radicals with paintings" (Zhang 2015). In one of his reports, he showed "the number 500 with the two zeroes resembling a pair of handcuffs. The cartoon was an indirect reference to a 2013 ruling that bloggers can be sent to jail for online posts containing false information which was reposted more than 500 times" (Zhang 2015). As with "Crazy Crab," "Zuozhongyou" was stopped by the authorities; his works were often censored before his account on WeChat (the Tencent messaging app) was shut down in 2014.

The active online cartoonist Wang Liming (pen name, Biantai Lajiao or Rebel Pepper) also lost his social media accounts to the censors before he fled to Japan when some Chinese newspapers labeled him a "traitor" (Zhang 2015; also Shi 2011). Until his self-exile, Wang was hard-hitting, even once caricaturing President Xi Jinping as a steamed bun surrounded by foods kowtowing to him as though he were emperor; on another occasion, he was shown in bed with a nationalistic blogger who had written negatively about the United States (Franchineau and Morillo 2015). Wang's understanding of government strategy was: "I know their [government's] bottom line. If you draw mostly as a hobby, they leave you alone. But if you draw to rally people around a political cause, you're crossing the line" (Jiang 2012). Given Wang's later fate, Wang either miscalculated the whereabouts of the line or the authorities moved the line.

Although he steered clear of targeting leaders—instead, aiming at society more generally—Beijing satirist Bai Budan also had his satirical microblog stopped by the government when he posted a cartoon showing Tiananmen Square immersed in red ink. Bai often shows his work in private exhibitions (Franchineau and Morillo 2015).

Mastering internet comics subterfuge for several years, beginning in 2009, Hutoon studio owner and animator Wang Bo (aka Pi San) created a mischievous character, Kuang Kuang, that became so popular as to lead to fan clubs in nearly every province and so provocative as to be deemed inappropriate and its creator fined by officials. The first appearance of Kuang Kuang was in *Blow up the School*, an attack on China's education system. Others, such as *Good Teacher*, about childhood frustrations with a rigid system, and *Crack Sunflower Seeds*, a tribute to his artist friend Ai Weiwei's detention as a government critic, are layered with meanings (Larmer 2012; "The Controversial Cartoons . . ." 2011). In Wang Bo's four-minute *Little Rabbit, Be Good*, Kuang Kuang has a nightmare about a place ruled by tigers who promise a "harmonious" forest (again mocking Hu Jintao's catchphrase) that turns out to be a living hell for the rabbit inhabitants, who suffer social ills similar to those in real-life China.

Because images are more difficult to block than keywords, and cartoons even more so, because they take additional time to decipher (especially if they have hidden meanings), satirical messages do find their way online, even if briefly. One recent sample of cartoons blocked by censors on Sina Weibo gives an idea about topics that are not to be discussed: air pollution, food safety, graft, arrests of activists, and official corruption (Williams 2014). Since 2007, the censors in many major cities use two cartoon police figures (a male and a female) to monitor content on China's largest internet portal; every thirty minutes, these cartoonized cops come onto the screen to give viewers an opportunity to report any illegal information they see online (Xiao 2007).

Chinese authorities stay in perpetual motion trying to block various tools utilized to bypass the "Great Firewall," China's sophisticated internet censorship system, set up in 2003 and considered the world's largest and most advanced such infrastructure. In 2015, the software they had to contend with was the VPN (virtual private network), usually a free service that unlocks parts of the Web supposedly controlled by the government (Editorial Board 2015; Lowenthal 2015; for background on China's Web control, see also Stevenson-Yang 2005: 6–10).

The "Great Firewall" notwithstanding, social media are considered by some young cartoonists as the salvation of Chinese political cartooning, with their use of modern styles, their ability to adapt to many situations, and their speedier drawing techniques that allow for quicker responses to the news.

The Government as User of Comic Art

Governments use comics, cartoons, and animation to educate, to propagandize, and to raise social consciousness levels. Sometimes, these categories overlap; sometimes, distinctions between them are hard to come by. For example, is a cartoon campaign urging birth control in China propaganda because it fits into the government's one-child policy, educational because it teaches people the dangers of overpopulation, and methods of controlling it, or social consciousness-raising because it makes people aware of a problem they had not thought

Fig. 5.19. One of six comic strips about President Xi Jinping released by Chinese state media in 2014. *Offbeat China*, March 10, 2014.

help from family planning officials, painted and displayed more than 12,000 cartoons in more than 200 villages, trying to persuade residents to have fewer children. The cartoons were colorful, with symbolic language aimed at often-illiterate farmers. Typical messages instructed on birth control practice, healthy maintenance of reproductive organs, and giving birth to a healthy baby. The cartoons lined the streets; in Beiguodong Village, a one-kilometer stretch of street was decorated with villagers' paintings ("Cartoons Urge Birth Control" 2000).

In Qiuxian, a county seat in Hebei Province, prosecutors found a way to make small-town officials aware of two vices they were notorious for—playing poker on the job and using their official powers for personal gain. With help from the Frog Cartoon Group, the county's chief prosecutor had a deck of playing cards made that in cartoon form depicted the fifty-two ways of abusing an office listed in the law books. Each card described the legal definition of a "crime of public office." For example,

> The king of spades depicts a crime that is much reported these days, the bribery of officials with sexual powers rather than cash. No statute specifically refers to sexual bribery, but the card is explicit: a man covered only by a towel luxuriates on a beach, shielded from the sun by a woman with her dress billowed out, forming an umbrella. (Eckholm 2002: A4)

Breaking with tradition and policy, Chinese state media in 2014 released a cartoon image of President Xi Jinping in an infographic about his busy schedule, to promote a "kinder, softer, and 'closer to the people' image" of the nation's top leader. Six comic strips, "Uncle Xi's Cartoon," appeared on iFeng.com, the website of a pro-Beijing television broadcaster in Hong Kong. The four-panel strips, some of which were based on real events, featured Xi conversing with villagers while sitting cross-legged, talking with sailors, discussing EQ with college-student village cadres, greeting a Wuhan woman with, "Hello, beautiful!" visiting locals in Xiangxi, and queuing for steamed buns in Qingfeng ("'Hello, Beautiful!' . . ." 2014).

much about previously? Any one of the three, or all of them together, could apply; it would depend on what the government agency termed the campaign or how it is interpreted by favorably impressed or skeptical participants and onlookers. Trust of the issuing government agency would be a decisive factor.

A few examples from many are presented here to show ways the Chinese government agencies have used comic art. An innovative approach was that in Wuzhi County (Henan Province, Central China), where farmers, with

Manhua and cartoon competitions have carried government-induced social consciousness-raising themes. CCP cadres in Henan Province received comic books reminding them to stay free of graft in the form of Spring Festival gifts in 2008. One hundred thousand copies of the pocket-size books were distributed by the Henan Provincial Commission for Discipline Inspection of the CCP (Yao 2008). Other government-related campaign subjects, particularly environment awareness, were adapted to manhua and cartoon competitions over the years. Standing out as a bit different was a cartoon competition in Hunan Province in which children were asked to draw Lei Feng, a young army man in the early 1960s, who spent all of his time and money helping needy people. He became a national icon in 1963 when Chairman Mao Zedong set him up as a role model for all Chinese.

state funding; as a result, some cartoonists became entrepreneurs, owning large companies, such as Beijing Heavycomics Culture Media and Shenjie manhua gongsi. Technologically, the internet, with its relative anonymity, opened up spaces for online comics, as well as political cartoons. Partly to plug up holes in the system, the government revised (and merged) media regulatory bodies and, on and off, tightened censorship restrictions.

Other significant changes occurred in comic art education, professionalism, the role of women, and the creation of a new group of cartoonists, more outward-looking, but still very much aware of the duties and shortcomings of cartooning under a Communist government.

Summary

The forty-one years from the end of the Cultural Revolution until the present have been transformative, in line with other periods in Chinese culture. Many adjustments had to be made in the art and cartooning sectors because of the rise of modernization, the switch to a market economy, and major innovations in technology. After some shifts of ideas in the 1980s, a certain degree of individualism and acceptance of Western art/cartooning was permitted. Policies, practices, and infrastructures were changed, with the establishment of new professional cartoon associations, such as the Cartoon Art Committee of China Artists' Association and China Journalistic Caricature Society, and cartoon magazines, such as *Satire and Humor* and *The World of Cartoons*. Old forms like lianhuanhua had a heyday in the mid-1980s, but, as with cartoon magazines by the late 1990s, moved aside to allow space for Japanese manga (initially, mainly pirated) and xinmanhua, a hybrid of manga and lianhuanhua.

With the market economy, the comics and animation industries could no longer completely depend on

二郎神
嘎妹
孙悟空

The story of China's animation and its rise to near the top in production globally by 2015 reaches back to the 1920s. It is a story marked by unswerving persistence, where animators in the beginning struggled to learn the secrets of making pictures move; survived wars and disastrous, stressful government campaigns and the Cultural Revolution, sometimes engaging in cartoon propaganda; sparked and nurtured two golden eras of exquisite, world-class animation; and stepped into a period characterized by norms of commercialism, bigness, and lower quality.

Chapter 6

Animation: From Hand-Crafted Experimentation to Digitalization

The Wan Brothers and the Origins, 1920s–1940s

Usually given full credit for being the originators of Chinese animation are the Wan brothers (twins Laiming, 1899–1997, and Guchan, 1899–1995, Chaochen, 1906–92, and Dihuan, 1907–?), with their *Danao huashi* (*Uproar in an Art Studio*). Contrary to common belief, however, they were not the only presence in China's earliest animation, despite being the dominant figures in the 1920s and '30s.[1]

What the Wan brothers accomplished under very adverse conditions from 1922 to 1941, was definitely praiseworthy: thirty animated works, including entertainment, advertising, and anti-Japanese propaganda films, some silent, others with sound, ranging from one to eighty minutes, and among them, the first in the categories of full animation, color, sound, feature-length, and paper cut. It is not a stretch to say the first twenty years of Chinese animation, with a few exceptions, belonged to the Wans.

Other early Chinese animation did not present much of a threat to the brothers. Two known 1924 works were *Guonian* (*Happy New Year*), a funny cartoon released in January that was produced by the Shanghai British and American Tobacco Company Film Department and drawn by artist Yang Zuotao, and *Gou qingke* (*Dog Treating Guests*), which came out in June, produced by Chinese Film Company and drawn with pen by cartoonist Huang Wennong (Zhang 2002: 26; see Zeng 1992). A

Fig. 6.1. Wan brothers: Wan Chaochen, Wan Laiming, and Wan Guchan. Courtesy of Shanghai Animation Film Studio.

live-action animated film of "more than 1,000 feet," *Dog Treating Guests* was described by Zhang (2002: 26) as a very funny story with quick movements. In 1925, two works were completed by Shanghai South Pacific Film Company: *Jinghuayuan* (*Good Fate*) and *Shaonian qiyu* (*Young Boys Adventure*). The directors and artists of these works are not known.

Several other early Chinese animated films known not to be associated with the Wans are *Wushiliunian tongshi* (*The 56 Years of Sorrow*), a 1935 production of Nanjing Central University Electronic Education Department, and *Yemingzhu* (*Night Pearl*), made in 1942 by Manzhou yinghua xiehui (Manchuria Film Association).

The Wan brothers, born in a large family in Nanjing, were absorbed with artistic activities from childhood, inspired by a mother with the ulterior motives of calming noisy children and occupying their time. She bought them art supplies and at night, showed them hand silhouettes and told them stories (Zhang 2002: 28). The boys were fascinated by moving images, as Wan Laiming (1981) recounted:

> I remember how we loved to play with the shadows of our hands from the weak light given off by an oil lamp when we were children. When we were a little older, we happened to see a shadow theatre performance, and were very taken with it. After that we spent all our evenings cutting out cardboard figures, which we fixed on sticks. Then, illuminating them with the oil lamp, we made their shadows move along the wall. It was a marvelous game. . . . I recall

another time, when seeing the shadow of trees glide along a wall at the mercy of the wind and become lifelike, we thought it very beautiful and decided that our cardboard silhouettes should become animated in the same manner as the tree branches when swept by the wind. From that moment on, the expression animated picture rooted itself in our childhood imaginations, but we were far from realizing that we had found our calling.

After graduating from high school at seventeen, Wan Laiming began drawing cartoons and making crafts, especially beginning in 1918, when he went to Shanghai alone, passed an examination to work at Commercial Press, Ltd., and started illustrating children's reading materials. Soon, he was made an editor of *Liangyou* (*The Young Companion*); he also published two art silhouette books on body beauty. Although Wan Laiming's main interest was animation, he continued his work as a print cartoonist and illustrator, serving as chief editor of *Phenomenal Cartoon* during its one-month existence in 1935, and helping to organize the first national cartoon exhibition in 1936.

Wan Laiming's three brothers joined him, one by one, at Commercial Press as they were graduated from Nanjing and Shanghai art schools. Together now, the Wans' resolve to learn to make pictures move was strengthened, especially after viewing cartoons by the Fleischer brothers in Shanghai theaters. Determined to learn animation principles, they visited theaters often, wrote to American and European animators for advice (to no avail), went to toy shops on Shanghai's Bund to inspect entertainment instruments from Europe, and continued to experiment (Bao 2000b: 6). Upon visiting the Great World Amusement Center, they saw a Praxinoscope, which made them understand that to make pictures move, film equipment was needed.

After working their full-day shifts, the Wans devoted their evenings and weekends contemplating, plotting, improvising, and experimenting. Wan Laiming spoke about those nights and days in several reports:

In 1922, my brothers received their degree from the School of Fine Arts and entered the cinema section of the Commercial Press. For my part, I was illustrating children's books. It was our persistent desire to produce a cartoon one day that led us to pursue our research. In the daytime, we worked, but at night we carried out our experiments at home. At the time, it was difficult because we lacked not only money but also materials. In the one and only little room we had, we owned nothing but a few lamps, some pencils, and an old camera. We had to do everything ourselves: write the scenario, think up the characters, draw the pictures, take care of shooting, developing, editing. . . . Day after day, night after night, our research absorbed us totally, leading us to forget all about meals, sleep, our families, our children, life. All the rest was secondary. (quoted in Quiquemelle 1991: 176)

He related how he and his brothers figured out the principles of animation:

We sat around a little wooden table [in their small room] and drew a small horse on the corners of a thick book. We drew more than 20 pages, then flipped the pages. But, my brothers felt the horse did not move. I thought why not? We realized the horse had to move in our drawing. We did a new experiment. We drew the horse running from a standstill to a slow run, then move quickly, slow down, and be still again at the end. The first page was a still page, each page moving a little, after 20 pages, the horse slowed down. I then flipped the pages. My brothers opened their eyes widely as they saw the horse move. . . . Unfortunately, this movement stopped in seconds. We were still not satisfied as it was very dull. So we started to work separately. On the book corners, I drew a cat, you [brothers] drew a rat. We drew tens of the cat chasing the rat. On the final pages, the rat is under the cat's paws, not daring to move. After we finished drawing, we watched it intently. This was the biggest discovery, a real miracle. That night was a memorable night for me and my brothers. . . . After several years' exploration, we finally found the key. . . . That night, we felt very excited; we laughed and sang songs full of tears in our eyes. . . . We drew and watched all night, sleepless.

But the Wans' troubles were not over, as Wan Laiming explained:

Though we found the secret of animation, we faced many difficulties hard to resolve. First, we did not have a place to experiment. We hardly could find materials to reference. Third, we didn't have money to buy the necessary machine and instruments. These three problems were just like three mountains. We did not have the capability of crossing one mountain at a time and we didn't want to stop half way. (quoted in Zhang 2002: 31–32)

They persisted methodically, making their room, just seven square meters, their workplace, Chinese shadow shows and foreign animation their references, and a still camera with a wooden box they refitted as a projector, some common bulbs, and pencils as their instruments and supplies. To pay for these sparse materials, the Wans decided not to spend any money on fish or meat for a year and not to make clothes for themselves during New Year festivities (Bao 2002a: 7). They "moved the stove out of the kitchen and covered the windows completely" to have a darkroom. According to Wan Laiming, they "drew every image carefully and shot it carefully. Then we went to the darkroom and developed. When it was very hot, we would be naked to the waist and worked in that very dirty, hard-to-breathe kitchen, bitten by mosquitoes till we had a rash all over our bodies" (quoted in Zhang 2002: 33).

Everything was learned through trial and error. Bao (2000a: 7) explained how the Wans tackled issues related to maintaining continuity of locations and a sense of perspective and distance:

> Thousands of drafts were drawn and it was difficult to make the characters move in the same position. Finally, they created a three-nailed stabilizer that regularized accurately the movements of the characters without losing the continuity of the locations—a primitive device that is still used to this day in the making of animated films.
>
> [To maintain perspective and distance], Brother Number Four would operate the camera, while Brother Number One and Two would hold up the drawn draftboards, and move one step at a time towards the camera. Number Three would manage the time by holding a stopwatch and controlling the movements. In order to economise on film, the brothers would rehearse their steps before every shot until everything could be coordinated. (Bao 2000a: 7)

After much experimentation and many failed attempts, Wan Laiming recounted, "One evening, on a white wall in our room, the drawings began to appear lifelike. They were animated. We were overcome with happiness" (quoted in Quiquemelle 1991: 176). Wan Laiming also said of this experience:

> My childhood dreams. . . . finally fulfilled by my hands and tears came out of my eyes. It's hard to say if it was happiness, excitement, or sadness. We projected again and again as if we did not see enough, until we thought the projecting machine couldn't work and then we stopped. (quoted in Zhang 2002: 34)

Hearing of the Wans' breakthrough, their employer (Commercial Press) requested they make a one-minute advertisement, which they completed at the end of 1922. Titled *Shu Zhendong huawen daziji* (*Comfortable Shu Zhendong's Chinese Typewriter*), the commercial was described by Wan Laiming (quoted in Quiquemelle 1991: 177): "Today that film would seem simplistic and a trifle ridiculous, but it does not alter the fact that it was the original model upon which we built all our following movies and that it gave us first-hand experience in the art of the production of a cartoon."

They completed two additional advertisements during the next two years before being hired by Changcheng (Great Wall) Film Studio as set-makers, with the intent to make an animated film in their spare time. Finished in 1926 and released in early 1927,[2] the Wans' work, *Danao huashi* (*Uproar in an Art Studio*), is usually considered China's first animated film. Combining real-life and cartoon figures, *Uproar in an Art Studio* was very much influenced by the Fleischer brothers' *Out of the Inkwell* series. In the Wans' film, an artist draws a small man who comes to life, leaves the drawing board, and causes havoc in the studio until the artist captures him and pins him to the drawing board.

Wan Laiming (quoted by Shi 1962, in Quiquemelle 1991: 177) said, "After such a promising start, we had to wait several years before we could make another cartoon, because the Shanghai producers regarded animation too costly both in material and personnel." But, though he was not listed among the credits for a 1927 production, *Yifeng shuxin jihuilai* (*A Letter Posted Back*), two of Wan Laiming's brothers were: Wan Guchan and Wan Dihuan as drawers and Wan Guchan also as photographer. The film was produced by Changchun Film Company and directed by Mei Xuechou, who also wrote the screenplay (Cheng, Li, and Xing 1995: 20; Zhang 2002: 35).

In 1930, Wan Laiming worked with his brothers for the production of *Zhiren daoluan ji* (*The Rebellion of the Paper Man*) for Great China Baihe Company. Like their two previous films, this one was imitative of American and European productions, blending live action and animation, an economical and time-saving process. *The Rebellion of the Paper Man* is similar to *Uproar in an Art Studio*: a painter is drawing; the ink metamorphoses into a small man who jumps out of the ink bottle, fights the painter, and hides under the bed until the painter gets him back into the bottle. Wan Laiming said that this film showed improvement, because it characterized real life in China and its movements were funny. He predicted that when businessmen saw audiences laughing, they would realize animated films are moneymakers and invest in producing them. He may have been correct, for then, Lianhua Studio, Shanghai's most successful film company, known for its high-quality work, asked the Wans to make animated shorts. It was then, according to Wan Laiming, that their working conditions improved tremendously (quoted in Zhang 2002: 36).

From 1931 to 1936, much of the animation produced by the Wans was of a propagandistic or educational nature, but their major achievement was making China's first animated sound film, *Luotuo xianwu* (*The Dance of the Camel*). They created six "educative" and "patriotic" films for Lianhua before moving to Mingxing Film Company in 1933, where, until war with Japan was declared in 1937, they made nine short films and lived "for the first time in comparative comfort and security" (Quiquemelle 1991: 177).

Anti-Japanese or patriotic in theme were *Guoren suxing* (*Citizens, Wake Up*), in 1931 or 1932; *Xueqian* (*The Price of Blood*) and *Jingcheng tuanjie* (*United Together*), both in 1932; *Loudong* (*The Leak*), in 1934; and *Guohuonian* (*The Year of Chinese Goods*), between 1931 and 1936. Taking stands against imperialism and feudalism were *Gou zhentan* (*Dog Detective*), 1931 or 1933 (Zhang 2002); *Minzu tongshi* (*National Sorrow*), 1933; *Xinchao* (*New Tide*), 1936; and *Hangkong jiuguo* (*The Motherland Is Saved by Aviation*), between 1931 and 1936. Educative, fable-based animation by the Wans were *Gui tu saipao* (*Tortoise and Rabbit Have a Race*), 1932, and *Feilaihuo* (*Sudden Catastrophe*) and *Huangchong yu mayi* (*Locusts and Ants*), both undated but probably between 1931 and 1936. Two other short films, *Feilaifu* (*Happiness Comes Flying In*) and *Dikang* (*Resistance*), both in 1935, carried Wan brothers' credits (Cheng, Li, Xing 1995).

Citizens, Wake Up was China's first fully animated film and the initial thrust in the anti-Japanese campaign. Using lion and whale allegories, the film called upon Chinese to give what they had to resist the Japanese. *United Together* depicts a leaf in the shape of Northeast China being eaten by a large worm (the Japanese). Chinese people in various ethnic costumes appear with spades and haul baskets of dirt to fill in the holes eaten by the worm. *Blood Money*, which mixes live action and animation, shows a girl student imagining a Chinese man giving blood to a package of goods made in China. The goods are turned into money used to make factories that produced food, clothes, planes, tanks, and cannons to defeat the Japanese goods (Zhang 2002: 38). *Dog Detective* also combines live action and animation to tell the story of a girl and her dog who find the source of the opium the Chinese are smoking to be an imperialist warship and proceed to burn it. Both *National Sorrow*, which relays how the Chinese government sold out the country by signing unequal agreements, and *New Tide*, which campaigns for new ideas against feudalism, were sound productions.

As the Wan brothers built their careers in the first half of the 1930s, they knew that to compete with European and American animation, they would have to convert to sound and orient their films more to Chinese culture. Knowing the Europeans and Americans would not help them, they fumbled and experimented until they found suitable optical sound recording techniques. When Mingxing Studio challenged the Wans to produce a sound animated film, they proceeded to make *The Dance of the Camel*, an Aesop's Fable about a camel invited to a banquet hosted by a lion. During the festivities, a bunch of monkeys are applauded for their dancing, prompting the camel to try, but the animal is booed off the stage. The brothers were unsuccessful in replicating the sound of the camel dancing until:

> Laiming suggested the use of Peking Opera percussion instruments and they appeared to produce a good effect. For the elephant drawing water with its trunk, the other Wan Brothers came up with several methods but settled on the use of a rubber tube. A bamboo flute was used to dub the sound of the camel doing a somersault on stage. As for the sounds of thrown objects at the camel, the filmmakers recorded the sound of real glass bottles being broken.

The most difficult part was that of the audience of animals bursting into laughter. At first, the sound of an audience laughing was recorded but the effect produced was lacking dimension and depth. After several failed attempts, the brothers decided to record the sound of laughter from several groups of people standing at different positions. The nearest group laughed first and loudest, followed by the second group and so on. (Bao 2000b: 11)

About the time they finished *The Dance of the Camel*, the Wans also created animation sections for two feature-length films: *The Beautiful Cigarette Girl*, in which the animation showed golden dollars assaulting Chinese factories, and *Scenes of Urban Life*, a famous film by Yuan Muzhi.

The Wans' second competitive strategy (employing a Chinese culture orientation) was rather contrary to their practices, for they regularly imitated Fleischer and Disney cartoons. But, in a July 1936 article, "Talking about Cartoons," in a Mingxing Studio periodical, they wrote that not only American cartoons but also German and Russian ones were very good, and that all three bore the characteristics of those cultures. Thus, they argued, "in a Chinese film, one ought to have a story based purely on real Chinese traditions and stories, consistent with our sensibility and sense of humor. . . . Also, our films must not only bring pleasure, but also be educational" (Wan Laiming, et al. 1936, quoted in Quiquemelle 1991: 178).

As Quiquemelle (1991: 178) and Cheng, Li, and Xing (1995) state, the early Wan works were not preserved, but the oldest to have survived—*The River Is Red with Blood* (1938)—supports the above theories: it is both Chinese and educational. Quiquemelle (1991: 178) wrote of it:

Sung by the Wuhan Chorus, it becomes a vehement criticism of the aggressive war fought by Japan against China. The representation of Yue Fei [the author of the poem on which the story is based] draws inspiration from ancient statues, but the style of the pictures is direct and caricatural, reminding one of the etchings made by contemporary artists.

The Wans were preoccupied, from 1937 to 1941, with making anti-Japanese and patriotic shorts and China's first feature-length cartoon. They were also dodging the Japanese invaders immediately after Shanghai was occupied in August 1937. They moved to Wuhan where they worked for China Film Studio, producing two episodes of *Kangzhan biaoyu katong* (*Anti-Japanese War Posters Collection*) and four of *Kangzhan geji* (*Anti-Japanese War Songs Collection*). When Japan occupied Wuhan in the autumn of 1938, Wan Chaochen escaped to Chongqing alone, where he made the puppet animation, *Shang qianxian* (*Go to the Front*) and *Wang Laowu qu dangbing* (*Wang Laowu Became a Soldier*). In April 1939, Wan Laiming and Wan Guchan returned to Shanghai, because the city's Foreign Concessions that embraced China's film (and animation) industry remained free of Japanese military until December 7, 1941. Animation had taken on added importance while the Wans were gone, especially after Shanghai investors saw the big stir caused by the release in China of Disney's *Snow White* in 1938.

After seeing that classic film, Wan Laiming and Wan Guchan decided to do a feature-length animated movie. Wan Laiming recalled:

In 1940–1941, I opened an animation section for the United China Company with my brother Guchan. At the time, the first American feature-length cartoon, *Snow White*, was a big success in Shanghai, receiving great acclaim. This made Chinese capitalists greedy, and so they proposed that we make a full-length Chinese cartoon. Inspired by a chapter from the ancient novel *Journey to the West*, "Lending the Fan Three Times," we produced *Princess Iron Fan*. It was clear to us that we had to arouse the national spirit of the public by stressing the need for resistance. The end of the shooting occurred just at the time of the invasion of the foreign concessions by the Japanese, so, when the prints came out, we had to cut in a song for Zhu Bajie, the pig, with the lyric "People Rise and Fight Until Victory." 7,000 feet long, it was the first feature-length Chinese cartoon. It played for a month and a half without a break in three cinemas in Shanghai. It was also shown in Singapore and Indonesia,

Fig. 6.2. The first Chinese feature-length animation *Tieshan gongzhu* (*Princess Iron Fan*), 1941. Courtesy of Shanghai Animation Film Studio.

and was warmly received everywhere. (Wan Laiming 1981, quoted in Quiquemelle 1991: 178–79)

The political and technical conditions under which *Tieshan gongzhu* (*Princess Iron Fan*) was produced were deplorable. Investors consistently cut corners, paying low wages when they paid them at all, setting a very close deadline to save costs, and scrimping on materials. The Wans resorted to hiring apprentices and teaching them the basics, and had to listen constantly to workers' complaints about the working pace and conditions, not to mention not being paid for several months. Some staff members wanted to give up, claiming, "We were drawing Monkey King, but our own ordeal was even more difficult than when Monkey King was passing the Fire-Spewing Mountain" (Bao 2000b: 11). Improvisation was necessary when adequate materials were not made available; for example, because of a lack of color negative film, the Wans used prepared ink to draw the fiery colors of the Fire-Spewing Mountain onto the celluloid itself.

The Wans, as usual, trudged on and found the head of a Shanghai group interested in art and culture, Sheng Peihua, who was willing to assume the production expenses of *Princess Iron Fan* on the condition it be shown in the group's three theaters.

Princess Iron Fan struck a note of patriotism throughout the country and in the Chinese diaspora of parts of Asia (Ehrlich and Jin 2001: 8). Film scholar Jin Tianyi (quoted in Ehrlich and Jin 2001: 8) said that then-sixteen-year-old Tezuka Osamu (1928–89), Japan's so-called "God of Manga," saw the film and said that it "showed clearly such a theme of resistance of the entire Chinese nation against the Japanese invaders' brutal devastation of China." Whether the message was as transparent as Tezuka claimed is questionable. There were subtle references and images, but the initial ending—"Get the final win in the anti-Japanese war"— was cut as the Japanese invaded the Foreign Concessions. In fact, Wan Laiming, talking about the danger of making *Princess Iron Fan*, said, "I'd been very upset if the Japanese had found it. If the Japanese had found the purpose of this film, I would be dead without a place to bury my body" (quoted in Zhang 2002: 47).

Quiquemelle (1991: 180) also dwelled on the trying conditions under which the crew worked, though she was very laudatory about the end product:

Animation: From Hand-Crafted Experimentation to Digitalization

This production on the "orphan island" of the French Concession in the middle of the war was a real feat not only on the artistic level but also on the technical level. Seventy artists, in two teams, worked without a break for a year and four months, all in the small room, in limited space, in the cold of the winter, and in the atrocious heat of the summer. To assure the accuracy of the movement, certain scenes were filmed with actors to serve as a guide to the artists. This film, with its many inventions, sparkles with humor, fantasy and poetry. It is a delight to the spectator. But it suits adults and older children better than very young children, who might be frightened by the violence in the fight scenes, underscored as it is by brutal music. Even if, at times, the influence of Disney is still noticeable, we are far from his sweetness and prettiness, far from America and its prosperity. *Princess Iron Fan* bears witness in its own way to the brutal reality of the daily violence in a country crippled by war, where it would have been impossible for any aware filmmaker to produce a film designed purely to amuse.

The enemy's invasion of the Foreign Concessions put a halt to the Wans' plans for a second feature to be called *The World of Insects*, which was also to be a veiled condemnation of the Japanese. They then started a new project, *Danao tiangong* (*Havoc in Heaven*), also from the novel *Journey to the West*, but it too was shelved when, according to Wan Laiming,

our boss suddenly ordered us to stop everything. At the time the cost of the film and the chemicals were increasing so much that the capitalist figured that selling the materials would bring him more money than our producing the film! Six months of effort were reduced to nothing, and the hopes of several years dashed. For my part, I put away my paint brushes. Our Sun Wukong [Monkey King] was over. Apart from our own grief, what saddened us most was to send away our team of specialists, which we had spent several years training. Each had to manage on his own, and it was with sad hearts that we ourselves also had to face up to changing jobs. At that time I was close to fifty [actually,

in 1941, he was forty-two] and I told myself that never again would I be able to work on this project. (Wan Laiming 1981, quoted in Quiquemelle 1991: 180)

After these setbacks, the Wans worked at whatever jobs were available or that they could generate. For example, Wan Laiming cut out silhouettes, which he sold to foreigners on streets in Shanghai. For a while, Wan Laiming and Wan Guchan lived in Hong Kong, where they commenced work on *The World of Insects* for Great Wall Film Company; again, the project was aborted for lack of capital and trained personnel. The brothers settled for jobs as set designers and special effects technicians for the remainder of their Hong Kong stay.

Although Wan Laiming thought his animation-making days were over in 1941, as stated above, he and two of his brothers became part of the crew of the newly established Shanghai Animation Film Studio in the 1950s. Wan Chaochen returned from the United States where he had emigrated in 1946 to study American animation techniques, and Wan Laiming and Wan Guchan left Hong Kong in 1954, to join what was to become the Shanghai Animation Film Studio. Wan Chaochen directed the studio's first color film, the puppet short *Xiaoyingxiong* (*The Little Heroes*) in 1953; Wan Guchan specialized in paper cut, a genre he conceptualized in 1950, and brought to the screen in 1958 with *Zhu Bajie chi xigua* (*Zhu Bajie [Pigsy] Eats Watermelon*), and Wan Laiming finally realized his twenty-year dream of producing *Danao tiangong* (*Havoc in Heaven*). The threesome directed other animated works in the 1950s and '60s: Wan Laiming—*Yewai de zaoyu* (*Experience in the Wilds*), and with Wan Guchan, *Wuya weishenme shiheide* (*Why the Crow Is Black*); Wan Guchan—*Guo houshan* (*Across Monkey Mountain*), *Jigong dou xishuai* (*Cricket Fighting by Jigong*), *Yutong* (*The Little Fisherman*), *Renshen wawa* (*The Spirit of Ginseng*), and *Jinse de hailuo* (*Golden Conch*); and Wan Chaochen—*Diaolongji* (*The Carved Dragon/Inscriptions of Dragons*).

Transition I: From Austerity to Prosperity

The latter part of the 1940s and the early '50s were a transitional period for China's animation, between a time when animators were few, scrounged on budgets in getting their films made, and worked under the aegis of rather unappreciative, miserly motion picture (not animation) studios, and a time when there was an abundance of trained talent, comfortable government sponsorship, a realistic working pace conducive to producing high-quality films, and a major studio devoted entirely to animation.

With the absence or inactivity of the Wans, others kept the country's animation alive, notably Fang Ming, Qian Jiajun, and Chen Bo'er.

Fang Ming (1919–99) actually was a Japanese animator (Mochinaga Tadahito), who had spent part of his youth in China, part in Tokyo. His father had taken the family to Manchuria when he accepted a position with the South Manchuria Railway Company. Spending his elementary school years in China, Mochinaga became familiar with Chinese culture which proved useful to him later.

On his occasional trips to Tokyo, he viewed early Disney cartoons which convinced him to be an animator. During three years as an art student in Tokyo, he learned animation techniques, and in 1938, "surprised the school instructors by making a short film titled *How to Make Animated Films* as his graduate work" (Ono 1999). When he was graduated, Mochinaga was hired by the animation department of Geijutsu Eigasha (GES, Art Film Company), where he worked with famed World War II animator Seo Mitsuse on *Ari-Chan* (*Ant Boy*) and *Momotaro, the Sea Eagle*, an important propaganda film commissioned by the Japanese Imperial Navy in 1943. It was with *Ant Boy* that Mochinaga designed and built Japan's first multi-plane camera. His first director's post was with *Fuku-chan's Submarine*, also an anti-enemy work derived from the very popular print cartoon strip "Fuku-chan" (Ono 1999).

A number of factors led to Mochinaga's return to Manchuria with his animator wife, Ayako, in June 1945:

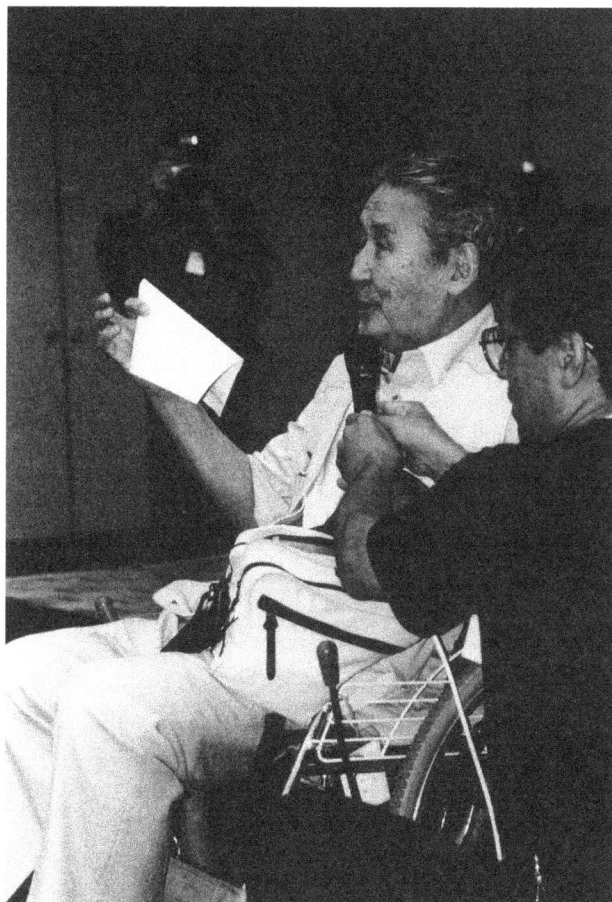

Fig. 6.3. Tadanito Mochinaga, Hiroshima, 1998. Photo by Namiki Takashi.

the deplorable state of war-wasted Tokyo, an air raid burning of his house, and his physical exhaustion after directing *Fuku-chan's Submarine* (Ono 1999). As an experienced animator, Mochinaga was recruited to join the art department of Man-El (Manshu Eiga Kyokai, or Manchukuo Film Association); with about 2,000 employees, it was one of Asia's largest studios. Under Japanese control since its establishment in 1937, Man-El produced cultural promotion films about and for Manchuria's puppet government. After the Japanese surrendered August 15, 1945, Man-El was disbanded as an organization and the rights to the former company were fought over by the Communist Party and Guomindang. The Communists prevailed and seized whatever equipment remained after Soviet looting and created Dongbei Dianying Zhipianchang (Northeast Film Company, renamed Northeast Film Studio, October 1, 1946), integrating Yan'an Film Studio in the process. Northeast Film Company moved to Xingshan in Heilongjiang Province on May 23, 1946, when the Guomindang overran Changchun. On October 20, 1948, the night after the Communist military forces recaptured Changchun, Northeast Film Studio workers seized film equipment left behind by the Guomindang, and six months later (April 1949), Northeast returned to the city (Zhou 2007: 216).

Ono's (1999) version, though not as full, is similar:

> Since a film studio was a valuable asset for both Mao Tsetung's Communist Forces and Chiang Kai-Shek's Nationalists, they fought over the ownership. Even the Soviet forces showed their interest in this studio, because of its scale and latest equipment. The whole of China plunged into civil war. When the Nationalists' attack on Chang Chun became intense in 1946, the studio staff, including Mochinaga, escaped and went further north. Arriving in the mining town of Hao Gang, they started the "new" Tong Pei [Dongbei] Film Studio from scratch. The shooting crew set out to the front lines and concentrated on making news films to inform people about the status of the civil war. Thus, this became the starting point for filmmaking in what is later referred to as New China.

As for Mochinaga, when Man-El disbanded upon Japan's defeat, the Japanese staff "was given the choice to return to Japan or to remain. It was not easy to return to Japan and because he had found joy working with the Chinese staff, Mochinaga chose to remain," according to Ono (1999).

That was a fortunate decision for Chinese animation because of the many contributions Mochinaga (and his spouse) made. Foremost, because of his experience, he had much to teach the novice Chinese animators,[3] and he helped them set up what became the Shanghai Animation Film Studio. Ono (1999) also credited him with making the first stop-motion puppet animation in China (and also, Japan). Mochinaga was also the animator of *Huangdi meng* (*Emperor's Dream*), 1947, directed by Chen Bo'er, and he was director-animator of both *Wengzhong zhuobie* (*Go after an Easy Prey* or *Turtle Caught in a Jar*), 1947–48, assisted by his spouse, Mochinaga Ayako, and *Xiexie xiaohuamao* (*Thank You Kitten*), 1950

Qian Jiajun (1916–2011) is seldom mentioned in the recounting of the history of China's animation, yet he was a guiding force and creative engine in the transitional period of the art. In some instances, colleagues received the accolades for his creations; one that readily comes to mind is the application of ink-wash painting techniques to animation.

A graduate of Suzhou Art School in 1935, Qian studied animation principles in his spare time, and, in November 1940, along with twenty young artists, made *Nongjia le* (*Happiness in a Peasant Family*), a black-and-white, patriotic, anti-Japanese short. Produced by Chongqing Lizhishe, the film tells the story of a girl, who, with her father, brother, and dog, defeat and send away marauding Japanese soldiers who invade their peaceful village.

In 1942, Qian joined and eventually became director of Chongqing Education Film Animation Studio, jointly established by the Education Department of Government Central Film Studio and Lizhishe. As head of animation, he created *Shengsheng buxi* (*Generation after Generation Never Stop*). He moved to Nanjing in 1946 with Lizhishe and planned to produce *Mifeng guo* (*Bees Country*), but it never made it through post-production. The following year, he joined the production team at Shanghai Chinese Press Editorial Office, which had been commissioned by UNESCO to produce *Ren yu shuangshou* (*People and Hands*). After 1949, Qian was hired by what became the Shanghai Animation Film Studio as an art designer, director, and its leading technician; there, and in various educational institutions, he mentored some of China's soon-to-be top animators.

Qian worked in key roles on some of China's classic productions. He was art director of the award-winning *Why the Crow Is Black* (1955–56); director of *Jiuselu* (*The Nine-Color Deer*) (1981); art director of *Jiao'ao de jiangjun* (*The Conceited General*) (1957), which ushered in a Chinese-style of animation; and technical director of two of Shanghai Animation Film Studio's four unique ink-wash painting films, *Xiaokedou zhao mama?* (*Where Is Mama?* or *Little Tadpoles Looking for Their Mother*) in 1960–61, and *Mudi* (*The Cowherd's Flute*) in 1963. He also directed at least two other works, *Ba luobo* (*Pulling the Radish*) in 1957 and *Yifu zhuangjin* (*One Piece of Zhuang Kam*) in 1959.

Qian should be remembered for his help in adapting ink-wash painting techniques to animation, something for which Te Wei is usually given full credit. More recent research by the authors of this book reveals that Qian, A Da (real name, Xu Jingda), and Duan Xiaoxuan (b. 1934) were actually the masterminds behind this invention. Writing immediately after Qian's death, Lei Xu (2011) reconstructed the story of ink-wash painting animation in this manner:

> Xu Jingda [A Da], a young man at the time who later found fame with *Three Monks* (1980), thought that, since people could print the works of famed artist Qi Baishi—whose *Eagle Standing on Pine Tree with Four-Character Couplet in Seal Script* recently set a record for contemporary Chinese art at auction when it sold for 425.5 million yuan ($65 million)—on wash basin, why couldn't they produce them in cartoon form?
>
> Xu invited Duan Xiaoxuan, a photographer, and Qian Jiajun, a leading technician at the Shanghai Animation Film Studio (SAFS), to realize his bold idea. After the first clip, featuring a frog jumping from a lotus leaf, was successfully produced, the entire studio was mobilized.
>
> Three months later, they completed the 15-minute *Baby Tadpoles*, hence opening a new chapter in animation: the birth of the first ink-wash film.
>
> Among those participating were some of China's top painters, such as Li Keran and Huang Yongyu. Li donated many of his buffalo paintings to SAFS and in 1963, the studio created China's second ink-wash-style animation, *The Cowboy's Flute* [*The Cowherd's Flute*], about a young cowboy, his extraordinary flute-playing ability and his faithful water buffalo. (More discussion of this chain of events is included later in this chapter.)

Though short-lived, Chen Bo'er (real name, Chen Shunhua, 1907–51) enjoyed an adventurous life as a film and stage actress and director, screenwriter, novelist, essayist, animator, documentary director, administrator, revolutionist, and educator. She acted in at least four films, including a starring role in China's first sound motion picture, *Taolijie* (*Fate of College Graduates*) in 1934, and two with her future second husband, Yuan Muzhi.

In 1929, Chen Bo'er was graduated from Shanghai Art University, where she met a Vietnamese Chinese, Ren Bosheng, whom she married in Hong Kong in 1931, and had a son by him. In 1934, she and the child went to Shanghai, where she began acting, including in an anti-Japanese film, *Babai zhuangshi* (*Eight Hundred Warriors*), and an anti-Japanese stage drama, *Baowei lugouqiao* (*Protecting Luguo Bridge*), both in 1937. Very active in the antiwar effort and rescue activities, she joined the Communist Party in 1937, and the next year, went to Yan'an with her son, where she directed and acted in several stage dramas and documentaries denouncing fascism, supporting Maoist principles, and attempting to change the popular image of women as insecure seductresses. Her films were among the first that showed feminine strength from a feminine viewpoint. As a leading figure in the Communist struggle for China, she traveled to cities and villages around the country in an effort to recruit women to join the Revolution (Wang Zheng 2012).

By 1947, Chen Bo'er had been sent north to help develop Northeast Film Studio and serve as its art director. That year, she organized and led the production of a seventeen-series documentary, *Minzhu dongbei* (*The Democratic Northeast*) and directed and wrote the screenplay for *Emperor's Dream*, a two-reel puppet animation film included in the fourth series of the documentary *Democratic Northeast*. *Emperor's Dream* portrayed Guomindang leader Chiang Kai-shek as a stooge of the United States, willing to give up numerous Chinese national rights in exchange for economic and military aid in his bid to be an "emperor." The film was based on a caricature of Chiang by Hua Junwu. The second animated film produced while Chen Bo'er headed the art department was *Go after an Easy Prey*, which was written by cartoonist Zhu Dan. It also denounced Chiang for being propped up by American imperialism.

The Guomindang leader is shown in a castle which turns into a jar and Chiang into a turtle; a People's Liberation Army soldier stomps the jar to pieces and holds the turtle [Chiang] by the neck.

Convinced that the studio should continue animation production, Chen Bo'er helped set up an animation division in the art department. Her choice to head such a division was political cartoonist Te Wei (born Sheng Song). In 1949, Te Wei and painter Jin Xi (Jin Shi, real name, Zeng Diping, 1919–97) were asked by the Ministry of Culture to go to the northeast, establish an animation group, and learn the art from Fang Ming, which they did.

Chen Bo'er and Yuan Muzhi, whom she married in 1947, moved to Beijing in 1949, where, a year later, she established Beijing Performing Art Research Institute, later to become the Beijing Film Academy. In the span of her forty-four-year life, Chen Bo'er starred in China's first sound film and became the country's first woman director and screenwriter, and at the beginning of the new China, she helped establish both the first people's film studio and film academy, pioneered the making of puppet and animation films, and wrote and directed the first documentaries. Despite these major accomplishments and the public reverence of her in the formative years of PRC, she is largely forgotten today.

The Shanghai Animation Film Studio and the First Golden Era

When Te Wei received the order from the Ministry of Culture, under a directive from Zhou Enlai, he was not enthusiastic about doing animation, because he dreaded "all those monotonous frames," but most of all, because he knew absolutely nothing about animation production (Te Wei, interview, 2001). Futhermore, he probably was not excited about moving to a much colder climate. Te Wei thought Chen Bo'er called on him because she knew of his print cartoons, which professionally dated back to 1935. He said he accepted the challenge, because "cartooning had similarities to animation except for its lack of movement" (Te Wei, interview, 2001).

The animation unit stayed in Changchun for about a year. In 1950, Te Wei and his staff felt Shanghai offered "better conditions" and with the sanction of the Ministry of Culture, they joined the Shanghai Film Studio, along with artists from the Wan Brothers, Central Academy of Fine Arts, the Art Institute of Suzhou, Beijing Film Academy, and other top institutions. Te Wei retained his position as head of the art department (Te Wei, interview, 2001).

Upon arriving in Shanghai in 1950, one of the first tasks Te Wei and his staff took on was to learn animation styles and techniques, which they accomplished primarily through "study and exploration." Te Wei (interview, 2001) talked about the challenges they encountered and decisions they made:

> In the 1950s, we thought we should have Chinese art films. The first animation was puppet. They were not called cartoons, but art films. When we closed the door to the US, you seldom heard of cartoons, only art or animation films. The staff at the time seldom said we should learn from Disney, but most of them liked Disney skills in movement, styles, etc. When the Guomindang left [1949], they left behind some Disney work, including *Fantasia*, which Chinese animators had seen. The word "animation" can include all aspects—paper cut, paperfold, puppet, etc. We didn't waste time over what to call it; we just did things to make a national identity-type animation. We also learned from the high skills of foreign countries.

In the early days, animators usually learned as they worked, the way Te Wei grasped animation skills and also the way he recommended to young artists. Yan Shanchun (interview, 2016) admitted he did not know about animation when he began working at the studio, which was the case with other newcomers. He said that Te Wei comforted them by saying "just work; you will learn from experienced senior animators." Although Qian Yunda (b. 1929) was graduated from Zhongnan Art School and studied at the Prague Arts and Crafts College, he learned much while making his seven-minute *La jinzhong* (*Pull a Metal Bell from a Pond*) in Prague. He

Fig. 6.4. *Jiaoao de Jiangjun* (*The Conceited General*), 1956. Courtesy of Shanghai Animation Film Studio and Te Wei.

said that the Czech studio photographer every night left the key with him, and during the night, "I stayed alone in the studio, and shot my film" (Qian, interview, 2016).

Te Wei (interview, 2004) said that, when the animators attended international festivals, they learned from the films that were screened. "I'm open-minded and learn from everyone, but not to duplicate their films," he added. Other studio pioneers said they were influenced by Disney, Polish, and Czech animation, as was the case with Zhang Songlin (interview, 2005), while making the humorous *Meitounao he bugaoxing* (*Scatter-brain and Crosspatch*, called *Mindless and Unhappy* by Zhang [interview, 2005]). As mentioned above, Qian Yunda spent five-and-a-half years (1954–59) in the Czech Republic; he studied with the puppet master Jiri Trnka.

No doubt, in the beginning, the country the Shanghai animators learned the most from was the Soviet Union. Te Wei (interview, 2001) explained that "every aspect of everything was learned from the Soviets at the time, because Soviet animation had high level skills and very healthy contents." Another reason was that the Soviet Union was the country friendliest to, and most ideologically aligned with, China. Ironically, Te Wei's enthusiasm for the Soviet model wore off when his studio's *Why the Crow Is Black* won an award at the 1955 Venice animation festival, and to the dismay of the Chinese animators, the judges mistook the film as a Soviet work. It was then, according to Te Wei, that he decided Chinese animation must reflect Chinese customs, stories, and techniques.

As a result, Te Wei (interview, 2001) said that he made his move to rectify the misunderstanding while directing *The Conceited General* in 1956, when he hung a slogan on the studio wall that implored animators to explore a national way of animation. Discussing *The Conceited General*, which, with its use of Peking opera-like movements, was the first such experiment, Te Wei (interview, 2001) said, "We had a clear idea to draw useful things from the traditional arts—local opera, drama, and Peking opera. From the models to the movements, we followed these operas. Most importantly, we invited opera teachers to the film studio to show us how to move."

Ehrlich and Jin (2001: 9) conceded that *The Conceited General* showed a "national spirit," but offered an earlier film, the award-winning *Shenbi Ma Liang* (*The Magic Paintbrush*), in 1955, as also being Chinese-styled. They wrote, "The backgrounds, puppets' clothing and the charming interactions between the people in the village were very much a part of the everyday living experience of the average Chinese." It was directed by Jin Xi and You Lei, the former sent with Te Wei to build the studio when it was in Changchun. Another pioneer lost in China's animation annals, Jin Xi directed *Xiaoxiao yingxiong* (*Little Hero*), in 1953, which helped set the pattern for children's entertainment, and *Kongque gongzhu* (*The Peacock Princess*), in 1963, described as, "First feature-length puppet animation that was based on a legend of the Thai [actually, it is Dai] people, something like the *Swan Lake* of the East" (Giesen 2015: 47). He also conceived *Afanti de gushi* (*Story of Effendi*), a thirteen-part, stop-motion puppet series, running from 1981 to 1988, directed by Qu Jianfang (b. 1935) and Cai Yunlan. It was the first animated series in China's history.

Though excellent works were made in the early 1950s, as just indicated, the first "golden age" of Chinese animation was 1957–1964. In October 1956, at a Beijing meeting of the Film Bureau of the Ministry of Culture, the reorganization of the Shanghai Film Studio was discussed and, as a result, three new entities were created, including the Shanghai Animation Film Studio. On April 1, 1957, a sign bearing the names "Shanghai

Fig. 6.5. *Caoyuan yingxiong xiaojiemei* (*Two Heroic Sisters of the Grasslands*), 1965. Courtesy of Shanghai Animation Film Studio and Qian Yunda.

Animation Film Studio" or "Shanghai Fine Art Film Studio" was put on the gate of the official residence of the former Shanghai mayor, thus, providing a home for the studio (Giesen 2015: 24).

Ehrlich and Jin (2001: 10) wrote about the boost this move gave to animation:

> In addition to the tremendous credibility given the Shanghai animators in 1957 by their new official status as the state "Studio," there was an influx of additional state support, new artists, equipment, and the encouragement for them to abandon the Soviet model of animation, to study animation being done throughout the west and to develop their own animation models that were more truly Chinese.

The Shanghai Animation Film Studio was established as an independent organization centrally controlled and financed by the Ministry of Culture and supervised by Te Wei. Initially, the studio had 200 employees and was designed to produce animated films for children "that were educational at the same time they were entertaining" (Ehrlich and Jin 2001: 9).

A number of factors were responsible for the first so-called golden age. First, no one seemed to care about how much money was spent; as animation critic/theorist/scriptwriter Chen Jianyu noted, "The government gave money and collected all the outstanding animators together. How long they took to produce, no one cared." Chen added that Te Wei and other animators were middle-aged, "with much energy," and as recent graduates of film and art academies, some mature at that time. Also helpful were a prosperous production system, three

generations of animators working alongside each other, and the level of government interest and support (Chen, interview, 2001).

Key to the studio's success was the "good atmosphere" alluded to by animators entering the profession at that time. Claiming that a congenial working atmosphere no longer exists, because of assembly-line production, Zhang Songlin (interview, 2005) said that during the "golden" eras, it was

> very strong. Every aspect from idea to screenplay until character design and beyond, we discussed together. No matter who the director was, he listened humbly to others' opinions. Every animator involved in a work thought of it as his [/her] own and talked about ideas. Every animation was the fruit of group effort. That's why the animation was so excellent—this gathering of all this wisdom and talent working together.

New animators learned work skills as well as human values, such as patience, humbleness, and cooperation, as neophyte Zhan Tong (interview, 1993) found out while working with pioneer Wan Laiming:

> I was at the studio from the very beginning and started my career from the very bottom—assistant to the assistant of background design. Starting at the bottom meant I went through all types of work. Wan Laiming told me "of the six masters of animation [writer, director, actor/actress, photographer, sound controller, and art designer], art designer is the lowest, and you are even third from the bottom among art designers." Mr. Wan said, "Don't be so picky." He was teaching me a working methodology and the principles of being a good man.

Chang Guangxi talked glowingly about learning much from husband-wife animators Yan Dingxian and Lin Wenxiao before being given a key animator role in 1963 on *Caoyuan yingxiong xiaojiemei* (*Two Heroic Sisters of the Grasslands*, 1965), about two Mongolian teenage sisters who risk their lives to save their commune's sheep during a snowstorm (Chang, interview,

2009). Ma Kexuan, who joined the studio in September 1959, used the word "lucky" when describing his experiences—lucky to have been "appointed" to the studio, to be mentored by Te Wei, Wan Laiming, and Qian Yunda, and to have learned animation during his first four years on masterpieces such as *Where Is Mama?* and *The Cowherd's Flute* (Ma, interview, 2005). Yet, on another occasion, Ma Kexuan (interview, 2011) challenged the common belief that Shanghai Animation Film Studio was a cooperative, unified place to work. He said people were divided in importance by their past affiliations: Considered first class were those who came from Beijing Film Academy, such as Yan Dingxian; second class were those who previously were at the Northeast studio in Changchun, such as Wang Shuchen and He Yumen (1928–98); and third class, graduates of art academies or art schools, such as Zhan Tong, A Da, and Ma Kexuan.

Knowledge, creative experimentation, and government collaboration characterized the initial golden age. The gaining of knowledge by the first two generations of Chinese animators has already been discussed. Some of the next generation, from 1959 to 1964, learned at an animation program in the Shanghai Vocational Film Training School, taught by Qian Jiajun and Zhang Songlin. Zhang (interview, 2005) recalled:

> At that time, we were all newcomers to the teaching field. It was a task for me. I told the leaders I came from animation practice and that I would not follow the educational way. I broke the old academy way. Normally, three years were used to train animators, but I agreed with the leaders who wanted it narrowed to two years. From high school graduates, I chose those who could draw well; I thought if a student could draw well, that was better than classroom knowledge.
>
> I divided the two years into four parts—in the first one-half year, students learned the fundamentals of drawing; the second phase, the skills of animation drawing; the third half-year, how to design and create characters; and finally, they were required to make a ten-minute animation film in the fourth half-year.

Zhang showed his students "hundreds of movies, famous US features and animation shorts, Soviet ones too—whatever we could get." He also set up music and acting classes and, "they listened to music from all over the world. I invited famous Shanghai musicians to lecture. We also had a performance class, because we thought to be a good animation designer, they needed to know acting. Students staged dramas" (Zhang, interview, 2005).

Chang Guangxi, denied admission to Tsinghua University because "my father was a Guomindang officer," went instead to the Shanghai Vocational Film Training School, where he studied with Zhang Songlin from 1960 to 1962. He said:

> I was very fond of animation from childhood. I decided if I couldn't go to the best university to study architecture, I would go to this animation school. . . . All the students in my class at this school and I created an animated film, *Mindless and Unhappy*, which has influenced many students until now. Zhang Songlin was the director and we students the key animators. (Chang, interview, 2009)

Chang went directly from the school to Shanghai Animation Film Studio, where his first assignment was to work on *Havoc in Heaven*, directed by Wan Laiming.

In 1964, the Shanghai Vocational Film Training School animation program was merged with the Beijing animation setup; the Shanghai teachers and students moved with the program. Zhang stayed behind and returned to the Shanghai Animation Film Studio, where he continued to write screenplays for *Banye jijiao* (*The Cock Crows at Midnight*, 1964), *Xiaobalu* (*Little Eighth Route Army*, 1974), and *Qiyi de mengguma* (*Fantastic Mongolia Horse*, 1989–90).

With plenty of time and resources available, a cooperative and trained staff, and Maoist admonitions since the Yan'an Talks about how culture should reflect a national spirit, the Shanghai Animation Film Studio turned into the sort of experimental workplace very seldom seen elsewhere in the world. After the Chinese-styled *The Conceited General*, with its application of Peking opera movements, became popular in art and public circles, the studio's experimentation with content, techniques, and basic raw material accelerated.

Studio photographer Duan Xiaoxuan (interview, 2016) told how the animators used life experiences and participatory engagement to prepare an animated film. She said that they put into practice Mao Zedong's principle that life is the source of art creation. For example, with the films *The Cowherd's Flute*, *The Deer Bell*, and *Feeling from Mountain and Water*, ten-person crews (usually, four animators, two background designers, and one photographer, director, producer, and music composer) went to the countryside for a couple of months to experience rural life and research the subjects of their films.

The crew of *The Cowherd's Flute* spent two months in Guangdong Province, where they observed the buffalos' movements, recorded the cowboy's life, and experienced rural living. Duan Xiaoxuan (interview, 2016), believing this to be the best way to create, said the crew got a taste of all types of pre-production, at the same time that they mingled with the cowherds. *Feeling from Mountain and Water* crew members hired a bus and went to the mountainous area of the Fuchun River in Zhejiang Province, a region Duan described as looking "like a painting." They invited two professors from the Zhejiang Art Academy, character designer Wu Shanming and background designer Zuo Hejun, to paint the mountains and river not with clear lines, but by spreading the ink to create a foggy atmosphere. Duan photographed the painters as they worked, after which the three of them discussed the results; Duan called this a new way to produce animation (Duan, interview, 2016). To prepare *Where Is Mama?* the animators studied the movements of tadpoles, shrimp, crabs, turtles, and other creatures, all of which were kept in a pond on the studio's grounds. Duan (interview, 2016) said, "We observed how tadpoles moved when they were happy and when they were not happy; we observed their emotions."

To emphasize the aesthetic effects, each of the studio's four ink-wash animated works used a different painter's style: *The Cowherd's Flute*, that of Li Keran;

Where Is Mama? Qi Baishi; *The Deer Bell*, Cheng Shifa; and *Feeling from Mountain and Water*, Wu and Zuo.

Qian Yunda (interview, 2016) cited two of his animated films that employed the life experience approach: For his favorite, *Red Army Bridge*, the crew went to a small mountain area in Hunan to experience walking on the same roads that the Red Army had, and for *Two Heroic Sisters of the Grasslands*, he and others participated in grasslands' life.

The raw materials used were also in experimental stages. Puppet animation, the first post-World War II animation, was, by the 1950s, in wide use, as was paper cut, which also had deep cultural roots. Wan Guchan and his twenty-two-year-old assistant, Hu Jinqing (b. 1936), worked for a year to make the first paper cut film, the award-winning *Zhu Bajie [Pigsy] Eats the Watermelon* (1958). Hu (interview, 2001) said paper cut was chosen for animation because it has a "long history and it is traditional. Our thinking was the more national a work was, the more international it would be." *Zhu Bajie [Pigsy] Eats the Watermelon* was followed by other paper cut works, such as *Yutong* (*The Little Fisherman*, 1959), *The Spirit of Ginseng* (1961), *Deng mingtian* (*Waiting for Tomorrow*, 1962), *Chabuduo* (*More or Less*), and *Hongjunqiao* (*Red Army Bridge*), both 1964. Hu Xionghua (1931–83) made *Waiting for Tomorrow* and *More or Less*.

Wan Guchan was the spearhead of paper cut; besides *Zhu Bajie [Pigsy] Eats the Watermelon*, he also directed *The Little Fisherman* and *The Spirit of Ginseng*. His assistant, Hu Jinqing, continued to refine paper cut animation, eventually surpassing his teacher in quantity and quality of work. After Wan Guchan's health suffered, Hu, in the 1960s, collaborated with Qian Yunda in making *Jinse de hailuo* (*Golden Conch*), a variation of Chinese shadow puppet and paper cut, and *Red Army Bridge* (Hu, interview, 2001). For about three years, Hu also experimented to find a way to combine paper cut with the ink-wash painting technique. He explained the difficulty of combining the two: "Paper cut is of two kinds—tough and soft. Ink wash is the soft way. With the tough method, you just follow the lines and cut, but

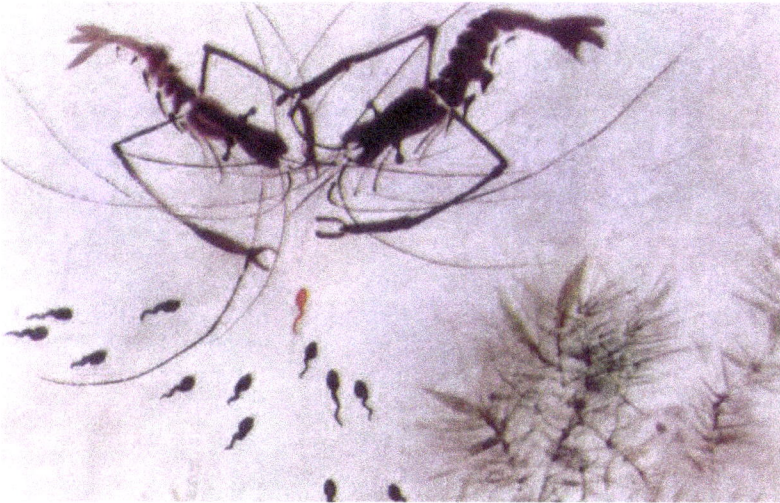

Fig. 6.6. *Xiaokedou zhao mama?* (*Where Is Mama?*) ink wash, 1960–61. Courtesy of Shanghai Animation Film Studio and Te Wei.

with the soft, if you add too much water, it will fade. The tough way is clear" (Hu, interview, 2001).

In the 1960s, Yu Zhenguang (1906–91) introduced the traditional Chinese folk craft of folded paper (later introduced in Japan as *origami*) to animation with *Congming de yazi* (*The Clever Ducklings*), a tale of ducklings who outwit and spook a cat that was chasing them. Another folded animated film, *Yike dabaicai* (*A Cabbage*), appeared in 1961, but the folded paper technique was not popular and was used in only several studio productions.

The technique resulting from the Shanghai Animation Film Studio's experimentation that caused a sensation was the aforementioned ink-wash painting, first used with *Where Is Mama?* and then *The Cowherd's Flute*. Rist (2016: 60), while studying landscape painting aesthetics and Chinese film, said that the "closest connections between classical landscape painting and Chinese films of the first seventeen years of the PRC" were these two animated works. The studio made only four ink-wash painting films while Te Wei was there; besides *Where Is Mama?* and *The Cowherd's Flute*, *Luling* (*The Deer Bell*, 1982) and *Shanshuiqing* (*Feeling from Mountain and Water*, 1988) came out of the second "golden" age after the Cultural Revolution.

Duan Xiaoxuan (interview, 2016) ventured reasons for the limited number of ink-wash animated films: 1. they are very expensive to produce; 2. they require special aesthetic effects, and 3. they need high-quality scripts, which increasingly became hard to find.

Where Is Mama? resulted from a hope expressed by the first mayor of Shanghai and future vice premier of China, Chen Yi, that one day ink-wash, mastered by famous artist Qi Baishi, would be animated. Contrary to what Duan Xiaoxuan is quoted as saying in this chapter, Te Wei said he took this as a challenge:

This type of painting was very famous and had a long history, so I thought we should do animation this way. Qi Baishi painted a lot of tadpoles and shrimp; we thought we'd make them move. We tried many ways before they moved. We made samples and showed them to the art association and got a strong positive reaction. (Te Wei, interview, 2001)

Where Is Mama? won five awards, including at Annecy, Cannes, and Locarno. Animator and scholar David Ehrlich described this method of animation as aiming,

to express the spirit of both the artist and what is being depicted, by the modulation of speed and pressure with which the fingers move the brush. Although the viewer of the finished painting is not witness to the movement of the hand that painted the picture, it is possible to experience that movement kinesthetically by looking carefully at the strokes of ink that it has left. (Ehrlich 2001: 11)

Other animators working at the time these ink-wash painting classics were made weighed in on various aspects of them. Hu Jinqing (interview, 2001) and Qian Yunda (interview, 2001) insisted ink-wash painting animation needs "good" scripts. Qian explained:

Some stories are not suitable for ink wash. The four ink-wash productions [from 1960 to 1988] were outstanding

Animation: From Hand-Crafted Experimentation to Digitalization

because the art and story forms combined very well. *The Deer Bell* was not as successful as the story was not suitable enough. Normally, animators find the content [story] and then a form that is suitable. It is different with ink wash— you find a content that fits the form.

Te Wei (interview, 2004) emphasized the need for much time, because ink wash "takes lots of work, doing it piece by piece." And, obviously, to make ink-wash painting animation, a keen knowledge of Chinese traditional painting is required, which almost all animators lack. Te Wei (interview, 2004) said that *Feeling from Mountain and Water*, which took a year to produce, was "rushed" in order to be entered in a festival, adding, "If we had had more time, we could have made it more perfect."

Much controversy lingers about the "inventor" of ink-wash painting animation. As stated earlier, Te Wei usually receives full credit, though others were heavily involved. One interpretation of this issue of the inventor came out of a discussion involving A Da's son, Xu Chang (aka Charles Zee), US animator David Ehrlich, film magazine editor Jin Tianyi, and the authors of this book that took place in Shanghai, June 9, 2005. According to Xu Chang, after Vice Premier Chen Yi expressed his desire to see ink wash applied to animation, the Shanghai studio staff scurried about trying to find a method:

> One day, my dad said excitedly, "I have an idea, but I'm not sure we can do it." He then went to his teacher Qian Jiajun's house to ask him what to do. Qian told him, "You can try to do it." So, A Da worked together with the studio photographer to make several pieces of film as samples to show to Te Wei to get his permission. Te Wei said, "OK, you can try it." (Xu Chang, interview, 2005)

From the beginning, credit was difficult to ascertain. When individual prizes were given at a competition in which one of the studio's ink-wash works was entered, the first prize went to the leader of the photographers on the project, Duan Xiaoxuan, second to A Da, and third to Qian Jiajun. Xu Chang (interview, 2005) explained that Duan Xiaoxuan told Te Wei that she had come up with

Fig. 6.7. Duan Xiaoxuan. Camerawoman of ink-wash animation films, June 11, 2016. Photo by Xu Ying. Courtesy of Duan Xiaoxuan.

the idea, and because Te Wei was powerful as studio head, his was the final word. Xu Chang said that Duan, as head of the photographers, had written down the steps she and the animators had employed in making ink-wash painting animation and had secretly kept them.

Duan Xiaoxuan's version differs from those of Xu Chang and Te Wei. Asked directly, "Who invented ink wash animation?" without hesitation, she said, "I was the first. In 1954, I wrote an application report to Te Wei and asked him to make Chinese painting into animation" (Duan Xiaoxuan, interview, 2016). She added that Te Wei thought about it for a while, and then, in 1958, at the advent of the Great Leap Forward movement, when big progress was on everyone's minds, A Da told Duan he had heard of her report and suggested they cooperate in experimenting with the technique. After ending their work days at the studio, A Da and Duan spent evenings deliberating about and trying different ways to create ink-wash animation. "A Da drew; I shot and printed out the film during the night, using a hair dryer to dry the film," Duan (interview, 2016) said. They showed their end product to Te Wei, who, according to Duan, said "we could do it."

Some time later, the Shanghai Animation Film Studio held an exhibition in Beijing to show off the animation industry's achievements. Vice Premier Chen Yi visited the exhibition and was told of the ink-wash animation experiments, to which, he replied, "If you can make Qi Baishi's shrimps move, that would be good," Duan related. The challenge was enthusiastically accepted, and Duan and other animators were divided into four research groups to study frogs, chickens, fish, and horses (the latter were dropped), all matching subjects in Qi Baishi paintings. They then produced a longer experimental animation short and showed it to Te Wei, who, according to Duan (interview, 2016), said two words: "Xing! Gan!" ("Okay! Do It!"). The story for *Where Is Mama?*—which the studio used for the first ink-wash animation—was found in a primary school textbook.

Duan filled in other details concerning the origins of ink-wash animation. She said Vice Premier Chen Yi's encouragement may have resulted from his friendly visits to the studio while he was mayor of Shanghai and occupied offices in the same building as the Shanghai Animation Film Studio. To support her claim to being the ink-wash animation inventor, she showed the authors of this book photographs of patent certificates and the 2nd Class National Invention Award that list her as first inventor because she first suggested the idea and used her photography skills. A Da is placed second for his artistic work, and Qian Jiajun, as general engineer, for his guidance on techniques. For example, originally the ink-wash animation experiments were in black-and-white; Qian guided the crew in using color (Duan, interview, 2016). Duan (interview, 2016) expanded on how the patent credits were ordered:

To apply for a patent, you have to give one person, not a group, as the inventor. I think the studio leaders, during discussions, decided who should be number one inventor by the number of contributions made.

Photography is the key to ink-wash animation. The special effects of ink wash require photography skills. Those skills are not like shooting regular animation. With ink wash, you have to shoot a scene many times to get the effects; to get the ink to spread, you need to shoot multiple layers, reprint many times, and research special effects.

Her reaction to the other claims for the invention:

Different people have different versions. I have heard them all, but the fact is, I am the only one to experience the whole process from beginning to end. Te Wei played an important role as supporter, but he did not participate in the experimenting with techniques.

Zhang Songlin's (and Gong Jianying) book, which credits Te Wei with creating *Where Is Mama?* (Zhang and Gong 2010), is not factual; a little bit of it is made up. When it was published, Yan Shanchun, Pu Jiaxiang [members of the *Where Is Mama?* crew] and I wrote a letter to the publisher and the studio leader, saying parts were not true. Te Wei was only the leader; he did not know the skills. I respected Te Wei, but he did not know the techniques.

Duan (interview, 2016) said that she did write down the process of ink-wash animation as it was being invented ("What I did; the conditions; how long each step took, a record of all scenes [in each of the four ink-wash animation films]") and has kept the notes in her apartment, not trusting the studio to keep them safe and not divulging their contents in agreement with patent requirements.

During the course of her dissertation research on the early history of the Shanghai Animation Film Studio, Daisy Yan Du (2014) also surmised that Duan Xiaoxuan had invented the technique. She wrote:

In 1958, the Communist Party advocated for technological innovation in all aspects of socialist production. As the person in charge of animation technology, Duan, with support from her colleagues, proposed to make ink-painting animated film. Her proposal was supported by the studio and Chen Yi. . . . After many trials and failures, they made *Little Tadpoles Look for Mama* [*Where Is Mama?*]. . . . The technique of ink painting has been a national secret since, but it is generally believed that the key resides in the photography, which Duan controlled. . . . It is only through the mediation of animation photography that the ink-painting technique can be reproduced on cell [*sic*].

Ma Kexuan (interview, 2011), who was an animator for *Three Monks* and co-director of *Feeling from Mountain and Water*, said, "There was a pattern of Te Wei taking the credit; three directors would make a classic

Fig. 6.8. *Yubang xiangzheng* (*Snipe-Clam Grapple*), paper cut, 1983. Courtesy of Shanghai Animation Film Studio and Hu Jinqing.

but only Te Wei would be credited to the fullest." As an example, he mentioned the credits for the latter film:

> Te Wei, Yan Shanchun, and I were co-directors. Te Wei said we should share the credits. We insisted Te Wei should be listed first, Yan second, and me third as I was the youngest. After this animation won the grand prize at the First Shanghai International Film Festival, Te Wei told Yan that because he had done a lot for this work, he would like to be the general director, and Yan and I would be credited as co-directors. But, later on, people only mentioned Te Wei as director.

Yan Shanchun elaborated on Ma Kexuan's comments. Answering a question posed by the authors of this book about the Shanghai Animation Film Studio's atmosphere—was it cooperative or conflictual?—Yan said that in the early days, harmony ruled, but later, a major conflict was "personnel arrangement" (Yan Shanchun, interview, 2016). By way of example, he explained how the directorship of *Feeling from Mountain and Water* evolved:

> On *Feeling from Mountain and Water*, Te Wei asked me to join as head of animation. Previously, on *The Cowherd's Flute*, I was in charge of determining how many layers of animation were needed, something I learned in 1962 from Qian Jiajun. Not many animators could do that. Later, I had been a director. When I joined *Feeling from Mountain and Water*, Te Wei assigned me to do layering, but I thought I should be director. Te Wei let me be the director, but, after that, he decided there would be three directors—Ma Kexuan, Te Wei, and me. After the film was completed, Te Wei asked if in the credits, he could be general director and Ma and I, directors. I was not comfortable with that as I did most of the work. Today, I would tell Te Wei, no way, but I respected him as the leader and said okay. (Yan Shanchun, interview, 2016)

It is very likely that Te Wei was credited with the invention because he was studio head, which was a common practice at the time. That was Te Wei's belief. When David Ehrlich asked Te Wei who invented ink-wash painting animation, his reply was, "I did. I made the decision to start making it." He said as much when we asked him what his proudest achievements were:

> I did one important thing; I explored national styles and ways for animation. I not only said what had to be done; I not only put a slogan on the wall [declaring the studio's films had to be Chinese-based and -originated], but I did something—made outstanding ink-wash films. (Te Wei, interview, 2001)

Besides co-directing *Where Is Mama?* Te Wei wrote the script and directed *The Cowherd's Flute* and later, as stated above, was general director of *Feeling from Mountain and Water*.

A third characteristic of China's first golden animation period, carried over to the post-Cultural Revolution times, was the government's cooperation, financial and administrative support, and, generally, hands-off policy. Besides providing the studio with facilities and supplies and not pressuring animators with strict or tight deadlines, the government also handled marketing and distribution, thus, freeing time for serious production creativity. The animated films did have political implications, but usually they were not blatantly obvious. Most often, they were more moralistic than propagandistic, as in one of Hu Jinqing's later paper cut films, *Yubang xiangzheng*

Fig. 6.9. *Danao tiangong* (*Havoc in Heaven*), 1961, 1964. Courtesy of Shanghai Animation Film Studio.

(*Snipe-Clam Grapple*, 1983), which sends the message that when the snipe and clam fight, only the fisherman wins.

In all probability, the authorities did not have to interfere with production. The animators knew their limits, having followed Mao's instructions about art and culture that dated to Yan'an, watched colleagues and friends imprisoned or sent to the rural areas because of accusations brought against them, and in many cases, experienced the same cruel fates themselves.

Animated films often related to historical events (e.g., *The Little Fisherman* and the Boxer Rebellion; *Banye jijiao* [1964], based on the autobiography of Red Army fighter Gao Yubao; and *Red Army Bridge* [1964], about a bridge repaired by Mao's army and then defended by peasants against Guomindang forces), or to Mao and his policies or heroism and current events showing China's triumphs (e.g., *Havoc in Heaven* [first part, 1961; second part, 1964], about which Ehrlich and Jin [2001: 11] wrote, "As a young conquering potent male who creates 'havoc' with the 'old boy' networks in Heaven, Monkey [King] proved to be the paradigm of the heroic rebel for Mao Tsetung," and *Chuang Tapestry* [1959], about the dangerous retrieval of a tapestry in Tibet, timed to be released in the same year when the PLA quashed the Tibetan uprising and forced the Dalai Lama to flee).

Government involvement in the Shanghai studio's animation was remembered in different ways by interviewed animators. *Red Army Bridge* director Qian Yunda said:

> At that time (1950–60s), political factors influenced art very much. The government had demands of us as filmmakers.

The government did not give us instructions; instead, it hoped we used animation to show modern class struggle and problems. Under this request/demand, I chose *Red Army Bridge* as a way to do this. (Qian, interview, 2001)

Zhan Tong offered this description of government-studio relationships:

> We produced films that followed the existing policy of China, that is, to serve the children. In addition, we did some international topics, such as American imperialism and an attack on Eisenhower. Also, some animation films were made in cooperation with the Great Leap Forward political movement, and there were a few adult animation films, but very few. These would be like new types; for example, one that might introduce a new porcelain product. (Zhan Tong, interview, 1993)

Te Wei's impression was that the government maintained a hands-off policy to help animation develop. He said:

> Seldom was there government control of the animation industry. Some believe there was so little government control so that the industry could develop smoothly. And some senior government leaders have been artists, literary and cultural workers, like Xia Yan, Chen Huangmei, and Premier Zhou Enlai. Even Zhou gave his attention, spiritual support, and suggestions to animation. I saw Zhou many times and he often talked about animation films. On one occasion, when he visited Southeast Asian countries, Zhou took Chinese animation with him to show. When he met Japanese delegates, he told them Chinese art films could find their own ways. (Te Wei, interview, 2001)

There was no disagreement on the role of government and political forces after the mid-1960s, the decade of the Cultural Revolution. What was put together in the first fourteen years of the studio (1950–64) was shelved or destroyed in a period of nearly the same length that followed. Many of the studio's works (including *The Cowherd's Flute*, *Havoc in Heaven*, and *Red Army*

171

Animation: From Hand-Crafted Experimentation to Digitalization

Fig. 6.10. *Mudi* (*The Cowherd's Flute*) ink wash, 1963. Courtesy of Shanghai Animation Film Studio and Te Wei.

Bridge) could not be shown in China again until the late 1970s or '80s, and new production all but dried up from 1965 to 1973. In fact, only two animated films were shown throughout the Cultural Revolution: the puppet films *The Cock Crows at Midnight* and *Two Heroic Sisters of the Grasslands*. Animators joined intellectuals and artists in rural settings, where they were given humiliating work and made to engage in self-criticism.

Te Wei as head of the studio was already criticized by party leaders (for not reflecting the class struggle) two years before the Cultural Revolution. He was ordered to write self-criticism, and when he could not comply, he was sent to a factory to work. When the Cultural Revolution started, for one year, he was isolated in a small room under very close supervision. Te Wei talked about that experience.

> In my tiny room, I had a table with a pane of glass on it. I drew many paintings on it. When I heard sounds—the guards coming—I erased the paintings with a wet cloth. I drew everything by imagination; I drew like I'd been there and saw it. This capability was from having drawn cartoons and animation. Later, when my job was feeding pigs [along with fellow animator A Da], I saw a lovely baby pig that I thought I would animate when I got out, but I didn't. One fat pig we named Wu Faxian, after one of the Gang of Four. A Da and I amused ourselves with humor at times. (Te Wei, interview, 2001; see also Chapter 4 of this book.)

Other animators besides Te Wei and A Da were cruelly treated during the Cultural Revolution. Zhan Tong, as related earlier, was sent to the countryside where his job was to find food for pigs (Zhan Tong, interview, 1993), and husband-wife animators Yan Dingxian and

Lin Wenxiao were made to work separately, away from their two children. Yan fed chickens; Lin planted vegetables (Ehrlich 2001: 14).

The animators gradually returned to the studio in 1973, producing mostly propaganda films, rendered in a realistic manner. Chen Jianyu thought this was a low point for Chinese animation, stating that portrayals of topics realistically does not constitute animation. He explained by giving examples;

> For example, a film called *Xiao Shi Zhu* (*Newcomer*) was made about a gymnast boy. Government leaders asked the animators to make it as real as real gymnastics. This is not animation. At the time, Chinese animation followed a circuitous route, away from animation's true nature. I emphasize an animation does not have a realistic character; it cannot be real. For example, let's say they made an animated feature about a barefoot doctor. If in a real film, an empathetic doctor first tested needles on himself before using them on his patients, the audience would be moved. But if you put a needle into a puppet in an animated version of the same story, the audience certainly would not be moved. It was so far removed from animation art that it was terrible. (Chen Jianyu, interview, 2001)

Three animated works came out in 1973, upon the return of some of the staff, according to Giesen (2015: 51). All of them dealt with wiping out enemies: in *Little Eighth Route Army*, a boy takes revenge against the Japanese army; in *Donghai xiaoshaobing* (*Little Sentinel of East China Sea*), a girl tracking chemical warfare workers seeks PLA help to destroy the enemy; and in *Xiaohaoshou* (*Little Trumpeter*), a shepherd boy learns to play the trumpet, joins the Red Army, and fights the Guomindang.

172

The Second Golden Age

If the Cultural Revolution obliterated the first golden age of the Shanghai Animation Film Studio, then, in a roundabout way, it also contributed to the birthing of a second, even more spectacular period. Te Wei, who had regained his position as head of the studio after the fall of the Gang of Four in 1976, strongly believed the second golden age yielded better work, stating:

> There were two ups and downs. 1960–64 was the first golden time with outstanding films. . . . The 1980s was also a golden period. The second era was much more intense than the first because all the artists had been oppressed during the Cultural Revolution and collected much energy as a result, and they wanted to do something. The level of work was much higher because all of them wanted to make their best works and they worked hard during that time. After the Cultural Revolution, animation films were revived and it is the best period. (Te Wei, interview, 2001)

Zhan Tong (interview, 1993) agreed, because, in his view, the second wave offered "improved methodology of presentation and better topics" and "all types of possibilities," while Chen Jianyu (interview, 2001) attributed the betterment to increased "use of Chinese art methods to create new ways and to show how Chinese animation was different from other countries" and to the elevation of the younger generation to directorships of films that they made into classics.

Actually, veterans and newcomers alike—animators such as A Da, Lin Wenxiao, Qu Jianfang, Zhou Keqin (b. 1946), Hu Xionghua, Hu Jinqing, Jin Xi, Qian Jiajun, Yan Dingxian, Wang Shuchen, Chang Guangxi, Zhong Quan, Ma Kexuan, Zhan Tong, Te Wei, Dai Tielang (b. 1930), and Wang Gang—made many puppet, paper cut, and cel works, as well as two additional ink-wash painting productions, which were shown (and captured awards) at international festivals.

Hu Jinqing was especially productive, making paper cut animated works such as the award-winning *Snipe-Clam Grapple* (1983), *Caoren* (*The Straw Man*, 1985),

Tanglang buchan (*Mantis Stalks the Cicada*, 1988), *Douji* (*Cockfighting*, 1988), *Zhuishu* (*Catching the Mouse*, 1988), *Qiangzhe shanggou* (*The Stronger Get Hooked*, 1988), *Bailu he wugui* (*The Egret and the Tortoise*, 1992), *Mao yu shu* (*The Cat and the Rat*, 1992), and *Xuehu* (*Snow Fox*, 1998).

The experimentation continued during the 1980s and '90s. Qian Jiajun used the Dunhuang Cave paintings (frescoes in an ancient Buddhist cave) as a source for *The Nine-Color Deer* (1981), a cel-animated film about a nine-colored, magical deer which helps all creatures, including a drowning merchant who later betrays his rescuer. Yan Dingxian and Lin Wenxiao also used Dunhuang Cave paintings and their stories in *The Deer Girl* (1993). Yan provided details on the conceptualization of their use of the cave paintings:

> The script for *The Deer Girl* was by a painter who had researched the caves. In the caves, there is one painting of several frames concerning a mother deer. It is a Buddhist story with a moral that people should not fight, but should be friends. I thought the story was good for modern times and adopted it to animation. We adopted both the story and art and followed the Dunhuang cave painting form. The deer is a symbol of good fortune. We made three animations about deer—*The Deer Fairy*, *Jia Zi Rescues Deer*, and *The Deer Girl*. (Yan, interview, 2001)

Another clever, out-of-the-ordinary film was the puppet animation *Lu yu gongniu* (*Deer and Bull*, 1992), created by a then-young Zou Qin (b. 1965), who spent a year bending strips of bamboo into shapes of animals with moving limbs, and animating them to tell a tale about the need to align against a common enemy. In the story, a deer and a bull share a water hole and defend it against a menacing lion. When the bull drinks almost all of the water, the two animals fight, at which time the lion moves in for the kill (Zou Qin, interview, 1993).

Different and experimental were *Yupan* (*Fishdish*, 1988), created by Fang Runnan (b. 1942), which blended cel with object animation, and Hu Yihong's (b. 1955) short, *Princess Lotus*. Ehrlich (2001: 22) said *Fishdish* portrayed a "painted fish [that] appears to swim off a real three-dimensional dish. . . . a unique film that expresses in its material form the permeable border line between reality and illusion." Describing *Princess Lotus* as an "expressionist 'dream-film,'" Ehrlich (2001: 22) said that it "wove reality and illusion together so seamlessly that we, the audience, are awakened from the illusion as abruptly as the protagonist awakened from his dream."

Like the first—only more extensively—the second golden era employed indigenous and sometimes-unique techniques, raw materials, and content, and both periods were marked by a distinct stylization that set Chinese animation apart from that of other countries. Teacher and researcher Zhang Huilin (2003: 70–79) showed how stylization with the influence of paintings and operas is perfectly represented in *The Conceited General*, *Havoc in Heaven*, and *Nezha naohai* (*Nezha Conquers the Dragon King*, 1979). Zhang Huilin explained that structures and facial makeup were done in a conscious effort to represent temperaments and mentalities; backgrounds are stage-like, and physical movements are similar to Peking opera. Metaphysical beauty, she said, was captured in lines that embody aesthetic values and signify feeling; zigzagging, long or short, thick or thin, straight or winding, they bring out subtle emotions. The action also possessed aesthetic value, Zhang Huilin said, giving the example of A Da's *Three Monks*, where each monk moves to a different rhythm (Zhang Huilin 2003: 70–79).

Another commonality of the two exceptional Chinese animation periods was the close connections between print cartooning and animation. As is common elsewhere, some Chinese animation scripts emanated from, or were based on, cartoons and comics, most notably, Wang Shuchen and Qian Yunda's *Yuanxing bilu* (*Show One's True Colors*, 1960), taken from Hua Junwu's satiric cartoon, *Eisenhower Shows His True Color*, portraying the United States as an aggressive Cold War invader, Qian's *Red Army Bridge*, adapted from Ke Ming's lianhuanhua of the same name, and A Da's *Sanmao liulangji* (*Wanderings of Sanmao*, 1984), a serial based on Zhang Leping's comic strip character. A puppet animation of

Fig. 6.11. Wang Shuchen. Courtesy of Wang Yiqian

Sanmao was also produced by Shanghai Animation Film Studio in 1958. Besides those mentioned above, other cartoonist masters worked on specific films. Of course, at least three of the founders of Chinese animation—Wan Laiming, Wan Guchan, and Te Wei—started their careers drawing cartoons. The Wans, who drew in the style of Aubrey Beardsley, worked for *Shanghai manhua* and *Liangyou huabao* as cartoonists. As already discussed, Zhang Guangyu (1900–65) began drawing satirical political cartoons in the 1920s and edited two humor/cartoon magazines before becoming character designer on *Havoc in Heaven*, which was released the year of his death; Hua Junwu served as screenwriter on *The Conceited General* and *Huangjinmeng* (*Dream of Gold*, 1963), in addition to lending his cartoons to at least two scripts; cartoonist/painter Zhang Ding was character designer on *Nezha Conquers the Dragon King*; and the so-called "Three Musketeers" of the Shanghai Animation Film Studio—Wang Shuchen, Zhan Tong, and A Da—were cartoonists (see Lent 2006). The title, as well as the "three horses" and "three carts," was given to these men by Te Wei, because he considered them as the mainstays of the studio.

Wang Shuchen (1931–91) began to work in animation when it was still being produced at the Changchun Film Studio in 1949. In 1954, he was character designer for Shanghai Animation Film Studio's first award-winner, *Haopengyou* (*Good Friends*), directed by Te Wei. Wang directed his first comedy, *Guohoushan* (*Pass over the Monkey Mountain*), in 1958, a simple story based on a

Fig. 6.12. *Nezha naohai* (*Nezha Conquers the Dragon King*), 1978–79. Courtesy of Shanghai Animation Film Studio.

Fig. 6.13. *Shanshuiqing* (*Feeling from Mountain and Water*) ink wash, 1988. Courtesy of Shanghai Animation Film Studio and Te Wei.

Chinese New Year's painting of an old man who tricks monkeys into returning straw hats they had stolen from him. The work differed from other Chinese animation of the time, as it was strictly entertaining, not meant to serve any ideological or educational functions. *Pass over the Monkey Mountain* and a later work, *Xuanmeiji* (*Selecting Beauty*, 1987), represented the national style Te Wei was calling for and used Chinese-type humor.

One of Wang Shuchen's most important animation films was *Nezha Conquers the Dragon King*, the first feature-length animation after the Cultural Revolution and China's first widescreen color animation. Besides co-directing the work, Wang was screenwriter, adapting the story in part from a classic novel, *Fengshen yanyi*. The film movingly tells the story of a brave child hero Nezha through five plots: he "is born, conquers

the Dragon King, kills himself, is revived, and seeks revenge" (Zhang Huilin 2002). Wang and his cohorts painstakingly assured that the work was genuinely Chinese, inviting Zhang Ding as character designer, absorbing traditional Door Gods and mural painting that was highly adorning and colorful in style, and using Peking opera and stringed-instrument music.

Toward the end of Wang Shuchen's career, he wrote the script for what became *Feeling from Mountain and Water*. He had intended it to be the backbone for a musical animation and gave it to Ma Kexuan for safekeeping, wanting to keep it out of the hands of the studio for the time being, according to Ma (interview, 2011). When the studio was searching for a good script for the upcoming first Shanghai International Film Festival, Ma Kexuan gave them Wang Shuchen's manuscript. Ma Kexuan (interview, 2011) regretted this action for the rest of his life. He said, "Wang Shuchen was very upset and angry with me, because he knew what would happen. He did not want the studio to have this script as he worried someone would steal his work. That was exactly what happened later. I feel so sorry for that."

Strangely, Yan Shanchun (interview, 2016) also took the blame for showing the script to Te Wei, as he related to the authors of this book. His account was as follows:

We were four in the same office, Wang Shuchen, Ma Kexuan, Qian Yunda, and me. We usually discussed art, not gossip. Once, while discussing art, Wang Shuchen showed the three of us his script [*Feeling from Mountain and Water*]. He told Ma and me that whichever of us who wanted to animate the story, he would give the script. Both

Animation: From Hand-Crafted Experimentation to Digitalization

Fig. 6.14. Zhan Tong in his Shanghai apartment unraveling the scroll he created. August 16, 1993. Photo by John A. Lent. Courtesy of Zhan Tong.

of us liked the script. We had not yet decided to apply ink wash to the script. For the next ink-wash animation, Te Wei already had a script, though it was not good for ink wash. Wang Shuchen had given the script to me, and I was the one who showed it to Te Wei. Te Wei immediately decided to use it. Wang Shuchen angrily said to me, "Why did you give it to Te Wei without my permission? Once he gets it, it will be his; all credit will go to him," which is what happened. I think the great achievements of *Feeling from Mountain and Water* should be credited to Wang Shuchen.

There is no easy way to sort out the discrepancies of the differing versions of this event without corroborating evidence, which the authors of this book have failed to uncover. While a bit far-fetched, it could be that both Ma Kexuan and Yan Shanchun showed Te Wei the script at different times. More likely, the contradictions resulted from memory lapse of one of the men, a problem that sometimes results from dependence on interviews.

Wang Shuchen acknowledged an indebtedness to cartooning, which he thought had aspects of literature, drama, and other interesting art forms that other paintings could not match. He spent much time reading widely about Chinese and famous foreign cartoon

masterpieces, trying to figure out how they were created, after which he drew his own cartoons. Wang's works, such as *Ganji* (*Go to the Local Market*), *Dumuqiao* (*Single Plank Bridge*), and *Changgonghao zuogongcha* (*Singing Is Much Better Than Conducting*) are examples of his ability to capture the essence of daily life with a sense of humor (Yong Fei 1997: 259; also see the personal account of Wang Shuchen's life written by his son [Wang Yiqian 2012: 292–304]).

Zhan Tong also recognized the importance of cartooning to his animation career, for he doggedly continued drawing cartoons even when he was chastised by his bosses for doing them. In the preface of a collection of his cartoons, Zhan Tong wrote:

> I will not hide this from you. Since my fate with cartooning, I have had many unhappy experiences and was criticized a lot. For example, after I moved to Shanghai and started to create animation in the animation studio, originally, I thought animation and cartoons were hard to be divided, no matter whether it was in idea creation or drawing techniques. To me, undoubtedly, drawing cartoons must be good for animation creation. On the contrary, a top leader called me to his office, put on a grave expression, and told me: "You draw fewer cartoons in the future so as to avoid objections." Some people kindly persuaded me: "It is useless to draw cartoons. There is no benefit for making animation. Otherwise, you will hurt someone." I am obstinate from my roots. No matter if you put on a grave expression or use kind persuasion, I don't care. I still happily draw my cartoons and never feel tired. (Zhan Tong 1993)

After winning a prize at an international cartoon competition in West Germany in 1980, he was publicly criticized and lost his merit commission for reasons unknown to him. He vowed never to attend another international cartoon competition.

Even before he began majoring in oil painting at Central Art Academy, fifteen-year-old Zhan drew anti-Guomindang propaganda cartoons at the request of the underground Communist Party. Zhan's version of how

Fig. 6.15. A Da. Courtesy of Xu Chang.

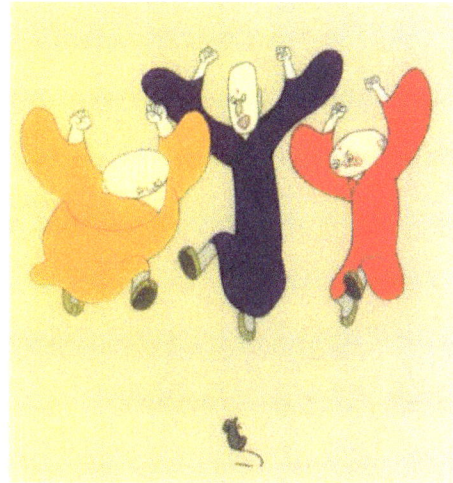

Fig. 6.16. *Sange heshang* (*Three Monks*), 1980. Courtesy of Shanghai Animation Film Studio and Xu Chang.

he ended up in animation and his initial experiences is as follows: "When I graduated in 1956, I was asked my choice of jobs. I said, first I was to be obedient to the assignment given by the Party; everyone said this. I said also I wanted to do children's drawings or cartoons. I was assigned to the animation team within the film studio" (Zhan Tong, interview, 1993; Lent 2001: 30).

Zhan produced a prodigious body of work during his nearly fifty-year career—thousands of cartoons, many of which won international and national awards; about forty animated films he wrote, directed, or designed, using celluloid, paper cut, and puppets; many essays and articles; and a theme park (based on *The Journey to the West*),⁵ which he designed.

Among animated works he directed solely or jointly were the puppet film *Qiguai de qiusai* (*Strange Game*, 1979), *Zhenjia Li Kui* (*Real Fake Li Kui*, 1981), *Jiaru woshi Wu Song* (*If I Were Wu Song*, 1982), and the paper cut work *Baxian yu tiaozao* (*Ba Xian and the Flea*, 1988). Additionally, he was character designer and art director of films such as *Zhu Bajie [Pigsy] Eats the Watermelon*, *The Carved Dragon* (1959), *Kanchai guniang* (*The Girl Who Cuts Firewood*, 1960), *Chabuduo* (*Almost*, 1964), *Renshenguo* (*Ginseng Fruit*, 1980), and *Xiaoxiongmao xuemujiang* (*Little Panda Learning to Be a Carpenter*, 1982). Zhan wrote screenplays for *Hualang yiye* (*One Night in an Art Gallery*), *Xiangbuxiang* (*Look Like or Not*), a simple story based on a comic strip, and *Yiban'er* (*A Half*, 1990), of which he was also director and

animation designer. *A Half* was critical of people who fail to finish anything. (Also see the personal account of Zhan Tong's life written by his son [Zhan Yong 2012: 321–31].)

Following graduation, in 1953 A Da began working at the Shanghai Animation Film Studio as an animator, art designer, and director. During his stay at the studio, A Da was involved in the production of more than thirty animated films. The works for which he was best known appeared after the Cultural Revolution, some even using knowledge gained in the countryside, as with *Hualang yiye* (*One Night in an Art Gallery*, 1978) and *Houzi laoyue* (*Monkeys Fish for the Moon*, 1980). As art director of the latter, A Da, when asked to create a dance for the monkeys, adapted from a peasant harvest dance he had watched while feeding pigs in the countryside (Ehrlich 2001: 19). A Da's next work, his signature *Sange heshang* (*Three Monks*), is based on a Chinese proverb that says when there is one monk, he carries two pails of water; two monks jointly carry only one pail; three monks carry no water at all. *Three Monks* captured four international awards and China's Hundred Flower Award; it was also shown on television stations in a number of countries. Other important works he directed include *Hudiequan* (*Butterfly Spring*, with Chang Guangxi, 1983), a music-oriented (without dialogue) story of lovers who die tragically but are transformed into inseparable, free-flying butterflies; *Sanshiliugezi* (*Thirty-Six Characters*, 1984), based on Chinese pictograms turned into living creatures; and the already mentioned *Sanmao* series.

Besides co-inventing the ink-wash painting technique applied to animation, A Da was also the first to use animation to make a documentary, about the Jinshan farmers' painting, *Hua de Ge* (*Songs of Painting*). His son described his procedure: "In this documentary, he used the splicing of shots, movement, and special effects as methods, with a high level of expression, making still pictures full of a moving sense and rhythm; even the animals in the pictures moved around" (Xu Chang 2012: 288–89).

Humor marked much of A Da's works, such as the ten-minute animation short *Xinzhuang de menling* (*New Door Bell*, 1986), about the frustrations a man faces trying hopelessly to get visitors to use his new door bell, and *Chaoji feizao* (*Super Soap*, 1986), in which people line up to buy a super soap that, in the end, turns all their clothes white. As a cartoonist, A Da won awards in China and abroad for works such as *Qiaoweiren* (*Clever Hypocrite*) and *Bian* (*Change*), and served as an officer in national and Shanghai artists and cartoonists associations.

Talented in crafts and music as well, A Da at one point organized a makeshift band at the studio. According to Xu Chang (2012: 290),

> He proposed using articles of daily life, including hard brush, washboard, DDT sprayer, etc., to form a "magic band" in the Shanghai Animation Film Studio. He himself held a feather duster as the conductor. This little band attended a theatrical festival under the Film Bureau and had a surprise effect. I think, even in today's *Up Show* television program, there are such makeshift kinds of performance that could not top A Da's band.

Chang Guangxi (interview, 2016) credited A Da's music inclination to a teacher at the Suzhou boarding school he attended, who encouraged him to listen to classical music. Perhaps that experience had something to do with A Da's belief that rhythm and timing are the most important elements of animation.

Little doubt exists that the heyday of Chinese animation were the years that the "Three Musketeers" were active at the Shanghai Animation Film Studio. There is even less doubt that A Da, Wang Shuchen, and Zhan Tong indeed helped to pull the animation cart to the top, responsible as they were for instituting a traditional style of animation, full of Chinese art, music, folklore, legends, and humor, and often closely tied to the cartooning that they each respected and practiced.

But it must be remembered that teamwork was a guiding force at the Shanghai Animation Film Studio (despite occasional disagreements and acts of jealousy), and if the "three horses" pulled the animation "cart" upward to success, they were supported by teams of "sidekicks" and "pushers," and they too had their individual accomplishments, a number worthy of worldwide notice. Many of these individuals have been profiled throughout this chapter.

While most of the recounting of the two golden eras has concentrated on men, women also played important roles, among them the already discussed Chen Bo'er, as well as Tang Cheng (1919–86), Lin Wenxiao, and Duan Xiaoxuan (b. 1934). It is understandable that these women (and the men who were not studio leaders) were not recognized separately during the golden ages, because the films (and all areas of art and literature) then were thought of as cooperative ventures, not individual accomplishments, in line with Maoist thought. However, it is difficult to fathom the lack of recognition given them in recent years as some animators have been singled out for attention.

Tang Cheng was co-director of two of the ink-wash painting films, *Where Is Mama?* (with Te Wei), on which she was also animation designer, and *The Deer Bell* (with Wu Qiang). She also co-directed the classic *Havoc in Heaven* (with Wan Laiming) and *Two Heroic Sisters of the Grasslands* (with Qian Yunda).

Because Tang Cheng's schooling was interrupted by health problems, she learned Chinese painting from her grandmother and father, both famed artists. Her father, who also taught art, became financially well-off, especially after he started and ran four Shanghai banks and purchased valuable property.

Despite the family wealth, Tang Cheng began her career in 1950 as a member of the art group of Shanghai Film Studio, where she was a crew member of several short films. In 1953, she became an assistant animation designer on *Caimogu* (*Picking Mushroom*) and then animation designer of *Kuakou de qingwa* (*The Braggart Frog*) in 1954. The same year, she joined the Communist Party. In 1958, Tang Cheng participated in the making of the first color animated work, *Why the Crow Is Black*, and *The Conceited General* and *Mutou guniang* (*The Wooden Girl*). When the Shanghai Animation Film Studio was set up in 1957, as a veteran, she was made the studio's group leader of animation, and from 1958 to 1960, acted as group director of the paper cut *Bayue shiwu qingfengshou* (*Celebrate the Harvest on August 15*) and three color animated films, *Laopopo de zaoshu* (*Grandma's Date Tree*, 1958), *Luobo huilaile* (*The Return of the Radishes*, 1959), and *Senlin zhiwang* (*King of the Forests*, 1959).

From 1960 to 1964, she was one of the directors of *Where Is Mama?* and *Havoc in Heaven*. A 2012 CCTV documentary claimed that Tang Cheng was in charge of most of the work on both films, that on *Where Is Mama?* Te Wei, who was listed as director, actually oversaw the art and Qian Jiajun, the technical aspects, and though Wan Laiming was billed as director of *Havoc in Heaven*, she usually was in charge, especially when Wan was hospitalized.

Her close friend, Duan Xiaoxuan, described Tang Cheng as a hard worker who did things her own way. As an example of how busy she was, Duan relayed how, when Tang Cheng was made a People's Congress member for Shanghai, she spent mornings doing her political work, went to the studio after lunch to direct *The Deer Bell*, returned to Congress work in the late afternoon, and went back to animation again in the evening (see the CCTV portrayal of Tang Cheng at www.1905.com/video/play/ . . . 2012-9-7, and website version at baike.baidu.com/2013-04-16).

Among Lin Wenxiao's achievements were significant co-directorships, three with A Da—*One Night in an Art Gallery*, a spoof of the Gang of Four, their ridiculous censoring of paintings and eventual humiliation at the hands of children; *Three Monks*; and *Nezha Conquers the Dragon King* (with Wang Shuchen and Yan Dingxian), about a mythological boy who fights and defeats the Dragon King and his three brothers, and analogous to the Gang of Four. She also directed *Xuehaizi* (*Snow Kid*, 1980), about the friendship between a young rabbit and a snowman that sacrifices its life to rescue the rabbit from his burning cabin. Among Lin Wenxiao's other credits were as co-director (with Yan Dingxian) of *Shuke he Beita* (*Adventures of Shuke and Beita*, 1989), a thirteen-episode TV series, and animation director of *Jinhou xiangyao* (*The Monkey King Conquers the Demon*, 1984–85), the studio's fourth feature-length film about the Monkey King.

Duan Xiaoxuan, by her count, was the photographer of "more than thirty" studio productions, including *Why the Crow Is Black*, *The Cowherd's Flute*, *Feeling from Mountain and Water*, *Havoc in Heaven*, *Where Is Mama?*, and *Little Carps Jump over the Dragon Gate*. She was also cinematographer of *Havoc in Heaven*, where she used many colorful effects, which she described: "The Monkey King's weapon is called the 'Jingu Bang.' It looks like a glittering red stick with yellow on both ends. In order to make it glow and sparkle, we employed multiple exposures, and it proved to be a very successful technique in the film" (quoted in Giesen 2015: 41).

In 1948, after passing an exam, fourteen-year-old Duan Xiaoxuan began an internship at Northeast Film Studio; she moved with the studio to Shanghai in 1950, when she became Te Wei's deputy director at age sixteen (Duan Xiaoxuan, interview, 2016). Her first assignment as photographer was on *Xiaoliyu tiaolongmen* (*Little Carps Jump over the Dragon Gate*) in 1958. To have that position, she was a "product of her times," according to Daisy Yan Du (2014), because after 1949,

179

Chairman Mao and his cohorts were determined to make everything new. They regarded the traditional family as a site of oppression and encouraged women to join socialist production as men's equals in the public sphere. . . . Encouraged by the slogan "whatever men can do, women can do too," women took jobs which were traditionally occupied by men. . . . It was in this special political context that Duan emerged as the first and only camerawoman in the state-owned animation industry in socialist China.

As discussed, Duan Xiaoxuan was instrumental in inventing ink-wash painting animation, which she continues to experiment with; in 1995, she and her colleagues used computers in the process, and even after retirement from the studio in 1998, she stayed active as a consultant and helped with the making of Yi Shi's three-minute, ink-wash animated section of *Hexie zhongguo* (*A Harmonious China*) at the 2010 Shanghai World Expo (Yan Du 2014; for a chronology of Duan's career, see Huang Zushen 2008: 353–56).

By the late 1980s, the glory days of the Shanghai Animation Film Studio were coming to an end. Te Wei stepped down as studio head in 1984, replaced by Yan Dingxian, who served in the post from 1985 to 1989. As already discussed, Te Wei was a director of the multiple prize-winning *Feeling from Mountain and Water* in 1988, an ink-wash painting production about a young boy who nurses an aging musician back to health. In the end, the old man disappears into the mountains, but not before handing over his *qin* (stringed instrument) to the boy. The scene is commonly interpreted as Te Wei, in the guise of the old man, making his exit to provide spaces for younger animators (see Giesen 2015: 73). Te Wei (interview, 2004) said that was not the intent: "It was a coincidence. When we made this work, the theme was to pass on knowledge, but the master is not me. The Shanghai Animation Film Studio wanted a new generation to take over. All departments wanted a new generation in. That's what they wanted to express in this film." One must also remember the script was written by Wang Shuchen, not Te Wei, and Wang had had other plans for the story.

Te Wei's accomplishments were recognized in 1995 when the international ASIFA presented him its lifetime achievement award. To Te Wei, it meant "I can draw a dot to my career." But, he hastened to add, that at eighty-six (and again at ninety, his ages when interviewed), he still wanted to make unique animation and was just waiting for the right script (Te Wei, interviews, 2001, 2004).

Animation critic/theorist Chen Jianyu said of Te Wei's work:

Te Wei's accomplishment as animator and artist is that he made several masterpieces—*Where Is Mama? The Conceited General*, *The Cowherd's Flute*, and *Feeling from Mountain and Water*. These works can go down from generation to generation. In 1999, the government chose the 100 outstanding films of China; only twenty animation works were represented and Te Wei's four were among them. Also, as a leader of the animation industry, Te Wei has had three accomplishments: 1. he founded a Chinese style of animation; 2. he established a highly talented group; under his leadership, the Shanghai Animation Film Studio developed from several to hundreds of staff, uniting seniors like the Wan brothers and cultivating the younger generation of animators; 3. he led both of China's golden eras of animation and most of the famous Chinese animation was made when he was the leader. In 1989, when the Chinese government chose four filmmakers as most outstanding of more than 50,000 people who had worked in the industry, Te Wei was one of them. (Chen, interview, 2001)

Beijing Science and Educational Film Studio

Though Shanghai Animation Film Studio dominated Chinese animation during the second half of the twentieth century, a few other studios functioned, notably Beijing Science and Educational Film Studio (BSEFS) and Changchun Film Group Corporation (CFGC).

BSEFS was founded in 1960 out of a workshop whose main task was to make science and educational films. They completed some animation designs or drew some details for the purposes of shooting science and educational films, but did not know very much about the conceptualization or production characteristics of animated films.

At the beginning of the 1980s, with an increase in the number of artists, the workshop was expanded into an Animation Department, which started to produce one-reel animated films in 1981. From the first cartoon, *Xiaoxiao jiqiren* (*A Little Robot*), the cartoonists of BSEFS not only sought a unique Chinese style, but also stressed form and philosophy. The one-reel cartoon *Hanniu yu mutong* (*A Ferocious Ox and a Buffalo Boy*, 1984), for example, was particularly popular. This story was about a cowherd boy who tamed a ferocious ox that most adults could not subdue with force.

With the Animation Department constantly enlarged by graduates from the Animation Department of Beijing Film Academy, production was increased, making it possible to produce animated films on a larger scale. A result was a long animated film, *Letu/Eden* (four reels), in 1986. The story, set in the distant past, featured a young warrior who saw his homeland being destroyed by a water monster. Deeply grieved, he decided to seek a happy place to rebuild the homeland. He was losing his fight with the water monster when he received enlightening guidance of a Red Snail fairy. She told him: "The happy land is under our feet." Further, he and the Red Snail fairy defeated the water monster and the young warrior finally was able to lead his people in building a new homeland near a beautiful lake.

One 1987 educational film made by animation at BSEFS was very successful both in China and abroad. *Renti de miniao xitong* (*Human Body's Urology System*, two reels) described the human body's urology system, detailing every organ and its structures and functions, for use in middle schools' physiology and hygiene lessons. It took pains to explain the excreting procedure and its importance. It was a subject that had never previously appeared in science or educational films.

In 1989, BSEFS produced a two-reel cartoon, *Lan Huahua*, with ink wash. It had a rich Chinese national style and strong, moving story. Based on the same named folk song, *Lan Huahua* told a tragic story, a sort of Chinese *Romeo and Juliet*, about a young married girl who grows up and falls in love with a shepherd. However, a wicked landlord's wife (who was Lan's mother-in-law) and a deified man discover the affair and ruthlessly sabotage the lovers' pleasurable feelings. Lan Huahua and the shepherd have no choice but to die together and float away with the torrential Yellow River. This cartoon's mold, color, and music were provided a strong distinctive flavor of Shanbei (north of Shanxi Province) (Cao, interview, 1999).

By the 1980s, BSEFS cartoonists steered from creating works for young children to those for adults, commencing work on three short animations (about ten minutes each), two of which—*Place Upside Down* and *Happy Birthday to Mom*—reflected the cartoonists' thinking about present situations.

As the 1990s began, BSEFS artists made several one-reel animated films and continued to regularly win awards. In 1991, they produced *Qisehua* (*A Flower with Seven Colors*), based on a Russian fairy tale about a little girl named Zhenzhen who received a magic flower with seven colors. With it, she could get whatever she wanted, but six of the petals did not bring her any happy feelings. Zhenzhen used the last petal to help a little boy lame in one leg to recover his health. As a result, she felt real happiness by unselfishly helping others. Another successful cartoon, *Fanglian yeye he yuanlian nainai* (*Square-faced Grandpa and Round-faced Grandma*, 1992), told a story that was full of philosophy: as the title suggests, a square-faced grandpa liked everything square, but a round-faced grandma loved all things round. The couple often quarreled, and in the end, they even destroyed their house for their favorite things. Eventually, they realized everything is square or round and that people can tolerate all things on Earth— a square object can exist in a round one, and vice versa. BSEFS produced *Be Similar* in 1992; totally made by computer, it was a coordinated effort with the Department of Computer of Beijing Industrial University. In 1993 and 1994, the BSEFS Animation Department produced animation series for the first time, starting with the seven-reel *Three Little Foxes*.

While BSEFS animation was garnering top awards in China and abroad, a total reform of film production and distribution in China nearly knocked the props from under the studio. A China Film Import and Export Company (CFIEC) contract to purchase three reels of BSEFS animated films annually was canceled, which was the entire production task assigned to the studio. But, in 1995, relief was in sight when BSEFS was combined with the Animation Department of China Central Television (CCTV), which requested thirteen television animation episodes yearly from BSEFS. Attaching great importance to animation, CCTV became a large investor in animation production (Cao, interview, 2001). Accordingly, BSEFS organized large-scale production of TV series beginning in 1996, including *Maomi xiaobei* (*A Story of Qiqi's Risky Experience*), *Elf-Huidouer* in 1998, and *A Story of Xiaobei's Vagrant Life* in 1999. Xu Ying (2000a: 65–66) compiled a list of twenty-five films and television series produced by BSEFS Animation Department between 1981 and 1999.

The head of BSEFS for many years was Cao Xiaohui, who began by drawing the backgrounds for the studio's first animated film, *A Little Robot*, in 1981, then moved to art designer for *Zhongli* (*Planting Pears*) in 1985, and finally director with *A Black Horse or a White Horse* in 1989. He also wrote the script for the latter, a humorous story about a horse in a stall described by one passerby as black, and by another as white, when actually the animal was a zebra.

Cao Xiaohui (interview, 2001) said BSEFS' production capability was hampered only by insufficient funding. From the studio's beginnings until the mid-1990s, BSEFS produced a total of thirty minutes a year, which were bought by CFIEC. Except for CFIEC, other buyers for animated shorts were not forthcoming, because these theatrical works did not make money. Once it was affiliated with CCTV, BSEFS finished 200 television episodes from 1995 to 2001. As the new century dawned, corporate sponsorship was sought; for example, the refrigerator/air conditioning firm Haier provided the finances for a children's animated show, *Haier xiongdi* (*Haier Brothers*). Haier chose the scripts, the series' direction, and its characters to promote the company's image. BSEFS, by 2001, was seeking additional corporate financing. Cao Xiaohui (interview, 2001) said that his studio differed from Shanghai Animation Film Studio, in that, "they can get bank loans, private and government money, and can do work for overseas clients." As mentioned often by other animators, a major issue for BSEFS artists after China's open door policy has been trying to satisfy both aesthetic and market demands. Cao Xiaohui (interview, 2001) explained:

> The Chinese have had the privilege of doing animation of special styles known throughout the world. Some believe we should not give this up, that we can use them at Annecy and other short film festivals. We used to produce animation for art's sake; but there were not enough markets. Now, we make a lot of animation to satisfy the market and our works have disappeared from the international festivals. It is one or the other.

Animation continued to be produced on and off at the Changchun Film Group Corporation (formerly Northeast Animation Studio and Changchun Film Studio). According to Yao Donghui (interview, 2009), who joined Changchun Film Studio in 1965, the animation made at the studio relied mostly on proverbs which were abandoned when many staff members left after CFGC went public in 2006. Previously, after Te Wei took studio talent to Shanghai in the 1950s, Changchun Film Studio animation closed, but was restarted in 1984. Animator Li Lekang (interview, 2009) felt that the studio made "good" animated films from 1984 to 1990, when government control was "looser" and animators had more freedom. He said that after 1990 and the Tiananmen Square demonstrations, the Communist Party took art creation "more seriously, strengthened control, and changed animation to a commercial basis, resulting in no more artistic work" (Li Lekang, interview, 2009).

Yao Donghui and Li Lekang, along with two other animators interviewed, Chen Xuhui (interview, 2009) and Guo Ye (interview, 2009), joined Dean Chang Guangxi as teachers at the Jilin Animation Institute in

Changchun. Originally known as Jilin College of the Arts-Animation School, the institute was started in June 2000; with more than 6,000 students, it is the largest animation education facility in China.

Transition II: From Planned to Market Economy Animation

As China increasingly moved from a planned economy to a market-driven one in the 1990s, animation production in Shanghai changed drastically. Previously, the Shanghai Animation Film Studio was subsidized to make 300 to 400 minutes of animation yearly, with the works guaranteed distribution through the China Film Corporation. This secure position broke down as Chinese animation was criticized as falling further behind market demands, as Japanese and American animation made deeper inroads into Chinese television, and as talented animators were seduced by higher wages to work for animation subsidiaries of foreign studios that sprouted along China's southern rim in search of cheaper labor.

To cope, the Shanghai Animation Film Studio branched from educational and artistic animation to a more commercial variety, and in 1991, joined with Yick Hee of Hong Kong to form Shanghai Yilimei Animation Company, Ltd., as its commercial wing. The government continued to pay for 300 to 400 minutes of animation, which met payrolls and covered about 70 percent of the studio's operating expenses; the rest had to come from work-for-hire with foreign companies (Jin Guoping, interview, 1993).

In 1994, the Chinese government set into motion a plan to help the studio survive. Shanghai Animation Film Studio was to produce mainly for Shanghai Television Station and to co-produce on a limited basis with foreign companies; the latter assignment meant that China provided the labor to make foreign-themed animation (Jin Guoping, interview, 2001). To the government, animation is predominantly a television medium. Through its Shanghai Television Station, the government pumped 49 million yuan ($6 million) into television animation from 1996 to 1999.

The studio co-produced two or three television shows yearly with foreign companies; the shows were aired in China and the co-producing country. As these changes occurred, the infrastructure of the Shanghai studio was revamped to meet market demands. A parent organization, Shanghai Animation Film and TV Group Co., was established, which subsumed Shanghai Yilimei Animation Company, Ltd., Shanghai Animation Film Studio, Shanghai Cartoon Culture Developing, Ltd. Co. (merchandising), Shanghai Animation Movies Drawing Studio, Cartoon Magazine Agency, Shanghai Animation Movies Special Training School, Cartoon Fan Club, and other enterprises.

Studio president Jin Guoping said that almost all production was for television, with the exception of the feature-length *Baoliandeng* (*Lotus Lantern*, 1999) and a few paper cut and puppet shorts for theaters. There was also another ink-wash short, *Yanzhen* (*Wild Geese Formation*), directed by Zhong Quan and Wang Gang in 1990. Otherwise, theatrical animation was and is almost nonexistent, according to Jin, mainly because of a lack of "talented, high-level staff." He elaborated that to make a feature in one or two years, several groups working simultaneously were needed, but the studio was hard-pressed to find one such group, and thus, it took three to four years to complete a theatrical feature (Jin Guoping, interview, 2001).

Although Jin encouraged animators to make short films of high artistic worth, the paucity of talent again was a stumbling block, and only one or two were made yearly. Jin explained:

The shorts that are made are not of international competition quality, because they do not have unique characteristics or high artistic levels. Younger animators get used to making TV and foreign company productions and seldom can they sit down, think, and do shorts in an artistic way. They don't have the time to explore new ways. They are not enthusiastic about doing artistic-level animation, because they must devote more time and attention to production and get less money in the end. (Jin Guoping, interview, 2001)

Zou Qin, who did the bamboo short *Deer and Bull*, was an example of a young animator torn between the artistic and commercial. He said,

When I started working in the studio, everybody liked to devote their lives to animation, to do the best work they could for China. Since 1986, with the "open door," everyone has come only to think how best to make as much money as they could on their own. I worked a whole year to make *Deer and Bull* and made only 800 yuan [$125 at the time] above my regular salary to do this. When I worked for Pacific Rim Studio in the South, I made 5,000 yuan a month doing very simple work that required no intelligence. That was several years ago [in 1990]. Now I could make 8,000 to 10,000 yuan per month working for a foreign animation producer. I returned to the Shanghai Animation Film Studio because I thought I could utilize my brain. Many Chinese animators are just copying the West now, whereas the older generation of animators were very individualistic and I want to be on an equal footing with them. (Zou Qin, interview, 1993)

The attraction of higher pay at foreign studios based in China created a gap between senior and younger animators, both in numbers and philosophies. Qian Yunda said that there were "no animators in the middle-age (forties) range, not only because of the Cultural Revolution (that is a remote reason), but because when the foreign companies came in the 1980s, the young went there to work" (Qian Yunda, interview, 2001). He also pointed to differences in approaches between senior and junior animators:

We used to call animation art films, but the young doubt this title. They think we seniors pay attention to art, but animation is more visuals and TV effects. They feel animation should be a film, not art. I think the senior generation did combine Chinese art into film and created a Chinese style. But now, the situation is more demanding in that

senior animators, because they must make TV animation for the commercial market, have to put more attention on film skills. Animation in China now faces two problems—how to make animation more like film and how to follow the market. (Qian Yunda, interview, 2001)

The pressure to convert to TV animation very quickly and to produce ever-increasing volumes for that medium—from 500 minutes of animation annually to 5,000 between 1995 and 2000—was staggering (Jin Guoping, interview, 2001). The result was that much discussion occurred concerning the artistic quality of Chinese animation and whether art films had a future.

Hu Jinqing believed the artistic films would not disappear, because studio administrators were committed to their production even if they lost money (Hu Jinqing, interview, 2001). Zhan Tong was optimistic that the tendency towards commercialization and Westernization would reverse itself.

In recent years, people are concentrating on making money. Fewer are willing to devote their lives to artistic pursuits. There are many Western influences, but this is temporary. Sooner or later, it will turn around. I've consulted with Japanese animators who said they had the same thing in the beginning, but later they overcame the situation. By way of a personal example, in 1987, my work was chosen to be shown in Bulgaria. I met with an animator there who wanted to tell me about how his country might lose its tradition to Western influences. Now I see the same here. But we will overcome this trend. At present, certain people are leaving cartooning to make money, but they will return, and they will again do Chinese style cartooning. (Zhan Tong, interview, 1993)

Told of Zhan Tong's prediction, Te Wei laughed and said, "I too can say the future is splendid, that the problem will be solved, but it is useless to say this. If I don't know the situation well, I should not say" (Te Wei, interview, 2001).

Te Wei did comment on foreign impacts and what the Chinese animators had to do to counter them:

When I was working, I put more attention on creation. Now retired, I feel some animators pay more attention to working for foreign companies; it's not their work, not Chinese animation. Working for the foreign companies means more pay, but it also means there is no time to do Chinese animation exploration. This is a bad impact. This situation has been around for years, not just recently. Chinese animators have tried to do something about the [drain of talent to] foreign work. Shanghai Animation Film Studio recently made *Lotus Lantern* which had market success. You can see Disney in it, but at least they tried. Seldom is there a film here like that these days; it is not common to make efforts at high-quality animation like *Lotus Lantern*. The artistic exploration and atmosphere are not strong in Chinese animation now.

Artistically and commercially, *Lotus Lantern* made contributions. We should not expect too much of these films, because rarely can the animators do the exploration they need. Nowadays, the animation competition worldwide is stronger and stronger. Chinese animators should take bigger steps like *Lotus Lantern*. After this success, others have made efforts to do features. Disney has its own ways and methods; Chinese animation must have its ways and methods to compete. But Disney and DreamWorks are too powerful and it is not easy to catch up with them. (Te Wei, interview, 2001)

Chen Jianyu thought that the Chinese had much to learn from foreign animators and welcomed the overseas production companies because they trained the younger generation in new concepts and techniques (Chen Jianyu, interview, 2001).

Throughout the final quarter of the twentieth century, there was considerable discussion about the amount of skill transferred to Asian host countries as they produced North American and European companies' animation features and television series. In most cases, Asian animation companies did tedious production jobs, not more creative pre- or post-production work (see Lent 1998: 239–54). The same was true in China. Jin Yunzhi (interview, 2005), vice president of Hangzhou

Mingxing Animation Co., said that in the beginning, his staff did the "hard work" but later (HMAC) learned advanced skills from the foreigners. Jin Yunzhi and company head Zhang Ningping started the first animation company in Hangzhou, Hangzhou Animation Production, Ltd. Co., which only did production work for overseas clients. The Japanese trained their staff. When the company later split up, some staff joined other animation studios, others, such as Zhang Ningping and Jin Yunzhi, started new companies, in their case, Hangzhou Mingxing Animation Co., in 1995. Zhang Ningping (interview, 2005) said that, with the new company, he thought they had to develop the Chinese animation industry, not just satisfy foreign demands. One way that HMAC accomplished this task was by writing and publishing textbooks for the growing numbers of Chinese animation students.

Yan Dingxian acknowledged that artistic animation was rarely made in China by the early 2000s, but he said it had not ceased altogether. He agreed with others that, with the new economy, it was necessary to follow market demands, "what the kids want to see" (Yan Dingxian, interview, 2001). Veteran animator Ma Kexuan, later a professor in digital art and design at Beijing University, felt that overall, the artistic aspects of animation have suffered at the demands of local governments to increase quantity. He said:

> This policy is against creative animation-making. The politicians promised the public they could have more productions. It's the concept of catching up, developing our own culture, economy. My personal opinion is that this concept killed animation creativity. I never cared about quantity, only about quality. . . . When the studio said the amount, not quality, was more important, I left. (Ma Kexuan, interview, 2005)

According to critic Chen Jianyu (interview, 2001), animation talent was "limited by the system"; animators were not free to retain high artistic quality because of sped-up TV production and the lack of higher-level staff, such as scriptwriters and designers. Zhang Songlin

Fig. 6.17. *Baoliandeng* (*Lotus Lantern*), 1999. Courtesy of Shanghai Animation Film Studio and Chang Guangxi.

(interview, 2005), also thought that production of television series was too fast, with "no time for revision. Now, one TV series [episode?] is done in a week. There is no time to think of quality. It is like a machine. Impossible." In her assessment of the contemporary situation, Duan Xiaoxuan (interview, 2016) felt that the Chinese industry developed too fast, that a great amount of work is produced but of very low quality. She said that the animation is not personal, that it must instead be a group effort with strong support from leaders. "In our day, we had a plus system—one person can do this plus another who can do something else, and so on" (Duan Xiaoxuan, interview, 2016). Along the same lines, Qian Yunda (interview, 2001) said that time must be set aside to learn how to apply film language and scripts to television. In a 2016 interview, Qian compared what was expected of animators in the pre-1980s controlled economy and today's market economy:

> Before, we did not think about marketing; instead, we were only concerned with whether leaders would approve our work and it would pass censorship and whether other artists recognized it as having artistic merit. With the market economy, the animators must add whether the audience

likes it. If animation concentrates on audience likes and making money, it is not good animation. Two points must be considered: animation without commercial ability to make money cannot exist and without artistic animated shorts, animation techniques cannot advance. (Qian Yunda, interview, 2016)

Chang Guangxi, who directed the commercially profitable *Lotus Lantern*, said that changes must be made to adjust to a market economy while retaining some Chinese traits:

> We must learn how to upgrade the concept of rhythm and readjust form and content for an international audience. During the Chinese animation history, there are many outstanding works with strong Chinese cultural traditions. It is a market economy and we should change contents to what audiences like to see, but follow Chinese traditions. We should do some changes to suit today's market. If we can't make money, we can't continue. (Chang Guangxi, interview, 2001)

Later, Chang Guangxi (interview, 2016) said that he was disappointed with the Chinese animation industry, because, 1. the old generation died or retired and the young animators are not mature; 2. production is completed too quickly; and 3. the leadership turnover is too frequent and studio leaders come from outside of the field.

Chang Guangxi's *Lotus Lantern* was touted as the first Chinese feature animation to signal the changes from traditional animation to further commercialization. Launched in 1995 by the Shanghai studio, with initial capital investment from the Film Bureau of the Shanghai Municipal Government and Shanghai Television Station, the production was completed on an unprecedented scale—a 12 million yuan ($1.5. million) capital investment, more than fifty characters, and eighty-plus artists. It was the first feature animation using computers and was involved in a merchandising (CD, book, comics, other merchandise) campaign. Xu Ying (2000b) said that the film moved closer to the Hollywood model than previous works, producing what the audience wanted, working out a soundtrack before designing picture frames, using images and performances of well-established film stars as the basis of character designs, and expertly choreographing dance sequences with respected artists in that field.

Chang Guangxi discussed the film's production costs and explained what contributed to its success:

> The most money ever was put into *Lotus Lantern*. This was because of a special atmosphere that existed. For more than ten years, there had not been an animated feature in the theaters and the studio was seeking a way to be successful in the market. *Lotus Lantern* was very successful.
>
> On an artistic level, it does not surpass older films, such as *Havoc in Heaven* or *Nezha Conquers the Dragon King*, but we tried to get experience dealing with the market through this work. Actually, the original budget of 12 million yuan is only 1 percent of a Disney or Japanese production. We used computers and Dolby sound, for example. *Lotus Lantern* was commercially successful for several reasons: 1. we chose a traditional Chinese story, a tale about people's relationships, their love. Audiences liked this. 2. we chose as our audience, those from very young to those over

Fig. 6.18. Chang Guangxi. Photo by Xu Ying. Courtesy of Chang Guangxi.

sixty. 3. we followed audience demands for characters and models. 4. we used new technologies and techniques, such as pre-production music played by an orchestra, special sound effects. 5. we dubbed famous actors and singers into the film. 6. we did promotional work; studio personnel from the president down promoted *Lotus Lantern* before it was distributed. At the same time the film was being distributed, a book, CD, and toys appeared. Also different is that *Lotus Lantern* was the first feature-length animation film that the studio had copyright to. We just learned from Disney the good things on how to get market success. (Chang Quangxi, interview, 2001)

Chang Guangxi also directed one of the earliest Chinese animated television series, *Fantastic Mongolia Horse*, released in 1990. In addition to his work, there were co-productions with Germany and Hong Kong in the 1990s, as well as a few other studio films and series. Among them were the already mentioned *Deer and Bull*, *Fox Dividing Flapjack* (1992, director, Jin Xilin), the thirteen-part TV series *Hula xiaojingang* (1993), the TV series *Datou erzi he xiaotou baba* (*Big Head Son and Small Head Father*, 1995), *Learned Cat Teaches Chinese Characters* (1998, director, Wu Guanying), an educational series, and *Zigu yingxiong chushaonian* (*Young Heroes*, 1995).

The Shanghai Animation Film Studio faced many competitors throughout the 1990s and 2000s, and, according to Giesen (2015: 76), it wasn't releasing new films anymore but was trying to protect its past. In 2013, unable to cope with cross-media, the prominent studio filed a lawsuit against Apple and a Chinese subsidiary claiming 110 of its productions had been illegally sold on iTunes, including Calabash Brothers and Black Cat Detective, and sought $500,000 in monetary damages.

The Post-2000 Movement to Giantism

Commencing about 2002 or 2003, Chinese animation entered an era of giantism with new production techniques/emphases, government relationships, and marketing orientations that made the former art form and industry model barely recognizable.

No other country has experienced the rapid acceleration China has had in total production minutes, number of studios, and growth of animation training programs and students. As stated before, at the close of the millennium, Shanghai Animation Film Studio, which still accounted for the majority of the country's production, had witnessed a staggering increase in yearly produced animation minutes from 500 to 5,000 between 1995 and 2000. Just six years later, China accounted for more than 80,000 minutes. Whereas previously, the Shanghai studio, Beijing Science and Educational Film Studio, and a very few other production houses operated, by October 2006, the number of animation and cartoon studios had skyrocketed to 5,473. Nowhere is this growth mania more noticeable than in education and training. By October 2006, China had 447 universities with established animation programs; a total of 1,230 universities housed schools and departments with animation and cartoon majors. By 2005, the country had already graduated 64,000 animation students; a year later, the number of students in animation programs was estimated to be 466,000.

The growth continued to soar, so that in 2013 (the latest year for which data were available), the industry generated 87 billion yuan ($14 billion) in revenue, had a total workforce of 220,000, and produced about 260,000 minutes of animation (Coonan 2014; see also Hudson Lockett 2015). As a major outsourcing station, China, that year, exported $160 million (up 22.8 percent year-on-year) worth of animation.

Each link of the industrial chain developed differently. The broadcast market declined during 2011–13, producing in 2013, 358 domestic television shows (down 9.37 percent year-on-year). On the other hand, the number of Chinese animated films in 2013 rose to thirty-three with box office revenues of 1.64 billion yuan (up 13.34 percent year-on-year). Climbing even higher, the domestic animation derivative market (toys, games, and other merchandise) rose by 20 percent year-on-year to 26.4 billion yuan ("Global and China . . ." 2014).

Despite gains in the animated films and derivatives areas, overall, Chinese animation experienced declines at the beginning of the 2010s. For example, in 2012, the output of the country's animation industry exceeded 100 billion yuan (about $16 billion). That year, the State Administration of Radio, Film and Television reported that 395 television animation productions, totaling 222,960 minutes, were made. Yet production was down 14.66 percent (forty shows) from 2011. Largely accounting for the drop was the low quality of television animated programs, prompting the government to prioritize high-quality works. A result was that of the 580 productions, totaling 471,000 minutes, planned for 2012, a large percentage never came to fruition ("China's US $16.3 bn . . ." 2013) .

A number of factors accounted for this transformation, including government involvement, foreign influences and connections, and digitalization advances.

Government Involvement

In the early years of the 2000s, the Chinese government began to take notice of animation in a manner similar to that of the South Korean authorities a decade before (see Lent 2004; Lent and Yu 1996)—requiring China's television stations to use more domestic cartoons, singling out nine cities as animation industrial bases, supporting many international animation festivals and extravaganzas, and encouraging the development of four national animation teaching and research bases (Beijing Film Academy, Chinese Arts University, Jilin College of the Arts, and Communication University of China). In 2004, the State Administration of Radio, Film and Television announced it was committing 1,000 hours of animation programming to its 2,000 television outlets, and a year later, sponsored the Promotion of Outstanding Domestic Animation Awards, whereby four works are nominated yearly by provincial and municipal broadcasters to be given priority on all channels. Of course, provincial and municipal governments have taken notice of these changes mandated from higher up.

Speaking at an animation festival in Changzhou in 2005 (at which the senior author of this book spoke), Director of Culture Market Department, Ministry of Culture, Liu Yuzhu, talked about areas where the Chinese government planned to help. He said that the central government will

1. increase investments and set up a special fund for animation. The government will help build a base for folk art, help in giving awards to artistic animation works.
2. improve enterprise competitiveness, providing substantial support for enterprises doing research and development. In addition to this financial support, the government will give favorable help to the software industry, such as software industry parks.
3. support animation bases integrating the industry and academic research. The industry is in bad need of high-end technical talents and more professionals will be cultivated. Institutes of higher learning and research institutes will be involved in training to provide high-level, high-end creative and marketable talents. Youngsters will be encouraged to enter animation through competitions and interest groups.
4. implement a complete industrial changeover for the animation industry. Production takes a

critical position. We will encourage separation of production and the broadcasting of animation and make full use of derivative products, such as toys, apparel, etc.
5. improve efforts in copyright regulation and crack down on piracy. We will also increase self-regulation in the animation industry. (Liu Yuzhu 2005)

Liu Yuzhu said that Chinese federal and state governments have instituted policy statements because of a number of obstacles to growth faced by the animation industry. Among these, he said, were a public mentality concerned with children's addiction to animation, the loss of the adult market for which animation is not geared, low-level quality and quantity of domestic animation (only one-half of the nation's needs are now met), lack of Chinese stories and a propensity to imitate, an immature industrial base with insufficient markets and loss of part of the local market to cheaper foreign animation, a non-integrated administrative structure of the industry, and a lack of sufficient professionals, especially screenwriters and market personnel with creative ideas (Liu Yuzhu 2005).

Foreign Influences, Connections

Foreign influences upon and connections with Chinese animation come through imported programming, subcontracting agreements, co-production arrangements, and international marketing attempts.

Much foreign animation has been screened in China; for example, a 2004 survey by China Mainland Marketing Research Co. found that of the top ten cartoon shows Chinese children watched, six were Japanese and two each were American and Chinese. One effect of such a high viewership of Japanese shows is reflected in the style adopted by many Chinese animators, whose artwork, stories, and characters are hardly discernible from anime. Trying to counter this trend, the State Administration of Radio, Film and Television in 2005 and 2006, levied rulings that limited the amount of

189

Fig. 6.19. *Xiyangyang he dahuilang* (*Pleasant Goat and Big Big Wolf*), 2008, a very lucrative television animation series.

foreign animation on television to 40 percent, barred foreign channels such as Disney, and banned TV shows and movies that blend animated elements with live-action performers, and eliminated foreign cartoons from the favored 5–8 p.m. time slot. Later, the restricted time was extended to 9 p.m.

Since transitioning to an open economy, China has in recent years had a number of relationships with foreign animation companies, allowing them to set up the already discussed offshore production houses in the 1990s to benefit from China's inexpensive labor pool, and entering into co-production agreements with others of them later.

Benefits from co-producing that accrue to Chinese studios include moving from strictly work-for-hire (as in subcontracting studios) to a more creative role in animation, enlarging capital investment pools, being involved in larger, more prestigious projects, and gaining a wider

distribution abroad. Also, because sales of animation in China were almost impossible because of widespread piracy, Chinese studios sought co-production deals in which they would share in profits (meager as they are) from North America and Europe.

In the last few years, Chinese (especially Shanghai) animation has attracted Hollywood investors in a "new wave of transnational co-operation [that] attempts to combine Chinese animation elements with Hollywood storytelling techniques . . . to create a new phase of Sino-US film co-production and to expand China's cultural presence in global markets" (Curtin and Li 2013). Reasons given for Hollywood to cooperate with Shanghai animation are as follows:

1. Drawing on past strengths, the animation infrastructure in Shanghai is growing, making it a

national leader and an attractive partner for joint ventures with American studios.

2. Co-productions allow greater access to the PRC for Hollywood partners and in turn provide their Chinese counterparts with Hollywood expertise in production and distribution.

3. Local media conglomerates are attractive co-production partners that can leverage creative, administrative, and distribution resources to support animated projects.

4. Even though the Chinese government still exercises significant control, new models of cooperation are expanding the creative capacity of Shanghai's animation industry. (Curtin and Li 2013)

Concerning the growth of the Shanghai animation industry, of the $52 million box office of fifteen animated features in 2011, more than 66 percent came from Shanghai-based companies; both Disney and Dream-Works have expanded their investments in the Chinese market, which should stimulate the local animation industry, and Shanghai Media Group has taken the lead in building the "brand value of its successful animation properties by turning them into franchises that can be exploited in comic books and theme parks." For example, 70 percent of the profit from the TV series *Xiyang-yang he dahuilang* (*Pleasant Goat and Big Big Wolf*) was generated by ancillary products and licensing (Curtin and Li 2013).

Chinese media conglomerates have become attractive partners for US firms such as the Walt Disney Company, which teamed up with Shanghai Shendi Group in the Shanghai Disney Resort venture, and DreamWorks Animation, which collaborated with China Media Capital, Shanghai Media Group, and Shanghai Alliance Investment to form Oriental DreamWorks. *Gongfu xiongmao 3* (*Kung Fu Panda 3*) was the first joint project of US and China DreamWorks (Barboza 2015: B1).

Shanghai Disney Resort, opened in 2016, is the Walt Disney Company's first mainland theme park. It includes six themed sections and venues for live entertainment,

a theater, two hotels, and the "tallest, largest and most interactive castle at any Disney theme park" (Barboza and Barnes 2015: B13). The China government approved the park on the condition that it reflects Chinese culture, prompting Disney executives to repeatedly use the catchphrase, "authentically Disney and distinctly Chinese" (Barboza and Barnes 2015: B13).

Live-action films adapted from US superhero comics have also caught the attention of Chinese media groups. In 2015, the Beijing-based film production group DMG entered into a partnership with Valiant Comics of New York. The deal included an eight-figure equity investment in Valiant and "'nine-figures of film-financing capital' for feature and TV projects." Valiant owns about 2,000 comic book characters (Betancourt and Cavna 2015).

Besides partnering with companies from the US, Australia, Canada, England, France, Spain, and other countries, and with Hong Kong and Taiwan, China helped spearhead a Northeast Asia animation consortium with Japan and South Korea in 2003 and 2004. The three countries with similar cultural, philosophical, and linguistic roots explored a number of possibilities of working together in animation, such as the joint production/distribution of at least eight television series, the trading of festival exhibition space, and the extension of meetings for future cooperation. Thus far, animators from the three countries are proud of their joint activities, pointing out that operational decisions and procedures and the division of credits have been executed democratically, allowing each company in these arrangements to reach its full potential.

More broadly, globalization has been an overarching aim of industry decision-makers in recent years, hoping to succeed in overseas sales of the country's animation and all the accompanying merchandise. So far, there have not been many rewards, because, first of all, the industry does not have enough experience globally (James Wang, interview, 2005), and second, the animators have not completely solved the difficult puzzle of meeting the expectations of hundreds of millions of Chinese at home while appealing to an international market

191

(Yan Dingxian 2006)—or as James Wang, founder and head of Wang Productions in Taiwan, who has done business on the mainland, said, "fitting into the world and yet finding the lost Chinese spirit" (James Wang, interview, 2005).

Perhaps Chinese animators face the same difficulties most others of Asia face in trying to export: 1. animation is produced expensively and sold abroad at low cost; 2. characters and stories do not have universal appeal; and 3. Chinese animation must break into an international market tightly controlled by transnational behemoths which determine who gets in and under what terms.

Digitalization Advances

A third factor that has drastically changed Chinese animation has been the widespread use of computers in studios. For the past fifteen years, Chinese animation has increasingly moved into the digital age with a number of state-of-the art computerized studios sprouting, including some with motion capture capacities. The hundreds of animation training programs that have come to the fore also concentrate on digitalization.

Although computer-generated animation has a number of benefits (especially for producers overseeing the budgets), some of its principles and modes of operation are contrary to what existed during China's golden eras. Critics in China and abroad have pointed out that digitalized animation is more formulaic, less spontaneous, and not as open to experimentation as traditional animation. They also bemoan the tendencies of 3D to be additive—too detailed—in an art form that traditionally reduced things to their essentials, and the marginalization of the animator who no longer feels as though he/she is creating the character, but instead, is part of a collection of people and programs. Computers also allow for faster production, both a blessing and a curse, in the sense that they support what the senior author of this book has termed, since the dawn of the 2000s, "fast food animation." An American animator with her own studio in Beijing declared that among the major problems of China's animation are young people who know

computer software but lack the fundamental principles of timing, stretching, etc., that are part of 2D animation (Bristow 2006).

On the other hand, China has witnessed a surge of independent animation since 2000, urged on by digital technology. Wu (2005: 21–25) identified three categories of this independent animation: 1. researchers in computer graphics and students of animation; 2. individual animators with backgrounds in professional animation working in non-government studios; and 3. independent Flash animators and self-taught animators.

Paola Voci calls this type of animation "*animateur* cinema," a digitalized, "local, Chinese cultural practice, separate from mainstream [i.e., institutional and governmental] animation and contributing to the same 'alternative' cultural space of independent DV [digitalized video] production" (2015: 279). In such works, Chineseness is not branded nor marketed, and often, the postings are not linear narratives and some are dissenting against the government and the CCP. Examples that Voci (2015: 275–78) gave are *Caonima* (*Grassmud Horse*), the Chinese title sounding like "fuck your mother," and the already discussed (see Chapter 5) *Xiaotu Kuang Kuang* (*Little Rabbit Be Good*, 2011), by Wang Bo (aka, Pi San or Pisan). *Grassmud Horse*, done by two anonymous individuals, uses animals to insult taboo subjects, often with puns. *Little Rabbit Be Good* is even more provocative and revolutionary, strongly criticizing Chinese scandals (Voci 2015: 277). Three overlapping groups similar to those identified by Wu make up animateurs: "Professional Flash animators/artists who choose to produce and circulate animation outside the institutional (commercial and/or artistic) channels; animation students, who can also be considered pre-professionals; and non-professional moviemakers, who can also be considered occasional animateurs" (Voci 2015: 268).

Opportunities for independent animators are provided in some Chinese art and film institutes, where students are encouraged to produce animation with a blend of digital technology, the visuality of Chinese painting, and classical elite literature, and to distribute their works on the internet or by DVD. There are Chinese internet domains, such as the Chinese Animation Association's chinanim.com, that offer stable channels for uploading independent animation.

Summary

For most of the 1950s through 1980s, China's animation was at its pinnacle of artistic achievement, with a blend of Chinese and foreign materials, techniques, and approaches and indigenous art and literature traditions. Some of the work of those periods stands alone in exquisiteness of conceptualization and execution, crafted by artists with almost limitless time and resources.

The picture changed after China abandoned its planned economy system in favor of a more open market economy. Time became of the essence, as many studios cropped up, each scrambling to support itself; production accelerated to feed the greatly augmented numbers of television stations and to satisfy demands of overseas clients; and mechanization quickly replaced handcraftsmanship.

Government support and interest were primarily directed at animation as a money-making product useful in filling gaps in television schedules, rather than an art form. In the process, with the exceptions of independent and university works, almost all of the types of previously made animation faded into the distance.

Chinese animation had become a culture industry with all of the inherent flaws discussed by Theodor Adorno (1991 [1975]): the transfer of the "profit motive naked into cultural forms," "eternal sameness," and "distribution and mechanical reproduction contrary to the technique of art."

Although not recognized until the past decade or two, comic art plays major roles in a country's politics and culture, whether campaigning for, propagating, or criticizing governmental or societal policies and norms through editorial cartoons, or providing entertainment through animation and comic books, or educating and raising the social consciousness of people through specialized cartoons and comics.

Dating to the nineteenth century, Chinese comic art has been involved in each stage of the country's modern history, serving as a reporter and critic of current affairs, a recorder of history, and a storyteller, jester, and educator. Carrying out these tasks was often difficult as cartoonists faced government restrictions, economic deprivation, and, at times, severe punishments, including imprisonment, banishment, and the curtailment of their work. At the same time, there were also rewards, as some of them helped set artistic policies for China, while many more fought the good fight during wars, the formation of a country, and the drive to so-called modernization.

We have sought to provide a comprehensive account of the history and contemporary status of China's comic art, while also trying to hone in on themes such as, 1. the common threads that ran through the history of China's comic art; 2. the outside factors that influenced the development and nourishment of Chinese comic art; 3. the links historically between Chinese cartoons and the country's more general art and literary professions; and 4. the relationship of art (specifically, comic art) to Chinese society.

In addition to the themes inherent in the answers to the latter three questions, other strings that tie together the history of Chinese comic art are the many crises of twentieth-century China (e.g., the overthrow of the Qing Dynasty, civil wars, the Japanese war, the establishment of the People's Republic of China, the Maoist campaigns and Cultural Revolution, and the conversion to a market economy) that cartoonists had to contend with, and the major adjustments Chinese culture and art had to make in how they were defined, organized, and regulated.

Chapter 7

Conclusion

As said earlier, political and social commentary cartoonists thrive on crises that provide them topics and individuals and institutions to satirize; this was evident in caricatures and visual depictions of the Qing Dynasty and warlords early in the twentieth century, of the Japanese military in the 1930s and '40s, and of the Guomindang and Chiang Kai-shek and the Communist Party and Mao Zedong for many decades. To be sure, not every crisis was openly criticized by cartoonists, who, on a number of occasions had to pull their punches, follow the Party line as to who or what should be attacked, or employ subtlety to get their messages across.

Recurrent crises during almost the entirety of the twentieth century and a rash of campaigns from 1949 until 1976 required major adjustments from time to time on what culture and art (including comic art) meant, what their purposes should be, and what mechanisms were needed to meet those goals. Especially during the Seventeen-Year Period (1949–66) and Cultural Revolution (1966–76), alterations in policies concerning art occurred at irregular intervals, sometimes contradictory in mission and design, causing confusion, anxiety, and hesitancy among cartoonists.

Other major changes, though perhaps marginally crisis-laden, required adjustments in the art and cartooning sectors. The rise of modernization, switch to a market economy, and increased use of the internet required artists to find alternate means of funding and new technologies with which to do their work.

From its beginning, Chinese comic art was influenced by outside factors; the earliest cartoon periodicals, some dating to the nineteenth century, assumed European or American names (e.g., *Punch*, *Puck*, *Charivari*), were published by foreigners, and used and arranged content in a Western manner. Outside influences existed at other times: Chinese cartoonists such as Liao Bingxiong, Ding Cong, and others admired and, to a certain degree, emulated foreign artists at the beginnings of their careers in the 1930s; cartoon and humor magazines, as well as daily newspapers, used cartoons and comic strips by Grosz, McManus, Covarrubias, Thurber, and others before World War II; foreign cartoonists Sapajou and

Schiff, working in China from 1925 to 1940 and 1930 to 1947, respectively, also left their imprints on Chinese cartooning; Soviet and Eastern European art and animation styles were popular in China in the early 1950s, and in the 1990s to the present, Japanese manga and US comic books have had impacts on lianhuanhua (their popularity nearly decimating the lianhuanhua industry) and the creation of xinmanhua. Obversely, there were other times when the country's leaders looked at foreign (mainly American) cartoon work with scorn and either banned or limited it, as in a recent decision to block foreign animation from primetime television.

Also long-lived in the history of Chinese comic art are the connections between cartooning and the larger art and literary professions, and between art (including comics and cartoons) and Chinese society at large.

Despite objections to the embrace of cartoons as one of the arts (at one time, an objection voiced worldwide), in China, the many links shared by the arts offset such protests. First of all, much of the early comic art was considered worthy of publication in top literary and pictorial magazines, and, later, in prestigious art periodicals, including *Fine Art*. The lianhuanhua, popular beginning in the 1910s, were also considered, in some quarters, as an appendage of literature, as they included classical legends, operas, and contemporary short stories. Second, a number of famous cartoonists were also prominent painters, muralists, calligraphers, script writers, and sculptors; among them were Zhang Guangyu, Ding Cong, Ye Qianyu, Zhang Ding, Liao Bingxiong, Wang Zimei, Feng Zikai, Zhang Leping, and Huang Yao, to name a few. Third, when China's culture was revamped after 1949, cartoonists played key roles in the reorganization of the art profession: Ye Qianyu and Cai Ruohong headed the newly established China Artists' Association; Zhang Ding was one of the top administrators of the Central Academy of Fine Art; and others, such as Hua Junwu, helped set policies for art. Another indication that cartooning was accepted by the art community was the subsequent creation of the Cartoon Art Committee under the aegis of the China Artists' Association.

Actually, a case for the legitimacy of comics was made as early as 1932 by the noted intellectual/writer Lu Xun, who defended comics by saying not only should they be considered works of art, but that they already had a place in the "Palace of Art." At the same time, the novelist and future minister of culture Mao Dun also supported comics. For a few years from the mid-1930s, cartoonists wrote treatises in an attempt to develop a sound theoretical framework for their profession.

Chinese comic art has always been tightly entwined with Chinese society and politics in that it has, at different times, served as a critic, watchdog, and promoter of sociopolitical matters. As already seen, the earliest Chinese cartoons played these roles, warning of possible foreign encroachments, chastising Qing and warlord officials for their ineptitude and corruption, and empathizing with the Republican goals of Sun Yat-sen. Depending on the openness of the government at any given time, cartoons continued to perform these functions as they have in any society.

Art generally, and comic art specifically, connected with society in other ways at other times. In the late 1930s, the New Art Movement spelled out what art and cartooning should be: appealing to the masses, more realistic, socially and politically motivated, propagandistic, and marked by a Chinese style with Western elements. Some of these characteristics were enounced by Mao Zedong while at Yan'an in 1942, and became integral to how art was to relate to society: i.e., as Westad (2003: 96) said, "to benefit China in its hour of need." Cartoonists acted as Chinese Paul Reveres, waking "their countrymen to action against the country's ills" (96) throughout most of the twentieth century.

Determining the "ills" of Chinese society usually is not the prerogative of the cartooning community. China has at its disposal tightly controlled, restrictive, and regulatory bodies and state-owned mass media that decide when the news and opinion gates are opened and when they are closed, and when they are opened, what is permitted to come through. By this arrangement, cartoonists waken "their countrymen to action against the country's ills," but only as defined by the state.

A, Geng. Cartoonist. Guiyang, November 23, 2013.

Bi, Keguan. Cartoonist; cartoon historian. Beijing, May 29, 2006.

Bi, Weimin. Cartoon historian; son of Bi Keguan. Beijing, December 5, 2014; Beijing, October 1, 2015.

Cao, Xiao Hui. Animator; general director, Beijing Scientific and Educational Film Studio, Cartoon Department of Film. Beijing, October 1999; Beijing, May 29, 2001.

Cao, Xiuwen. Farmer painter. Fengjing Town, May 28, 2010.

Chang, Guangxi. Animator, director, Shanghai Animation Film Studio. Shanghai, June 17, 2001; Changchun, September 14, 2007; Guiyang, August 8, 2010; Shanghai, June 10, 2016.

Chang, Joe. Animator. Hangzhou, June 4, 2005.

Chang, Tiejun. Cartoonist. Beijing, November 26, 2013.

Chen, Huifang. Farmer painter. Fengjing Town, May 28, 2010.

Chen, Huiling. Cartoonist. Nanjing, May 15, 2009.

Chen, Jianyu. Animation critic, scriptwriter. Shanghai, June 14–15, 2001.

Chen, Jinghe. Son of Chen Huiling. Nanjing, May 15, 2009.

Chen, Xing. Cartoonist. Hangzhou, June 4, 2005.

Chen, Xuhui. Faculty member, Jilin Animation School. Changchun, June 1, 2009.

Chen, Yuli. Founder, co-director, Frog Cartoon Group. Qiuxian, May 28–31, 2009.

Chen, Zhong. Cartoonist, Frog Cartoon Group. Qiuxian, May 29, 2009.

Chua, Soo Teng. Research manager, Huang Yao Foundation. Singapore, November 27, 2016.

Cui, Zhenguo. Painter; former vice president, China Artists' Association; wife of Wang Fuyang. Beijing, August 22, 2004.

Deng, Weizhi. Vice chairman, Cultural Committee of China. Shanghai, August 13, 1993.

Ding, Cong. Cartoonist; first chair, Cartoon Art Committee. Beijing, December 20, 2002; Beijing, May 30, 2006; Beijing, July 2, 2007.

Ding, Weimin. Design artist, Shanghai Yilimei Animation Co. Shanghai, August 14, 1993.

Dong, Mingguo. Director, county propaganda. Qiuxian, May 28–29, 2009.

Du, Jianguo. Cartoonist, *Good Children*. Shanghai, August 16, 1993.

Du, Peng. Cartoonist. Nanjing, May 20, 2009.

Duan, Xiaoxuan. Camerawoman, Shanghai Animation Film Studio. Shanghai, June 11, 2016.

Fang, Cheng. Cartoonist; former art editor, *People's Daily*. Beijing, June 10, 2001; Beijing, August 11, 2002; Beijing, August 22, 2004; Beijing, June 12, 2005; Drexel Hill, PA, October 5–16, 2005; Beijing, May 29–30, 2006; Beijing, June 29, 2007; Beijing, June 10, 2008; Beijing, May 24, 2009; Beijing, August 2, 2010; Beijing, October 30, 2011; Beijing, May 20, 2012; Beijing, August 24, 2012; Beijing, June 11, 2013; Beijing, September 14, 2013; Beijing, November 30, 2013; Beijing, December 6, 2014; Beijing, September 26, 2015; Beijing, June 9, 2016; Beijing, December 7, 2016.

Appendix

Interviews Conducted by John A. Lent and/or Xu Ying

Fang, Tang. Cartoonist, *Southern Weekend*. Guangzhou, January 5, 2002.

Feng, Yiyin. Cartoonist; daughter of Feng Zikai. Shanghai, January 10, 2002; Shanghai, June 8, 2005; Shanghai, June 10, 2016.

Guo, Ye. Faculty member, Jilin Animation School. Changchun, June 1, 2009.

Han, Shangyi. Cartoonist; member, National Salvation Cartoon Propaganda Corps. Shanghai, August 15, 1993.

He, Wei. Art editor, *Workers Daily*. Beijing, May 28, 2001; Beijing, June 3, 2001; Beijing, December 16, 18, 2002; Beijing, August 22, 2004; Beijing, May 28, 2006; Beijing, June 3, 2007; Beijing, July 10, 2007; Beijing, May 24, 2009; Beijing, August 2, 2010; Beijing, October 30, 2011.

Hong, Huang. Cartoonist. Shanghai, August 15, 1993.

Hong, Jinfeng. Puppet animator, Shanghai Animation Film Studio. Shanghai, August 15, 1993.

Hu, Jinqing. Animator, director, Shanghai Animation Film Studio. Shanghai, June 17, 2001.

Hu, Yanting. Cartoonist, Frog Cartoon Group. Qiuxian, May 28, 2009.

Hu, Yihong. Animator, director, Shanghai Animation Film Studio. Shanghai, June 17, 2001.

Hua, Junwu. Cartoonist; co-founder *Satire and Humor*. Beijing, June 13, 2005; Beijing, May 31, 2006.

Huang, Wei. Instructor, Art Design College, Zhejiang Gongshang University. Hangzhou, June 3, 2005.

Huang, Yuanlin. Cartoonist; cartoon historian. Beijing, June 1, 2001; Beijing, August 22, 2004.

Ji, Chunbai. Vice president, Cartoonist Association of Wuhan. Wuhan, June 8, 2004.

Ji, Shixiao. Vice president, Cartoonist Association of Wuhan. Wuhan, June 8, 2004.

Jia, Fou. Professor, Animation School, Beijing Film Academy, Communication University of China. Beijing, May 30, 2001; Beijing, December 20, 2002.

Jiang, Yousheng. Cartoonist; co-founder, *Satire and Humor*. Beijing, December 17, 2001; Beijing, May 29, 2006.

Jin, Guoping. Vice president, later president, Shanghai Animation Film Studio. Shanghai, August 13, 1993; Shanghai, June 17, 2001.

Jin, Yunzhi. Animation director; vice president, Hang Zhou Mingxing Animation Art Design Co. Hangzhou, June 3, 2005.

Li, Aijun. Director of county culture bureau. Qiuxian, May 28–29, 2009.

Li, Binsheng. Cartoonist, *Beijing Daily*. Beijing, November 27, 2013; Beijing, April 30, 2015; Beijing, May 16, 2015; Beijing, July 11, 2015; Beijing, September 29, 2015; Beijing, January 3, 2016; Beijing, June 16, 2016; Beijing, December 7, 2016.

Li, Jianhua. Cartoonist, *China Daily*. Beijing, May 31, 2001; Beijing, September 18, 2002; Beijing, December 18, 2002.

Li, Lekang. Faculty member, Jilin Animation School. Changchun, June 1, 2009.

Li, Qin. Secretary, Tourist Company, Communist Party. Fengjing, May 28, 2010.

Li, Qingai. Co-director, Frog Cartoon Group. Qiuxian, May 28–31, 2009.

Li, Weiwei. Biographer and daughter of Wang Zimei. Beijing, December 4, 8, 2016.

Liao, Bingxiong. Cartoonist; member National Salvation Cartoon Propaganda Corps. Guangzhou, January 4–5, 2002.

Liao, Ling-er. Liao's biographer; daughter of Liao Bingxiong. Guangzhou, January 4–5, 2002.

Liao, Lingsi. Folklorist; son of Liao Bingxiong. Guangzhou, January 5, 2002.

Lin, Qin. Cartoonist. Shanghai, August 15, 1993.

Liu, Fumin. Design artist, Shanghai Yilimei Animation Co. Shanghai, August 14, 1993.

Liu, Rendao. Editor-in-chief, *Art Magazine*. Beijing, May 30, 2006.

Lu, Shengzhang. Animator; dean, animation, Beijing Broadcasting Institute. Beijing, December 20, 2002.

Luo, Jianglin. Vice dean, Jilin Animation School. Changchun, May 31, 2009.

Ma, Kexuan. Animator, Shanghai Animation Film Studio. Changzhou, September 29, 2005; Beijing, October 26, 2011.

Mai, Fei (Fei Mak). Cartoonist; leader, National Salvation Cartoon Propaganda Corps. New York City, June 16, 2006.

Miao, Yintang. Science cartoonist. Beijing, December 16, 2002; Beijing, August 22, 2004; Beijing, May 30, 2006; Beijing, June 5, 2007; Beijing, May 23, 2009.

Mu, Xiaoya (Michelle). Executive director general, Asian Youth Animation and Comics Competition. Beijing, September 21, 2013.

Pan, Shunqi. Cartoonist, editor, *Modern Family*. Shanghai, August 16, 1993.

Qian, Yunda. Animator, director, Shanghai Animation Film Studio. Shanghai, June 17, 2001; Shanghai, June 11, 2016.

Qiao, Ling. Cartoonist. Beijing, October 11, 2002.

Qu, Jianfang. Animator; chairman, Afanti International. Guiyang, September 10, 2007.

Quan, Yingsheng. Cartoonist; proprietor, director, Beijing Heavy Comics Culture and Media Co., Ltd. Beijing, October 28, 2011; Beijing, November 1, 2011; Beijing, August 24, 2012.

Ren, Guangqiang. Cartoonist, Frog Cartoon Group. Qiuxian, May 28–29, 2009.

Shen, Jun. Wife of Ding Cong. Beijing, December 20, 2002; Beijing, July 2, 2007; Drexel Hill, PA, October 2009; Beijing, August 2, 2010; Beijing, October 30, 2011; Beijing, June 10, 2013; Beijing, September 13, 2013.

Shi, Cuiting. Author; wife of Huang Yuanlin. Beijing, December 9, 2014.

Shi, Meicheng. Cartoonist, editor, *World of Cartoons*. Shanghai, August 16, 1993.

Sun, Jihong. Son of Fang Cheng. Beijing, October 30, 2011; Beijing, June 9, 2016.

Sun, Li-jun. Chair, Animation School, Beijing Film Academy. Beijing, May 30, 2001.

Sun, Shaobo. Cartoonist, editor, *World of Cartoons*. Shanghai, August 16, 1993.

Sun, Xiaogang. Cartoonist; son of Fang Cheng. Beijing, June 9, 2016.

Tan, Mayling. Daughter-in-law of Huang Yao. Taipei, July 25, 2005.

Te, Wei. Animator; director, Shanghai Animation Film Studio; leader, National Salvation Cartoon Propaganda Corps. Shanghai, June 16, 2001; Shanghai, June 12, 2004.

Wang, Fuyang. President, Beijing Artists' Association Cartoon Art Committee. Beijing, May 31, 2001; Beijing, December 16, 2002; Beijing, August 22, 2004; Beijing, June 12, 2005; Beijing, May 29, 2006.

Wang, Jiajun. Huashi Film/TV Culture Communications Co. Shanghai, June 8, 2005.

Wang, Lei. Animation professor, deputy dean, animator, Communication University of China. Beijing, May 26, 2009.

Wang, Liuyi. Co-founder, director, Asian Youth Animation and Comics Competition. Beijing, September 18, 2013.

Wang, Wei. Cartoonist, painter, *lianhuanhua* artist. Beijing, August 25, 2012.

Wong, Carolyn. Founder, director, Huang Yao Foundation; granddaughter of Huang Yao. Taipei, July 25, 2005; Singapore, November 27; Singapore, December 1, 2016.

Xia, Dachuan. Cartoonist. Beijing, May 31, 2006; Beijing, October 28, 2011.

Xia, Lichuan. Cartoonist. Beijing, May 31, 2006.

Xiao, Guo. Manager, King of Comics Internet Café. Shanghai, June 8, 2005.

Xie, Chun-yan. Cartoonist. Shanghai, August 16, 1993.

Xu, Chang. Animator; son of A Da. Shanghai, June 9, 2005.

Xu, Jin. Cartoonist, *Workers Daily*. Beijing, November 29, 2013.

Xu, Keren. Cartoonist; director of special articles, *World of Cartoons*. Shanghai, August 16, 1993.

Xu, Pengfei. Former chief editor, *Satire and Humor*; chair, Cartoon Art Committee. Beijing, June 11, 2001; Beijing, June 12, 2005; Beijing, May 29, 2006; Beijing, July 11, 2007; Beijing, June 16, 2008; Beijing, October 28, 2011.

Yan, Dingxian. Animator, director, Shanghai Animation Film Studio. Shanghai, June 17, 2001.

Yan, Shanchun. Animator, Shanghai Animation Film Studio. Shanghai, June 11, 2016.

Yao, Donghui. Animator, faculty member, Jilin Animation School. Changchun, June 1, 2009.

Ying, Tao. Cartoonist; co-founder and former editor, *Satire and Humor*. Beijing, May 29, 2006.

Yu, Gangzhi. Vice president, Cartoonist Association of Wuhan. Wuhan, June 8, 2004.

Yu, Yanyu. Marketing manager, Shanghai Animation Film Studio. Seoul, Korea, August 13, 2003.

Yu, Yatang. Head, Zhejiang University Press. Hangzhou, June 3, 2005.

Yue, Fenghua. Project manager, *China Daily* website. Beijing, May 31, 2001.

Zhan, Tong. Cartoonist/animator. Shanghai, August 15–16, 1993.

Zhan, Yong. Cartoonist; son of Zhan Tong. Shanghai, August 15, 1993.

Zhang, Ding. Cartoonist; painter; member, National Salvation Cartoon Propaganda Corps. Beijing, June 15, 2005.

Zhang, Guoqiang. Shanghai Animation Film Studio. Seoul, Korea, August 13, 2003.

Zhang, Liming. Owner, China animation company. Seoul, Korea, August 16, 2003.

Zhang, Linlan. Deputy editor-in-chief, *Xinmin Evening News*. Shanghai, August 16, 1993.

Zhang, Ningping. President, Hangzhou Cartoonists Association; director, manager, Hang Zhou Mingxing Animation. Hangzhou, June 3, 2005.

Zhang, Shupeng. Chancellor, Huashi Media Arts Academy. Shanghai, June 8, 2005.

Zhang, Songlin. Animator; vice president, China Animation Association; president, Jilin Academy of Arts; animator, screenwriter, Shanghai Animation Film Studio. Hangzhou, June 1, 2005.

Zhang, Yaoning. Cartoonist; director, Art Department, *China Daily*; secretary, general director, China News Cartoon Institute. Beijing, May 31, 2001; Beijing, December 10, 2014.

Zhang, Ying. Board chair, School of Software and Microelectronics, Peking University; wife of Wang Wei. Beijing, August 25, 2012.

Zheng, Huagai. Military cartoonist; historian. Beijing, December 16, 2002; Beijing, June 12–13, 2005; Beijing, May 31, 2006; Beijing, June 12, 2008; Beijing, August 2, 2010; Beijing, October 29, 2011.

Zheng, Huawei. Secretary, China News Cartoon Institute. Beijing, December 10, 2014.

Zheng, Xinyao. Cartoonist; chief, Art Department, *Xinmin Evening News*. Shanghai, August 16, 1993; Shanghai, June 14, 2001.

Zhou, Jie. Vice president, *China Daily* website. Beijing, May 31, 2001.

Zhou, Jin. Instructor, Animation School, Beijing Film Academy. Beijing, May 30, 2001.

Zhu, Cheng. Cartoonist; director, Redman Cartoon Competition. Fuzhou, October 2, 2011; Beijing, October 28, 2011.

Zhu, Genhua. Cartoonist, *People's Daily*. Beijing, May 27, 2009.

Zou, Jingquan. Vice president, Cartoonist Association of Wuhan. Wuhan, June 8, 2004.

Zou, Qin. Animator, Shanghai Yilimei Animation Studio. Shanghai, August 13, 1993.

Notes

Chapter 1

1. The magazine's name has variously been translated as *The Illustrated Lithographer*, *The Lithographic Studio Illustrated*, and *Dianshizhai Pictorial*.

2. Theobald (2012) said that *Dianshizhai huabao* was "sold separately or as a free supplement to subscribers of . . . *Shenbao*." Zhang (2001: 122) called it a "complimentary supplement."

3. Tongmenghui was an underground resistance group founded in August 1905 by Sun Yat-sen (1866–1925) and other Chinese revolutionaries in Japan. In 1906, a branch was started in Singapore. Tongmenghui moved from Tokyo to Shanghai in November 1911.

4. The duplicity of the Manchu government was the theme of a highly recognized cartoon in *Wushan quannian huabao*. Called "Two Faces: Domestic and International," it depicted the government's double dealing policy of brutal suppression domestically and complete kowtowing to foreign powers.

5. Shen (2001: 100) described Zhu's illustrated lithograph: "It was called *huihui tu* (chapter pictures), because it had one illustration for each chapter, *hui*. By putting the text and picture into a single composition, huihui tu is close in format to the later lianhuanhua."

Chapter 2

1. Most "Sanmao" strips were reprinted many times as collections, particularly *Sanmao liulangji*, which, after 1949, contrasted pre-Liberation wretchedness with the uplifted living conditions under Mao. The post-Liberation series, such as *Sanmao yingjiefang* (*Sanmao Meets Liberation*), *Sanmao aiyundong* (*Sanmao Loves Sports*), *Sanmao aikexue* (*Sanmao Loves Science*), *Sanmao xue Lei Feng* (*Sanmao Learns from Lei Feng*), *Sanmao riji* (*Sanmao's Diary*), and *Sanmao jinxi* (*Sanmao Yesterday and Today*), lost their spark, serving as educational and rhetorical tools "to draw a symbolic line for children between old and new China" (Farquhar 1995: 154). Sanmao now was shown as a bright, studious boy and as a teacher, imploring friends not to smoke, be selfish, or show off (see Peng 1980: 2). Farquhar (1995: 154) labeled these stories as "unspeakably dull, even tiresome."

"Sanmao" remains China's most popular comic strip after more than seventy-five years, still featured in films, stage shows, and new book compilations in China and abroad (some pirated versions). Merchandise carrying Sanmao's name and image includes toys, clothing, shoes, and souvenirs. A famous Taiwanese writer adopted San Mao as her professional name, and a hotel, park, museum, and three schools (kindergarten, primary, and arts) were named after either Sanmao or Zhang Leping. In 2015, Sanmao received the Heritage Award at the 42nd Angoulême International Comics Festival in France.

2. "Niubizi" sometimes is called "Willie Buffoon," which is incorrect. Huang Yao signed his cartoons "W. Buffon," the "W" standing for

his surname Wong (his name before conversion to Huang according to Hanyu Pinyin), "buffoon" for clowns in a circus.

3. The materials were preserved by noted author/intellectual Lu Xun, who, in a preface to a subsequent publication, wrongly credited everything to Yin Fu. After Liberation, Lu Xun's widow (Xu Guangping) donated the poems and illustrations to the government, where the illustrations were ascertained to be the works of Liang.

4. Barmé (2002: 93–94) discussed the "Manhua Society of Shanghai" (no doubt the same organization), a group of eleven artists who rejected Westernized names (*katong* [cartoon], *fengcihua* [satirical painting], *chouxiang* [caricature], or *youmo* [humor]) in favor of the Japanese *manga* as the loan word to describe their work as *manhua*. He credited the society with producing a collection of Huang Wennong's strong political cartoons and *Shanghai manhua*.

5. Another popular foreign-born cartoonist working in Shanghai between the world wars was Friedrich Schiff (1908–68). Born in Austria, Schiff was a cartoonist in China from 1930 to 1947, when he returned to his native country.

6. Gan (2008) divided Feng Zikai's cartoons into periods of paintings for old poems, of children, of society, and an ode to nature.

7. Bi and Huang (1983: 56) quoted Lu Xun as saying "the crucial point about cartoons is their honesty, they must accurately depict the appearance of things and people, that is, their essence."

8. Bevan (2016: 214 note) quoted *Shenbao* as reporting on November 3, 1936 (11), that "more than 300" exhibits were displayed. The following day, *Shenbao* wrote that only 200 of the original 700 works were exhibited.

Chapter 3

1. Song Meiling (1897–2003), the wife of Chiang Kai-shek, figured prominently in politics. As Madame Chiang Kai-shek, she helped her husband publicize his cause in the United States. In 1943, she became the second woman to ever address a joint session of the US Congress, pleading her case for aid to China.

2. Benedict Arnold (1741–1801) was a military general during the American Revolution who defected to the British Army. Shi Jingtang (892–942) was a military general for the Later Tang Dynasty in China who rebelled to overthrow the Later Tang. Qin Hui (1090–1155), a chancellor of China's Song Dynasty, was labeled a traitor for aiding in the persecution and execution of Yue Fei, a Song general. Wu Sangui (1612–78) was the military general instrumental in the fall of the Ming Dynasty. Eventually, he was considered a traitor to both the Ming and Qing dynasties.

3. This section depends heavily on Jeremy Taylor's research, for the reason he states: "The work of Chinese cartoonists who published their illustrations in the popular press in occupied China from 1937 to 1945 has largely escaped the attention of scholars of both the occupation itself and the broader field of cartoon history" (Taylor 2014: 1). Bi Weimin (interview, 2014) said that his father, historian/cartoonist Bi Keguan, did not deal with collaborationist cartooning in his books and articles, because "there is no information available on this [in China]."

4. Another cartoonist, Fang Cheng, went to Hong Kong in 1948, but claimed, by then, the Guomindang, sensing defeat, tried to recruit famous artists to move to Taiwan (Fang Cheng, interview, 2001).

5. One might also challenge Westad's claim that "throughout the civil war, the direct CCP influence on writers and artists was negligible, in spite of the Center's repeated instructions to its agents in GMD areas to recruit 'progressive artists and scholars'" (2003: 97), on the grounds that a rather large number of cartoonists did support the CCP. In the case of the cartoonists we interviewed, most already leaned to Communism before the Civil War began.

6. What became known as the Shen Chong Incident put a strain on US-China relations. Starting at Peking University and spreading nationwide, student demonstrations, petitions, and pickets were held in support of Shen Chong and in denouncement of US military stationed in China. The soldier accused of the rape, William Gaither Pierson, was found guilty by an American military court martial in early 1947, a ruling that was overturned later that year by the Navy and War Department in Washington, DC. Shen Chong was attacked on her return from a movie. Attempts were made by the two soldiers to besmirch her reputation, calling her a prostitute (for further details, see Hong Zhang 2002: 81–122; Cook 1996: 65–97; Xu Liping 2012, 2015: 58–60; Cathcart 2008: 140–54). The subject of the rape never came up in the many days the authors of this book were in her company.

7. An older sister, Liang Xueqing, was an accomplished oil painter and headed various advertising art departments (Laing 2004: 172).

Chapter 4

1. Although Li Binsheng was hesitant to continue cartooning after the Cultural Revolution (instead, he concentrated on his Peking opera acting), he did continue to create drawings meant to improve social conditions. One that he drew for *Beijing Daily* in 1982 made fun of poor telephone connections. Using "Yugong yishan" (old fool moves the mountain), a parody in which an old fool tries to move a mountain, and believes if he can't, his son will, and if his son can't, his grandson will, and so on, Li Binsheng drew "Yugong da dianhua" (old fool making a phone call). The cartoon shows four individuals of different generations ready to take on the onerous task of the father to get through on the telephone. The caption reads: "No matter how hard it is to get through the 46 Bureau, at least, after I die, I have my son; after he dies, I have my grandson." A government official thanked *Beijing Daily* for bringing attention to the phone problem and assured them the phone

system would be improved (Li Binsheng, interview, 2016; see cartoon at http://www.chinaqw.com/news/200810/16/134093.shtml).

2. According to Bi Keguan (2002: 61–64), the cartoon was created by Weng Rulan, a student of a middle school attached to the Art Academy.

3. In line with revised notions concerning the perpetrators of the Cultural Revolution (that the blame lies with others in addition to the "Gang of Four"), Liao Bingxiong added himself and Chinese people who passively accepted their own fate. In an interview (2002) we had with Liao, he candidly said, "I think the 'Gang of Four' was really the 'Gang of Five' with Mao at the head. He was a bad king."

4. The eight model operas, expanded by the end of the Cultural Revolution to eighteen, were revolutionary and modern in themes and heroes portrayed: kings, emperors, and beauties were out; stories of recent revolutionary struggles, the People's Liberation Army, the bravery of the people, and Maoist thought were featured.

5. Zhao Hongben was "condemned, struggled, and nicknamed 'The Comic Tyrant of the South'" for his lianhuanhua *Sun Wukong Thrice Defeats the White-Boned Demon*, with his Red Guard accusers claiming, "(1) His demon is considered much too beautiful, (2) His hero, Sun Wukong, is not enough of a hero to hold up to Cultural Revolution standards of scrutiny, and (3) The comic contains too much 'lewd sexual material'" (Mittler 2012: 340).

6. During the Cultural Revolution, the intellectuals were added to the list of eight condemned classes and were perceived as the worst, thus "stinking nine."

7. Edgar Snow was a US journalist who, in 1936, interviewed Mao Zedong in Shanxi and then stayed on with CCP forces for a few months, after which he wrote *Red Star over China* (1937).

Chapter 5

1. In an interview (2016) with Xu Ying, Li Binsheng told how an incident he was involved in probably inspired Liao to draw "Self Mockery." He remembered:

> After I regained my position at *Beijing Daily*, a French cartoon researcher came to interview me. He had intended to interview me at my apartment, but at that time, I was not allowed to receive interviews at home. So, the foreigner interviewed me at my office with another colleague of mine present. I was very nervous and answered the questions carefully. I remember one of the questions was, "Why were there guards at the gate of *People's Daily*?" I was not prepared to answer such kinds of questions, so I replied over-cautiously and with hesitancy. Later, the Frenchman went to Guangzhou and interviewed Liao Bingxiong at his apartment, not office. He asked Liao why he could interview Liao at his apartment but not at mine. He also told Liao how I answered questions with hesitancy and caution. A couple of days later, Liao called me and

told me to watch for his [Liao's] new cartoon in the newspaper soon. That cartoon was Liao's "Self Mockery" with the broken jar. Though Liao drew himself, the idea was inspired by my experience with the foreign interviewer. No one knows about this story.

2. Titled *Xingqiu dazhan* (*Star Wars*), the 1980 lianhuanhua stayed close to George Lucas's plot, though visual disparities and bizarre cultural references were prevalent (Reed 2014).

3. Not all Chinese cartoonists were enamored with manga. Older cartoonists, most of whom drew humor or political/social commentary cartoons for decades, labeled manga style as "ugly" (Liao, interview, 2002; Chen Huiling, interview, 2009), damaging, and non-relevant, having a pernicious effect upon the Chinese style (He Wei, interview, 2001; Zheng Xinyao, interview, 2001).

At times, manga have been trotted out as scapegoats during China's internal strife. In 2014, while students held pro-democracy demonstrations in Hong Kong, the state-owned *Chengdu Daily* published an editorial suggesting that the manga *Doraemon* was part of a Japanese plot to indoctrinate Chinese youth like those protesting in Hong Kong (Minter 2014).

4. Coco described a *tu wen* as image and text with a "loose cartoony" style, thus, easier and faster to make than manhua. An import from Japan, the tu wen genre has become a popular form among Chinese artists (Gravett, 2008).

Chapter 6

1. The names and descriptions of Chinese animated films were verified by sourcing Fu Hongxing's encyclopedia (2012), a more reliable and fuller account.

2. Confusion surrounds the production and release of *Uproar in an Art Studio*. Some sources list 1926, others 1927. The film was probably finished in late 1926 and released in 1927. Other sources, such as Leigh (1989: 85), Gilsdorf (1988: 20), and *Shanghai Animation Film Studio* (1987: n.p.), claim 1920, probably an error in translating "1920s." Similar problems exist concerning titles, translations varying so widely that a title sometimes counted as two separate films.

3. Mochinaga also taught animators in Japan, the most famous being Kihachiro Kawamoto (1925–2010), who became the country's most noted puppet animator. In the early 1950s, Mochinaga trained and helped Kawamoto make his first puppet animation work, an Asahi Beer commercial in 1953. For a while, Kawamoto worked as an assistant animator and puppet maker for Mochinaga (Yokota 2003: 29–30).

Kawamoto's famous *Fushanosa* (*To Shoot without Shooting*), 1988, was actually made in Shanghai with a Chinese crew. The story was inspired by the Chinese classic, *Chuang Tzu* (Yokota 2003: 41).

4. Te Wei mentioned Wu Faxian as one of the "Gang of Four," which he was not. However, Wu was a member of the Lin Biao Clique, which was tried and condemned together with the "Gang of Four."

5. The Shanghai Western Journey Paradise was located for a brief time in Putuo District (nine kilometres from Shanghai center) before it was demolished. Taking up 44,240 square feet, it contained twenty-four views and 316 characters from the novel. Opened on August 1, 1992, it took two years to design, and used as building materials gypsum and plastic made to look like stone. The facility fully used modern technology, with sound and lighting effects throughout and moving characters synchronized to music. It cost 15 million yuan ($3 million) to build (from notes of visit by John A. Lent, August 14, 1993).

Zhan Tong designed most of the characters. He said:

> Local organizers wanted to change the characters because I exaggerated them. I kept to the originals with very exaggerated features. The local peasants did not like my designs, so like Rodin, I changed them a little or at least made it look like I changed them. I kept the original designs or the peasants there would have sold them. The studio took the job of doing Paradise because there was money involved. The studio head came to my house a few times to convince me to design it. I made 600 original designs back and forth. I was forced to take the task as no one else could do it. I am not satisfied as it is not my best originality. (Zhan Tong, interview, 1993)

Bibliography

http://www.baike.com/wiki/%E9%83%81%E9%A3%8E. Accessed Oct. 4, 2015.

A, Geng. 2013. Interview with John A. Lent, Guiyang, China, November 23.

Adorno, Theodor W. 1991 [1975]. "Cultural Industry Reconsidered." In *The Culture Industry: Selected Essays on Mass Culture.* London: Routledge.

Ah, Ying. 1982. *Essays on Art.* Beijing: People's Art Publishing House.

Allen, Kerry, and Barney Rowntree. 2015. "Japanese Comics That Are Too Racy for Chinese Censors . . . but Still Popular Online." *BBC Trending* July 27. http://www.bbc.com/news/blogs-trending-33652502. Accessed August 1, 2015.

Altenhenger, Jennifer. 2013. "A Socialist Satire: *Manhua Magazine* and Political Cartoon Production in the PRC, 1950–1960." *Frontiers of History in China* 8 (1): 78–103. http://journal.hep.com.cn/fhc/EN/10.3868/s020-002-013-005.3. Accessed December 21, 2014.

Andrews, Julia F. 1990. "Traditional Painting in New China: Guohua and the Anti-Rightist Campaign." *Journal of Asian Studies* 49 (3): 555–77.

Andrews, Julia F. 1994. *Painters and Politics in the People's Republic of China, 1949–1979.* Berkeley: University of California Press.

Andrews, Julia F. 1997. "Literature in Line: Picture Stories in the People's Republic of China." *Inks* November: 17–32.

Bader, A. L. 1941. "China's New Weapon—Caricature." *American Scholar* April: 228–40.

Bao, Jigui. 2002a. "China's First Animated Short, *Tumult in the Studio.*" *Hong Kong Film Archive Newsletter* No. 2 (May): 6–7.

Bao, Jigui. 2002b. "China's First Animated Sound Film, *The Dance of the Camel.*" *Hong Kong Film Archive Newsletter* No. 13: 11–2.

Barboza, David. 2015. "China Escalates Hollywood Partnerships, Aiming to Compete One Day." *New York Times* April 6: B1.

Barboza, David, and Brooks Barnes. 2015. "Disney Unveils Attractions at Shanghai Theme Resort." *New York Times* July 16: B3.

Barmé, Geremie R. 2002. *An Artistic Exile: A Life of Feng Zikai (1898–1975).* Berkeley: University of California Press.

Barolsky, Paul. 1978. *Infinite Jest: Wit and Humor in Italian Renaissance Art.* Columbia: University of Missouri Press.

Betancourt, David, and Michael Cavna. 2015. "As China Seeks American Fare, Valiant Buoyed by Deal for a Universe of Films." *Washington Post* March 19. http://www.washingtonpost.com/news/comic-riffs/wp/2015/03/19/as-china-seeks-american-fare. Accessed March 20, 2015.

Bevan, Paul. 2010. "The Cartoonist Hu Kao and Shanghai Modeng." *Polyvocia—the SOAS Journal of Graduate Research* Vol. 2 (March): 64–70.

Bevan, Paul. 2016. *A Modern Miscellany: Shanghai Cartoon Artists, Shao Xunmei's Circle and the Travels of Jack Chen, 1926–1938.* Leiden and London: Brill.

Bi, Keguan. 1981. "Jindai baokan manhua" ("Cartoons in Modern Journalism"). *Xinwen yanjiu ziliao* (*Research Materials on Journalism*) 8 (November): 68–87.

Bi, Keguan. 1982. *Zhongguo manhua shihua* (*Talks on the History of Chinese Cartoons*). Jinan: Shandong renmin chubanshe.

Bi, Keguan. 1988. "He Wei—Eager to Promote Workers' Cartoons." *Wenhuibao* (Hong Kong) November 18.

Bi, Keguan. 2002. *Manhua de huayuhua: bainian manhua jianwen lu* (*Cartoon Conversations and Pictures: A Record of Experiences of One Hundred Years of Cartoons*). Beijing: Zhongguo wenshi chubanshe.

Bi, Keguan. 2005. *Zhongguo manhua shihua* (*Talks on the History of Chinese Cartoons*). Tianjin: Baihua chubanshe.

Bi, Keguan. 2008. "Caricatures Praising Major Victories in the Anti-Japanese War to the Memory of 70th Anniversary of July 7 Battle." In *Amusing Park. Chinese Cartoon. Chinese National Essence*, 137–44. China Yiyuan Press.

Bi, Keguan, and Huang Yuanlin. 1983. *Zhongguo manhua shihua* (*Chinese Cartoon History*). Jinan: Shandong renmin chubanshe.

Bi, Keguan, and Huang Yuanlin. 1986. *Zhongguo manhua shi* (*A History of Chinese Cartoons*). Beijing: Wenhua yishu chubanshe.

Bi, Weimin. 2014. Interview with John A. Lent and Xu Ying, Beijing, China, December 5.

Blyth, R. H. 1959. *Oriental Humour.* Tokyo: Hokuseido Press.

Bo, Songnian. 1995. *Chinese New Year Pictures.* Beijing: Cultural Relics Publishing House.

Bristow, Becky. 2006. Untitled talk. Presented at International Animation Artists Salon, Wuhan, China, November 3.

Bristow, Michael. 2010. "Chinese Paper Prints 'Tiananmen' Cartoon." *BBC News* June 3. http://news.bbc.co.uk/2/hi/asia-pacific/8719284. stm. Accessed July 22, 2015.

Brook, Timothy. 2007. "Occupation State Building." In *China at War: Regions of China, 1937–1945*, edited by Stephen R. MacKinnon, Diane Lary, and Ezra F. Vogel, 22–43. Stanford, CA: Stanford University Press.

Buchanan, Clare. 2014. "Bringing Animation Dreams to Life." *China Daily* July 30: H2.

"'Bunny Suicides' Cartoon Book Pulled in China After Boy, 12, Kills Himself." 2008. *This Is London.* http://thisislondon.co.uk/news/article-23555143-details. Accessed September 14, 2008.

Cai, April. 2006. "Chinese Economy Enjoys Comic Relief." *Asia Times* August 10. www.atimes.com. Accessed March 2, 2014.

Canaves, Sky. 2015. "Xi Jinping on What's Wrong with Contemporary Chinese Culture." *China Film Insider* October 26. http://www.chinafile.com/reporting-opinion/culture/xi-jinping-whats-wrong-with-contemporary-chinese-culture. Accessed November 10, 2015.

Cao, Weidan. 2010. "The Mountains and the Moon, the Willows and the Swallows: A Hybrid Semiotic Analysis of Feng Zikai's 'New Paintings for Old Poems.'" *International Journal of Comic Art* 12 (2/3): 251–67.

Cao, Xiaohui. 1999. Interview with Xu Ying, Beijing, China, October.

Cao, Xiaohui. 2001. Interview with John A. Lent and Xu Ying, Beijing, China, May 29.

Cao, Xiaohui. 2005. "The Structure and Development Direction of Animation Education in China." KOSCAS. *Cartoon Animation Studies* 9: 391–407.

Cao, Xinzhe. 2002. "The Past and Present of Lianhuanhua Publication in China." *Books and Information* No. 4: 56–59.

Cartoon Art Committee of Chinese Artists' Association. 1987. *Selected Works of Chinese Cartoonists.* Chengdu: Fine Arts Publishing House of Sichuan.

"Cartoon Shows Political Shift." 2011. *rfa* January 2. http://www.rfa.org/english/news/china/cartoon-12212010163719.html. Accessed January 2, 2011.

"Cartoonist: Nie Jun." 2005. October 15. http://english.cctv.com/program/cultureexpress/20051015/100681.shtml. Accessed October 19, 2005.

"Cartoons Come to Stay." 1931. *The New China* February: 101.

"Cartoons Urge Birth Control." 2000. *People's Daily* January 26. http://english.peopledaily.com.cn. Accessed November 20, 2000.

Cathcart, Adam. 2004. "Cruel Resurrection: Chinese Comics and the Korean War." *International Journal of Comic Art* 6 (1, Spring): 37–55.

Cathcart, Adam. 2008. "Atrocities, Insults, and 'Jeep Girls': Depictions of the U.S. Military in China, 1945–1949." *International Journal of Comic Art* 10 (1, Spring): 140–53.

Cha, Kai-Ming. 2007. "Thinking, Writing and Making Comics in China." *Publishers Weekly* October 16.

Chang, Guangxi. 2001. Interview with John A. Lent and Xu Ying, Shanghai, China, June 17.

Chang, Guangxi. 2009. Interview with John A. Lent, Changchun, China, September 14.

Chang, Guangxi. 2016. Interview with John A. Lent and Xu Ying, Shanghai, China, June 10.

Chen, Huiling. 2009. Interview with John A. Lent and Xu Ying, Nanjing, China, May 15.

Chen, Jack. 1938. "China's Militant Cartoons." *Asia* May: 308–12.

Chen, Jack. 1939. "Why They Go to Yenan." *Asia* 39 (1).

Chen, Jianyu. 2001. Interview with John A. Lent and Xu Ying, Shanghai, China, June 16.

Chen, Leonard. 1980a. "Cartoons Ain't Just for Fun." *Free China Weekly* August 31: 3.

Chen, Leonard. 1980b. "How Cartoons Have Been Used." *Free China Weekly* May 18: 3.

Chen, Leonard. 1980c. "Stories Behind Some Cartoons." *Free China Weekly* May 25: 3.

Chen, Shangyu. 1996. "Popular Art and Political Movements: An Aesthetic Inquiry into Chinese Pictorial Stories." PhD dissertation, New York University.

Chen, Xiao. 1952. "Jiaqiang dui xin lianhuantuhua bianhui yu chuban gongzuo de sixiang lingdao." *Wenyibao* No. 55: 20–21.

Chen, Xuhui. 2009. Interview with John A. Lent and Xu Ying, Chang-chun, China, June 1.

Chen, Yuli. 2009. Interviews with John A. Lent and Xu Ying, Qiuxian, China, May 28–30.

Cheng, Hsi Chang. 1931. "The Children's Page in Chinese Newspapers." *The New China* February: 103–4.

Chesneaux, Jean, Umberto Eco, and Gino Nebiolo. 1971. *I fumetti di Mao.* Bari, Italy: Editori Laterza.

Chew, Matthew M., and Lu Chen. 2010. "Media Institutional Contexts of the Emergence and Development of Xinmanhua in China." *International Journal of Comic Art* 12 (2/3, Fall): 171–91.

Ch'i, Cheng. 1974. "New Serial Pictures." *Chinese Literature* No. 2 (February): 112–13.

Chiang, Wei-pu. 1959. "Chinese Picture Story Books." *Chinese Literature* 3 (March): 144–47.

"China Challenges Manga Supremacy." 1996. *Comics Forum* 1 (12, Autumn): 4.

"China Draws Upon Humour." 1987. *Asiaweek* October 30: 53.

"China's Cartoon." 2008 (March 1).

"China's US$16.3bn Animation Industry Expected to Decline." 2013. *China* Daily June 4. WantChinaTimes.com.

"Chinese Animation: What's Ahead." n.d. ca 2013. *China Cinema.* Accessed April 16, 2015.

"Chinese Cartoons of the Day." 1936. *Asia* August: 507.

"Chinese Children Get Japanese Propaganda." 1938. *Asia* November.

Chinese Modern Art Volumes Committee, ed. 1998. *Chinese Modern Art Volumes Cartoon.* Tianjin: Tianjin People's Fine Arts Press.

Christiansen, Linn A. 2015. "Reading Liao Bingxiong. Chinese Cartoonist of the 20th Century." MA thesis, University of Oslo.

Chu, B. F. 1938. "Chinese Cartoonists in War-time." *Far Eastern Mirror* (Hong Kong) April 21: 72–73.

Clunas, Craig. 1997. *Pictures and Visuality in Early Modern China.* Princeton, NJ: Princeton University Press.

Cody, Edward. 2007. "Cartoonist's Social Spoofs Attract Young Chinese." *Washington Post* January 26: A12.

"The Controversial Cartoons of Pi San." 2011. *International New York Times Magazine* October 30. http://www.nytimes.com/interactive/2011/10/30/magazine/26mag-chinese-animations.html?_r=0. Accessed June 5, 2015.

Cook, James A. 1996. "Penetration and Neocolonialism: The Shen Chong Case and the Anti-American Student Movement of 1946–47." *Republican China* 22 (1, November): 65–97.

Coonan, Clifford. 2007. "Chinese Officials Continue 'Death' Crackdown." *Variety* July 27. http://www.varietyasiaonline.com/content/view/1750/53/. Accessed July 27, 2007.

Coonan, Clifford. 2014. "China Animation Revenues Rise to $14 Billion in 2013." *Hollywood Reporter* July 13.

Creemers, Rogier. 2013. "SARFT and GAPP To Merge." China Copyright and Media March 10. https//chinacopyrightandmedia.wordpress.com/2013/03/10/sarft-and-gapp-to-merge/. Accessed March 6, 2014.

Crespi, John A. 2011. *China's Modern Sketch—1. The Golden Age of Cartoon Art, 1934–1937.* Cambridge, MA: Massachusetts Institute of Technology, Visualizing Cultures. http://ocw.mit.edu/ans7870/21f/21f.027/modern_sketch_02/ms_visnav02.html. Accessed October 14, 2013.

"Criticizing Everything—An Interview with Chinese Satirist Crazy Crab of Hexie Farm." 2012. *China Change* June 5. http://chinachange.org/2012/06/05/criticizing-everything-an-interview. Accessed June 5, 2015.

Curtin, Michael, and Yongli Li. 2013. "Shanghai Animation Attracts Hollywood Investors." Casey-Wolf Center Media Industries Project July 22.

Damluji, Nadim. 2011. "Can the Subaltern Draw? Defining Manhua—or a Translated Marketplace in Contemporary China." *The Hooded Utilitarian* June 1.

de Smedt, Marc. 1981. *Chinese Erotism.* New York: Crescent Books.

Denyer, Simon. 2013. "Chinese Censors Crack Down on Cartoon Violence." *Washington Post* October 15.

Ding, Cong. 2002. Interview with John A. Lent and Xu Ying, Beijing, China, December 20.

Ding, Yanzha, and Yu Zhi. 2011. *Fengqing Shanghai Memory—Zhang Leping bixiade sanshiniandai* (*Local Conditions and Customs of Shanghai's Memory—Zhang Leping's Drawings of the 1930s*). Shanghai: Shanghai Dictionary Press.

Dong, Mingguo. 2009. Interview with John A. Lent and Xu Ying, Qiuxian, China, May 28.

"Drawing on Creative Enterprise." 2014. *Beijing Review* October 16. http://gbtimes.com/search/site/%2a/author/user%3a2800. Accessed March 2, 2015.

Driscoll, Ian. 2003. "After Tiananmen Satire with Savvy." *Financial Times* April 26/27 (Weekend): 8.

Du, Jianguo. 1993. Interview with John A. Lent, Shanghai, China, August 16.

Du, Ying. 2014. "Shanghaiing the Press Gang: The Maoist Regimentation of the Shanghai Popular Publishing Industry in the Early PRC (1949–1956)." *Modern Chinese Literature and Culture* 26 (2): 89–141.

Duan, Xiaoxuan. 2016. Interview with John A. Lent and Xu Ying, Shanghai, China, June 11.

Dunn, Richard L. 2006. "Elusive Target: Bombing Japan from China." Warbird Forum. www.warbirdforum.com/elusive.htm. Accessed October 19, 2013.

Eckholm, Erik. 2002. "Chinese Prosecutors Deal a Full Deck of Warnings." *New York Times* March 25: A4.

Editorial Board. 2015. "China's Losing Battle with Internet Censorship." *Chicago Tribune* January 31.

Edwards, Louise. 2013. "Drawing Sexual Violence in Wartime Japan: Anti-Japanese Propaganda Cartoons." *Journal of Asian Studies* 72 (3): 563–86.

209

Ehrlich, David. 2001. "Vignette: A Da, China's Animated Open Door to the West." In *Animation in Asia and the Pacific*, edited by John A. Lent, 17–20. Sydney: John Libbey.

Ehrlich, David, and Jin Tianyi. 2001. "Animation in China." In *Animation in Asia and the Pacific*, edited by John A. Lent, 7–29. Sydney: John Libbey.

Esseltrom, Erik. 2015. "Red Guards and Salarymen: The Chinese Cultural Revolution and Comic Satire in 1990s Japan." *Journal of Asian Studies* 74 (4, November): 953–76.

"Experts Call for Innovation at South China Comic Expo." 2014. *Global Times* October 6.

Faison, Seth. 1999. "If It's a Comic Book, Why Is Nobody Laughing?" *New York Times* August 17.

Fang, Cheng. 1980. "Profound Memory." In *A Selection of Chen Jinyan's Art Works*, edited by Fang Cheng, preface. Beijing: People's Fine Arts Press.

Fang, Cheng. 2001. Interview with John A. Lent and Xu Ying, Beijing, China, June 10.

Fang, Cheng. 2006. "What Is Humor?" *International Journal of Comic Art* 8 (2): 347–62.

Fang, Cheng. 2007. "Fang Cheng's Theories on Humor and Cartooning." *International Journal of Comic Art* 9 (2): 478–510.

Fang, Tang. 2002. Interview with John A. Lent and Xu Ying, Guangzhou, China, January 5.

Farquhar, Mary Ann. 1995. "Sanmao: Classics Cartoons and Chinese Popular Culture." In *Asian Popular Culture*, edited by John A. Lent, 139–58. Boulder, CO: Westview Press.

Farquhar, Mary Ann. 1999. "Comic Books and Popularization." In *Children's Literature in China: From Lu Xun to Mao Zedong*, 191–248. Armonk, NY: M. E. Sharpe.

Feng, Yiyin. 1998. *Xiaosa fengshen: wode fuqin Feng Zikai (God of Wind with Grace and Ease: My Father Feng Zikai)*. Shanghai: Eastern Normal University Press.

Feng, Yiyin. 2002. Interview with John A. Lent and Xu Ying, Shanghai, China, January 10.

Fernandez, Rebecca. 2008. "Benjamin: The Leading Contemporary Manhua Artist." *El Publico* March 14. Reprinted on Paul Gravett web. March 23, 2008. http://www.paulgravett.com. Accessed April 21, 2013.

"55 Years of Innovation." 1982. *Asiaweek* December 24–31: 26–27.

Findlay, Ian. 1984. "Drawing the Party Line: From Fallen Leaders to Consumeriser." *Far Eastern Economic Review* November 15: 108.

Flath, James A. 2004. *The Cult of Happiness: Nianhua, Art, and History in Rural North China*. Seattle: University of Washington Press.

Ford, Peter. 2015. "Popularity Carries a Sting for China's Exiled 'Rebel Pepper' Cartoonist." *Christian Science Monitor* May 28. http://www.csmonitor.com/World/Asia-Pacific/2015/0528/Popularity-carries-a-sting-for-China-s-exiled-Rebel-Pepper-cartoonist. Accessed May 29, 2015.

Franchineau, Helene, and Isolda Morillo. 2015. "Cartoonists a Casualty of China's Intolerance of Dissent." Associated Press November 1. http://news.yahoo.com/cartoonists-casualty-chinas-intolerance-dissent-055649360.html. Accessed November 5, 2015.

Fu, Hongxing, ed. 2012. *Encyclopedia of Chinese Films: Volume of Animated Films (1923–2010)*. Beijing: China Broadcasting and Television Chubanshe.

Fu, Shen C. Y. 1994. "Puns and Playfulness in Chinese Painting" *Asian Art and Culture* 7: 47–65.

Galias, Chester. 2008a. "Dragon Reawakened: China's Animation Industry Reclaims a Glorious Past and Is Fast Catching up with Its American and Japanese Counterparts." *China Business Philippines* June: 14–17.

Galias, Chester G. 2008b. "Through Artists' Eyes." *China Business Philippines* June: 20–21.

Galikowski, Maria. 1998. *Art and Politics in China, 1949–1984*. Hong Kong: Chinese University Press.

Gan, Xianfeng. 2008. *Zhongguo manhua shi (The History of Chinese Cartoons)*. Jinan: Shandong huabao Publishing House.

Giesen, Rolf. 2015. *Chinese Animation: A History and Filmography, 1922–2012*. Jefferson, NC: McFarland.

Gilsdorf, Ethan. 1988. "Chinese Animation's Past, Present, and Future: The Monkey King of Shanghai." *Animato* Winter: 20–23.

"Global and China Animation Industry Report." 2014. *Research in China* June.

Goldman, Merle. 1981. *China's Intellectuals: Advise and Dissent*. Cambridge: Harvard University Press.

Gough, Neil. 2015. "China Moves to Crack Down on Counterfeit Disney Products." *New York Times* November 6: B2.

Gravett, Paul. 2008. "Coco Wang: Wild China." March 3. http://www.paulgravett.com/articles/122_coco/122_coco.htm. Accessed March 5, 2008.

Guo, Ye. 2009. Interview with John A. Lent and Xu Ying, Changchun, China, June 1.

Han, Shangyi. 1991. Personal communication to HongYing Liu-Lengyel.

Han, Shangyi. 1993. Interview with John A. Lent, Shanghai, China, August 15.

Harbsmeier, Christoph. 1984. *The Cartoonist Feng Zikai*. Oslo: Universitetsforlaget.

Harder, Hans, and Barbara Mittler, eds. 2013. *Asian Punches: A Transcultural Affair*. New York and Heidelberg: Springer.

Hays, Jeffrey. 2012 "Animation in China." *Facts and Details* December. http://factsanddetails.com. Accessed April 16, 2015.

He, Ting. 2012. "Farewell to My Father." *International Journal of Comic Art* 14 (1): 332–38.

He, Wei. 1989. *Retrospective, Exploration, and Thinking*. Beijing: Workers Press.

He, Wei. 2001. Interview with John A. Lent and Xu Ying, Beijing, China, May 28.

He, Wei. 2002. Interview with John A. Lent and Xu Ying, Beijing, China, December 18.

He, Wei. 2009. Interview with John A. Lent and Xu Ying, Beijing, China, May 24.

"'Hello, Beautiful!' Says Chinese President Xi Jinping in Official Cartoon." *Offbeat China* March 10.

Henriot, Christian, and Wen-hsin Yeh. 2004. "Introduction." In *The Shadow of the Rising Sun: Shanghai under Japanese Occupation*, edited by Christian Henriot and Wen-hsin Yeh, 1–14. Cambridge: Cambridge University Press.

Hogan Lovells. 2013. "Will the Merger of SARFT and GAPP End the Turf War over Control of the Internet?" *Corporate China Alert* June.

Hong, Huang. 1993. Interview with John A. Lent, Shanghai, China, August 15.

Hong, Yu. 2007. *Jindai Shanghai xiaobao yu shimin wenhua yanjiu: 1897–1937 (A Study on Modern Shanghai Tabloids and Popular Culture: 1897–1937)*. Shanghai: Shanghai shudian.

Hong, Yuan. 1995. "Revive Lianhuanhua." *Study on Publication and Distribution* No. 4: 17–18.

Hong, Zhang. 2002. *America Perceived: The Making of Chinese Images of the United States, 1946–1953*. Westport, CT: Greenwood Press.

Hong, Zicheng. 2007. *A History of Contemporary Chinese Literature*. Leiden: Brill.

Hooper, Terry. 2007. "Yishan Li: Rising Manga Artistic Talent." July 17. http://blog.360.yahoo.com/blog-epFXsZ85dKlqC7tDmPACPKTch PEXBA-7. Accessed July 20, 2007.

Hu, Jinqing. 2001. Interview with John A. Lent and Xu Ying, Shanghai, China, June 17.

Hu, Kao. n.d. "Zhanshi de manhuajie" ("Cartoonists during the War"). In *Kangzhan yu yishu* (Chongqing: Duli chubanshe): 8.

Hu, Liqing, Zhenque Zhao, and Wei Zhao. 1986. "Hua Junwu Giving Soldiers a Cartoon Lecture." *Workers Daily* December 23.

Hua, Junwu. 1963. "Some Thoughts on Cartooning." *Chinese Literature* No. 10.

Hua, Junwu. 1984. *Chinese Satire and Humour. Selected Cartoons of Hua Junwu (1955–1982)*. Translated by W. J. F. Jenner. Beijing: New World Press.

Hua, Junwu. 1989. *Dangdai zhongguo manhua (Cartoons from Contemporary China)*. Beijing: Xinshijie chubanshe

Hua, Junwu. 1990. "Preface." *Military Camp Humor Cartoon Selection*.

Hua, Junwu. 1998. "Army Humor." *Satire and Humor* October 5.

Hua, Junwu. 2005. Interview with John A. Lent and Xu Ying, Beijing, China, June 13.

Huang, Mao. 1947. *Manhua yishu jianghua (Lectures on Cartoon Art)*. 2nd ed. Shanghai: Shanghai yinshuguan.

Huang, Miaozi. 1938. "Kangzhan yilai de zhongguo manhua" ("Chinese Cartoons Since the Beginning of the War of Resistance"). In *Quanguo manhua zuojia kangzhan jiezuo xuanji*, edited by Huang Miaozi, preface. N.P.: Zhangwang shuwu.

Huang, Nicole. 2005. *Women, War, and Domesticity: Shanghai Literature and Popular Culture of the 1940s*. Boston, MA: Brill.

Huang, Yao, ed. 1940. *Yazhou zai manhua zhong (Asia in Cartoon)*. Chongqing: Minjian chubanshe.

Huang, Yong. 2001. Interview with John A. Lent and Xu Ying, Beijing, China, May 30.

Huang, Yuanlin. 1981. "The Earliest Lianhuanhua in Existence in China." *Arts* No. 4: 17–18.

Huang, Yuanlin, ed. 2000. *Bainian manhua (Hundred Years of Cartooning)*. Vols. 1, 2. Beijing: Xiandai chubanshe.

Huang, Yuanlin. 2001. Interview with John A. Lent and Xu Ying, Beijing, China, May 28.

Huang, Yuanlin. 2011. *Huang Yuanlin manhua. Wenji. (Vols. 1–2). (Huang Yuanlin Cartoons. Essays Collection. [Vols. 1–2])*. Beijing: Wenhua yishu chubanshe.

Huang, Zushen, ed. 2008. *Jinguo fengcai (Female Charisma)*. Beijing: Zhongguo huabao chubanshe.

Hung, Chang-tai. 1990. "War and Peace in Feng Zikai's Wartime Cartoons." *Modern China* 16 (1, January): 39–83.

Hung, Chang-tai. 1994a. *War and Popular Culture: Resistance in Modern China, 1937–1945*. Berkeley: University of California Press.

Hung, Chang-tai. 1994b. "The Fuming Image: Cartoons and Public Opinion in Late Republican China, 1945 to 1949." *Comparative Studies in Society and History* 36 (1, January): 122–45.

Hung, Chang-tai. 2011. *Mao's New World: Political Culture in the Early People's Republic*. Ithaca, NY: Cornell University Press.

Hung, Chao-chun. 2014. "Cartoon Sites Censored in China for 'Inappropriate' Content." WantChinaTimes.com. Accessed March 9, 2015.

Hung, Yu. 1967. "Hua Junwu Is an Old Hand at Drawing Black Anti-Party Cartoons." *Chinese Literature* No. 4.

Hunter, Edward. 1953. *Brainwashing in Red China: The Calculated Destruction of Men's Minds*. New York: H. Wolff.

Hwang, John C. 1978. "Lien Huan Hua: Revolutionary Serial Pictures." In *Popular Media in China*, edited by Godwin Chu, 51–72. Honolulu: East-West Center.

Hyers, Conrad. 1994. "Humor in Daoist and Zen Art." *Asian Art and Culture* Fall: 31–46.

Inge, M. Thomas. 2004. "Chinese Comic Books." *Big Little Times* 23 (2, March–April): 10–15.

Inouye, Rei Okamoto. 2010. "Theorizing Manga: Nationalism and Discourse on the Role of Wartime Manga." *Mechademia* 4: 20–37.

International Cartoon Competition on Environmental Protection 2013 Works. 2014. Beijing: China Daily.

Ishii, Kenichi. 2013. "Nationalism and Preferences for Domestic and Foreign Animation Programmes in China." *International Communication Gazette* 75 (2): 225–45.

"The Jack Chen Archives at the Hoover Institution." 2013, March 7. http://oia.stanford.edu/news/jack-chen-archives-hoover-institution. Accessed June 19, 2015.

Ji, Zhi. 1942. "Guanyu 'muke' manhua" ("About Woodcut Cartoons"). *Xinhua ribao* March 19: 4.

Jia, Fou. 2001. Interview with John A. Lent and Xu Ying, Beijing, China, May 30.

Jiang, Steven. 2012. "'Pandaman' Creator Finds Political Cartoon a Risky Business in China." cnn.com January 23. http://www.cnn.com/2012/01/23/world/asia/china-pandaman-cartoons. Accessed August 3, 2015.

Jiang, Weipu. 1989. "Endless Life Source: Thoughts on the Lianhuanhua Works of 7th National Art Exhibition." *Arts* No. 12: 8–10.

Jiang, Weipu. 2000. "Facing the Centennial: Thoughts on Popular Art Forms of Lianhuanhua, New Year Paintings and Posters." *Arts* No. 2: 73–77.

Jiang, Yihai, ed. 1989. *Manhua zhishi cidian (Dictionary of Cartoon Knowledge)*. Nanjing: Nanjing University Press.

Jiang, Yousheng. 2002. Interview with John A. Lent and Xu Ying, Beijing, China, December 17.

Jiang, Yousheng. 2006. Interview with John A. Lent and Xu Ying, Beijing, China, May 29.

Jie, Ziping. 2004. *Faded Memory: Lian Huan Hua.* Taiyuan: Shanxi Ancient Book Press.

Jin, Guoping. 1993. Interview with John A. Lent, Shanghai, China, August 13.

Jin, Guoping. 2001. Interview with John A. Lent and Xu Ying, Shanghai, China, June 17.

Jin, Yunzhi. 2005. Interview with John A. Lent and Xu Ying, Hangzhou, China, June 3.

Judge, Joan. 1996. *Print and Politics: "Shibao" and the Culture of Reform in Late Qing China.* Stanford, CA: Stanford University Press

Kushner, Barak. 2006. *The Thought War: Japanese Imperial Propaganda.* Honolulu: University of Hawai'i Press.

Kushner, Barak. 2013. "Unwarranted Attention: The Image of Japan in Twentieth-Century Chinese Humour." In *Humour in Chinese Life and Culture*, edited by Jessica M. Davis and Jocelyn Chey, 47–82. Hong Kong: Hong Kong University Press.

Laing, Ellen Johnston. 2004. *Selling Happiness: Calendar Posters and Visual Culture in Early-Twentieth Century China.* Honolulu: University of Hawai'i Press.

Laing, Ellen Johnston. 2010. "*Shanghai Manhua*, the Neo-sensationalist School of Literature, and Scenes of Urban Life." MCLC Resource Center October. http://mclc.osu.edu/rc/pubs/laing.htm. Accessed February 7, 2014.

Lam, Wo-Lap. 1982. "Vagabond Waif of Shanghai." *Asiaweek* August 13: 32–33.

Lam, Wo-Lap. 1983. "Sketching China's Scoundrels." *Asiaweek* September 2: 52.

Landsberger, Stefan. 2001. *Chinese Propaganda Posters: From Revolution to Modernization.* Amsterdam: Pepin Press BV.

Larmer, Brook. 2011. "In China, an Internet Joke Is Not Always Just a Joke." *New York Times Sunday Magazine* October 26:MM34.

Larmer, Brook. 2012. "Little Rabbit Be Good." *World Policy Journal* Summer. http://www.worldpolicy.org/journal/summer2012/little-rabbit-be-good. Accessed June 5, 2015.

Lei, Xu. 2011. "Chinese Painting-Style Animation Now All but Extinct." *Global Times* September 4.

Lengyel, Alfonz. 1989. "China. Brief Cartooning Tradition." *Witty World International Cartoon Magazine* No. 8 (Summer/Autumn): 16–18.

Lent, John A. 1992. "Chinese Comic Art: Historical and Contemporary Perspectives." *Asian Culture* 24 (4, Winter): 27–46.

Lent, John A. 1994. "Comic Art." In *Handbook of Chinese Popular Culture*, edited by Wu Dingbo and Patrick Murphy, 279–306. Westport, CT: Greenwood.

Lent, John A. 1998. "The Animation Industry and Its Offshore Factories." In *Global Productions: Labor in the Making of the "Information Society,"* edited by Gerald Sussman and John A. Lent, 239–54. Cresskill, NJ: Hampton Press.

Lent, John A. 1999a. "Asian Comic Art." *Art Asia Pacific* No. 21: 66–71.

Lent, John A., ed. 1999b. *Pulp Demons: International Dimensions of the Postwar Anti-Comics Campaign.* London: Associated University Presses.

Lent, John A. 2001. "Zhan Tong, A Stickler to the Chinese Style." In *Animation in Asia and the Pacific*, edited by John A. Lent, 29–32. Sydney: John Libbey.

Lent, John A. 2004. "Korean Animation: From Adolescence to Adulthood, 1998–2003." *Asian Cinema* Spring/Summer: 151–68.

Lent, John A. 2006. "Asian Animation Relative to Asian Comics." Main speech, International Animation Artists Salon, Wuhan, China, November 2.

Lent, John A. 2012. "Sanmao and Tokai: Popular Street Urchins of Asian Comic Strips." *International Journal of Comic Art* 14 (1, Spring): 35–50.

Lent, John A. 2014. "Allied, Japanese, and Chinese Propaganda Cartoon Leaflets During World War II." *International Journal of Comic Art* 16 (1): 258–301.

Lent, John A. 2015a. *Asian Comics.* Jackson: University Press of Mississippi.

Lent, John A. 2015b. "Personal Remembrances: Interviews with Seven Recently-Deceased Giants in Cartooning and Animation." *International Journal of Comic Art* 17 (1, Spring/Summer): 598–630.

Lent, John A., and Xu Ying. 2001. "Animation in China Yesterday and Today—The Pioneers Speak Out." *Asian Cinema* 12 (2): 34–49.

212

Lent, John A., and Xu Ying. 2003a. "China's Animation Beginnings: The Roles of the Wan Brothers and Others." *Asian Cinema* 14 (1): 56–69.

Lent, John A., and Xu Ying. 2003b. "Chinese Women Cartoonists: Historical and Contemporary Perspectives." *International Journal of Comic Art* 5 (2, Fall): 351–67.

Lent, John A., and Xu Ying. 2003c. "Timeless Humor: Liao Bingxiong and Fang Cheng, Masters of a Fading Chinese Cartoon Tradition." *Persimmon* Winter: 1–6.

Lent, John A., and Xu Ying. 2004. "Chinese Cartoon Master Liao Bingxiong: A Poor Kid, Brave Caricaturist, and Kind Grandpa." Paper presented at Popular Culture Association conference, San Antonio, Texas, April 7.

Lent, John A., and Xu Ying. 2007. "Liao Bingxiong: A Chinese Style Man with Universal Values." *International Journal of Comic Art* 9 (1): 650–67.

Lent, John A., and Xu Ying. 2008. "Cartooning and Wartime China: Part One—1931–1945." *International Journal of Comic Art* 10 (1): 76–139.

Lent, John A., and Xu Ying. 2012. "Quan Yingsheng and the Blendings of Traditional Chinese Painting with Comic Books." *International Journal of Comic Art* 14 (1): 492–506.

Lent, John A., and Yu Kie-Un. 1996. "Oversea [*sic*] Marketing: Strategies of Korean Animation Through AnimEast '95." *Animatoon* 2 (4–1): 38–41.

Li, Binsheng. 2013. Interview with John A. Lent and Xu Ying, Beijing, China, November 27.

Li, Binsheng. 2015. Interview with Xu Ying, Beijing, China, July 11.

Li, Binsheng. 2016. Interview with Xu Ying, Beijing, China, January 3.

Li, Binsheng. 2016. Interview with John A. Lent and Xu Ying, Beijing, China, June 16.

Li, Jia. 1985. *Manhua qutan* (*On Cartoons*). Hefei: Anhui Fine Arts Publishing House.

Li, Lekang. 2009. Interview with John A. Lent, Changchun, China, June 1.

Li, Qingai. 2009. Interviews with John A. Lent and Xu Ying, Qiuxian, China, May 28–30.

Li, Qun. 1937. "Xuanchuanhua zai nongcun" (Propaganda Drawings in Rural Areas). *Dikang sanrikan* 17 (October 13): 8.

Li, Raymond. 2013. "Merger of Media Regulator and Censor, but No Culture Super-Ministry." *South China Morning Post* March 11.

Liao, Bingxiong. 1940. "Guanyu manmu hezuo" ("On Cartoon and Woodcut Co-operation"). *Jiuwang ribao* February 22: 4.

Liao, Bingxiong. 2002. Interviews with John A. Lent and Xu Ying, Guangzhou, China, January 4–5.

Liao, Ling-er, and Zhang Hongmiao. 2002. *Gei shijie ca ba lian: Liao Bingxiong huazhuan* (*Wiping the Face of the World: Liao Bingxiong's Illustrated Biography*). Guangdong: Huacheng chubanshe.

Liew, Jonathan. 2009. "Chinese Comics Ready to 'Open Minds'—but Sex Is Still Out." *Telegraph* October 19. http://www.telegraph.co.uk/expat/6350389/. Accessed October 25, 2009.

Lihu, Yuxue. n.d. "Humor Flowers Blossoming in Military Camp Humor Group of an Artillery Brigade of Beijing Military Region." *Zhongguo mei shu bao* (*China Art Report*). Undated clipping provided by Zheng Huagai.

Lin, Qin. 1993. Interview with John A. Lent, Shanghai, China, August 15.

Lin, Yang. 1997. "Lianhuanhua in China: Yesterday, Today and Tomorrow." *Encyclopedia* No. 8: 42–43.

Lin, Yutang. 1936. *A History of the Press and Public Opinion in China*. Chicago: University of Chicago Press.

Liu, Ting. 2009. "Conflicting Discourses on Boy's Love and Subcultural Tactics in Mainland China and Hong Kong." *Intersections: Gender and Sexuality in Asia and the Pacific* 20 (April). http://intersections.anu.edu.au/issue20/liu.htm

Liu, Yiding. 2004. *Chinese News Cartoon*. Beijing: China Youth Press.

Liu, Yuzhu. 2005. Keynote speech, China International Cartoon and Digital Arts Festival, Changzhou, China, September 28.

Liu-Lengyel, HongYing. 1993. "Chinese Cartoons as Mass Communication: The History of Cartoon Development in China." PhD dissertation, Temple University.

Liu-Lengyel, HongYing. 1999. "Fang Cheng." In *The World Encyclopedia of Cartoons*, edited by Maurice Horn, 266. Philadelphia, PA: Chelsea House.

Liu-Lengyel, HongYing. 2001. "Man Hua: Cartoons and Comics in China before 1949." *Comics Journal* 233 (May): 43–45.

Lockett, Hudson. 2015. "One Frame at a Time. China's Animation Industry Tries to Find Its Feet." *China Economic Review* January 26.

"Look Who're Cartoon Characters." 1986. *Malaya* (Manila) August 19: 6.

Lowenthal, Tom. 2015. "China Doubles Down on Counterproductive Censorship." Committee to Protect Journalists January 28. Accessed January 29, 2015.

Lu, Xing. 2004. *Rhetoric of the Chinese Cultural Revolution: The Impact on Thought, Culture, and Communication*. Columbia: University of South Carolina Press.

Luo, Quangqiang. 1995. "A Cartoonist Beloved by Workers—Famous Cartoonist He Wei." *Shou gang gong sibao* (*Capital Steel Company Newspaper*) November 24.

Ma, Ke. 1963. "Cheers to the New Achievement of the Serial Pictures." *People's Daily* December 29.

Ma, Kexuan, 2005. Interview with John A. Lent, Changzhou, China, September 29.

Ma, Kexuan. 2011. Interview with John A. Lent and Xu Ying, Beijing, China, October 26.

MacConaughy, Walter. Reports to the State Department, 1950–1951. Records of the Office of Far Eastern Affairs. Records of the Department of State. Record Group 59. National Archives at College Park, Maryland.

Macdonald, Sean. 2011. "Two Texts on 'Comics' from China, ca.1932: 'In Defense of "Comic Strips"' by Lu Xun and 'Comic Strip

Novels' by Mao Dun." *ImageText: Interdisciplinary Comics Studies* 6 (1). http://www.english.ufl.edu/imagetext/archives/V61/Macdonald/?print. Accessed July 25, 2012.

Magistad, Mary Kay. 2012. "Why Chinese Political Humor Is Spreading Online." PRI January 10. http://www.pri.org/stories/2012-01-10/why-chinese-political-humor-is-spreading-online. Accessed June 5, 2015.

Mai, Fei. 2005. "I and 'Cartoon Propaganda Brigade.'" October 27. Manuscript given to John A. Lent by Mai Fei.

Mai, Fei. 2006. Interview with John A. Lent and Xu Ying, New York City, June 16.

Mao, Mingsan. 1986. "*The Military Camp Humor* Opens up a Fresh Outlook." *Jingji ribao* (*Economic Daily*). Undated clipping provided by Zheng Huagai.

Martin, R. Orion. 2014. "Lianhuanhua: China's Pulp Comics." *Comics Journal* October 17. http://www.tcj.com/lianhuanhua-chinas-pulp-comics/. Accessed October 18, 2014.

Martin, R. Orion. 2015. "Chinese Web Comics: Scarlet-Faced Dog and Bu Er Mia." *Comics Journal* July 31. http://www.tcj.com/chinese-web-comics-scarlet-faced-dog-and-bu-er-mia/. Accessed July 31, 2015.

Mcauliffe, Anneliese. 2015. "China Accused of 'Tricking' Dissidents into Deportation." *Aljazeera* November 29. http://www.aljazeera.com/news/2015/11/china-accused-tricking-dissidents. Accessed December 5, 2015.

Meyers, Chris. 2011. "Chinese Woman Gets Top Prize in Japan Manga Awards." Reuters Life! February 23. http://www.reuters.com/article/2011/02/24/us-japan-comics-award-id. Accessed February 24, 2011.

Miao, Yintang. 2002. Interview with John A. Lent and Xu Ying, Beijing, China, December 16.

Minter, Adam. 2014. "China's Cartoon Crackdown." *Bloomberg View* October 2. http://www.bloombergview.com/articles/2014-10-02/china-s-cartoon-crackdown. Accessed November 14, 2014.

Mittler, Barbara. 2007. "Between Discourse and Social Reality: The Early Chinese Press in Recent Publications." *MCLC*. February. http://mclc.osu.edu/rc/pubs/reviews/mittler2.htm. Accessed February 15, 2014.

Mittler, Barbara. 2012. *A Continuous Revolution: Making Sense of Cultural Revolution Culture.* Cambridge, MA: Harvard University Asia Center.

Moritz, Frederic. 1973. "Chinese Comics Teach Mao's Lessons." *Christian Science Monitor* August 15: 9.

Mu, Hui. 1991. "Cartoons in Ming Dynasty." *Outlook Weekly* 22: 36.

Mufson, Steven. 1996. "China's 'Soccer Boy' Takes on Foreign Evils." *Washington Post* October 9: A31–32.

Murck, Alfreda. 2000. *Poetry and Painting in Song China. The Subtle Art of Dissent.* Cambridge: Harvard University Asia Center for the Harvard-Yenching Institute.

Nebiolo, Gino. 1973. *The People's Comic Book.* Translated by Endymion Wilkinson. Garden City, NY: Anchor Press.

Ningmeng. 1996. "Wenlushi: Ping riben shaonü manhua" ("Testing the Water: Comment on Japanese *shojo manga*"). *Shaonian manhua* (*Youth Comics*) 2: 64.

Okamoto, Rei. 1996. "Portrayal of the War and Enemy in Japanese Wartime Cartoons." *Journal of Asian Pacific Communication* 7 (1/2): 5–17.

Okamoto, Rei. 1997. "'Fuku-chan' Goes to Java: Images of Indonesia in a Japanese Wartime Newspaper Comic Strip." *Southeast Asian Journal of Social Science* 25 (1): 111–23.

Okamoto, Rei. 1999. "Pictorial Propaganda in Japanese Comic Art, 1941–1945: Image of the Self and the Other in a Newspaper Strip, Single-Panel Cartoons, and Cartoon Leaflets." PhD dissertation, Temple University.

Oliver, Andy. 2008. "Manhua–Chinese Comics Now." *Broken Frontier* March 11. http:www.brokenfrontier.com/lowdown/details.php?id=1232. Accessed March 17, 2008.

Ono, Kosei. 1999. "Tadahito Mochinaga: The Japanese Animator Who Lived in Two Worlds." *Animation World Magazine* 4 (9, December).

Pan, Lingling. 2008. "Post-Liberation History of China's *Lianhuanhua* (Pictorial Books)." *International Journal of Comic Art* 10 (2, Fall): 694–717.

Pan, Lynn. 2008. *Shanghai Style Art and Design between the Wars.* San Francisco: Long River Press.

Parton, James. 1877. *Caricature and Comic Art in All Times and Many Lands.* New York: Harper and Brothers.

Pekarik, Andrew J. 1983. "The Cave Temples of Dunhuang." *Archeology* 36 (1): 20–27.

Peng, Shan. 1980. "Picture Story Books of China." *Asian Culture* January: 2–3.

Perry, Elizabeth J. 2002. "Moving the Masses: Emotion Work in the Chinese Revolution." *Mobilization: An International Journal* 7 (2): 111–28.

Peskin, Max. 2013. "Can Animation Cure What Ails the Chinese Movie Industry?" *Tea Leaf Nation* June 7. Accessed April 16, 2015.

"Psychological Warfare: I. Chinese Propaganda." 2000. *Online Documentary. The Nanking Atrocities.* www.nankingatrocities.net/Propaganda/propaganda01.htm. Accessed October 19, 2013.

Qian, Yunda. 2001. Interview with John A. Lent and Xu Ying, Shanghai, China, June 17.

Qian, Yunda. 2016. Interview with John A. Lent and Xu Ying, Shanghai, China, June 11.

Qu, Jianfang. 2007. Interview with John A. Lent and Xu Ying, Guiyang, China, September 10.

Quan, Yingsheng. 2011. Interviews with John A. Lent and Xu Ying, Beijing, China, October 28, November 1.

Quan, Yingsheng. 2015. Correspondence to John A. Lent, May 14.

Quiquemelle, Marie-Claire. 1991. "The Wan Brothers and Sixty Years of Animated Film in China." In *Perspectives on Chinese Cinema*, edited by Chris Berry, 175–86. London: British Film Institute.

Raugust, Karen. 2008. "Challenges Ahead for China." *Animation World Network* August 20.

Rea, Christopher. 2013. "He'll Roast All Subjects That Might Need Roasting: Puck and Mr. Punch in 19th Century China." In *Asian Punches: A Transcultural Affair*, edited by Hans Harder and Barbara Mittler, 389–422. New York and Heidelberg: Springer.

Rea, Christopher. 2015. *The Age of Irreverence: A New History of Laughter in China*. Oakland: University of California Press.

Reed, Ryan. 2014. "Chinese 'Star Wars' Comic Book Unearthed, Featuring Chimp Chewie." *Rolling Stone* May 28.

Ren, Guangqiang. 2009. Interview with John A. Lent and Xu Ying, Qiuxian, China, May 28–30.

"Research and Markets: Animation Industry in China: Strategies, Trends & Opportunities 2013." 2013. Business Wire. Research and Markets May 23. http://www.researchandmarkets.com/research/h3jw2j/animation. Accessed April 16, 2015.

Rigby, Richard. 2007. "Sapajou and 'Shanghai's Schemozzle.'" In *Shanghai's Schemozzle. Volumes 1 and 2 Together*, Sapajou, with R. T. Peyton-Griffin, 7–15. Hong Kong: Earnshaw Books.

Rist, Peter. 2016. "Renewal of Song Dynasty Landscape Painting Aesthetics Combined with a Contemplative Modernism in the Early Work of Chen Kaige." In *The Poetics of Chinese Cinema*, edited by Gary Bettinson and James Udden, 51-77. New York: Palgrave Macmillan.

Rowe, David Nelson. 1939. "Japanese Propaganda in North China, 1937–1938." *Public Opinion Quarterly* 3 (4, October): 564–80.

Royaards, Tjeerd. 2012. "They Fear the Truth, They Fear Cartoons." *Cartoon Movement* January 23.

Rubens, Doris. 1939. "Japanese Propaganda Efforts in Shanghai." *China Weekly Review* August 12: 332–35.

Saeki, Satoshi. 2007. "China Deems 'Death Note' Manga Bad Influence." *Yomiuri Shimbun* June 6. http://www.yomiuri.co.jp/dy/national/20070606TDYO1002.htm. Accessed June 17, 2007.

"Sanmao, China's Favorite Son Turns 70." 2005. *Shanghai ribao* (Shanghai Daily) July 28.

Sapajou, with R. T. Peyton-Griffin ("In Parenthesis"). 2007. *Shanghai's Schemozzle. Volumes 1 and 2 Together*. Hong Kong: Earnshaw Books.

"Sapajou, Old Shanghai's Great Cartoonist." 2002. *Shanghai Star* May 30. http://appl.chinadaily.com.cn/star/2002/0530/cul8-2html. Accessed May 7, 2009.

Schurmann, Franz. 1968. *Ideology and Organization in Communist China*. Berkeley: University of California Press.

Scully, Richard. 2013. "A Comic Empire: The Global Expansion of *Punch* as a Model Publication, 1841–1936." *International Journal of Comic Art* 15 (1): 6–35.

"A Second Cultural Revolution." *Marketing Week* August 21. http://www.marketingweek.co.uk/cgi_bin/item.cgi?id-6111&d=259&h=263&f=3. Accessed August 23, 2008.

Shanghai Animation Film Studio, 1957–1987. 1987. Shanghai: Shanghai Animation Film Studio.

Shen, Bochen. 1918. "Benkan de zeren" ("The Responsibilities of the Magazine"). *Shanghai Puck* No. 1: 1–2.

Shen, Jun. 2002. Interview with John A. Lent and Xu Ying, Beijing, China, December 20.

Shen, Kuiyi. 2001. "*Lianhuanhua* and *Manhua*—Picture Books and Comics in Old Shanghai." In *Illustrating Asia: Comics, Humour Magazines, and Picture Books*, edited by John A. Lent, 100–120. Richmond: Curzon.

Shen, Tongheng. 1991. Personal communication to HongYing Liu-Lengyel.

Sheng, Dalong. 2012. "Recalling My Father Bit by Bit in His Daily Life." *International Journal of Comic Art* 14 (1): 305–20.

Shi, Cu. 1962. "Donghua manhua" ("About Cartoons"). *Dazhong dianying (Popular Film)* No. 5–6.

Shi, Jiangtao. 2011. "Chinese Cartoons of Gaddafi Mock Beijing's Policy." *South China Morning Post* October 25. http://topics.scmp.com/news/china-news-watch/article. Accessed November 21, 2011.

Shi, Jicai. 1989. "Introduction." In *Cartoons from Contemporary China*, edited by Hua Junwu, 12–15. Beijing: New World Press.

Shi, Jinan. 1986. "Let the Military Camp Be Full of Humor." *Zhan you bao (Fellow Army Daily)*. March 18.

Silverberg, Miriam. 2006. *Erotic Grotesque Nonsense: The Mass Culture of Japanese Modern Times*. Berkeley: University of California Press.

Song, Wenwei. 2004. "Cartoon Art Seeking Rebirth." *China Daily* September 29.

Stember, Nick. 2014. "Don't Call It 'Manga': A Short Intro to Chinese Comics and Manhua." March 19. http://www.nickstember.com/dont-call-it-manga-short-introduction-chinese-comics-manhua/. Accessed November 14, 2014.

Stevenson-Yang, Anne. 2005. "Can China Co-Opt the Web?" *Far Eastern Economic Review* October 5: 6–10.

Sugiura, Yukio. 1993. Interview with John A. Lent, Tokyo, Japan, November 6.

Sullivan, Michael. 1996. *Art and Artists of Twentieth-Century China*. Berkeley: University of California Press.

Sullivan, Michael. 2006. *Modern Chinese Artists: A Biographical Dictionary*. Berkeley: University of California Press.

Sun, Lijun. 2001. Interview with John A. Lent and Xu Ying, Beijing, China, May 30.

Sun, Shaobo. 1993. Interview with John A. Lent, Shanghai, China, August 16.

Sun, Xiaogang. 2016. Interview with John A. Lent and Xu Ying, Beijing, China, June 9.

Taylor, Jeremy E. 2014. "Cartoons and Collaboration in Wartime China: The Mobilization of Chinese Cartoonists under Japanese Occupation." *Modern China* June 10. http://mcx.sagepub.com/content/early/2014/07/02/0097700414538386. Accessed November 14, 2014.

Taylor, Jeremy E. n.d. "Enemy of the People: Visual Depictions of Chiang Kai-shek." Arts and Humanities Research Council. http://www.hrionline.ac.uk/chiangkaishek/background/. Accessed November 21, 2015.

Te, Wei. 2001. Interview with John A. Lent and Xu Ying, Shanghai, China, June 16.

Te, Wei. 2004. Interview with John A. Lent, Shanghai, China, June 12.

Theobald, Ulrich. 2012. "Chinese Literature: *Dianshizhai huabao* The Illustrated Lithographer." *China Knowledge* May 28. http://www.chinaknowledge.de. Accessed February 15, 2014.

"Tibetan Rock Dog Rocks On." 2009. *People's Daily Online* April 22. http://english.people.com.cn/90001/90782/91341/6642265.html. Accessed April 23, 2009.

Utley, Freda. 1939. *China at War*. London: Faber and Faber.

Various speakers. 2005. Launching of Anti-Japanese Cartoon Website (commemorating sixtieth anniversary of end of "anti-fascist war"). *China Daily* building, Beijing, China, June 15. (Authors of this book were guests.)

Vincent, Danny. 2009. "China's Manga Drive Is All 'Fake.'" *National* June 10.

Voci, Paola. 2015. "DV and the *Animateur* Cinema in China." In *DV-Made China: Digital Subjects and Social Transformations after Independent Film*, edited by Zhang Zhen and Angela Zito, 260–88. Honolulu: University of Hawai'i Press.

Wagner, Rudolf G. 2011. "China 'Asleep' and China 'Awakening.' A Study in Conceptualizing Asymmetry and Coping with It." *Trans Cultural Studies* No. 1: 4–139.

Wan, Laiming. 1981. "Fifty-five Years of Activity in the Art of Animation." *Donghua yishu shengya wushiwu nian* No. 1.

Wan, Laiming, Wan Guchan, and Wan Chaochen. 1936. "Talking about Cartoons." *Mingxing huabao*.

Wang, Dazhuang. 1991. Personal communication to HongYing Liu-Lengyel.

Wang, Fuyang. 2001. Interview with John A. Lent and Xu Ying, Beijing, China, May 31.

Wang, Fuyang. 2002. Interview with John A. Lent and Xu Ying, Beijing, China, December 16.

Wang, James. 2005. Interview with John A. Lent and Xu Ying, Taipei, Taiwan, July 27.

Wang, Jiajun. 2005. Interview with John A. Lent and Xu Ying, Shanghai, China, June 8.

Wang, Nianyi. 1988. *1949–1989 niande Zhongguo—dadongluande niandai* (*China, 1949–1989—Years of Great Turbulence*). Zhengzhou: Henan renmin chubanshe.

Wang, Wei. 2012. Interview with John A. Lent and Xu Ying, Beijing, China, August 25.

Wang, Xiaoqing and Mei Ke. 2012. "China's Subsidized Cartoons, Comics Tickle Few." Caixin Online. August 7.

Wang, Yang. 2005. "The Dissemination of Japanese Manga in China: The Interplay of Culture and Social Transformation in Post-Reform Period." MA thesis, Lund University.

Wang, Yiqian. 2012. "Memory of the Past." *International Journal of Comic Art* 14 (1): 292–304.

Wang, Zhaowen. 1980. *Wang Zhaowen wenyi lunji* (*Collected Writings on Art*). 3 vols. Shanghai.

Wang, Zheng. 2012. "When Talented Women Became Socialist State Power Holders: Chen Bo'er and the Paradigm of Socialist Film in the PRC." Lecture presented at University of Michigan Center for Chinese Studies, Ann Arbor, November 14.

Wang, Zimei. 1935. "Zhongguo manhua de fazhan yu zhanwang" ("The Evolution and Prospect of Chinese Cartoons"). *Manhua shenguo* 2: 2–3.

Wei, Junyu. 2008. "'Cartoon King' Compelled to Leave China before the Olympics." *Epoch Times* August 6.

Wei, Shaochang, ed. 1998. *Miss Bee*. Jinan: Shandong Pictorial Press.

Wen, Yuqing and Ho Shan. 2015. "Thailand Repatriates Chinese Dissidents Who Sought Political Asylum." *Radio Free Asia* November 16. http://www.rfa.org/english/news/china/repatriation-11162015113959.html. Accessed December 5, 2015.

Westad, Odd Arne. 2003. *Decisive Encounters: The Chinese Civil War, 1946–1950*. Stanford, CA: Stanford University Press.

Wing. 2006. "Comic Books of Chinese Ancient Masterpiece Published in Japan." *China View* October 8. http://www.newsgd.com/culture/culturenews/200610080030.htm. Accessed December 18, 2015.

Wong, Carolyn. 2005. Interview with John A. Lent, Taipei, Taiwan, July 25.

Wong, Carolyn. 2006. "Learning about My Grandfather." *International Journal of Comic Art* 8 (1, Spring): 45–70.

Wong, Carolyn. 2007. "Niu Bizi and Other Cartoons: Huang Yao's Legacy." *SPAFA Journal* 17 (1): 28–31.

Wong, Carolyn. 2008. "Huang Yao and His Cartoon, 'Niu Bizi,' in China, 1934–1947." *International Journal of Comic Art* 10 (2, Fall): 669–93.

Wong, Edward. 2012. "China's President Lashes Out at Western Culture." *New York Times* January 4.

Wong, Wendy Siuyi. 2002. *Hong Kong Comics: A History of Manhua*. New York: Princeton Architectural Press.

Wren, Christopher S. 1984. "China Is Said to End a Campaign to Stop 'Spiritual Pollution.'" *New York Times* January 24.

Wu, Chen. 2010. "Growing Pains of China's Animation Movie." English.news.cn February 15.

Wu, I-Wei. 2013. "Participating in Global Affairs: The Chinese Cartoon Monthly Shanghai Puck." In *Asian Punches: A Transcultural Affair*, edited by Hans Harder and Barbara Mittler, 365–89. New York and Heidelberg: Springer.

Wu, Jijin. 2003. "Art during the Cultural Revolution Period." *Hundred Year Tide* 19: 54–63.

WuDunn, Sheryl. 1990. "Chinese Cartoonist Is the Master of the Fine Line." *New York Times* December 31: 2.

Xiao, Qiang. 2007. "China Censors Internet Users with Site Bans, Cartoon Cop Spies." *SFGate* September 22. http://www.sfgate.com/opinion/article/China-censors-Internet-users-with-site-bans-2501596.php. Accessed March 9, 2015.

Xiao, Tie. 2013. "Masereel, Lu, and the Development of the Woodcut Picture Book in China." *CLCWeb: Comparative Literature and Culture* 15 (2). http://dx.doi.org/10.7771/1481-4374.2230. Accessed March 5, 2015.

Xiao, Xiao-lan. 2011. "Preface." Catalogue of Huang Yao Exhibition. Shanghai: Shanghai Art Museum.

Xie, Bo. 1991. *Ye Qianyu zhuan* (*Biography of Ye Qianyu*). Changchun: Jilin Art Publishing House.

Xin, Lin. 2015. "Fears Grow for Chinese Activists Detained by Thai Police." *Radio Free Asia* November 5. http://www.rfa.org/english/news/china/fears-grow-for-chinese-activists. Accessed December 5, 2015.

Xing, Zhao. 2010. "Comic Strip Sparks Chinese Success Debate." July 22. http://www.cnngo.com/shanghai/life/it-difficult-be-righteous-person-china-8578604. Accessed July 23, 2010.

Xu, Chang (Charles Zee). 2005. Interview with David Ehrlich, Jin Tianyi, and Xu Ying, Shanghai, China, June 9.

Xu, Chang. 2012. "Recalling Ah Da." *International Journal of Comic Art* 14 (1): 283–91.

Xu, Haiou. 1999. "Discussing the Rise and Fall of Lianhuanhua in China." *Journal of Suzhou Institute of Silk Textile Technology* No. 6: 51–54.

Xu, Jin. 2013. Interview with John A. Lent and Xu Ying, Beijing, China, November 29.

Xu, Keren. 1993. Interview with John A. Lent, Shanghai, China, August 16.

Xu, Liping. 2012. "Qingguo zhi jiaren—Ji Shen Chong zibai" ("The Beauty of My Country—Record on Shen Chong's Confession"). *Pingguo ribao* (*Apple Daily*) August 12; abstract in *Wenzhai* 2015 (7): 58–60.

Xu, Pengfei. 2001. Interview with John A. Lent and Xu Ying, Beijing, China, June 11.

Xu, Pengfei. 2005. Interview with John A. Lent and Xu Ying, Beijing, China, June 12.

Xu, Ying. 2000a. "Animation Film Production in Beijing." *Asian Cinema* 11 (2): 60–66.

Xu, Ying. 2000b. "'Lotus Lantern' and the Disneyization of Chinese Animation Film." Paper presented at Asian Cinema Studies Society, Norman, Oklahoma, May 19.

Xu, Zhihuo. 1994. *Zhongguo meishu shetuan manlu* (*Brief Accounts of Chinese Art Groups*). Shanghai: Shanghai shuhua.

Xuan, Wenjie. 1979. "Kang-Ri zhanzheng shiqi de manhua xuanchuan-dui" ("Cartoon Propaganda Brigade in Anti-Japanese War Time"). *Meishu* (6, July 25): 37–38.

Yamamoto, Kenta. 2014. *The Agglomeration of the Animation Industry in East Asia.* Tokyo: Springer Japan.

Yan, Dingxian. 2001. Interview with John A. Lent and Xu Ying, Shanghai, China, June 17.

Yan, Dingxian. 2006. "The Cultivation of Animation Talents Through Practice." Paper presented at International Animation Artists Salon, Wuhan, China, November 2.

Yan, Du (Daisy). 2014. "Socialism and the Rise of the First Camera-woman in History of Chinese Animation." *Animation Studies* December 3. http://blog.animationstudies.org/?p=977. Accessed May 5, 2015.

Yan, Shanchun. 2016. Interview with John A. Lent and Xu Ying, Shanghai, China, June 11.

Yang, Chih-shih, ed. 1988. *Cartoonists' Roll of ROC.* Taipei: Chinese Cartoonists Association.

Yang, Gladys, and Xianji Yang. 1992. "Ding Cong and His Cartoons." In *Wit and Humour from Ancient China,* by Ding Cong, 5–7. Beijing: New World Press.

Yang, Lina. 2014. "China Launches 'Spring Wawa' Design Competition Overseas, Promotes Spring Festival Culture." Xinhua March 17. http://news.xinhuanet.com/english/china/2014-03/14/c_133184699.htm. Accessed November 18, 2015.

Yao, Donghui. 2009. Interview with John A. Lent, Changchun, China, June 1.

Yao, Siyan. 2008. "Comic Book a Reminder for Chinese Cadres to Avoid Graft." Xinhua January 8. http://news.xinhuanet.com/english/2008-01/08/content_7386500.htm. Accessed January 8, 2008.

Ye, Xiaoqing. 2009. "Political Cartoons in Commercial Advertising in Early Twentieth Century China." *Asian Social Science* 5 (10). http://www.ccsenet.org/journal/index.php/ass/article/view/3974/0. Accessed February 9, 2014.

Yi Guo, James. 2015. "Conceptualizing the Freedom of the Press in Chinese Political Cartoons." *International Journal of Comic Art* 17 (2, Fall): 217–37.

Yimen. 1997. *Dreams of Spring: Erotic Art in China. From the Bertholet Collection.* Amsterdam: Pepin Press.

Ying, Tao. 2006. Interview with John A. Lent and Xu Ying, Beijing, China, May 29.

Yokota, Masao. 2003. "The Japanese Puppet Animation Master: Kihachiro Kawamoto." *Asian Cinema* 14 (1, Spring/Summer): 28–44.

Yong, Fei, ed. 1997. *Chinese Modern Cartoonists Dictionary.* Hangzhou: Zhejiang People's Press.

217

Yu, Feng. 2010. "Shanghai di manhua shidai" ("Shanghai's Cartoon Era"). In *Yu Feng sanwen jingxuan (Selected Essays of Yu Feng)*. Beijing: Renmin wenxue chubanshe.

Yu, Guo. 2000. "The Rise and Fall of Xiaorenshu." *Wind of March* No. 12: 37–40.

Yuan, Quan. 2015. "War Artist's Paintings Bring History to Life." ShanghaiDaily.com July 17. http://www.shanghaidaily.com/feature/people/war-artists-paintings-bring-history-to-life. Accessed June 27, 2016.

Yue, Xiaodong. 2010. "Exploration of Chinese Humor: Historical Review, Empirical Findings, and Critical Reflections." *Humor* 23 (3): 403–20.

Zeng, Guangchang. 1992. "Chinese Early Animation." *Jiangsu Film* December.

Zhan, Tong. 1993a. Interview with John A. Lent, Shanghai, China, August 15.

Zhan, Tong. 1993b. *Zhan Tong Cartoon Collection*. Jinan: Shandong Art & Literature Press.

Zhan, Yong. 2012. "Recalling My Father—Zhan Tong." *International Journal of Comic Art* 14 (1): 321–31.

Zhang, Aixue. 2009. Interviews with John A. Lent and Xu Ying, Qiuxian, China, May 29–30.

Zhang, Ding. 2005. Interview with John A. Lent and Xu Ying, Beijing, China, June 15.

Zhang, Huilin. 2002. *Ershi shiji zhongguo donghua yishushi (20th Century Chinese Animation Art History)*. Shanxi: Peoples' Art Press.

Zhang, Huilin. 2003. "Some Characteristics of Chinese Animation." *Asian Cinema* 14 (1): 70–79.

Zhang, Leping. 1963. *Sanmao liulanji xuanji (Selection of the Wanderings of Sanmao)*. Shanghai: Shanghai ertong chubanshe.

Zhang, Leping. 1983. *Sanmao conjunji (Sanmao Joins the Army)*. Chengdu: Sichuan shaonian ertong chubanshe.

Zhang, Linlan. 1993. Interview with John A. Lent, Shanghai, China, August 16.

Zhang, Ningping. 2005. Interview with John A. Lent and Xu Ying, Hangzhou, China, June 3.

Zhang, Shaoqian. 2014. "Combat and Collaboration: The Clash of Propaganda Prints between the Chinese Guomindang and the Japanese Empire in the 1930s–1940s." *Transcultural Studies* No. 1.

Zhang, Shupeng. 2005. Interview with John A. Lent and Xu Ying, Shanghai, China, June 8.

Zhang, Songlin. 2005. Interview with John A. Lent and Xu Ying, Hangzhou, China, June 1.

Zhang, Songlin, and Gong Jianying. 2010. *Shui chuangzao le. "Xiaokedou zhao mama"—Te Wei he zhongguo donghua (Who Created "Little Tadpoles Looking for Mama"?—Te Wei and Chinese Animation)*. Shanghai: Shanghai renmin chubanshe.

Zhang, Yaoning. 2001. Interview with John A. Lent and Xu Ying, Beijing, China, May 31.

Zhang, Yaoning. 2014. Interview with John A. Lent and Xu Ying, Beijing, China, December 10.

Zhang, Yaoning, and Zheng Huagai, eds. 2013. *Zhongguo bainian xinwen jingdian manhuajuan (Chinese 100 Years News Classic: Cartoon Volume)*. Beijing renmin chubanshe.

Zhang, Yingjin. 2001. "The Corporeality of Erotic Imagination: A Study of Pictorials and Cartoons in Republican China." In *Illustrating Asia: Comics, Humour Magazines, and Picture Books*, edited by John A. Lent, 121–36. Richmond: Curzon.

Zhang, Yiqian. 2014. "Cartoonists Team Remembers Suffering during Cultural Revolution." *Global Times* April 18. http://www.globaltimes.cn/index.html. Accessed November 11, 2014.

Zhang, Yu. 2015. "Changing Times Have Traditional Political Cartoons on the Wane in China." *Global Times* February 2.

Zhao, Elaine. 2014. "China's Cartoons Finding Their Way Home to Roost." http://www.creativetransformations.asia/2011/02/chinas-cartoons-finding-their-way-home-to-roost/. Accessed November 10, 2015.

Zheng, Huagai. 1987a. "Hua Junwu and *Military Camp Humor*." *Haerbin ribao* April 11.

Zheng, Huagai. 1987b. "Military Camp Humor: Political Department of 51392." *The World of Cartoons* April.

Zheng, Huagai. 2002. Interview with John A. Lent and Xu Ying, Beijing, China, December 16.

Zheng, Huagai. 2005. Interview with John A. Lent and Xu Ying, Beijing, China, June 12.

Zheng, Huagai. 2007. "Jiang Yousheng—Yige cong paohuozhong zuochulai de manhua dashi" ("Jiang Yousheng—A Cartoon Master Who Evolved from Gunfire and Smoke"). *Art* No. 8: 119–24.

Zheng, Huagai. 2008. "He Was Such a Kind Person—Eulogistic Comments on Chinese Cartoonist Wang Fuyang, 1935–2008." *International Journal of Comic Art* 10 (Spring, 1): 543–52.

Zheng, Huagai. n.d. "I Love Military Cartoons." Manuscript provided by Zheng Huagai, April 2015.

Zheng, Xinyao. 1993. Interview with John A. Lent, Shanghai, China, August 16.

Zheng, Xinyao. 2001. Interview with John A. Lent and Xu Ying, Shanghai, China, June 14.

Zheng, Yang. 2013. "Chinese Cartoonists Take Center Stage." *Chinafrica* Vol. 5 (September).

Zhong, Yanling. 2004. "An Elementary Introduction to the Rise and Fall of China's Traditional Picture-Story Book." *Library Construction* No. 1: 107–8.

Zhou, Jin. 2001. Interview with John A. Lent and Xu Ying, Beijing, China, May 30.

Zhou, Raymond. 2006. "Animated, but Not Yet a Cash Cow." *China Daily* June 12: 1.

Zhou, Yuanzhi. 2007. "Capitalizing China's Media Industry: The Installation of Capitalist Production in the Chinese TV and Film

Sectors." PhD dissertation, University of Illinois at Urbana-Champaign.

Zhu, Genhua. 2009. Interview with John A. Lent and Xu Ying, Beijing, China, May 27.

Zhu, Guorong. 1990. *China Art: The Ultimate*. Shanghai: Knowledge Publishing House.

Zhu, Helena. 2008. "Award-Winning Cartoon Artist Forced out of China." *Epoch Times* September 19.

Zou, Qin. 1993. Interview with John A. Lent, Shanghai, China, August 13.

Zürcher, Erik. 1994. "Middle-Class Ambivalence: Religious Attitudes in the *Dianshizhai huabao.*" *Études chinoises* 13 (1–2): 109–143.

Additional Sources

Bai, Chunxi, et al. 1989. "Illustrated History of the Development of Chinese *Lianhuanhua*." *Lianhuanhua Art* 1 (February): 114–29; 12 (April): 77–127.

Chen, Guangyi. 1979. "The Origins of the Term *Lianhuanhua*." *Studies of Lianhuanhua* 15: 66–69, 71.

Chen, Guangyi. 1981. "Producing *Lianhuanhua* for Most of My Life." *Studies of Lianhuanhua* 25: 70–77.

"Comics, Animation Industry Gets Boost in China." 2008. *People's Daily Online* January 24. http://english.people.com.cn/90001/90776/6344256/.html. Accessed January 24, 2008.

Dai, Yangfan, ed. 1993. *Zhang Leping manhua xuan* (*Zhang Leping's Caricatures*). Shanghai: Shaonian ertong chubanshe.

Ding, Cong. 2004. *Ding Cong manhua xilie—Ding Cong lao manhua* (*Series of Ding Cong's Cartoons—Ding Cong's Old Cartoons*). Beijing: Shenguo dushu xinzhi sanlian shudian.

Ding Cong. 2004. *Wode manhua shenghuo* (*My Cartoon Life*). Beijing: Wuzhou chuanbo chubanshe

Feng, Lei, ed. 1999. *Lao manhua—IV* (*Old Cartoons—IV*). Jinan: Shangdong Pictorial Press.

Gao, Made. 2007. *Wode manhua shenghuo—Gao Made* (*My Cartoon Life—Gao Made*). Beijing: Zhongguo luyou chubanshe.

Hua, Junwu, ed. 1998. *Zhongguo xiandai meishu quanji—manhua* (*China Modern Art Collection—Cartoon*). Tianjin: Tianjin renmin meishu chubanshe.

Hua, Junwu. 2003. *Hua Junwu ji—Manhua ji I* (*Hua Junwu Collection—Cartoon Collection I*). Shijiazhuang: Hebei jiaoyu chubanshe.

Hua, Junwu. 2005. *Manhua yisheng* (*Cartoon Life*). Beijing: Xinshijie chubanshe.

Huang, Mao. 1942. "Manhua de xuanchuan fangshi" ("Propaganda Methods of Cartooning"). *Kangjian tongsu huakan* July 1: 18–19.

Huang, Ruogu, and Yiqui Wang. 1986. "From Gongyili to Taoyuan Road—A Special Distribution System of Old *Lianhuanhua*." *Lianhuanhua Art* 11 (3): 115–19.

Huang, Ruogu, and Yiqui Wang. 1989. "It Is the Real Old Brand, Beware of Imitations." *Lianhuanhua Art* 9 (1): 118–22.

Huang, Ruogu, and Yiqui Wang. 1993. "The Concise History of Shanghai *Lianhuanhua*." *Shanghai meishu tongxun* (*Shanghai Art Information*) 45: 12–19, 115–19.

Huang, Yuanlin, ed. 2000. *Bainian manhua* (*Hundred Years of Cartooning*). 2 Vols. Beijing: Xiandai chubanshe.

Liao, Bingxiong. 2005. *Woyou yizhibi—Liao Bingxiong geshiqi manhua jingxuan* (*I Have a Brush—Choice Cartoons of Liao Bingxiong*). Guangzhou: Jinan daxue chubanshe.

Liu, Zheng, Ci Liqun, and Zhang Zikang, eds. 1994. *Zhongguo manhua shuxi—Ding Cong juan* (*The Series of Chinese Cartoons—Issue of Ding Cong*). Shijianzhuang: Hebei jiaoyu chubanshe.

Liu, Zheng, Ci Liqun, and Zhang Zikang, eds. 1994. *Zhongguo manhua shuxi—Ye Qianyu juan* (*The Series of Chinese Cartoons—Issue of Ye Qianyu*). Shijianzhuang: Hebei jiaoyu chubanshe.

Liu, Zheng, Ci Liqun, and Zhang Zikang, eds. 1994. *Zhongguo manhua shuxi—Zhang Leping juan* (*The Series of Chinese Cartoons—Issue of Zhang Leping*). Shijianzhuang: Hebei jiaoyu chubanshe.

Liu, Zheng, and Liao Ling-er, eds. 1998. *Zhongguo manhua shuxi—Liao Bingxiong juan* (*The Series of Chinese Cartoons—Issue of Liao Bingxiong*). Shijianxhuang: Hebei jiaoyu chubanshe.

Shen, Kuiyi. 1997. "Comics, Picture Books, and Cartoonists in Republican China." *Inks* November: 2–15.

Zheng, Yimei. 1979. "A Memory to Some Cartoonists." *Fengci yu youmo* (*Satire and Humor*) No. 3.

Zhong, Wenlong, and Dong Xiaoming, eds. 1990. *Hua Junwu manhua* (*Hua Junwu's Cartoons*). Hangzhou: Zhejing renmin meishu chubanshe.

Zhou, Limin, and Wang Xiaodong, eds. 2004. *Manhua shenghuo, 1934–1935—Lao Shanghai qikan jingdian* (*Cartoon Life, 1934–1935—Old Shanghai Journals Classics*). Shanghai: Shanghai shehui kexueyuan chubanshe.

Additional Sources

Page numbers in **bold** refer to illustrations.

226

234

www.ingramcontent.com/pod-product-compliance
Lightning Source LLC
Chambersburg PA
CBHW061219270326
41926CB00032B/4777